SUPER SECRETO
The Third Epoch of Cryptography

Theo Tenzer

Theo Tenzer

SUPER SECRETO

The Third Epoch of Cryptography

Multiple, exponential, quantum-secure
and above all, simple and practical

Encryption for Everyone?

Impressum

Tenzer, Theo: SUPER SECRETO - The Third Epoch of Cryptography:
Multiple, exponential, quantum-secure and above all,
simple and practical Encryption for Everyone?
Norderstedt 2021, ISBN 9783755761174.

In collaboration with Jo van der Lou.

1. Edition.
© 2021 Theo Tenzer – Manufacturing and Publisher: BoD
– Books on Demand, Norderstedt.
Further bibliographic information at: https://portal.dnb.de.

»I am sorry,
if I don't understand all of this!
Sorry if I go home!

You call me and you say you're late
and you're already way too late!

I need power for my netbook.
No power in my netbook.
Baby, lend me your Lada.
Come on, please lend me your loader,
I need power for my netbook.

I NEED MORE ELECTRICITY! «

Quoted and translated according to
Bungalow, Annett Louisan,
Kitsch.

Content

9

PREFACE:
REGARDING THE GLOBAL CRISIS OF PRIVACY - THE AWAKENING OF ENCRYPTION AND ITS WAY INTO THE THIRD EPOCH OF CRYPTOGRAPHY ●

Encryption is
- like math -
there for everyone.

based on Jimmy Wales,
Founder of Wikipedia.

Dear Reader*,

You have never been to an introductory workshop in Cryptography - or to a so-called »Crypto Party« - to encounter the art of encryption?

We are in the 21st century in a global Privacy crisis. Not only are the private data made available by us being collected and stored more and more, but also data traces that can be viewed on the Internet, personal interests, and behavioral preferences as well as the content of e-mails and chat messages from all of us are intercepted, analyzed, and linked together in a targeted manner.

Encryption can help protect this data. To communicate confidentially, fear-free and tap-proof, simple and practical encryption is required for everyone. But can it really be available to everyone?

---

* Terms for persons used in the book can include female, diverse, and male genders.

11

The current discussions about encryption include a Right to Encryption as well as encryption restrictions. In particular, it is about so-called »end-to-end encryption«, according to which only two friends know a common key for a secure communication channel. Third eavesdroppers are excluded with end-to-end encryption.

The magic of replacing legible characters with other apparently random and therefore illegible characters had been almost religious for centuries: only those initiated into the invention of a secret language could crack the messages. Encryption remained Super Secreto – Top Secret – Streng Geheim, as it is called in Latin-American or German. Reason enough to choose »Super Secreto« as the title for the book in your hands.

In recent years, many authors, scholars, and journalists have contributed to making the topic of Cryptography and the knowledge of the fundamentals and methods of encryption accessible and understandable to a wider public.

From the point of view of mathematics or computer science, these introductions are usually rich in technical, detailed knowledge: They explain calculations with prime numbers, the application of action and process operations, i.e., the so-called algorithms; or it is about the use of computers to automatically confirm that we are only we when we do something or communicate on the Internet.

And reports from the point of view of the history of science are rich in historical events: how *Gaius Julius Caesar* is said to have given the rider of a horse a message encoded according to a self-invented pattern in order to have a better influence on his strategic position in achieving sole rule in Rome; just as popular: how the Queen of Scotland, *Mary Queen of Scots*, encrypted her letters to the conspirators against *Queen Elizabeth I* in order to usurp the English crown; or how *Alan Turing* played a key role in

12

the deciphering of the German radio messages encrypted with the »Enigma« machine in England during the Second World War.

Many people who communicate over the Internet today want to understand clearly how encryption works in their messenger and how Cryptography increases our security on the Internet: Because they want to be sure that their communication is also protected electronically and not viewed by third parties and can be monitored.

Nevertheless, executive state authorities such as the FBI, Europol, or the police station on the next street in our neighborhood want and must be able to read and monitor communications from criminals. But they can't. Because it is technically very difficult in Cryptography without a key, i.e., hardly possible, or: not possible at all.

In the public debates and rhetorical wars of words - the so-called »Crypto Wars« - by politicians, computer scientists and civil rights activists about the further development and the sense of the use of encryption, everyone is involved today. Encryption is no longer an issue for the military or state governments. In today's age of smartphone and pocket computers, encryption is now available to everyone.

And: encryption is developing rapidly thanks to open-source programming and new innovations. This *Transformation of Cryptography* is primarily characterized using better algorithms, processes, and protocols as well as longer and more diverse - and therefore more secure - keys: Ever more sophisticated math is calculating - ever faster - in our messengers the secret, so-called »cipher text«, with a large number of corresponding keys.

The Third Epoch of Cryptography is becoming more present

But now, the *Third Epoch of Cryptography* is even more present: More and more quantum-computers calculate with ever increasing computing speed. It is measured in the unit of quantum bits, or QuBits for short.

While the QuBits of a quantum-computer could still be counted on one hand a few years ago, the computing speed has meanwhile increased more than tenfold and in a few years should not only be three-digit, but also four-digit. In addition, individual quantum-computers are now interconnected to form entire networks over long distances or even via satellite.

Multi-Encryption

Further adjustments to increase security take place: *Multi-Encryption*, so-called »super-encipherment«, i.e., the application of repeated, possibly multiple encryption to already existing encryption respective already encrypted text - as said: the cipher text - is creating further fundamental transformations. What does this double, triple or even multiple encryption mean for the telegraphy of the future? We want to explore these and other questions in this volume.

Better algorithms for encryption

The aforementioned super- and quantum-computers with their faster and new quality dimension of computing capacity also require new or different algorithms for more security on the Internet and for encryption: the well-known and widely used RSA algorithm is considered to be - in view of the fast quantum-computers - critical or as no longer secure, not to say: as broken.

And other algorithms such as McEliece or NTRU - which are in spite of that considered so far secure - have heralded a fundamental change in applied programming - similar to the change that we are currently experiencing with the decarbonization of energy: Cars no longer run-on liquid petrol, but switch to electric drive, fed by regenerative methods of energy generation: sun, water, wind, geothermal energy... The engine, with its technology and driving force, is changed.

Software with the RSA encryption, which is often used but is considered to be potentially insecure given the fast supercomputers - officially confirmed since 2016 -, has reached the end of the product life cycle, or at least needs to be updated or supplemented by better standards.

Beyond Cryptographic Routing
with Exponential Encryption

However, not only better algorithms or multi-encryption help against cracking encryption, but also new ways of routing and exchanging message and data packets on the Internet. For example, the Echo protocol, which has been developed for a number of years, supplements the encryption with a theory and practice of graphs, i.e., which routes on the Internet our messages take as multi-encrypted packets.

This new form of routing with encrypted data packets is called *Exponential Encryption* according to this concept: Routing is carried out on the basis of cryptographic processes without destination information in the route, so that we speak of »*Beyond Cryptographic Routing*«: Routing takes place without targeted routing.

And accordingly, all nodes are reached by potentially exponential replication of the message and its forwarding. This means that routing is robbed of its identity: Routing without routing - in an age that, in terms of innovation, lies beyond the status of routes that would be network-related or even cryptographically identified.

Abstinence in key transmission

And: In the past, both - the key and the encrypted text - had to be transmitted (over one of these routes) to the recipient. In today's electronic Cryptography, it is no longer absolutely necessary to transfer the keys: the risky transport route for the keys can be omitted!

Yes, today, even with our beloved messengers, it is no longer necessary to have a *Transmission of Keys on the Internet* for later decryption. »A key has to be given to the other person to be able to open a door?«, some will ask.

It is about the fascination of how Cryptography became abstinent in the transmission of keys through process-oriented mathematics, so-called »Zero-Knowledge proofs« - and this political and technical innovation and science portrait is also about the impact it has on the state governments' desire for duplicate keys: In the following, the special features of the new keys called »Juggerknaut Keys« and »Secret Stream Keys« will be further explained with regard to their fundamental character and their transforming effect in the field of applied Cryptography.

Democratization thanks to open sources

And finally, *encryption has been democratized*: thanks to open-source software, it is now available to everyone and knowledge about it is no longer elitist but secularized and democratized in the hands of all citizens who access this available knowledge in the field of Cryptography, and expand their skills in using or even developing encrypting software applications.

Questions and answers in a broad learning dialogue

Modern encryption therefore not only raises many questions, for example by or from which computing capacity in QuBits (and with which corresponding time period) an algorithm can be broken; or whether multiple encryption applied one after the other lead to higher security; or whether learners or criminals compile machine code themselves, i.e., are able to and will convert it into an executable software program for encryption?

At the same time, applied Cryptography also offers numerous answers to the challenges of the (natural) sciences, society and our modern times: Smart programming can already equip mobile communication devices with encryption. Their algorithms also prove to be secure against expanded computing capacity and strengthen cyber-security on the Internet. But they also no longer allow governmental authorities to investigate the encrypted message packets.

In the public discussions of these different approaches, political and social actors in particular must be included in order to analyze security through encryption and also security during and in spite of the use of encryption.

We all need to update our knowledge, skills and experience in the field of encryption

A third of cryptographic applications and programs are produced in North America and also in Europe, where in the leading countries Germany, England and France around half of the applications are open source, that means the machine code can be viewed by anyone who is capable to understand, and the functionality and programming can be comprehended.

Enthusiasm for sending secret or indecipherable messages over the Internet is shown not only by students and a completely new audience of readers in these countries of North America and

Europe, but also in the other countries in which the secret service network of the *Five Eyes* - that is, the countries Australia, Canada, New Zealand, and the United Kingdom - and/or where their attentive observers are at home.

At the same time, however, this also means that countries such as Russia, China, India and Islamic and Arab countries as well as other states that, for political reasons, shape or try to block the Internet according to leadership-relevant opportunities, have - in addition to the learners and the scientists at the schools and universities of these respective countries - great interest in entering into a dialogue about encryption and its function in the *Third Epoch of Cryptography*.

In short, these global actors, an alliance of interested parties, are also thinking about how to not only make messengers and the code of encrypted messages more secure, but also how to crack them! And: how to tap data at a suitable location and save it permanently - or how to protect personal data through technical measures or laws that apply to everyone.

This means that the question is how the mathematics behind encryption can also be understood and used politically.

Can mathematics be a basic right or be banned? And if we did not learn Cryptography in early school such as languages, sports and mathematics, when is a suitable time to get excited about it, e.g., if it is to be used individually, for civil, professional, social or military purposes? Ultimately, this dialogue about encryption and its software always remains connected with the citizens and learners. And also, with the issue of protecting their Privacy.

Many previous writings on Cryptography are not only strictly relevant to the subject, but are also simply out of date and remain on the threshold of the *Third Epoch of Cryptography*:

In a last chapter, for example, reference is often made to the encryption standard »PGP« - Pretty Good Privacy - (which will be explained later) without discussing the prospect that this is based on algorithms that could be out of date by time. In the open-source variant (and in the following) »PGP« is also called »GPG«, derived from »GNU Privacy Guard«. But GPG might soon have to be checked and provided with the better McEliece algorithm as a possible alternative.

Or a preview of the technical discussions about »PQ« - post-quantum Cryptography - is dared: Since the first topical conference in 2006, it has been about encryption of e-mails and also about the (un)probable possibility of breaking this encryption by quantum-computers and their fast calculation methods based on quantum mechanical states.

Often such an outlook remains in the panel of experts or is recommended with the reassuring message that consumers will not be able to buy a super-computer in the next super-market in the coming years.

Numerous references in these overview-works are made to the 1970s, 1990s or 2000s - but that was many decades ago!

It therefore remains correct to continue addressing this continually rousing and at the same time highly interesting topic of Cryptography with its modern and epoch-making developments as well as its practical questions and solutions to encryption and decryption not only in the natural sciences and humanities, but also in the general public in particular; even to promote it. Yes, the task remains to discover an encryption program for yourself as a good practice!

There is a need to discuss multiple, exponential, quantum-secure and, above all, simple and practical encryption for everyone, which nevertheless may not be available to everyone at all?

This volume would like to invite you, the reader, in understandable language to enter this dialogue and to a critical, i.e., inquiring discussion about these standards and developments in the field of Cryptography - and to encourage you to get to know cryptographic functions and to think it through. And probably simply to use such software programs.

Acknowledgments: A Big Thank You !

In life, we all sometimes need a mentor here and there for the first insights and steps into new topics to be deepened. With a personal and narrative mediation, we find and found access to what was previously uncharted territory.

At that time, I also had this mentor or tutor for a first access to the field of Cryptography and I would like to thank him very much for it - as well as all other participants in the creation of this book on the subject of encryption and its implications in technical, political and social terms.

I would also like to thank the other helpers such as colleagues in the publishing/manufacturing house, teachers, booksellers and librarians who work tirelessly to ensure that the content of modern non-fiction books is understandable to us citizens and that their ideas are an initiation of interest and enthusiasm.

Ultimately, this also ensures the ability to reflect and act in the assessment and application of encryption technology on a broad basis.

Last but not least, I would like to thank all readers who set out to get to know the contents of this portrait from different perspectives in order to mark the beginning of a new era with its cryptographic functionalities and necessities as well as to assess technical, social and economic consequences and opportunities.

My special thanks go to my long-time comrade, colleague and good friend *Jo van der Lou*, with whom I often discussed ideas and thoughts via a messenger, sometimes unencrypted, sometimes encrypted (not because the content of the conversation required confidentiality, or because we always want to have this standard set, but because we were just testing another messenger or GPG) and received numerous suggestions and impulses in this exchange, including on personal, family or professional topics. Without him, this book - *»Super Secreto«: The Third Epoch of Cryptography* - would never have been possible.

Many thanks to all who have contributed to providing themselves and others with initial or extended access to the subject of *Encryption for Everyone*, and who take part in the discussion about whether it is really available, can or may be available to everyone - and what role we, as learners, and teachers, have to play in this.

Theo Tenzer on Mai 24, 2021.

1 FEAR-FREE, CONFIDENTIAL AND SECURE – DOES DEMOCRACY NEED THE RIGHT TO ENCRYPT? •

The demands for a *Right to Encryption* on the one hand, and the demands for a restriction on encryption on the other, are a long-standing story: The public discussions[1] can already be found in the 1990s, then at the turn of the millennium, as well as around 2010 and finally again in the decade from 2020 - and again and again in the middle of this never-ending story of erosion, retention or the attempt of a re-definition of Privacy.

Those who want to restrict encryption, e.g., to better grasp criminals, realize that they cannot implement this extensively because of technical circumstances. And they recognize that encryption is needed in all areas of life, so that it would have devastating consequences if it were to be restricted or even abolished. Those who only want their Privacy protected by encryption - not only secure, but also tap-proof - recognize that the technology could potentially also be used by criminals - and therefore authorities not only want access to communication, but also need it.

This is how these findings lead to the formulation: We want to achieve »security through encryption and security despite encryption«. From a technical point of view, however, this claim is tantamount to squaring the circle, because there is just as little »a little bit encrypted« as there is »a little bit pregnant«.

The proposal to ban the sending of encrypted messages on the Internet is therefore always on the agenda: Terrorists, it is said at the beginning of every discussion, made use of the most modern communication technologies. And: The exchange of encrypted messages on the Internet poses serious problems for the authorities.

Because encryption is not forbidden, terrorists and other criminals can communicate freely and unobserved over the international data networks and exchange their criminal plans: »This idea is anything but new«, summed up the book author *Christian Meyn* already for the 1990s, because even then the Member of Parliament *Erwin Marschewski* demanded an initiative e.g. in the German Bundestag for a crypto law, which should regulate a reservation of approval for encryption procedures and a collection point for the deposit of keys.

As a member of the so-called G10 Commission of the German Bundestag, he was involved in decisions on the necessity and permissibly of all restrictive measures implemented by the federal intelligence services (like BND, BfV, MAD) in the area of secrecy of letters, mail and telecommunications.

The interior minister at the time also spoke out in favor of a place where the keys could be deposited[2]. Private encryption was defined and understood as a public problem[3]. However, there was no law to issue private keys for encryption or state decryption in the following decades.

Today it is also evident that installing surveillance software - a so-called »Trojan« - on the mobile communication devices of people to be observed requires the help of the telecommunications provider or, probably, the manufacturer of the smartphone operating systems. And even after a court decision, these inquiries to companies or overseas cannot be made without further formalities. And: they often cannot be processed or answered in a timely manner.

After all, breaking the encryption, the cipher text, will probably[4] hardly be possible - despite increased investments in computers with high computing capacity.

The political discussion of the demands for a softening of encryption thus alternates between the three paradigms, (a) we do not want to break encryption because it weakens the security systems, (b) we must, however, be able to break encryption to avoid criminal offenses or demand the surrender and state collection of keys, up to (c), we use surveillance Trojans to access the plain text before encryption or after decryption.

On the other hand, there are those, often civil rights activists, who want to legally establish a Right to Encryption in order to protect personal, family and professional Privacy.

So, what remains for the correct use of encryption?

1.1   The first act:
Main role of the European parliamentarians ●

The *European Council* therefore came up with the idea of adopting a resolution for the entire European continent, so to speak, according to which the so-called end-to-end encryption should be restricted across Europe.

With end-to-end encryption, user Alice and user Bob exchange their keys - and from now on third parties can no longer investigate this connection. This is different with point-to-point encryption, which decrypts a server in the middle and then encrypts it again for forwarding. Here a server in the middle can read all messages.

A central example of this difference between point-to-point encryption and end-to-end encryption is the German state DE-Mail: Ten years ago, on behalf of the German Federal Government, DE-Mail was launched for secure communication with authorities.

Over the years around 85 out of 92 German federal authorities have been connected via DE-Mail. However, DE-Mail was offered without end-to-end encryption, i.e., there is an intermediate point in which the mails can be decrypted. So, the encryption was just a point-to-point encryption. As a result, we see, that this was not accepted by the citizens.

The CEO *Timotheus Höttges* of (among other) executing Deutsche Telekom finally criticized the mail service sharply in an interview with the well-known YouTube channel »Jung und Naiv«: DE-Mail was »over-complicated« and a »dead horse«. Despite investments in the three-digit million range and running annual costs in the six-figure range, »there has never been anyone who has used this product«, which is why the service was discontinued[5].

After completing his studies, *Timotheus Höttges* joined a management consultancy and worked there as a project manager in the »Services« division before moving to Telekom, those perspectives can certainly also be transferred to IT services.

And yes, who wants to set up an extra e-mail address for a service just for communication with authorities, which should then only be used for private purposes without secure end-to-end encryption? This is comparable to a Lufthansa direct flight with »only« one stopover.

Figure 1: End-to-End-Encryption

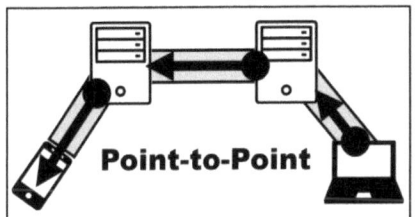 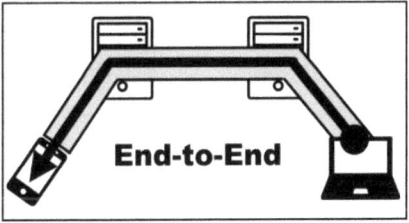

Source:[6]

End-to-end encryption characterizes encryption from Alice to Bob without interruption or gaps, even if the connection is forwarded via intermediate stations. Only the two can read the message. Point-to-point encryption, on the other hand, only encrypts the transport route to the next station. The intermediate stations can unpack the encrypted package, read it and encrypt it again before it is sent on.

According to the idea of the *European Parliament* and the given EU resolution on encryption, commercial providers of telecommunications services are now obliged to keep a copy of the encryption key available in case of need.[7]

This applies in particular to users of end-to-end encryption, since the keys to open the encrypted messages are with the users at the ends of the encryption channel. This duplicate key is not a master key (since this technically, depending on the encryption method, cannot be generated as a third, passable key), but a copy of the original key and should therefore also be designated as a *duplicate key* - or better called: a *copy* (e.g., in a third hand).

However, with this requirement to store cloned keys in government hands or access them with government authorization, encryption would become less secure in both basic encryption methods: symmetric keys (identified by a shared password as a secret) as well as the public keys of asymmetric encryption (and thus also the respective private keys of this so-called »Public Key Infrastructure« (PKI)) would be attacked. The following parts of the book explain the differences between the two types of encryption in more detail.

But it is already clear from the political initiative to store keys: for both types of encryption, copies of keys always require procedures for the copying process, for checking-out the selection, for transport routes, for storage, for indexed assignments to the encrypted messages and also are authorization concepts needed in order to then being able to view the content. Respective, first of all, it is necessary to define who is allowed and should have access to the keys. All of these processes can reduce security, so that in addition to the two communicating parties and the patrolling state, unwanted fourth parties could gain access to the keys - and thus also to the content of the messages.

Was the European idea for this amendment to the law a good idea?

1.2   The second act: Big Five & Five Eyes - Main roles of more than five (secret) agents ●

It then came to light (in quasi another act in this story) that this European initiative to issue keys for encryption by the so-called Organization of the *»Five-Eyes«* (abbreviated: FVEY), the worldwide espionage alliance consisting of the five countries Australia, Canada, New Zealand, England and the USA and in this case plus India and Japan was supported and prepared with[8].

Because not only in Europe, but also in the USA, there are similar efforts to take the keys for the encryption of their communication out of the hands of the citizens: with the proposed EARN-IT-Act[9], the use of the end-to-end encryption can be made practically impossible.

But: What use is a key if the associated messages are not copied, stored and accessible in the same way - i.e., also physically?

And: Basically, banning cipher text on the Internet may not be possible and also not wanted: Who wanted to do without banking, home office, online shopping and other secure transmissions, especially in critical infrastructure such as the energy industry or healthcare? Finally, it is also not possible to forbid, for example, free Linux machines on which cipher text is also still being generated[10].

At the same time, after the European initiative for this resolution, which was co-sponsored by the Five-Eyes, there were reports from Google, Apple, Microsoft Teams, and the video portal Zoom, to name just a few, that they expand end-to-end encryption. They will introduce encryption, e.g., even for simple

SMS/RCS messages or video chats, as we have been using it for many years as a standard with market-leading text messengers.

These companies are in good company among the »Big Five« US technology companies. They are the American technology companies Google (Alphabet), Amazon, Facebook, Apple and Microsoft. The Big Five are also abbreviated with the acronym GAFAM, which stands for Google, Amazon, Facebook, Apple and Microsoft. All of these companies have seen rapid growth in the last decade and all of them have a corresponding influence on encryption in their Internet offerings.

Figure 2: Big Five Companies of the Internet: GAFAM

Big Five Companies	Employees	US$ Sales billion	US$ Revenue billion
Google (Alphabet)	127.498	275.900	161.857
Amazon	1.225.300	225.248	280.522
Facebook	52.534	133.376	70.697
Apple	137.000	323.888	274.515
Microsoft	166.475	301.300	143.000

Source:[11]

Commentators have raised the effects of these technology giants on data protection, market power, freedom of speech, encryption technologies and censorship as well as national security and law enforcement as issues and criticize their power[12]. On the other hand, companies remain popular by offering consumers free services - in return for disclosing their personal data, interests, habits and communication content - and thus their Privacy as a whole.

The perfidious system may also consist in the fact that the companies say, give your personal data only to us, and to no one else on the Internet, - therefore they are in favor of encryption not only for technical reasons, but also for market reasons. Also for strategic considerations: A police officer or the Federal

Intelligence Service of any European, American or worldwide country should only ask Google during an observation about the data, not Apple or a European mail provider, and certainly not Europol!

Strong encryption not only establishes and cemented the communication channels, but also the power of the intermediary servers or platform providers on which conversions from plain text to cipher text take place: our smartphones. The policewoman, who has to ask Google or WhatsApp in the Facebook group as part of investigative work, will only be able to make her inquiries in non-English mother-language in the long term if there exist also appropriate alternatives to mail and messaging in her own country, in addition to the central five American technology giants.

Possibly in this sense, after the EU resolution, the rejection of a key release or the approval of encryption culminated in the following demand from Apple: Through its software boss *Craig Federighi*, the company announced to those responsible in Europe in terms of politics, on the contrary: support for end-to-end encryption must be expanded and reinforced. [13]

Craig Federighi is known in the public image for his energetic presentations of new Apple software functions and his distinctive humor about his (sometimes longer) hair, which is why he has been nicknamed »Hair Force One«, if not the Apple Boss personally calls him »Superman« at the karaoke parties he organizes for his colleagues.

Even if Apple steadfastly emphasizes that it does not want to decrypt its own telephone devices for police investigations, this may also only be part of official rhetoric. Because it can be assumed that even Apple will not be able to avoid in the background when observing crime providing insight into the messages of customers in the case of specific investigation inquiries outside the public.

At the time, for example, a judge in California ordered the company to help FBI investigators obtain data stored on an Apple cell phone. It was about *Syed Farook*'s iPhone, who killed 14 people together with his wife in San Bernardino. Apple was able to stand firm until a third party, the Israeli company Cellebrite, was supposed to pull the coals for Apple out of the fire and decipher the cell phone.

But the *Washington Post*[14] finally reported that the FBI (according to anonymous »people familiar with the matter«) instead paid »professional hackers« who were using an allegedly unsettled security hole in the iPhone software. So, the help of Cellebrite was no longer needed. The image as a confidential partner was saved: Apple was off the hook and was not considered a company that was misappropriating data. And there was no third company that had proven that it could crack Apple's encryption.

Once again elegantly taken the curve to lull the public and customers into security that their encryption is safe in the hands of this company and that the secret services, as can be assumed, still run their filters and analyzes in the background (as with other GAFAM Tech companies).

But what happens if users now start to set up end-to-end encryption themselves, and really nobody can look inside along the way? Civil rights activists understand encryption very differently, namely as protection of Privacy. - Private life in their own four walls and the associated communication with family and friends, as a rule and in their opinion, is nothing which should be exposed to the state and government organizations - if there are no illegal machinations behind it.

Since not only the state, technology companies, as well as suppliers and service providers monitor, evaluate data, and sacrifice economic processes in the market, the protection of private data and private communication is of particular importance. Finally, *Edward Snowden*'s papers[15] in the summer of 2013 proved that the American surveillance organizations store and analyze all content and data on the Internet. His revelations give insights into the global extent of surveillance and espionage practices by the American and British intelligence services and sparked the NSA affair that has made him live in exile in Moscow since that time.

Edward Snowden has received several awards from non-governmental organizations for his publication: he received the Honorary Prize of the Right Livelihood Award (also known as the Alternative Nobel Prize) and was even nominated for the Nobel Peace Prize two years later.

The only thing that helps against the worldwide surveillance measures he has uncovered is encryption, which civil rights activists believe should be strengthened. And from this context of having to expand encryption to protect citizens, there is also the longstanding political demand for a Right to Encryption. In Germany, for example, it is represented by the liberal party of the Free Democrats. The party »Die Linke« also represents this right for citizens as well as conservative party politics in their program consistently and very clearly speaks in favor of end-to-end encryption and wants to implement a Right to Encryption - simply and above all for everyone available.

There are also approaches in the social democratic party when the chairwoman *Saskia Esken* - in the sense of the quotation from the fourth German Chancellor *Willy Brandt* with his demand: »Dare more Democracy« - still formulated a few years ago: »Dare more Encryption!«.[16] This catchphrase was seen as a social awakening hoped for by many and a necessary social dialogue that had to be conducted.

On the part of *Saskia Esken*, it was a fitting headline based on this, when she was not yet a party leader of a ruling party, and furthermore, because she previously was trained as a state-certified computer scientist and then also worked in software development. Encryption was a fundamental aspect of her training!

However, this document later disappeared from the official Internet pages of her online blog and should only be found in the deep archives of the Internet via detours. She was apparently whistled back by those involved in party politics in the government and henceforth holds back rather with brief general statements on the subject - as in the following Twitter message after repeated requests to comment on the further implementation of the European initiative and resolution of the mandatory key handover: »Encryption protects the Privacy, security and confidentiality of communication - for each of us and even more so for those who particularly need this protection: journalists and lawyers, but also politically active people who are threatened by authoritarian regimes.«

As well as adding, months later: »I reject state Trojans in the hands of the services. That just can't be. The majority of the party opted for this path, and I respect this majority. I share the motivations for effective law enforcement. However, I still consider the agreed means (use of #StateTrojan) to be wrong.«[17]

Party members at the grassroots asked themselves whether, as party leader, she would still vote for the implementation of the EU resolution to abolish end-to-end encryption in her own country and why she wrote two years earlier that her party would not go along with it?

Jimmy Schulz, Member of Parliament, who died far too early from pancreatic cancer, and who grew up in the eastern part of Germany - the GDR -, spoke very clearly in an emotional and moving speech in the German Bundestag a few years ago about the need for a Right to Encryption for every citizen.

He was also the chairman of the Digital Agenda committee, which deals with other members of parliament with digitization, networking and digital change. He represented a vision of security in confidential communication and freedom from fear in open and private speech, and even liked anonymous communication options. He illustrated his liberal claim with experiences from the unjust state of the GDR and the surveillance of the citizens there by the organization of state security at the time, also abbreviated as »STASI«:

»That we have the opportunity to walk down these corridors, these halls (of the German Bundestag) and move freely in this house, to be part of Democracy - for which people fought for centuries and gave their lives because they to stand up for these Basic Rights and our Privacy - that is a tremendous privilege for us today!

We send unencrypted e-mails like postcards that in case of doubt anyone can read. This also applies to the popular messenger systems if they are unencrypted.

In the analog world, reading along can be prevented by an envelope - in the digital world this is done using encryption technology. They ensure that only you and the person you are speaking to can read the content of a message. The encryption technologies act like a closed envelope with a seal.

In the analogue and digital world, we need the same rights and opportunities: Privacy in today's digital space must also be protected. (..)

And this topic haunted me all my life: Because I still have that click in my ear, that click when they have been observing us. (..) Every time we called the family left behind, we were sure that they were listening. Every time we visited (.. the family), we were sure that they would overhear. We had to go to the laundry room, or go into the kitchen, turn the water tap on, just to make sure they weren't listening.

I grew up in a time when every phone call by us was monitored!

But what does this eavesdropping do: It's scary! It forces fears to speak freely and openly, to express one's opinion, and one is frightened of the consequences of what one has said. Something like that must never happen again! (..).

Encryption is a fundamental pillar for guaranteeing our Fundamental Rights. (..) The Secrecy of Correspondence as well as Postal and Telecommunications Secrecy are inviolable. This principle must also apply to electronic communications. This is what the Federal Constitutional Court for the Federal Republic of Germany also says (..) - we have a Fundamental Right to guarantee the confidentiality and integrity of IT systems (..). A Right to Encryption must therefore be demanded, in which all providers are obliged to offer services encrypted as standard: end-to-end secure. Not only secure, but tap-proof - only then can everyone (including those with no technical knowledge) be sure of communicating confidentially.«[18]

Logically, in accordance with his parliamentarian resolution, Parliament should therefore call on the government to »oblige telecommunications and telemedia providers to offer their communications services in the standard form tap-proof end-to-end encrypted.« [19]

Figure 3: Storming of the STASI headquarters in the German Office for National Security in 1990

Source:[20]

Storming of the headquarters of the Office for National Security (AfNS) on January 16, 1990 in Berlin: At a demonstration in front of the building of the former AfNS in Normannen- and Ruschestrasse, which the New Forum had called for, thousands demanded the complete dissolution of the office: Everything must be done to ensure that a spying apparatus like the State Security (STASI) - controlled by an Office for National Security (AfNS) - never emerges again as a party's instrument of power.

Politics - and especially politics in Germany against the background of historical experiences in the eastern part of Germany - must ultimately make itself honest in a set theory: whether it wants encryption for everyone, for no one, or especially wanting it for journalists, priests, and lawyers, but not for criminals! And whether there is a right to it or not, and how a balance can be found with regard to desired or necessary measures for decoding or monitoring plain text.

Following the European advance, lawyers as well as IT associations and other institutional organizations speak out in unusual clarity in favor of maintaining end-to-end encryption and against its intended restriction.

The federation of lawyers, *Bundesrechtsanwaltskammer* (BRAK), rejects the European initiative and calls for the formula »security despite encryption« to be refrained from as long as it is aimed at breaking the encryption[21]. Then the BRAK followed up in its magazine to all members and discussed whether legal communication should not even be done exclusively with end-to-end encryption and how this could then be implemented in practically every lawyer's office. [22]

However, the encryption of lawyers to clients is only one aspect. The connections to colleagues and to the courts should also be discussed. In Germany, a »special electronic attorney's mailbox« (short: beA) is provided for this purpose, the connections of which are only encrypted point-to-point via the German Bundesrechtsanwaltskammer; the continuous chain of confidentiality can be broken at any time by »recording«. It's the same dilemma as with DE-Mail.

The German government considers this risk of decryption to be »acceptable«[23]. However, several lawyers, together with the *Society for Freedom Rights* (GFF), are suing the fragile system and want to achieve end-to-end encryption[24]. This is to be decided with a constitutional complaint against the previous legal situation. After all, lawyers also see the protection of mandate secrecy as a constitutional requirement.

The association of public prosecutors and judges called *Neue Richtervereinigung* (NR) requests for more effective end-to-end encryption to be strengthened instead of weakened[25]. The *German Lawyers' Association* (DAV) also rejects such legislative provisions »in general.«[26] Who can give European parliamentarians better recommendations in this context than public prosecutors?

Even according to the ecclesiastical data protection in the Catholic Church, which demands special confidentiality for pastoral care and knows its own church laws, »a selected open-source messenger should _always_ have end-to-end encryption.« [27] Reliable security is even more important when it is about the »digital confessional« in the »Faith 2.0« program: Praying and confessing online, as offered by Einsiedeln Abbey in Switzerland, for example, with the platform »The Golden Ear«[28]: A monk of the monastery designated by the _Mishpaha_ (Hebrew for: family), the head of the 42-strong all-male community, grants the highest level of confidentiality online - in other words: so that it can be said confidentially in text form what one would otherwise not dare to express. And this requires tap-proof end-to-end encryption so that the ›Golden Ear‹ does not become the ›Golden Gazette‹ - a well-known tabloid magazine for gossip.

In particular, technicians, developers and computer scientists confirm to the political elite that a weakening of the encryption must instead be converted into a strengthening and practical application of end-to-end encryption.

The project of the end-to-end encrypting messenger GoldBug, whose name is a reminiscence based on the short story of the same name by _Edgar Alan Poe_ from 1843 about a so-called »cryptogram« (a puzzle with necessary logical combinations), explains for example in the public debate: »How should a key be secured that is sent through end-to-end encryption in order to set up further (regular) encryption?

With the announcement that they want to restrict end-to-end encryption, politics is shaking at the foundations: with software providers, with encryption methods, with transport providers and with (temporary) storage of cipher text, the so-called »hosters«. Ultimately, every email inbox is addressed.

And: Cipher text can still be generated at any time with open-source software and open-source Linux systems and inserted into existing channels and software programs. With simple »Copy & Paste«: copy,... and paste. Those who want to act illegally, on the other hand, will also use illegal tools; - but taking away everyone's security means greater harm and risk than leaving encryption in everyone's hands!« Another aspect is that the key generation is often not done centrally, but decentralized on the users' devices: »Neither symmetric nor asymmetric encryption still needs centrality« continues the project in an interview with the well-known portal *Winfuture*. [29]

The messengers Delta-Chat, Smoke-Chat, RetroShare and Threema, for example, also work according to this principle of decentralized keys on the users' devices.

The Threema developers make it clear in an interview with the newspaper »*Die Welt*«: »The encryption is carried out decentralized by the users. Therefore, app providers have no way of viewing the communication. Crime is a social and not a technological problem: one should therefore not solve a social problem with a few by weakening everyone's Privacy. Privacy is a Human Right and must also exist in the digital space.«[30]

That Democracy needs Cryptography, the GoldBug project in the aforementioned interview formulates this argument in a nutshell as follows: »Creating cipher text is like baking bread - and is not printing counterfeit money: If every communication sound of a person should be inspected like every data packet - what kind of society do we live in? Anything that leaves our mouths (digitally) confidentially - i.e., not intended for third parties - cannot and must not be subject to infiltration or distribution control in a free society«[31] - on the contrary, Privacy must be better protected by encryption and thus against automatic scanners in order to preserve democratic processes.

Should the Privacy guaranteed by the digital secrecy of letters be sacrificed in favor of transparency in communication by criminals?

Thus, after this argumentation, the political formula becomes fragile: »Encryption must not protect criminals« - because encryption is accessible and available to everyone, and at the same time it applies: »Criminals must not force the removal of protection through encryption for everyone«.

In times of the corona pandemic, for example, it would be a logic that would mean: Because of some opponents of vaccination who practice vandalism against vaccination centers, vaccination is suspended for everyone. Because encryption also wants to provide all citizens with the necessary online security and »vaccinate« their systems and Internet communication channels, that is to say: protect them.

In an interview with *Spiegel-Online* magazine, the developer of the Signal messenger finally formulated: »You can't take the encryption away from criminals«[32]. - This sounds like a requirement, but it is just a technical description. In such a way that encryption technologies like oxygen are available to everyone. Taking encryption from the Internet is like taking oxygen from life.

Several messenger providers finally got together and announced in a joint statement that from a technological point of view it is impossible to grant access to end-to-end encrypted content without endangering the security of the entire system.

And: you don't even want to state it - just a few weeks later, several European e-mail providers have teamed up once more and again issued a joint declaration: In an open, democratic society, it should not happen that the protection of the digital Secrecy of Letters is weakened and encryption is abandoned, because strong end-to-end encryption is absolutely necessary[33].

And: you can hardly tell, a further, third time, again a few weeks later, after the messengers, after the e-mail programs, the ten large classic European telecommunications companies and organizations around the *Federal Association of IT Security* (TeleTrusT) including Google and Facebook came up in their declaration »Against an unlimited expansion of surveillance and for the protection of encryption« and called among other things: »No further legal measures to be taken that would weaken or break the encryption.«[34]

And: you can hardly tell, a further, fourth time, two weeks later this call was supplemented with another two dozen associations - and renewed with the question of how a resistance to advice could be overcome.

And: you can hardly say it a fifth time: A few weeks later, major providers of Internet infrastructure across Europe, the tech companies that offer us the Internet lines, came together in a declaration: Calling on the occasion of their *RIPE conference* these experts in IP address management are urging companies and administrators of networks to finally turn on encryption as standard and to interfere louder, otherwise the monitoring and cracking of encryption would result in a »huge phishing campaign against everyone« - and then there is just no longer an investigation in the specific suspected case, which is covered by a law and approved by a judge.[35]

But you can hardly say it a sixth time: A few weeks later, more than 60 further companies, associations and individuals from civil society and business came together and clearly criticized the national legislative processes of the government from the EU initiative and on IT security. The signatories include the digital-political think tanks of major parties in Germany such as D46 (SPD), Load (FDP) and Cnetz (CDU), the Association of the Internet Industry Eco and civil society actors such as the Chaos Computer Club or Reporters Without Borders. A total of over 70

European representations. *Rainer Rehak*, who studied computer science and philosophy in Berlin and Hong Kong and researches systemic IT security and who has also signed as co-chair of the forum for computer scientists for peace and social responsibility, sums up: there is EU-wide for the weakening of the end-to-end encryption »insufficient support in business and society«[36].

And furthermore, you can hardly say it and report about a seventh initiative: a few weeks later scientists are calling for the resignation of the German Interior Minister for his totalitarian surveillance fantasies. But more on that later.

And finally, we confess the eighth initiative: the Global Encryption Day (Globalencrypt.org) is founded in which more than 153 companies and organizations call for strengthening encryption mechanisms worldwide. In addition to the Tech Company Facebook and Apple, well-known Non-Governmental-Organizations (NGOs) such as the Electronic Frontier Foundation, the World Wide Web Consortium and the Internet Society are signatory. Strong encryption is called »essential technologies«, which helps to support the confidence in online services and hedge the data from governments, companies, as well as the population.

In more than seven initiatives, we find a European mix of associations and organizations which alert with public incendiary letters and design now an Encryption Day every year worldwide on October 21st: But can a libertarian position to release the encryption of intentions to restrict - qua political »K.O.«[37] because of technical constraints or a de-facto creation of facts - already be declared the winner?

And isn't a restrictive position also a necessary point of view in order to understand »citizens as a security problem«[38] - if they cannot be taken as a basis as sovereigns?

Because some people could use encryption for criminal purposes, should and must it be withdrawn from all?! As already mentioned, this would be tantamount to the argument that all people, including surgeons, should have their knives removed because few people rammed them into other people's stomachs to kill them.

In the meantime, the situation has also changed: in the past, people wanted to move towards a libertarian position because there was hardly any encryption. Today it is open source and available to everyone, we are already in a free and libertarian situation: instead, some want to use encryption more restrictively and weaken it with back-doors.

The head of Apple, *Tim Cook*, put *Encryption for Everyone* in a nutshell: »The reality is this: if you put a back door in, that back door is for everybody, for good guys and bad guys«[39]. In other words: This knife, this technology - but potentially also a back door intended in it - is or would be available to everyone.

Tim Cook was personally recruited for the company by Apple founder *Steve Jobs* and followed him after he retired. Even during his early employment as a manager for the operational business, *Tim Cook* made many political statements and publicly addressed the reformation of international and national surveillance, the improvement of cybersecurity, national production as part of digital sovereignty, his pride in God's greatest gift to him, being gay and the activities necessary to protect the climate and the environment.

If one wants to relate this technical argumentation to a libertarian as well as a restrictive position on the use of encryption, a new formula should therefore, according to this view, be better: »Security with Encryption and No Security without Encryption«, or in other words: »Encryption despite Crime and against Cyber-Crime«.

Crimes that still exist in real life must be combated by further, other means. Encryption must be applied and secure so that it does not cause any damage - or the damage is even greater if it is not used!

In the course of the public discussion on the EU resolution, the German association *Gesellschaft für Informatik* (GI) took up exactly this reasoning a few days later and emphatically demanded »to stand up for a strong European Right to Encryption: Whoever weakens the encryption, weakens the IT-Security and thus sovereignty as a whole«.

With around 20,000 personal and 250 corporate members, this Society for Computer Science is the largest and most important specialist society for computer science in German-speaking countries and represents the interests of computer scientists in science, economy, public administration, society and politics. They all speak out »vehemently against weakening (end-to-end) encryption by duplicate keys.«[40]

Other European IT organizations such as the *Federal Association for Information Technology, Telecommunications and New Media* (Bitkom) or the *Association of the Internet Industry* (ECO) have expressed themselves in a similar way to the above-mentioned association.

The turning away from the weakening of end-to-end encryption also applies if the chat is concerned with threats, for example from »terrorism«[41] or so-called sinner rings or »shadow armies«[42] in the police and military or, if applicable, in the case of threats. Also potentially with priests in the church: should at this point, a demand of the women's movement *Maria 2.0* be added that abusive priests should not rather be redeemed from the elusiveness-illuminated celibacy and that all church offices vacancies are to be filled by all people regardless of biological sex and social gender, instead of just ridding them of encrypted network connections to their sinful accomplices in the Catholic Church?[43]

Or in reference: may (right-wing) extreme chat groups in the police like in Frankfurt or, for example, suspected cases in the Hamburg fire brigade - as an Engelwerk, so to speak - remain inaccessible? Internet columnist *Sascha Lobo* used the corresponding Danish term »hyggelig«[44] to refer to this well-being.

Sascha Lobo is referred to by some media as the »class representative for Web 2.0«. For his commitment he was awarded the Signs Award for »Visions in Communication«. At the same time, using the example of Holocaust denial in Germany, he spoke out in favor of regulating certain opinions on the Internet - and in the above column he also addressed the well-being of uncontrolled extremist groups which are also familiar with other communities.

The Engelwerk (Latin also: Opus Sanctorum Angelorum) was for a long time a spiritual movement that was viewed as a sect within the Catholic Church that was beyond the control of the Church: there have been murders and series of sexual abuse in the history of the Engelwerk community, which, however, presented itself to the outside world as if this ring of sinners were in full communion with the Catholic Church. Unimaginable if this sect formation had already been a network of laptops communicating in encrypted form back then?

›Philip B.‹ asks on Twitter: For more than a decade, hundreds of abuses in the Catholic Church by priests have been known. Why aren't the churches searched? Why aren't there raids on priests nationwide? Also in their online communication. A senior public prosecutor and spokesman for the Cologne Public Prosecutor's Office answered him the question on the phone why the public prosecutor's office had never searched despite complaints, legal proceedings and massive amounts of information: »We considered it reasonable not to search.«

And is such an exemplary, customary operational declination of the effects of encrypted chats already clear for other people such as dealers with drugs or weapons as well as contract killers?

Civil rights activists criticize that encryption is too often presented in connection with serious criminal crimes and that groups of criminals (for weapons, drugs, terror, etc.) are enumerated. The legitimate protection of the electronic Secrecy of Letters for all citizens should therefore not be presented in the media unilaterally in the light of serious criminals.

In addition to this background, there is finally the preparation of a further act in EU politics - in which a search filter is now supposed to completely monitor the electronic plain text communication of all citizens without cause.

With this follow-up legislation, the European Commission wants to prepare the introduction of chat control as an obligation for everyone in Europe. And if end-to-end encryption has been compromised with messengers, it may also apply to those. This type of chat control is currently only used by US providers.

In this context, the European parliamentarian *Patrick Breyer* refers, for example, to the legal opinion of a former judge of the European Court of Justice, according to which comprehensive message screening violates Telecommunications Secrecy[45]: Even according to the case law of the European Court of Justice, a permanent automated analysis of the communication of all chats and e-mails is only proportionate if it is restricted to suspects.

Patrick Breyer, who moved into the European Parliament as the top politician of the Pirate Party, already dealt with the systematic recording and storage of telecommunications traffic data for state purposes with the subject of data retention in his exam and has since been involved in the *data retention working group for data protection and civil rights* (AK Vorrat). *Patrick Breyer* is a father himself and wants his child to be effectively protected not only online. And that it may still grow up with private rooms and private talks, because children and adolescents also have a right to privacy - a fundamental right broken by illegal exception regulations like chat-control. What is a chat-control in the text-based messenger could soon be named in voice-based services such as Alexa, Bixby, Siri or Google a dialogue-control?

Because already today IP telephony and group chat apps such as Clubhouse, Skype or Alexa transcribe, archive, and search all spoken dialogues possibly also as text. Presidium spokesman of the Society for Computer Science (GI) *Hartmut Pohl* stands therefore next to *Patrick Breyer*: Europe wants either built-in back-doors or a secret online search for everyone through the scanning of the terminals: by searching all memory contents of all clients, servers and hard disk or cloud storage. Such a chat control 2.0 violates the European fundamental rights!

In addition, *Patrick Breyer* published a survey[46] according to which 72% of Europeans reject suspicious-less message and chat checks on everyone - with the argument that totalitarian methods are also used with this instrument, which are incompatible with a Democracy.

The legal system says that total monitoring of communication or the communication behavior of everyone is not proportionate, and the political system nevertheless implements this against the will of the majority of the citizens - in part, possibly with assignments of and shares for the technology companies. What kind of totalitarian practice and totalitarian goal is this and what a repressive method against the majority to conduct this public dialogue in the context of felons ... What is right and wrong here? - asked commentators from this group online.

In this context, civil rights activists also point out our own daily social duty to maintain a ›social glue‹: Has it got to do with encryption in chat groups, if we do not recognize radical right-wing police officers (at least in the case of personnel selection and proficiency testing or) in daily cooperation on the patrol or at lunch and whistle them back with moral courage? Does it have anything to do with the police if they are not observing priests or their own people?

Granting and restricting encryption remains difficult: Granting encryption to the good guys, such as journalists, police officers, priests and lawyers, but not to bad dealers with illegal goods, intentions or views, remains a difficult and much-discussed undertaking, especially technically and politically.

The association *Gesellschaft für Informatik* (GI, society for computer science) provides us with guidance: The fight against crime should in any case »not be at the expense of the safety of users - citizens, companies and authorities.«[47]

»Accordingly, it is to be rejected to oblige service providers to hand over keys, passwords, etc.,« pointed out the *German Federal Commissioner for Data Protection and Freedom of Information* (BfDi) in his statement on the »Right to Encryption« already a year earlier.

In terms of the intensity of the intervention, this would be tantamount to a secret »infiltration of an information technology system«, without, however, simultaneously being able to comply with the necessary technical and organizational measures with which this measure can be designed in a controllable manner. Because: this secret infiltration - the so-called »online search« with which the use of the IT system of a user is monitored and his or her storage media are read out - is constitutionally only permissible within very narrow limits.[48]

The German *Federal Office of Justice* (BfJ) has now published the statistics on the surveillance of telecommunications: The number of initial and extension orders for »classic« telecommunications surveillance was 18,255 (the majority of these are violations of the Narcotics Act and (computer-) fraud and gang theft. And for the online search, 578 judicial decisions on particularly serious crimes were passed (according to § 100b StPO such as murder and manslaughter, terror, gang theft or counterfeiting and money laundering, etc.), of which a total of 368 were actually carried out (in 2019).

The numbers from a daily online search in Germany caused quite a stir. But these statistics, published for the first time, had to be revised a few weeks later because of journalistic research. Inadvertently, some department heads gave incorrect and excessive information: Online searches using so-called Source-Telecommunication-Monitoring (in short: Sources-TCM) and Trojans are therefore »not an everyday tool«.[49] After all? - so far so good?

Finally, the *Council of European Professional Informatics Societies* (CEPIS) also highlighted the economic consequences of restricting encryption at European level: »The initiative endangers not only the informational self-determination of EU citizens but also the protection of company and business secrets. It is ultimately hindering the necessary digitization of the European economy.«

At the same time, this *Council of European Professional Informatics Societies* (CEPIS) and the *Gesellschaft für Informatik e.V.* (GI) came together on an European level and added a Right to Encryption *in Europe* to the political demand from a professional point of view, which should finally be codified[50].

The *European Cybersecurity Agency* (ENISA) had already published a study entitled »Data protection and Privacy in design« a few years earlier, which also recommends encryption programs for European economic processes, that are secure, and which must be taken into account already in the outline of an IT system architecture. [51]

The software developer *István Lám* therefore summarizes the risk of industrial espionage from a European perspective as follows: »Unfortunately, many European politicians only partially understand how end-to-end encryption works. They think it is possible to see some data for law enforcement without compromising the security of the system. Unfortunately, that is impossible. The incorporation of government back doors into encryption technology would cause great economic damage. Every company would have to fear for its trade secrets.«[52]

The Hungarian programmer *István Lám*, currently head of the Tresorit company, which offers client-side encrypted cloud storage, was already a few years ago included on the European list of »30 under 30« by Forbes magazine for his future-oriented views and work in the technology sector.

The *European Committee for Technology Assessment in the EU Parliament* (STOA) even recommended promoting existing user-friendly end-to-end encryption solutions for e-mail, messaging, chat etc. in its expertise on the subject of »mass surveillance«. Also requested: Dedicated funding or participation in open-source software to implement end-to-end encryption solutions.[53]

»We want to become the No. 1 encryption location in the world«[54] - the German *Ministry of the Interior* also summed up this goal a few years ago in harmony with the technical experts at European level. This task was also formulated in the overarching contract of the German governing parties of the *grand coalition*: User-friendly »end-to-end encryption should be available to everyone«[55].

This agreement of the governing parties, the parliamentary demand for a Right to Encryption, as well as the expressed advice and recommendations of the technicians, data protectionists, lawyers, churches and also representatives of companies, to strengthen the end-to-end encryption, been led into an upside down standing world by those responsible in Europe only a few time later: Instead of *more* end-to-end encryption, encryption should now become *more fragile and easier to intercept* - at least for commercial providers in Europe.

As a consequence, users of Internet communication will (and have to) rely on open-source programs and their own private chat servers in the future if the citizens of Europe want to continue communicating at this established level: fear-free, confidential and tap-proof.

1.3   The third act: Main role of novella ●

But this unusual story, in which many social actors take part, continues (in the third act) as the European requirements then flowed into country-specific regulations:

Only a few days later after this EU resolution to unleash the keys for encryption, first mover Germany, for example, already presented the draft of its amendment to the IT Security Act: the publication date was on a Wednesday afternoon. The main change in the - as is the term technicus - »regulatory regime« on the 180 relevant pages in the package with over 460 pages of amendment to the law was the change that (encrypting) messengers (§ 3) are now also included in the scope of application: namely telecommunication systems, telecommunication networks and telecommunication services that are provided within the scope of this Act (§ 1.2). So far, only those Internet and telephone service providers who are linked to a specific number have been included. This stipulates that the new law now also applies to »interpersonal communication services« (item 61) or to systems, networks and services that generally send »signals«.

So, everything that transmits is a telecommunications system.

And: The operation of a publicly accessible telecommunications service is to be reported and is therefore subject to registration (§ 5)[56].

Service providers based outside the EU should also potentially be held legally accountable: Regulations on inventory data information (§ 171) up to and including sanctioning measures, which are implemented via a so-called »sector organization« - according to Article 30 of the EU Code for electronic communication – and could go beyond.[57]

The political highlight of this amendment from number-based services to signal-oriented services continued to be the rush-hour procedure with which it was carried out shortly before Christmas: the option to submit customary statements ended 24 hours later: Thursday, 2:00 p.m.

Experts from the *Critical Infrastructures Working Group* (AG KRITIS) headed by Manuel ›HonkHase‹ Atug burst the collar when asked to comment on the latest draft within 24 hours: »Such a short period is a ministerial middle finger in the face of civil society!«[58], it was reported probably from the environment of the working group, which has set itself the goal of improving IT security and the resilience of critical infrastructures (KRITIS) with a group of experts. Founder and spokesman Manuel Atug is therefore invited to the committees as an expert in hearings in legislative processes such as the amendment to the IT Security Act.

Following this impulse, fifteen associations and organizations turned to the ministries with an open letter[59] and clear demands. The good practice culture of the participation of civil society and the acquisition of external expertise for proposed legislation should no longer only be simulated: A few days for a quick review are now more rule than exception, but unacceptable for a competent discussion of often complex proposed legislation and their technology assessment in the field of IT.

On the short message service Twitter, said *#Middlefinger* was converted into the slogan *#EvenMoreSoNow* (#JetztErstRecht): This term referred to an action to increase the sending of cipher text in the channels of the Internet. In defiance, users will now send increased cipher text to the Internet - and even more so now - increasingly encrypt more texts and files.

For example, with the e-mail-based Delta-Chat-Messenger or the simple SmokeStack chat server and its freely available and open-source messenger derivatives - as well as RetroShare or the communication function of Freenet ... Or the well-known encryption suite Spot-On, for example, on a small Raspberry-Pi computer that can regularly send encrypted packets with the so-called »Impersonator« function, but which (before encryption) only contain random words and no real chat or message text with meaning. Real fake news. There are many ways of sending cipher text automatically and regularly - with or without a presumption of meaning in the message.

The lawyers *Martin Delhey* and *Christoph R. Müller* then followed up the discussion *»Jetzt erst Recht«* in their article with precisely this title in the *Berliner Anwaltsblatt*, not to mention the newly introduced key management in the concept of the state regulatory regime for the secure communication of lawyers only to be proven as unsafe, but also afflicted with serious security deficiencies.

Martin Delhey sees the conceptual orientation of his law firm as a manufacturer for law, which stands for independence, creativity and technical excellence. *Christoph R. Müller* also works as a lawyer in Leipzig and as a lecturer, an educational assignment at private educational institutions is also important to him.

In the opinion of the two lawyers - *Niklas Luhmann* as the most important German-speaking representative of the sociological system theory sends his regards - there would be a self-referential circular conclusion of an auto-poietic system[60]. This means: The structure of the central key management proposed at European level is simply incompatible for the legal system with the basic idea of end-to-end encryption, which requires secure communication, especially without an intermediary.

In terms of content, the novella-amendment specifically means that (signaling) messenger providers should now also archive keys and give them out if necessary. Here, too, at the national level of the EU, using Germany as an example, the decentralized key generation on the users' devices and temporary, so-called ephemeral keys, which may not be accessible in the haze of volatile designs or, as we will see further below, which do not even have to be transmitted over the Internet, are not taken into account!

And the amendment logically means that, in addition to keys, the associated messages and IP addresses must also be given further focus!

It also means and defines that a modem or router at home is just as publicly accessible as a mailbox at home; just as a node of the randomization network Tor or a private chat server can be reached at home. Who wanted to distinguish or register them all?

Where no one complains, no one judges - and those with technical skills will continue to have private chat servers for the family, class or sports group at home. With the approximately 6000 public servers of the Tor randomization network, which may then be more closely monitored, however, with this amendment, around 1/6 of these servers just in Germany will soon cease to exist because they are unregistered.[61]

And at the same time, such a communication router - or technically often referred to as a so-called »listener« - can still be present at each of the 65,535 ports of an IP address. Does a

European government now want to control and monitor over 65,000 potential »sleepers« behind every IP address - if we supplement the technical term »listener« (or: listening server) like that? That would be a complex undertaking, although such port scans could run and computers could easily monitor 65,000 port entries per IP address.

However, the new IPv6 protocol expands these possibilities again and requires more extensive security concepts or makes the request to monitor, track and potentially bring any port-node and any unidentified data-packet on the Internet to court, also seem nonsensical. It would be total surveillance.

The new data retention - a so-called ›matrix monitoring‹ based on the film of the same name - is therefore not only the storage and monitoring of IP addresses, but also of all ports and data packets. Will politicians soon be demanding complete matrix monitoring of all communication systems at all ports?

In the science fiction film »The Matrix«, the young hacker Neo receives a mysterious message on his computer screen that he should »follow the white rabbit« (a quote from Alice in Wonderland). The next morning, while working as a software developer, he is called by a mysterious protagonist named Morpheus, who explains to him that the world, he believes he lives in, is just a simulation and that he would be just a trapped slave in this computer-generated dream world, the matrix. Agents guard the matrix and its communication channels and act like protection programs against human revolutionaries like Morpheus and Neo who hack into the matrix through ports of telephone lines in order to free people. However, this is dangerous because if you believe you are dying in the matrix, or if you lose your port to the matrix, you will actually die. Does this mean that real people also die when all electronic communication systems at all available ports are subjected to total surveillance?

And if no scans for listeners at IP addresses or port numbers are carried out in order to find unregistered Tor or chat servers or messenger services, the situation might first have to be assessed on the basis of the existing cipher text streams in the data line: With that, however, we are already in a society that casts doubt on any sending of cipher text - and thus also on our security standard in many areas, including those that are system-relevant.

Just three months after the EU resolution, the *Rostock Higher Regional Court* (OLG) in Germany carried out precisely this, the legal presumption of innocence to be overturned: Even the use of crypto-cipher text »indicates a conspiratorial behavior to commit and cover up criminal offenses and justifies urgent suspicion«[62], it said in this judgment.

In an analogous example, the legal question is: If a person carries a crowbar, may that be enough for a conviction or even just a search for a possible break-in?

The presumption of innocence is one of the fundamental principles of the rule of law in legal proceedings and is today recognized by most countries in the world. This »In dubio pro reo« (»in case of doubt for the accused«) goes back to the French Cardinal *Jean Lemoine* (1250-1313) and *Friedrich Spee*, who wrote this (in 1631) in his Cautio Criminalis, an extensive work against the practice the witch hunts, which were rampant at the time, took up and deepened.

The contributions to the discussion on the new data retention, who communicated when with whom on which port, and on the criminalizing of cipher text through the reversal of the presumption of innocence, resulted from the reaction of many Twitter users that it would soon be time to send automated cipher text as »sovereignty noise« into the lines of the Internet.

For example, the user ›BitMagier‹ writes: »If end-to-end encryption should really be criminalized in the future, permanent

»noise connections« will ensure that you can no longer distinguish between noise and encrypted communication«!

The female user ›Sunrise‹ adds: »The regulatory regime's compulsory control will end in a catastrophe. As soon as encryption has been banned by one of the governments, a crypto storm of apocalyptic proportions will sweep across the earth and encrypt everything that comes into contact with it«.

The use of a virtual private network (VPN) channel, for example from your own open-source firewall PFSENSE, in which the VPN server is already implemented, to your own mobile phone or your own web server, is completely sufficient - if so-called »Impersonator-Noise«, meaningless cipher text to simulate an encryption of a chat, is to be sent through the line.

At the same time, hundreds of thousands of employees or learners are connected to the company or educational network every day with an end-to-end encrypted VPN tunnel and, like an encrypting messenger, only send real cipher text to the Internet. Addressing pupils in hybrid digital lessons using »home schooling« via a VPN connection in a pandemic time also remained free of third-party interferes.

Figure 4: Connection of the home office workstation with a VPN tunnel to the company network

Source:[63]

In a VPN network, a VPN client creates an encrypted connection as a tunnel through the Internet to a VPN server. The connection is encrypted end-to-end. Only cipher text is visible on the Internet. This tunnel can also be used to send cipher text from a messenger to a private server.

Lawyers will therefore deal with the definition of when a listener on a port, and not a server on an IP address, is considered commercial, public or private or semi-private or unregistered. And whether port users who access unregistered telecommunications systems to the public are partly to blame if third parties use these in-future criminalized telecommunications systems - or whether the port providers of unregistered telecommunications systems are solely responsible. As well as: whether it is technically proportionate and feasible to create account-based ports in order to exclude the public from previously accessible telecommunications systems on these ports for messenger chats.

So, will users be allowed in the future to send nonsensical cipher text as noise through their own network connection? Who wanted to forbid people in the home office from using the VPN channel whose end node could be a VPN port to a wild chat server or the productive company network? Sending chat cipher text through a VPN channel is advanced multi-encryption, the different architectures and case constellations of which would or will keep lawyers busy for years. Especially since many employees in the home office are equipped with the standard of a VPN channel by the IT departments and are further equipped according to the corporate novellas and security requirements.

It was precisely because of these and other questions that the hearing on the IT Security Act 2.0 was rescheduled after the turn of the year: Over a dozen organizations and associations took part and any comment hardly left a good hair on the law project. In particular, the exclusion of open-source providers was criticized and also the expanded role of the *Federal Office for Information Security* (BSI), which is now given different powers - some also say: hacker powers - to act in the event of security gaps in future: the BSI may perform port scans and use so-called honeypots as Trojans. The port scans for unregistered telecommunications systems may begin now.

With 799 new jobs, which cost 74.24 million euros in personnel costs, the office should be a key player in the fight against automated server networks, neglected devices in the Internet of Things - that would be telecommunications systems on a Raspberry-Pi computer, for example -, and nodes for the dissemination of defined software.

The publicist, network activist and Member of Parliament, *Anke Domscheid-Berg*, who took part in the hearings, summed up for all the statements that she had not seen in all those years within German Bundestag that ALL experts - including those invited by the government - would have torn a draft bill so devastatingly in the air as it happened in this committee at the hearing on the security law #ITSig20. Security measures in IT are correct and important, but authorizations and knowledge should not be superimposed for and with monitoring and surveillance measures. *Anke Domscheid-Berg* is also a member of the

»Artificial Intelligence« Enquete-commission and advocates gender equality and women in management positions, a topic that she addressed early on with a study on »Female Leadership in Europe« as an IT strategy consultant.

Cultural-politician *Konstantin von Notz* works today as a lawyer and faithful Protestant in the »IuK«-commission - Information and Communication - at the Parliament's Council of Elders, which is responsible, among other things, for the IT equipment of the parliament's offices. In addition, he warned the German Bundestag and also in view of the IT security needs of the country's general energy and water supply: »The hut is burning brightly« - what is needed in the legislation is more secure end-to-end encryption, less mass surveillance and more open-source[64], so the now defined and recommended leadership duties for an online living together.

But the dispute over the control intentions of the ministries of the interior took another round after a short time: two interior ministers led by social democrats (from Lower Saxony and Mecklenburg-Western Pomerania) followed suit - and demanded identification on the Internet, e.g. for messengers and social networks. In the reform of the Telecommunications Act (TKG), according to this catalog of requirements, operators of so-called number-independent telecommunications services such as e-mail providers or messengers are to be obliged to »collect and verify user identification features and, in individual cases, make them available to the security authorities.«[65]

That would be a real name requirement with verification of the identity card via the telephone number or directly via the identity card, as is the case with the allocation of SIM phone cards.

The personal data on the real name should be saved across the board as a counterpart to the communication messages of the citizens for the purpose of possible future criminal prosecution. This identification is to be supplemented by address, date of birth and location information during operation - which in the 5G network is even more precise to the nearest centimeter than has previously been the case.

But this is nothing more than (data) retention of people, which has a different quality than IP data retention for Internet connections. (And even so, this difference cannot even justify IP data storage in advance.)

The question arises why the human number, which will be mentioned here later on and was decided at the same time, was not mentioned as a clear identification feature in this context? - We'll come back to that.

The users would always first have to carry out an identification process or show their ID before they can communicate electronically and would be forced to deposit their verified data with numerous companies all over the world. Often these are companies with advertising-financed, data-driven business services, to which the verified data of the users would be delivered on a silver platter under the justification of security measures.

Linus Neumann, a spokesman for the Chaos Computer Club, rates this request on the well-known *Netzpolitik* portal as follows: »That would be an unprecedented attack on European values and the free Internet. Things that we normally use to differentiate ourselves from China. This attack on everyone's freedom of communication and the freedom of expression of minorities is unparalleled and would be an immoderate attempt to restrict Fundamental Rights. Storing personal data of innocent citizens without cause is also disproportionate and permeated by authoritarian thinking, which contradicts the German Basic Law«[66].

Linus Neumann is not only a consultant for IT security, but as a qualified psychologist, he also considers attacks on human beings' values as critical and therefore recommends an independent and evidence-based security policy in IT, in which measures that restrict Fundamental Rights in particular should be evaluated in advance with regard to their effect.

A real name requirement not only makes it possible to find a speaker on the Internet, but also requires the permanent storage of the chatting from yesterday, which the Internet often never forgets - the first Federal Chancellor of the German Republic, *Konrad Adenauer*, in his well-known bon mot, at least for the fleeting spoken words, »did not care«. He is supposed to have said: »What do I care about my chatting from yesterday, nothing prevents me from becoming wiser?« The procedure would be an infinite inadequacy documentation.

By the way, *Konrad Adenauer* was also an inventor and pioneer of ideas and applied for numerous patents. However, since he was often unsuccessful in registering his curious inventions, he did not mention this in his memoirs. For example, the »device to protect against glare from headlights of oncoming vehicles, consisting of a head-shield or glasses« was created. This was rejected by the patent office in 1937, on the grounds that this was nothing new - today, when ›driving‹ on the Internet, he could certainly have used such a head screen against the data-screening activities of the technology agencies and to protect Privacy?

To no longer be able to contribute opinions on the Internet under a pseudonym has been studied far too little in a behavior-controlling component with its negative and positive effects of permanent storage in a global public.

The passages on the online identification requirement were no longer included when the reform of the German *Telecommunications Act* (TKG) was passed. Not yet. And yet the mail providers like GMX have already started quietly to obtain identification from customers without a stored mobile number. Otherwise, it will no longer be possible to send e-mails.

Only a few weeks later, the Partner Search Platform Tinder - part of the Facebook Group – created technical facts: the clear name & person identification has (at first optionally) been implemented.

In addition for this purpose, operators of public cellular networks across the EU must now »provide an unencrypted surveillance copy in their roaming contracts in the EU.«[67] Only encryption for text and audio via roaming that is set up by end users themselves will remain unaffected.

Germany is just one example of how a country is implementing the EU amendment into country-specific legislation - if different laws then have to be harmonized in all EU countries, there is already a call for an EU-wide regulation to be drawn up that the police and the judiciary have access to encrypted content and can also view and copy it unobserved. This European »legal framework for decryption«[68] should also affect hardware manufacturers. This is diametrically opposed to the elaboration of a »European Right to Encryption« called for by the numerous associations and organizations above.

1.4 The fourth act:
Nobody intends to monitor:
On the crisis of Privacy in the 21st century •

But it comes - in a fourth act just a few days later - even worse: Together with the *IT Security Act* 2.0 and the amendment to the *Telecommunications Act* (TKG), the new BND law was also introduced before Christmas: The *Federal Intelligence Service of Germany* (Bundesnachrichtendienst, BND) can now ask foreign intelligence agencies for mass surveillance of communications.

In addition, this organization itself can continue to subject 30 percent of the Internet traffic from the existing national telecommunications networks to strategic telecommunications intelligence[69]. It is known from the Snowden papers that the USA, for example, uses the programs XKEYSCORE and PRISM to permanently record and monitor almost 100 percent of Internet traffic: »Permanent Record«[70] is also the book title of the documentation by *Edward Snowden*, who uncovered this as a former employee of the American National Security Agency (NSA). And it is increasingly true: The Facebook group with WhatsApp will soon control more than half of the world's population!

For 100 percent surveillance in Germany, for example, the new 70-30 rule now applies: 30 percent domestic surveillance, the rest is regulated »out-bound« - that is, outsourced abroad and monitored overseas through targeted inquiries. The German *Federal Intelligence Service* (BND) will be allowed to spy on up to 30 percent of all networks globally, carry out secret online searches and cooperate closely with the NSA.

This law[71] resulting from the amendment with its extended monitoring options applies not only to the police and trusted people (V-persons) in the criminal investigation offices, but also to the *Federal Intelligence Service* (BND, with 6500 employees and a budget of 1022 million euros), also for the Agency for *Protection of the Constitution* (Verfassungsschutz, federal and state governmental, with 3864 employees and a budget of EUR 476 million) and in the field of defense for the *Military Counterintelligence Service* (MAD, with 1,255 employees and a budget of EUR 113 million). And: The police can continue to monitor, now supplemented by the tool of a so-called state Trojan.

Figure 5: Overview of selected surveillance

Surveillance measures of individuals	Basis in the (German) law	Approval by	Implementation in cooperation with	If necessary, protective shield to be overcome
Observation (classic)	§ 28 Abs. 2 Nr. 1 BPolG	Law court	In-house	Wearing a hat on your face.
Eavesdropping as communication surveillance	§ 100a StPO	Law court	Elektronic-Provider	Speak softly in the basement.
State Trojans: Source-TCM (with additional app)	§ 100a StPO	Law court	Telephone manufacturer / SIM-Provider	TEE: Trusted Execution Environment.
Provider-Fork: Cipher-Text-Copy	§ 100a StPO	Law court	Internet-Provider	Multi-Encryption.
Online-Search by state	§ 100b StPO Abs. 1	Law court	Operating Sys. manufacturer	Firewall like PFSENSE.
Key-Logging: Keyboard taps in plain text	§ 100b StPO	Law court	*Without add. App:* Apple / Google	Open Keyboard -App / TEE.
Use microphones from **speaking devices**	§ 100a & 100b StPO	Law court	*Without add. App:* Amazon / Apple / Google	Device has been removed.

Observation is traditionally the covert, targeted and systematic monitoring of people, groups of people, facilities or things and is to be distinguished from other surveillance measures such as online searches and telephone surveillance. If the phone or apartment is tapped, it is also referred to as eavesdropping. Surveillance programs that are secretly installed on suspects' devices are colloquially known as state Trojans. The aim is to monitor ongoing communication. If the Internet line is tapped and copied (forked) at the provider, one speaks of a provider fork, which can include plain text, cipher text and visited websites if these were not fed through an alternating VPN / TOR tunnel. If the entire target device is searched, it is referred to as online search. Keylogging of text entries on the smartphone through the keyboard app as well as the use of the microphones of voice-controlled devices are usually addressable via the device or the operating system and do not require any additional installation.

In addition to fundamental criticism of surveillance measures, some now fear that the work of the services and the police in this area cannot be clearly separated. The doctrine that »everyone is allowed to do anything« violates the principle of separation between the police and the secret services (in Germany). The installation of a state Trojan on the end devices is still not clearly distinguishable from the online searches (because this has completely different and higher requirements) and is comparable to the approval requirements for classic surveillance measures. And: The Office for the Protection of the Constitution is not only authorized to observe groups of people with anti-constitutional tendencies, but also individuals (which is currently in Germany not allowed). With its split into federal and state levels, the Office for the Protection of the Constitution gets an unconstitutional egg with imbalances and legal uncertainties that may need to be synchronized further in the nest, not to say: net-work, with the state trojan for source telecommunications monitoring (Sources-TCM).

Because now all 19 secret services in Germany get state Trojans. Internet providers need to help with the installation. Including Source-TCM-plus, i.e., other agencies may use this, not only for ongoing communication, but also for stored communication from the past, which is an online search.

In addition: From now on, the telecommunications of the citizens can be monitored preemptively, any cases - even without a specific initial suspicion.

The constitutional lawyer *Benjamin Rusteberg* sums up why a mishmash of online searches and state Trojans would lead with a clear eye to the unconstitutionality and misuse of the instruments for the police and secret services for the analysis of groups as well as individuals: The state Trojan for secret services is an extremely difficult intervention, that meets the requirements of proportionality in Germany in any case not enough. In this way, not only a copy of the communication is diverted, but also targeted manipulation of private data is made possible: everyone could have everything played on their computers without denying it or being able to defend against it. The German G10 commission, which actually approves interventions by secret services in advance, is now outside the field and even with the police, subsequent judicial approvals are only retrospective. This means that in ostensibly urgent cases the door is open to all those interested in all-round surveillance[72]. Google, Apple and Microsoft as well as Amazon Alexa become accomplices in the implementation of surveillance. Even the Scientific Service of the German Bundestag had already raised these points of criticism in advance. [73] The Federal Council then approved the state Trojan for the secret services and suspended it for the next time for the federal police.

As another result, the *Max Planck Institute for Research into Crime, Security and Law* has now developed a category-based concept on the basis of material collections from the *DigitalCourage* association, which can be used to compile a surveillance accounting system (Überwachungsgesamtrechnung, ÜGR). This is like a monitoring barometer[74], because the efforts to monitor in Germany and Europe or on the Internet are never ending.

The so-called data retention - the storage of IP addresses, who was in electronic contact with whom for how long - was initially rewritten unchanged in this German legislative package, although such storage is temporarily suspended after a court order, as there are Europe-wide several lawsuits constitutionally pending against the mass surveillance of all citizens without cause; - and in England legally was already considered not compatible.

Overall, it is a general attack by numerous political actors on the Privacy of Internet users. Much more: There is a worldwide crisis of the private sphere in the 21st century: The capitalist mode of production[75] with its exchange of goods also enables the trade in private data, so that the use of surveillance techniques for profit purposes and the monopoly of means of communication are connected with it.

And at the same time, it is about state power - against the citizens - combined with a struggle of the politicians for an understanding of technology and its procedural complexity and sufficient accuracy: Do Germans distribute the stars and filter criteria particularly comprehensively and thoroughly during the next indexing? The corona pandemic already showed how unvaccinated people and those against vaccinations can be indexed and excluded from civil liberties. And anyone who does not reveal own data or does not make it decipherable is also considered suspicious. Everyone who did not go through the previously voluntary X-ray body scanner will have experienced this in an airport control: It was reported that some passengers were then manually scanned twice as critically, even shoved.

Analogously, it can mean: Whoever does not make their private data available, does not allow it to be screened, or even encrypts it, is particularly spied on and checked? That would be a behavior-based control beyond any assumption of innocence: Who is not a member of WhatsApp is already considered strange and tomorrow will certainly be suspicious? Encrypted messengers should be understood as protection of Privacy and not as an indication of the need for surveillance - just as the envelope is supposed to protect the letter in the analog world and it must not be opened by curious interest by couriers. Letters are not postcards with envelopes that can be viewed by everyone, but rather sealed writings that need to be protected.

Who is more likely to understand the technical tools, including encryption and their social consequences for society, the economy, the education system and the rule of law, and assess them in the interests of everyone - those with a technical, civic or political interest? How do we notice that or when interest in news content and sanction-driven fear or total control with reporting and identification override a Right to Privacy? Is it necessary to assess in which areas restrictive decision-making options are discriminatory against human dignity?

In any case, power imbalances in digital communication could only be countered in the future through decentralization instead of centralization of our information technologies and communication structures: People then take care of the infrastructure of their electronic communication at the ports they can use instead of leaving it to providers who cannot adequately guarantee their Privacy.

Does such an extended, central matrix surveillance soon lead back to a »niche society«, as it was previously ascribed to the GDR? The term niche society was coined in 1983 by the publicist *Günter Gaus*, who had lived in the 1970s as head of the permanent representation of the Federal Republic in East Berlin of the GDR. Subcultures, which were only accessible to a limited extent to state censorship because they were organized in private circles, offered spaces for retreat and development, which sometimes gave the impression of a society in niches for everyday life in the GDR[76].

Does that mean today that if cipher text is criminalized, the socialization of cipher text will no longer take place publicly, but only in the private niche of insiders in the secured network?

Technically translated, this means the formation of a trust network, a so-called »Web-of-Trust«. Users only establish an encrypted connection with trusted friends in order to communicate with them and share information and files. - And if necessary, they network in the background with the same users who activate their port or server to the outside world with friends.

An obligation to report or register communication options can lead to a comparable situation in which one not only has to look for access to a wifi network in order to send a chat message, but also to find an undiscovered but public access to a non-registered chat server to be able to send a cipher text *without a stored key*. If - according to this law - it should now apply: Sending an encrypted chat message - without depositing the key in a state repository or with state access - is a criminal offense.

For example, the Tor network for anonymous surfing could then be converted to a network not with public access, but to a network in which the access is only known to friends. This then represents a transformation of the network access from a public peer-to-peer (P2P) access to an account-based friend-to-friend (F2F) access - as in the architecture of Freenet or RetroShare and other networks has already been implemented as a model. The only difference is that these are not yet prepared for surfing the web, as is the case with the Tor, I2P, Wireguard or Psiphon networks. The future will show which of these candidates will offer (so-called »remote«) web surfing via the computer of friends as a supplementary option.

Figure 6: Trusted friend-to-friend (F2F) connections in a web of trust

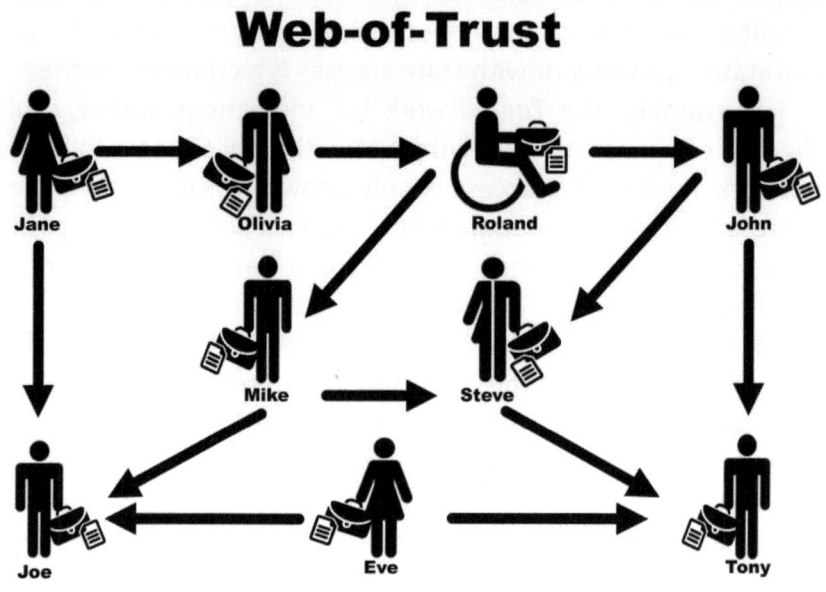

Source:[77]

In a trusted network (WoT, Web-of-Trust) only friends connect to known friends whom they know and whom they trust. The connections are encrypted. Another node in the network cannot establish a connection if the corresponding trust has not been confirmed. These connections can be used to forward messages and access websites. Telecommunications systems remain private through these friend-to-friend (F2F) networks and are not public and therefore not reported or identified. Since only secure connections exist, a group that is secured in this way could implement these network activities in a less visible niche.

Does the restriction, prohibition or even criminalization of encryption soon lead to the fact that even more people may seek protection in a solidarity or gang-like niche, as was the case under the state security regime in the GDR? If the web is no longer explored publicly and encrypted communication is no longer sent publicly via appropriate service providers, but rather designed from a private niche with private, encased technology that is protected or unregistered in a network, which may be less transparent and therefore less observable?

A Right to Encryption, on the other hand, protects against communication drifting into a niche that is no longer observable because it is private. And the Right to Encryption also guarantees well-trained citizens and, ultimately, qualified staff in a country that not only wants to be the »world champion in encryption« (see above), but also has to be in decryption, since other countries projects, units and platforms also train and offer this standard and the qualified staff. To do this, we would also have to put encryption technology with appropriate communication servers in the hands of interested parties?

So, will this European attack on end-to-end encryption and its electronic communication servers in the coming decade - just like the American attack on encryption in the 1990s - mean that not only GPG remains a standard as it was then, but will the modern methods of the currently discussed end-to-end encryption continue to establish themselves in the end?

And how do innovative encryption technologies develop further: For example, the so-called »Cryptographic Calling«, which is explained in more detail below, i.e., the immediate renewal of end-to-end encryption within an ongoing online session? Or e.g., the 2-Way-Calling described below, in which each side contributes half of a password for a common password to be created? Or a Cryptographic Calling with asymmetric temporary keys of the secure McEliece algorithm? Or also Cryptographic Calling with the so-called »Fiasco-Forwarding«-Keys, in which up to a dozen keys are derived per message?

Who wanted to save all these keys of the different methods, export it and assign it to the messages, time stamps and ports? Especially if these keys - as we will see below with the Juggerknaut Keys and Secret Stream Keys - are no longer transmitted over the Internet in the Third Epoch of Cryptography?

Tim Cook, the head of Apple, made forward-looking statements about this technical effort and the current issues. He does not want to take on the role of a new STASI: »We (technicians) don't feel like we should be in the middle of it [messaging]. I'm the FedEx guy. I'm taking your package and I'm delivering it. I just do it like this. My job isn't to open it up, make a copy of it, put it over in my cabinet in case somebody later wants to come say, I'd like to see your messages. That's not a role that I play. It's not a role that I think I should play. And it's certainly not a role I think you want me to play.«[78]

That sounds not only very sophisticated, well-considered and pointed, but also very clear and under pressure! As seen above in the San Bernadino case, the police authorities did not get the green light from Apple for decryption processes, at least in public. And technically speaking, technology companies do not want to and cannot start hoarding every key. There is also a question of liability for them. The trustee concept with regard to the keys, messages and an index of who sent what message text to whom and when, is rejected not only by users, but also by business. And a purely state trust for the sorting of keys would possibly be neither effective nor efficient in view of the rapid innovation and the high volume of cross-border messages.

Since we now know that the (let's call it) »attempt across Europe« to make the issue of keys mandatory was also shaped by the Five-Eyes and the leading United States of America, this can also be understood as a »staged revolving door effect«: Apple will be brought to the north via the European route and will be forced to keep keys for the US market and at the same time for the whole world, if European countries will do so. A ›firing stage two‹ of the demand for the unleashing of copied keys may still be expected. And: Europe will then stand in the role of a stirrup holder for a global erosion of data protection. Or in the eyes of those who want to decrypt: have set a new standard. This could also apply in the future to Apple, which can then no longer refuse - if European companies take the lead in collecting keys.

At the same time, technicians also know that with the trust of customers they have a high level of responsibility for their personal data and communication and that any expansion or publicity of investigation cases can mean the end of their business fundamentals. Who would have left their phone in the responsibility of the NSA if that intelligence agency had been a phone operator when *Edward Snowden* felt he had to say they were storing and filtering everything? The big technology groups of the GAFAM group do nothing else today: save the data of their customers and search it for advertising and profit purposes - and probably also for national security.

And yet *Tim Cook*, as the head of Apple, at the *»International Privacy Conference of Data Protection and Privacy Commissioners«* - an international data protection conference - in Brussels deliberately refrained from speaking about his company in his opening speech with the title: »About ethics: Dignity and respect in data-driven life«, when he stages his company as a model student in the discipline of data protection and Privacy protection: »In contrast to Facebook, Google and many of our Californian neighboring companies, Apple does not make its money collecting data about its users and then to sell advertising space on their screens. Apple is a hardware company that earns billions from the sale of computers, tablets and smartphones and wants to become world champion in data protection«[79]. So no word about alleged measures to support national security. Should one already note at this point: »Canary, I hear you trap!«? - we will come back to that later.

Research by the *New York Times*[80] recently showed how Apple is compromising with the regime when it comes to encrypting user data in China in order to secure the benevolence of the dictatorship. Apple transports its digital keys, which are used to encrypt the data, to China, where they do without the established security devices in which the keys are stored. A Chinese state-owned company has direct access to the servers with the private data. With this, Apple is now sending the signal: If the pressure is just high enough, civil rights activist *Tim Cook* will no longer be seen: He not only makes himself untrustworthy as a protector of Privacy worldwide, but this investigative research also shows that a published image not must match the actions behind the scenes.

The *New York Times* also reported with *CNN* that Apple spied on over 100 opposition and media accounts under the administration of former US President *Donald Trump*. *Tom Burt*, Microsoft's corporate vice president for customer security and trust, told members of the House Judiciary Committee that federal law enforcement in recent years has been presenting the company with between 2,400 to 3,500 secrecy orders a year, or about ten to fifteen per workday for years and demanded that infinite measures be limited in time and that the target person be informed afterwards[81].

Also, Apple will not offer its VPN with secure keys called Private Relay in China, Belarus, Colombia, Egypt, Kazakhstan, Saudi Arabia, South Africa, Turkmenistan, Uganda and the Philippines.

Human Rights remain as a slogan on the company website - this is known as »green-washing« - something like: falsely conjuring up the blue of the sky.

The European blueprint for legally overturning end-to-end encryption turns out to be a - political and social, if not as feared economic - fiasco: Especially when a European country like Germany wants to become again a master in - then electronic - awarding of stars and filter criteria in a full index of plain text or at first triggers a search for cipher text senders on unregistered ports.

If Turkey and Prime Minister *Recep Tayyip Erdoğan* were in the EU, he would soon be able to search all chats and e-mails for the keyword of his opposition enemy »Fethullah Gülen« and to be able to remove thousands more journalists, teachers and judges from the civil service, who have spoken textually on this keyword or even only researched? - as happened in the last few years with over 70,000 state employees in the Turkish »waves of purges«[82].

In a telephone conversation at the time, *Recep Tayyip Erdoğan* instructed his son to get the money out of the house as quickly as possible. He admitted the authenticity of further telephone calls. *Recep Tayyip Erdoğan* himself suspects that these corruption allegations are a conspiracy of the Muslim preacher *Fethullah Gülen*. His Gülen movement is trying to form a »state within the state« and wants to harm him and the party before the 2014 election. Even if many observations assume *Fethullah Gülen* as Erdoğan's opponent and the actual mastermind of the corruption affair, these opposition questions were followed by numerous dismissals from professional existences among the supporters of *Fethullah Gülen* who communicated about it.

Back then, in Turkey there were these encryption apps no such mature: Delta-Chat, which encrypts the chat well for the transport, or the FDroid-App Smoke-Chat, which also encrypts the chat well on your own device; or an IPhone if the keys are or should be in good hands, not in your own hand, but in the hands of Apple.

Even if technical tools are not a solution to free speech, which is seen as a political problem in Democracy, in emerging state authorizations they remain a building block for the protection of Privacy. Because: the names are interchangeable, whether they are called *Fethullah Gülen* in Istanbul, *Joshua Wong* in Hong

Kong, *Maryja Kalesnikawa* in Belarus or *Alexei Navalny* in Moscow or those who think along and express their own opinion orally or textually, be it publicly or privately to friends. Encryption can protect free speech and democratic research and discussion processes by people who are described by others as unpleasant representatives of divergent opinions.

The example of the 34-year-old journalist and human rights activist *Omar Radi* from Morocco shows that telephone computers are the preferred target for surveillance. According to Amnesty International, he was spied on by Moroccan authorities using the Israeli software »Pegasus«.

The software »Pegasus« from the Israeli company NSO is one of the most powerful surveillance tools in the world. The espionage program can be installed remotely in secret, without the target person being aware of it. No physical access to the device is necessary. Amnesty International security experts found that numerous journalists' telephones had been infected with the »Pegasus« Trojan in order to carry out extensive and unnoticed spying. The *BBC* reports on a list of more than 50,000 monitoring victims for the Pegasus Trojan.[83]

More and more of such tools »Made in Israel«, now well over a dozen, are specialized for eavesdropping on our phones and are also reaching countries that are tracking opposition, critical journalists or activists for Human Rights.

Omar Radi wanted to report on corruption in his country and on the links between companies and the political elite. He had also been critical of the Moroccan royal family. Technically, the Internet browser on *Omar Radi*'s smartphone was then redirected and the »Pegasus« spyware software was installed on the Moroccan's device. In an interview with the research network *»FB Stories«*, *Omar Radi* describes when he was targeted by Moroccan investigative authorities: »I live in an authoritarian police state. They know everything about me. They have all my messages, my photos - all of my private life.«[84] The Moroccan authorities reject the allegation of the use of Israeli espionage tools.

In such cases, encryption can under certain circumstances also support Democracy: If free speech in public is not opportune, encryption at least secures our Democracy and its right to freedom of expression in personal 1:1 chat and message exchange. Even if what-is-not-visible could possibly be dismissed as a potential conspiracy or message of hate by those who cannot look into this cipher text.

However, there is not only indirected mass surveillance in underdeveloped democracies, it also takes place in industrialized countries - and targeted surveillance is also supplemented, as is the case with already mentioned journalists, for example. The piquant thing is: In addition to journalists, politicians can also be affected as the main target group. Ultimately, all public actors can be affected. The higher up they are, the sooner. Politicians and public administration are perhaps even more interesting than journalists.

For them, espionage by other states is a potential danger if encryption is not used. And the offices of Members of Parliament, as well as media houses, are sometimes very negligent in this area. It is therefore intolerable for some technology journalists that citizens cannot communicate with them and political officials in encrypted form. Every website of Members of a Parliament should, for example, include the possibility of being able to send an encrypted e-mail. For example, by disclosing your own public GPG key, you already have the option of encrypted emailing: it doesn't take much to set up. Some media are well positioned: the magazine *Der Spiegel* in Germany, for example, computer portals and weekly magazines have set up secure channels for potential informants in addition to an e-mail address: so-called exclusive mailboxes.

Journalists who have found their first access to digital Cryptography have already set up this type of email encryption.

The *German Association of Journalists* (DJV) therefore calls (in the public discussion and in comparison, to lawyers quite late) to put plans to weaken the secure encryption of digital communication to the files forever. Journalists would not only be affected in their contacts with whistle-blowers if government agencies had the opportunity to follow the communication. »That would mean the end of informant protection: journalists must continue to have the opportunity to research and exchange ideas with informants without being targeted by investigators. Anything else would be a marginalization of research«[85], warns the DJV. The editorial secrecy is also wasted, since the Executing Services can use surveillance Trojans under the new Surveillance Act even with those who are subject to professional secrecy.

On the contrary, the legislature must protect itself against this: because, as in Germany, it must also be constitutionally bound with regard to the Fundamental Rights of digital communication: All Fundamental Rights of communication become impaired if individual communication is either disturbed or, in particular, made accessible to an authoritarian regime via the dependence on technology providers. Because whoever has to anticipate potential disadvantages will adapt their communication behavior - which represents a considerable impairment of freedom. This applies in particular, for example, if a powerful actor gains a sufficiently substantial mastery of knowledge through his technical influence on the communication networks, which he can use against political opponents or unpleasant external perception. In this respect, Fundamental Rights protection obligations for adequate communication security apply, which are also binding on the legislature.[86]

The media organization ›Reporters without Borders‹ will file a constitutional complaint.

Edward Snowden called for equation of smartphone Trojans with nuclear weapons and a corresponding international ban. Trading with nuclear weapons is not allowed, so that the trade in surveillance software should not be allowed: who find a way to hack an iPhone, have also found a way to hack everyone. This could break the smartphones cost-efficiently, and from the currently 50,000 targets quickly become 50 million goals. This industry should not exist according to him. And what if we come to the realization that our phones are no longer safe without such additions? Germany's IT security authority BSI spoke because of Pegasus a cyber security warning with a categorized IT threat of level two (of four)[87]. Organizations such as Amnesty International (AI) promoted recognition and encryption tools.

1.5   The fifth act: Apple's Falls - create reality through technological power as fifth state power after legislative, judiciary, executive and the media ●

But before the political or statutory situation of a legal framework for decryption could be discussed, Apple has already made facts through technical measures: Apple could not allow the external Trojan (Pegasus) of a third company - similar to the attack by the external company Cellebrite - and internalized the espionage as »Trojan by Default« into its own operating system. As follows: All pictures, also excerpts and size or quality changes (resizing), as well as texts - are checked for Apple devices through their scanners with so called hashes, short identification numbers. With the argument »to protect the children«, Apple searches the data of the customers on their devices and thus enables »mass surveillance throughout the world«, in turn, *Edward Snowden* at Twitter took the point. The system could be used »very easily to scan private content on everything you or a government want to control. Because countries have different definitions, which is acceptable«, criticized also WhatsApp-boss *Will Cathcart* on Twitter. Whether he saw the status of his own filter and surveillance machinery endangered? *Will Cathcart* is referred to by the Facebook CEO as a narrower familiar and »one of the most talented executives of our company«, after all, he was originally trained at Google and since the start, he has been responsible for the development of anti-spam filter technologies at Google's products, including Gmail.

Also, US civil rights organizations such as the *Center for Democracy & Technology* (CDT) ran storm against the Apple project, to use a so-called ›nude-scanner‹ or ›naked-filter‹. They are called naked scanners, not because the filters are looking for pictures with bare people, but because the scan processes take place prior to potential encryption in the plain text or on the plain image. It's not about Apple searching on its servers and is reporting illegal results to the police. All GAFAM-providers already make this. It is about that even the decentralized phones will be searched.

How the Civil Rights Organization *Electronic Frontier Foundation* (EFF)[88] further persists: The abuse cases of these naked scanners are easy to imagine: governments that outlaw homosexuality might require a classifier to be trained to restrict apparent LGBTQIA content, or an authoritarian regime might demand the classifier to be able to spot popular satirical images or protest fliers of the opposition to the regime.

The filter scanner of the operating system should also be installed in each approved application via API interface. It is comparable as if the sugar industry does not attach the sugar to the milk product for usual 13%, but the cow is already directly to feed with sugar. Have we all become digital stuffing geese? Tomorrow fed with compliant thinking specifications, at least today rightly exempt from potentially not compliant content, which is necessary to be defined further? Or is the state-initiated AI-control comparable to an insulin pump integrated on or in the organism? How far or deep may state control of the mind be anchored?

Not only civil rights activists and employees of Apple, but worldwide also the associations of journalists (such as DJV, ORF Council, Swiss Media Union SSM, EFF, Section Media Verdi and more) see a threat to privacy and press freedom in the Apple scan: This international coalition of more than 90 civil society organizations requested apple not to scan on their servers and especially not to scan on the decentral devices, our smartphones. Apple has abandoned its once-famous commitment to security and privacy.

Also, it is to ask, why this US-tool is controlled first or so far only through the Apple operating system and not via Android of Google? While at this time in Afghanistan the US-troops are deducted and the Islamist terror group Taliban opens up the power to itself again, may be assumed that the phones that can only know one of the two operating systems have been fully indexed as US-Solves have stood in addition to allies and population. So that after the crushing of the crowd, which could act from an orbit of the Geo-observation of the smartphones as an animal heap, this surveillance system can also probably find the previous contact persons in a remote maintenance at any time. The contact people continue to be found by smartphone: to monitor Afghans via Android is cheaper than to displace Taliban by troops on-site? Country intervention is replayed by computer operation. The goal, no Afghan sleepers attack the USA, has been achieved, was the justification of the troop deduction. Because the state members of this country can now be monitored about the smartphones? When the Taliban took over the power in Kabul, an ISIS terrorist has blown up himself, 169 Afghans and 13 US soldiers into the air. The American president threatened with retaliation - but already the next day the newspapers reported: »The goal is killed!« The high-ranking coordinator of the terror militia ISIS was quickly found in his geolocation because he was indexed with his smartphone: without a court process, a targeted air strike with a drone of type »MQ-9 Reaper« could be carried out against him.

Apple's Fall of Man is a global total surveillance by the back door, where phones work against their users: this is a historical bait and creates a precedent — and the problem would be also, that publicly barely no one is brave enough to pronounce, to enter the retention of privacy under purchasing the risk of less cases with illegal content. Who wanted to accept this risk in the own family and society?

Though this will be an »infrastructure for mass surveillance and global censorship and clearly a back-door«[89] - even if child protection, to which the National Center for Missing and Exploited Children continues to take care of, would be undoubtedly an important goal. The basic pillar of legal states that citizens are not systematically monitored and spied on, is also a priority.

Probably the tremendous media echo about Pegasus was also needed and helpful in advance to introduce and justify such a total world surveillance – prepared and done by the U.S., and not Israel again. *Erich Honecker*, former chairman of the State Council of the GDR, would appreciate this NEW GLOBAL STASI with millions of small computer-boards as ›Unofficial Collaborateurs‹ (IM, German: ›Inoffizielle Mitarbeiter‹), which were one of the most important rule instruments and supports of the dictatorship power of the GDR?

A dream of *Erich Mielke*, who was mainly responsible for the expansion of the security organs of the GDR into a comprehensive control, surveillance and suppression system, and a nightmare for *George Orwell*, who as the most important writer of English literature with his future vision of a totalitarian state in the Books ›Animal Farm‹ and ›1984‹ became world famous.

The classical separation of powers in the state through legislative, judiciary and executive has not only been extended by the media, but also by (stage ordered) control through technology companies. With the result of unclear and / or totalitarian effects.

*

The president of the *Society for Computer Science* (GI), and professor at the University of Hamburg, *Hannes Federrath*, also developed the web anonymizer software JonDo a few years ago to protect anonymity and unobservability on the Internet. The program was developed as an alternative to the well-known Tor network with state research funding, which still exists today - also with a payment option.

He finally sums up this discussion about scanning of clear data and texts and restrictions on encryption as follows: »Attempts to restrict encryption not only endanger the informational self-determination of citizens, but also the protection of company and business secrets. By undermining all efforts towards legally binding corporate communication by weakening encryption, the necessary digitization of our economy is ultimately hindered. We also need reliable, confidential communication for the formation of political will and the creation of a free society.

The basic Right to Encryption is important for our Democracy - just as postal secrecy is in the analogue world. Secret communication can neither be effectively prevented with a second key nor with a ban on encryption. Otherwise, unobservable communication with Steganography could also be used«[90].

So, let us take a look at what Steganography can mean to complement and replace Cryptography.

2 26 SHADES OF GREY - THE SEARCH FOR HIDDEN MULTI-ENCRYPTION IN STEGANOGRAPHY ●

In addition, it should be pointed out to good practice that not only keys - as we will see below - can be excluded from transmission on the Internet, but also cipher text (as well as plain text) cannot be recognized as such. This is called Steganography.

Steganography is the science or art of the hidden storage or transmission of information in a carrier medium. Let us think of this as a container in which the information or the cipher text can be stored virtually invisibly. It is often understood as a sister science to Cryptography.

With steganographic processes, for example, the color of a pixel point in an image in the red-yellow-blue spectrum can take on a different RGB value and thus represent a secret cipher. With the naked eye, nobody will notice that a gray may have turned into a darker gray: a mouse gray, ash gray, dusty gray - or maybe a flaming, fresh stone gray in the sense of the humorist *Loriot* can be suggested? 26 Shades of Gray. And all the letters of the alphabet are defined.

The following table on Steganography in pixel points of an image shows that if an 8-digit number value for the color red (RRRR RRRR) in a pixel point of the image (e.g., pixel No. 1) takes on a different value in the last two digits (here: 00), we can then expect that this pixel point will not be perceived differently by the human eye. Nevertheless, it is a slightly changed red tone in the last two digits of the red value of a pixel point.

Figure 7: Steganography in pixel points of an image

Pixel number	1
Message / letter (of the cipher text)	G
Position in the alphabet	7
Position binary (filled)	000111
red color value before coding	RRRR RRRR
green color value before coding	GGGG GGGG
blue color value before coding	BBBB BBBB
red color value after coding	RRRR RR00
green color value after coding	GGGG GG01
blue color value after coding	BBBB BB11

Source:[91]

The letter G is represented in binary with 000111 and embedded in the first pixel of an image with this binary number over the RGB value, in which the red value at the end with 00, the green value at the end with 01 and the blue value at the end with 11 is adjusted. The human eye does not see any change in color. An analysis of the pixel points of the image does not know the changed (significant) pixels.

Before exchanging the changed image, it should be defined by default or known individually at which pixel position the Swiss cheese has its holes, so to speak, at which pixel the changed color values are located. So is that why photographers always want to hear a »cheese« when they are taking pictures?

If we do not recognize that encryption essentially means security and protects us, then the phrase »going dark« (also: »getting grey«) can mean in a few years that no more plain text (as visible cipher text) is sent to the Internet, but cipher text. Text wanders into the dark - via Steganography!

Encryption must therefore be thought of as »going the extra mile for more security«[92].

Encryption in a network forms a »bright net« (light, transparent network) and not a »dark net« because it offers protection against third parties and the sending of cipher text is visible - even if (hopefully) there is only a small percentage who would like to define illegal and thus criminal processes over it. According to this argument, the real dark net is only found in steganographed plain text or cipher text.

Political intervention in the security of end-to-end encryption could bring the barrel to overflowing - is it a so-called »tipping point«, a turning point? If encryption is criminalized, by definition only criminals encrypt! But how could you distinguish this criminalized cipher text from good and bad people? And it can be assumed that the encryption will not be omitted in the future, because cipher text in the data lines is increasing more and more: Browser manufacturers also announced that the transmission of websites takes place in the standard as HTTPS, i.e., encrypted (and not unencrypted as HTTP). This will give the sending of encrypted cipher text over the Internet a further boost.

Accessing websites in encrypted form, but not being allowed to access encrypted chat messages, could subsequently establish a niche society for communication, as described, if the population still wants to encrypt messages: Such a niche can arise when groups are decoupled into their own networks, as it is already known when nations are decoupled into their own networks, for example in Russia this has been set up with #RuNet, which is self-sufficient if necessary. Russia wants to be able to decouple its Internet internationally at any time. Then the Internet will no longer be a globally transparent communication medium but will be subject to national sovereignty (albeit without encryption) and thus also limit or exclude global economic processes.

Likewise, the political tendency or a political compulsion to hide cipher text using steganographic functions can lead to even less transparency than before. Then senders of cipher text may begin with a decoupling of the visibility of the cipher text through steganographic processes in the sending of messages: encryption then becomes hiding (from Cipher to Conceal, FC2C).

Because the use of Steganography aims at secrecy and confidentiality. The information is hidden in the communication in such a way that third parties have no clue of a second message it contains when looking at the carrier medium. This also ensures that the hidden information does not become known to third parties, which means that secrecy is guaranteed - as is the case with Cryptography.

The functional principle of Steganography is based on the fact that outsiders do not recognize the existence of the steganographed information. In this way, Steganography also differs from Cryptography, in which outsiders know about the existence of information, but are not able to understand the content because of the encryption.

2.1   We play Halma: with the null cipher ●

Another practical example illustrates how information can only be seen through appropriate focusing or filtering: If Alice does not send her friend Bob a cipher text, but instead a message in the form of a (unimportant) poem, in which the first letters of the lines are read one after the other form the actual message, the outside Walter can see that Alice is sending a message to Bob, but the content that Walter perceives does not correspond to the relevant message from Alice to Bob.

The probability that Walter will change or block the message will therefore be low because of a lack of interest. The algorithm, which works steganographically in this way, is referred to as the so-called »null« cipher (also German for »zero« and known as concealment cipher). In the null cipher, the plain text is integrated into another text. This could also be a cipher text. The reader only has to delete more letters in order to decipher the actual message.

This means that most of the characters in such a cryptogram are to be assessed with zero (i.e., as to be skipped), only a few characters are significant or meaningful and count towards the actual message. Some other signs can also provide additional information about the significant signs.

The null cipher works like a Halma or Man, Don't Get Angry game: to get to the next significant character, simply a few characters are assigned to skip, that are not significant, and thus get the value of zero. It is like in life: meaning is created by letting »rubbish« - in this case: words while reading - swim by. One such technique was used by a prison inmate, for example, where whole words were interspersed in an inconspicuous letter. The letter read as follows:

«SALUDOS LOVED ONE SO TODAY I HEARD FROM UNCLE MOE OVER THE PHONE. HE TOLD ME THAT YOU AND ME GO THE SAME BIRTHDAY. HE SAYS YOUR TIME THERE TESTED YOUR STRENGTH SO STAY POSITIVE AT SUCH TIMES. I'M FOR ALL THAT CLEAN LIVING! METHAMPHETAMINES WAS MY DOWN FALL. THE PROGRAM I'M STARTING THE NINTH IS ONE I HEARD OF A COUPLE WEEKS BEFORE SEPTEMBER THROUGH MY COUNSELOR BARRIOS. BUT MY MEDICAL INSURANCE COVERAGE DENIES THEY COVER IT. I'M USING MY TIME TO CHECK AND IF THE INSURANCE AGENT DENIES STILL MY COVERAGE I'M GETTING TOGETHER PAPERWORK SAYING I TESTED FOR THIS TREATMENT REQUIRED ON THE CHILD CUSTODY. THE NINTH WILL MEAN I HAVE TESTED MY DETERMINATION TO CHANGE. ON THE NEXT FREE WEEKEND THE KIDS ARE COMING, BUT FIRST I GOTTA SHOW CAROLINA I'M STAYING OUT OF TROUBLE WAITING TO GET MYSELF ADMITTED ON THE PROGRAM. THE SUPPORTING PAPERWORK THAT THE FAMILY COURTS GOT WILL ALSO PROVE THERE'S NO REASON NEITHER FOR A WITNESS ON MY CHILDREN'S VISITS.

OF COURSE MY BRO HAS HIS MIND MADE UP OF RECENT THAT ALL THIS DRUG USAGE DON'T CONCERN OUR VISITS. I THINK THAT MY KIDS FEEL I NEED THEIR LOVE IF I'M GONNA BE COOL. GUILTY FEELINGS RISE ON ACCOUNT OF THE MISTAKES I COULD WRITEUP. FOR DAYS I'M HERE. HE GOT A GOOD HEART. SHOULD YOU BE HAVING PROBLEMS BE ASSURED THAT WHEN YOU HIT THE STREETS WE'LL BE CONSIDERING YOU...«

If you only use every fifth word, you can reconstruct the hidden text in which it is recommended to attack or blackmail someone (in this drug trafficking environment) if the person does not report in time ... »he should be hit«.

TODAY MOE TOLD ME ...
I FEEL - IF GUILTY OF WRITEUP - HE SHOULD BE HIT.

However, the US police agency FBI was able to decipher this letter from the high-profile prison inmate based on a detailed investigation[93].

2.2 Thanks to the stencil filter: I can see what you cannot see! •

The Grille Cipher also works according to these steganographic principles. It hides superfluous information so that only the relevant information comes to light. It is also called Fleißner's stencil in the German speaking region – according to the Austrian Colonel *Eduard Fleißner von Wostrowitz*. The French writer *Jules Verne* described, among other things, the encryption process with the Fleißner stencil in his novel *Mathias Sandorf* in 1885. However, the idea goes back even further to the »Cardan grid« invented by the Italian mathematician and great polymath of the

Renaissance *Gerolamo Cardano* and named after him (around the year 1550; however, with the Fleißner stencil, this Cardan grid was additionally different times rotated 90 degrees).

Gerolamo Cardano has worked on a large number of areas of knowledge in the form of lectures and writings, ranging from medicine, mathematics, philosophy, comparative religious studies, physics, chemistry, engineering, pharmacy, psychology and dream interpretation, astronomy and astrology to architecture and the history of science. So everything that schools are trying to teach us nowadays.

The Cardan grid played a significant role in the encryption of messages related to Steganography in the early modern period.

Figure 8: Cardan grid or Fleissner stencil for a Grille Cipher

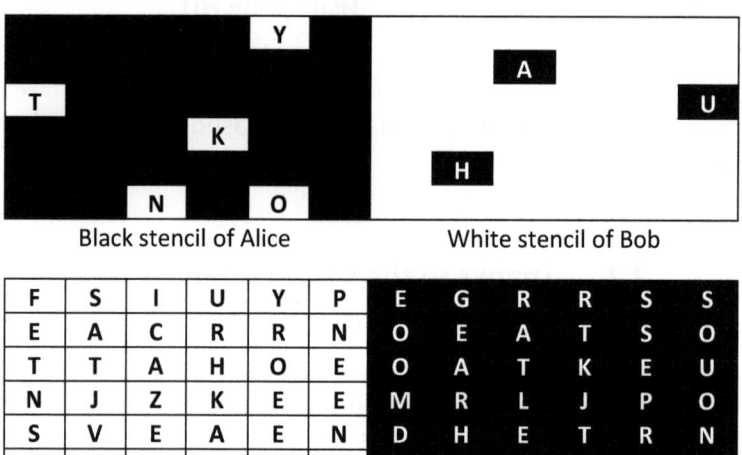

Black stencil of Alice						White stencil of Bob					
F	S	I	U	Y	P	E	G	R	R	S	S
E	A	C	R	R	N	O	E	A	T	S	O
T	T	A	H	O	E	O	A	T	K	E	U
N	J	Z	K	E	E	M	R	L	J	P	O
S	V	E	A	E	N	D	H	E	T	R	N
T	L	N	O	O	U	Y	X	E	T	S	E

Source:[94]

In the figure above, there is a white table and a black table (English: Grille), the cells of which are filled with random letters. The upper part of the illustration shows a black and a white stencil. If you put it on, the password TNKYO results from the black stencil and the white stencil reads HAU. Both parts can be combined to form a common password TNKYOHAU, which Alice and Bob use together.

With this method, the cells are determined using a stencil in a matrix, table or grille, which, for example, result in a password such as »TNKYO« from Alice's black stencil or the password »HAU« from Bob's white stencil (read from right to left).

Originally, such a stencil with its holes could also be placed over a letter text and thus bring out the desired, selected words, which then resulted in a new sentence or a different meaning.

These two character strings, which can be seen from the stencils in the above example from Alice and Bob, could finally be combined to form a common password »HAUT-NKYO«. (It is a so-called »2-Way-Calling« according to the method of »Cryptographic Calling« explained in more detail below: both give one half to the common password).

The two-character strings result in a new password that is only visible via steganographic processes. It can then be used by both for further (symmetric) encryption (i.e., with a password), e.g., as part of multi-encryption.

Let us further imagine such a 6x6 matrix filled with numbers, and that it was exchanged by Alice and Bob in another, unobserved and a channel in the past, so that the content is known on both sides, but not by current observers of their communication. Even with this 6x6 table there are, depending on the number of holes (2, 3, 4 or more characters ... from 36), a variety of possible templates with which Alice can then create a password consisting of characters, numbers or letters, only becomes visible when Bob tells her: Choose template No. 13!

Who would recognize the number 13 for the stencil or the 36 characters in the matrix as a key element? Short identifications such as the number 13 as an indication of the stencil 13 can refer to a filter of a key spectrum that remains secure for normal chat messages but is not visible as a transmitted key: because the key to creating the password is the stencil and not the number 13.

The coordinates of the punched-out fields are another key element of this steganographic tool.

The daily crossword puzzle in the public newspaper takes on a whole new meaning: Alice and Bob solve the crossword puzzle, communicate using the number of a stencil, for example as mentioned: Stencil No. 13, place it over the box of the crossword puzzle in the daily newspaper and receive a password read from left to right that was not transmitted over the Internet and therefore cannot be stored with corporate actors. Such manual passwords for establishing (symmetric) end-to-end encryption can already be stored in numerous messengers today. The process is abbreviated as »BYOK« or »CSEK«: »Bring your own Keys« or »Customer Supplied Encryption Keys«.

We also see such specifically placed characters or significant points every day in the office: Who knew that when we fetch a color copy from the printer in the office, this page can be invisibly marked with tiny yellow dots? We have them in front of our eyes, but we don't see them! - (which sometimes happens to some with work).

This is necessary so that no color copies of banknotes are made or color copies can be identified from which copier or printer they come from. However, this also means that copies or printouts of sensitive documents - such as letters from doctors, bank statements, tax returns or company balance sheets - can be traced back to the owner of the printer and the time at which they were created. This traceability is not even known to many users and is also not accessible. Because the code is not disclosed by the manufacturers. Xerox is one of the few manufacturers who writes openly: »The digital color printing system is equipped with a forgery-proof identification and banknote recognition system in accordance with the requirements of numerous governments. Each copy is provided with an identifier which, if necessary, enables the printing system with which it was made to be identified. This code is not visible under normal conditions.«[95]

This color printer marking - also called »Machine Identification Code« (MIC), yellow dots, tracking dots or secret dots - is a digital watermark that many (though not all) color laser printers and copiers put on every printed page. Inconspicuous signs on a carrier medium of our everyday life: the copy paper from our printer.

2.3   The Bacon's Cipher: Change instead of illusion •

If a text or a string of characters is hidden and invisible through Steganography, it can be plain text, or it can also be multi-encrypted cipher text with computers, or simply so-called encoded text with little effort. So it's not just about hiding plain text, but also cipher text can be »interspersed« in cipher text at defined positions and thus become virtually invisible. And even with the simpler encoding there can be advantages if the result of the encoding, i.e., the cipher text, consists only of a sequence of two characters, i.e., 0 and 1 or A and B (which can also be easily converted into 0 and 1).

Encoding can be an assistant or a preliminary stage in the process of Steganography, so it is included here.

For a simple encoding - if there is no computer available - the cipher by *Francis Bacon* - also called Bacon's cipher or Baconian cipher - from 1605 gives us a good example: *Francis Bacon* was an English philosopher, lawyer and statesman and is considered a pioneer of so-called »empiricism«, according to which theory and knowledge are based or should be based on experience. In addition, *Delia Bacon* claimed - a coincidental name identical without being related to him - many years later that *Francis Bacon* wrote the works of *William Shakespeare*. In her book *The*

Philosophy of Shakespeare's Plays (1857) she developed the view that behind the Shakespeare plays there was a group of writers with and around *Francis Bacon*. However, this claim is rejected by Shakespearean scholarly research. Maybe just a wild idea from this dark-haired teacher with a strong will because of the fact that they have the same name?

Figure 9: The Bacon's Cipher

SIGN	CODE	BINARY	SIGN	CODE	BINARY
A	aaaaa	00000	N	abbab	01101
B	aaaab	00001	O	abbba	01110
C	aaaba	00010	P	abbbb	01111
D	aaabb	00011	Q	baaaa	10000
E	aabaa	00100	R	baaab	10001
F	aabab	00101	S	baaba	10010
G	aabba	00110	T	baabb	10011
H	aabbb	00111	U	babaa	10100
I	abaaa	01000	V	babab	10101
J	abaab	01001	W	babba	10110
K	ababa	01010	X	babbb	10111
L	ababb	01011	Y	bbaaa	11000
M	abbaa	01100	Z	bbaab	11001

Source:[96]

The Bacon's Cipher maps the alphabet in binary with zeros and ones and also displays them as A or B letters, which can easily be embedded in steganographic methods.

The word STEGANOGRAPHY, after the Baconian cipher, results in the following encoded character string, which at the end was padded with three random digits (one also says technically: cryptographically »salted«):

baaba_baabb_aabaa_aabba_aaaaa_abbab_abbba_aabba_aaaaa_abbbb
_aabbb_abaaa_aabaa_babbb_babbb_babbb.

It is also possible to display this character string in other blocks:

baa_babaa_bbaab_aaaab_baaaa_aaabb_ababb_baaab_baaaa_aaabb_b
baab_bbaba_aaaab_aabab_bbbab_bbbab_bb.

The first three letters can now also be removed and remain secret as the key to this rotation. Even if a computer can convert this string back immediately today, it was an additional protection at the beginning of the modern era - and it can still be today, in connection with Steganography.

Because this encoding with a and b could also be hidden in the form of zeros and ones as seen in the color values of an image - at defined pixel positions of the image.

**10010_10011_00100_00110_00000_01101_01110_00110_1000
1_00000_01111_00111**

In addition to hiding, which is more reminiscent of an illusion, a (previous) metamorphosis, a transformation (encoding) can also be used, which can then be hidden again - in a simplified manner. And the whole thing can be done not only for plain text, but also for cipher text. It can also be hidden in a carrier medium as a converted string of zeros and ones.

So why should the Delta-Chat-Messenger described later send cipher text via the e-mail infrastructure used and not better send images as attachments to an e-mail, in which the cipher text is additionally encoded and invisible via zeros and ones is let in?

And this is exactly what security researcher David Buchanan has successfully done. Via the messenger Twitter: He has published[97] several pictures as PNG files on his Twitter account, in which MP3 and ZIP files were steganographically integrated without it being directly visible. Up to 3 MB could be incorporated into the pictures.

Because of security concerns, such uploads are actually cleaned up by the services through conversion. In the specific case, however, the information was attached to the IDAT information of the images and not removed by Twitter. This is because images larger than 3 MB are converted to JPG format.

So, he was able to publish a PNG picture that says: »Save this picture and change the extension to .zip«. The source code used, including an explanation, can be found in the archive disguised as an image. A second picture can be saved as an audio file »for an MP3 surprise« and then played back in the music player after the file extension has been renamed .mp3.

2.4   Hiding and Mixing by Transformation: The XOR Function ●

Relevant information may not be evident or may even be modified beforehand using a calculation operation. In the data world, this skillful modification and mixing can furthermore be mapped by the so-called »XOR function«. This exclusive-or-gate, also called XOR-gate is a gate with two inputs and one output, where the output is logical »1«, when »1« is present at only one input and »0« at the other. That is, a so-called »truth table« looks like this:

Figure 10: Truth table of the XOR operation

A	B	Y = A $\veebar$ B
0	0	0
0	1	1
1	0	1
1	1	0

The XOR truth table has a gate with two inputs, which can be 0 or 1. Depending on the constellation, the output can be 1 or 0. The output is set to 0 if both inputs have the same character. The signs of both entrances are, as it were, »merged« with one another to a new result: a transformation is present.

With the help of such an exclusive-or link, two-character strings that are binary converted into zeros and ones can be merged with one another.

A message to be encrypted (plain text) is first encoded as a bit sequence. A second bit sequence, which is just as long as the message, is used as a key. The cipher text is created by exclusively-or-linking the first bit of the message with the first bit of the key, the second bit with the second and so on. If you then carry out the same exclusive-or link with the cipher text and the key - quasi backwards - you will get the original message or the second character string used (this is already available as the key).

Thus, two data series of zeros and ones are mutually transformed in such a way that from the available result of the »mixed« number series of zeros and ones, either one file or the other file or series of numbers can be reconstructed. The steganographic process is a special one here: Cipher text is still visible, or it can be seen that it is a sequence of zeros and ones, but the hidden message does not necessarily have to be plain text can also be in a key of the same length!

This is how the Offsystem and Offload programs work, for example - even if, as said, the file or sequence of numbers is conspicuous as a quasi-cipher text (i.e., encoded text) in the form of zeros and ones. The row of numbers transformed into it is not noticeable. So, this is more of a coding than an encryption, but a reverse conversion requires knowledge of the corresponding mathematical operations (such as XOR) or the second character string. The following applies: An obvious file and a hidden file (or their number strings) can be formed (back) from it depending on the mathematical operation, so that this transformation comes close to steganographic thinking. This method can also play a role when it comes to »weaving« (a second) cipher text into (a first) cipher text, i.e., the carrier medium is cipher text and not plain text.

The Offsystem program will be explained further below, for example, how a film by *James Bond* with its binary number series of 0 and 1 is virtually merged with a film by *Mickey Mouse* and also with its binary number series of 0 and 1. Depending on the operation either one string of numbers can be restored as a Bond film or the other string of numbers as a Mouse film. Without further knowledge, the copyright on the mixed hero thread remains questionable, since it is again only a sequence of zeros and ones (see also below). The Offsystem is therefore also defined by the authors on their website as a Bright-Net and not as a Dark-Net, as the newly formed series of numbers has almost nothing to do with the original works. Hiding qua transformation is not a (shorthand) illusion but creates something completely new: a phoenix from the ashes, who, however, is able to know its roots.

2.5   Deniable cipher text:
A new direction of research or just a salted message? •

In order to hide files in a file system on a hard drive, journalist and Wikileaks spokesman *Julian Assange* worked from 1997 to 2000 (together with *Suelette Dreyfus* and *Ralf Weinmann*) on a (now deleted) system called Rubberhose (previously also called Marutukku[98]).

Julian Assange's libertarian worldview, his way of working and his Wikileaks project to publish secret government documents had a major impact on traditional media companies: They adopted many of the Wikileaks innovations, such as installing technology to send encrypted or anonymous messages, promoting digital issues in journalism and the encouragement of reporters to protect their sources through better internet security - also, for example, by mixing files into other files in his prototype mentioned above.

Furthermore, the Offsystem described was created for the appropriate mixing of files by means of XOR operations from 2003 - as well as later also a function for the hard disk encryption Truecrypt or VeraCrypt, which also opens a secret partition depending on the password entered, but without the corresponding password brings the illusionary world of another partition to light. Such software features are designed to be resistant to attacks from people willing to torture those who know the keys to decryption.

In science and applied programming, Cryptography and Steganography are combined with research questions and prototypes that will continue to attach great importance to the topic of »deniable cipher text« in the future (deniable encryption). In Cryptography as well as in Steganography, plausible deniability of cipher text or encryption refers to techniques with which the existence of an encrypted text or an encrypted file can be denied.

It is about the sense that an attacker cannot prove that there are (further or derivable) strings that are either cipher text or contain a second cipher text, which of course could also be converted to plain text.

This can be achieved in that an encrypted message can be decrypted into different meaningful plain texts depending on the key used.

With simple means it is possible to convert two cipher texts as seen with the XOR function of the program Offsystem into a third text sequence, and later to split the text sequence again into two cipher texts and to convert a desired cipher text into readable plain text.

Two different cipher texts can also be displayed alternately in a character string A1B1A2B2A3B3 per character block and after separation result in either cipher text A (A1A2A3) or cipher text B (B1B2B3). If the character string A1B1A2B2A3B3 were to be encrypted again in the case of multi-encryption, the cipher text of the second conversion then changes back to the first cipher text after the separation like a chameleon, which will and may be the desired readable plain text after a further conversion or password entry.

The aim is to leave the other, second cipher text potentially undecrypted, hidden and deniable. The characters of the second cipher text B1B2B3 could be random characters that fill up the first cipher text, so-called »cryptographic salt« - but who would suspect a message or a second encrypted container in it? If you order a book online, you do not suspect that there may be a second short story printed on the outer packaging!

This deniable cipher text can today be related not only to the cipher text, but also to the keys. As we will see below, keys no longer have to be transmitted over the Internet according to the innovations presented in applied Cryptography and are therefore also deniable!

Will this research direction of »deniable cipher text« or »deniable keys« and also »deniable signatures« (so-called »Vanishing Fingerprints«, see also below) become another, third sister science of Cryptography and Steganography, or is it their link?

Soon after the EU resolution on the mandatory issuance of copies of the keys it is determined that this is technically and socially a difficult undertaking, a marginalization of the sending of cipher text in general - and not only with regard to the non-disclosure of keys – may occur and, as indicated, lead to an increased steganographing of cipher text.

A future political and social organization will also ask itself whether it wants to know how cipher text is transported or not, and whether it wants end-to-end encryption as a security standard for everyone - or not - and thus the dispatch of cipher text with potentially illegal content may not be able to be prevented for possibly a few people.

Computer-based Steganography is an important tool for opponents of legal encryption restrictions. A few years ago, specialist author of numerous books, *Klaus Schmeh*, put their argument in a nutshell in his book »Hidden Messages« on the subject of Steganography: Restrictions of encryption »are useless because they can be circumvented with the help of computer-based Steganography without great effort.« [99]

What specialist authors have been representing for many years was then also underlined by the *Association of Management Consulting, Accounting and IT* (UBIT) for the European initiative to abolish end-to-end encryption. Chairman *Alfred Harl* announced: »The abolition of secure encryption enables the abuse of personal rights and actually drives criminals to use other channels that are more difficult to monitor,« and recommended the retention of recognizable end-to-end encryption in view of steganographed or, even deniable cipher text on the part of the professional association, which, with more than 73,000 members across Europe, is one of the largest and most dynamic professional associations for the interests of entrepreneurs in the fields of management consulting, accounting and information technology. [100]

The applied Steganography is successful if the yellow (or our blind) dots have not yet been noticed on a color page of a printer or copier - or a future messenger only communicates by sending randomly selected images into which a McEliece cipher -Text could be embedded invisibly.

3 WITH LEARNING CURVES: BACK TO THE FUTURE OF A NEW WHATSAPP? ●

For the future, the respective national gap must be assessed, falling behind the technical standard and thus also behind the education and training standards of other countries with their experts on these topics with restrictions on encryption and Steganography. Open-source encryption projects are to be taken into account across national borders. In order to hunt down criminals, other methods of combating crime from a wide range of actors may also have to be focused.

Such an envisaged and now beginning slowdown of encryption technologies must also be judged based on the needs of the citizens: All those involved in the process of this assessment must ask themselves whether this means a delay in encryption technologies or an acceleration in their use would improve learning- and protection-experience for the future of our society as a whole. How is the German Chancellor *Angela Merkel* supposed to have asked in a different context with a double pleonasm: Do we want to be the last when strolling? Because if you stroll around, you will end up in one of the last places...

3.1   The sixth act: Main role of teachers ●

The response to the European initiative to limit end-to-end encryption with a resolution to the European countries finally culminated in an open letter from the social and scientific movement   »Scientists4Crypto«[101]   to   the   European parliamentarians: Over 427 cryptographers as well Education officers at universities from 27 countries on the day of the first subscription alone appeal firstly to the retention of end-to-end encryption and secondly to the retention or expansion of the educational processes on the subject of secure Cryptography - and do not advocate their restrictions.

The point of view of the teachers at universities corresponds in terms of the demand aspect of education policy to some extent with the view of the establishment of computer science as a compulsory subject already in elementary schools. According to a study, the majority of teachers in Germany wanted compulsory computer science lessons in schools a few years ago. Around three quarters (73 percent) of the teachers agree to the demand to introduce computer science as a compulsory subject nationwide. Without a fundamental understanding of how computers and software work, our world can hardly be understood today: Basic IT knowledge will be required in more and more industries, and in future also increasingly in classic production, according to the study by the *Federal Association of Information Technology, Telecommunications and New Media* (Bitkom) with more than 2,700 member companies.

In the years to come, a whole decade later, some federal states are now implementing this compulsory subject for training in the use of computers.

In the training of police officers, in addition to English-language skills for cross-border cooperation inquiries in Europe and overseas, training goals in the field of computer science, hardware, software and especially Cryptography with their police work areas of cryptographic analysis, cryptographic investigation, cryptographic forensics and cryptographic cooperation are more central than ever. Because: the teachers in police schools on the subject of digitization and Cryptography have so far been rare. The market for IT specialists in the civil service is practically empty. The problem has been known for years. Unfortunately, countermeasures were taken far too late.

Even the German Federal Intelligence Service has to advertise its IT staff with funny job advertisements: with the

#followtheglitchkarnickel campaign and a computer-animated rabbit, the Federal Intelligence Service tries to reach developers and IT specialists directly with a choice of words, cyber aesthetics and a special image program. Do you want to attract staff by restricting essential training content such as encryption technologies and then advertising in job advertisements with a white rabbit for getting into a rabbit hole?

My name is Harvey and I don't know anything - it is reminiscent of the 1950 film »My Friend Harvey« by *Henry Koster*, which is based on the play of the same name by *Mary Chase*. *Elwood Dowd* is a lovable, quirky and unshakably friendly middle-aged man. For several years now, his best friend has been an imaginary creature in the form of a 2.10-meter tall, white bunny named Harvey, with whom he wanders through town for hours and invites strangers to his favorite bar for a drink with himself and Harvey. The problem, however, is that even if the landlord and the other guests accept Harvey's existence, Harvey is invisible to everyone except Elwood. A symbol for invisible personnel policy and non-existent technical training content on the central topic of encryption, which no one has seen or should no longer see? More than four hundred teachers in the subjects of programming, computer science and Cryptography throughout Europe have a different opinion and are updating their curricula.

3.2   The seventh act: Main role Europol and the police officers •

The cross-continental uprising of the university teachers in this previous sixth act is finally answered in Europe in the seventh act: Europol, the police authority of the European Union based in The Hague, announced a few days later that it will support national countries in deciphering cipher text.

Following the example of the German *Central Office for Information Technology in the Security Sector* (ZITIS), the

European Council wanted to improve the capabilities of reading encrypted content already two years earlier at Europol and its *European Center for Cybercrime* (EC3). Now, in the course of the balance of power and the spectacle to restrict encryption, a decryption platform within the EC3 institutions with 86 positions has been approved[102]. How many QuBits their super-computers contain, and whether they outstrip the Bavarian pug-speed* of the German platform ZITIS with the same purpose for decrypting cipher text, however, remained unknown (*their location in Munich once conspicuously advertised Transrapid-speeds in the traffic connection between the airport and the main train station).

Trafficking activities of serious criminals with weapons or drugs have already been discovered in the past because their communication channels were monitored by these police institutions: After officers had succeeded in deciphering millions of chat messages from the underworld of organized drug and gun crime, tons of cocaine, gun deals, torture chambers and contract killings were reported[103]. Anyone who looks at the pictures of the torture chambers of this Europol case, for example, does not want to keep a password for themselves or will be grateful that police officers (can) find serious criminals through online surveillance.

The conservatively oriented party politicians in Germany emphasize that the rule of law must defend itself appropriately and decisively if it is attacked at its core, because everything else would be the German Weimar, and one does not want to go back there. The democratic Weimar Republic could not defend itself against its enemies and went under when the National Socialists began to rule in Germany in 1933. Democracy therefore needs ways to decipher the communication between right-wing groups and criminals.

The commentator ›Mecki‹ speaks out in a forum: »Encryption is not the problem, so attacking it is also not the solution, because encryption is a tool and tools do not cause problems unless they were considered to cause problems. Weapons produce problems because they were intended to hurt or kill people. Burglary tools create problems because they were intended to break in apartments. But encryption itself does nothing bad. It does not harm anyone, it does not hurt anyone, it does not allow attacks on infrastructure or security procedures. On the contrary: Encryption protects. Everything that enables encryption is, confidential communication. But in a world in which the existence of confidential communication represents a problem for the ›public security‹, there is certainly a lot wrong - But nothing can be repaired by an attack on encryption, because basically public protection (in such abstract sense) is generated by the removal of freedom«: That would be the beginning of each totalitarian state!

And there remains the question of what the police can and should do if they cannot decipher: Shouldn't the fight against crime then also be given a focus through other and complementary measures? In many cases, there is already sufficient information for an investigation. It is then more important to reduce complexity, to stick with the suspect, and to act efficiently and with focus. *Sascha Lobo* pinpointed this approach a few years ago as follows in his column: »The rational approach (against terrorism) would be the admission that the point is not to get new data, but to better evaluate what has long been available. The seemingly rational approach, however, will prevail: more surveillance. More data. The irrationality behind it is: We can't find the needle in the haystack, so we need more hay. That sounds so disturbing; but it is seriously a matter of the European strategy...«[104]

3.3 The eighth act: Main role John Doe – Trust is good, encryption is better •

So how can a solution perspective look like, and what do consumers like »John Doe« want?

When it comes to radio communications, it is well known that for reasons of safety and emergency calls, amateurs must not disturb the »thin« connections for sea and air traffic with cipher text or audio noise. And it's widely accepted! Paragraph 8 of the German *Amateur Radio Ordinance* (AFuV) states succinctly and briefly: »Amateur radio traffic must not be encrypted to conceal the content; Control signals for earth and space stations of the amateur radio service via satellites do not count as encrypted transmissions. The broadcast of misleading signals, of permanent broadcasts and of radio-like performances as well as the use of international emergency, urgency and safety signs of the maritime and aviation radio service is not permitted.«[105] to be sent encrypted by radio over the blue of the ether. Neither the constant noise of the laundry room nor the Saturday evening show of the Song Contest may be sent digitally or encrypted by radio over the blue of the ether by amateurs.

Why shouldn't this security standard also apply to an Internet line? Just because this is not a scarce commodity and is used every day (and not episodically as with emergency calls on amateur radio), should it not be possible to ban cipher text from it? As mentioned: We are deciding against any security, including when it comes to banking and shopping. With their radio license, radio operators have more or less obtained a tested driver's license - do we want to establish this license test for sending messages on the Internet as well? The comparison with amateur radio, however, lags insofar as it is not about bandwidth that is too tight. The feared interference is because of the fact that control signals sent via radio have so far been unencrypted - this is the only reason why they can be interfered with. And: emergency signals can still be transmitted in clear language. Amateurs simply may not and shouldn't disturb professional radio.

Citizens, however, neither want to disturb nor acquire a comprehensive license driver's license in order to be able to send an electronic message on the Internet. If necessary, you want your internet chats to be protected against being read by employers, intermediary administrators of servers and possibly the advertising industry with just a simple safeguard.

And if necessary, the online search or the state Trojan with source telecommunication monitoring (Source-TCM) of the plain text, e.g. by tapping it via the keyboard application of the smartphone, are still available for police authorities. - In addition to the attempts to break the encryption with a lot of computing power in their netbooks, or with more complex algorithms to have the encrypted message broken by the super-computer in the rabbit hole described above using platforms with analysts specially set up for this purpose.

Likewise, the providers of telecommunications systems could be legally bound to a *principle of the market location* of the respective police authority, as will be discussed further below on the interoperability and congruence of messengers.

So, what speaks against leaving the people with the algorithms RSA and elliptic curves such as ECDSA, which are no longer considered secure under the appropriate conditions, and not granting NTRU and other quantum-computers secure algorithms? This would affect a regulation agreement based on the respective key length resulting in the formula: »Simple encoding of a message: yes - secure encryption of a message larger than key size RSA-8192: no« - any computer Trojan, bot worm or ransomware virus (such as Nemty) already uses this key size as the standard.

Would *Jimmy Schulz* turn in his grave if the encryption were only »secure« but not »tap-proof« - with regard to messages from the citizen to a state executive? Don't we citizens have to be tap-proof - with key sizes larger than those of those cheap computer infections - in order to rule out a new STASI 2.0? And what is the practical application for system-relevant computers to secure them using high-grade encryption?

The elimination of the public mathematical knowledge of encryption is hardly possible, as is the exclusion of cipher text in the data lines: the particularly secure McEliece encryption has been known for many decades after its publication in 1978 and has also been implemented in various messengers. Any discussions about encryption and its weakening require engineers and technicians to implement the most secure technology in each case if it is to withstand attacks. Capped encryption would be like a speed limit of 40 miles per hour on our highways.

Europol does not emphasize IT security thanks to encryption in the event of attacks by hackers on authorities, hospitals, newspaper printers and other, in particular, system-relevant infrastructure, but this is highlighted by the German *Federal Office for Information Security* (BSI) in its annual security status report[106]. Four weeks after the European November initiative to restrict encryption, there was no daily newspaper in Germany because of an attack (at the Funke media group[107]) and only emergency editions could be produced for Christmas. More than 6,000 workstation computers had to go through a »washing street« to be able to access a new, secure network.

At the *US-Conference of Mayors* (USCM) even 227 mayors, for example from Atlanta, Baltimore or Riviera Beach in Florida, vowed in a resolution not to pay any more money to attackers in the future, who with so-called »ransomware« in numerous Government computers and urban e-mail systems have penetrated because they were inadequately secured with firewalls and encryption[108]. Too little encryption and security enabled the encryption of the systems by hackers on their part - which could only be released against a digital Bitcoin ransom, as the US Conference of Mayors pointed out.

The US-government even had to declare a state emergency when the controlling computers of the Colonial Pipeline[109], whose security was also based on encryption, were attacked with ransomware and then encrypted from the attack side. Since no more oil could be forwarded, tank trucks had to be used to transport emergency rations of oil from Texas to New York. The press was clearly trying to update its articles, so that it was not US-President *Joe Biden*, who had just come into office, that declared the state emergency because of encryption and inadequate IT security, but rather vaguely »the government,« as it was called. Nonetheless, within three days he signed a so-called »Executive Order«[110] that national cybersecurity had to be strengthened: unencrypted data should be secured with »multifactor encryption«, i.e., multiple secured encryption that will be deepened later.

First quintessence: John Doe, the working population and their infrastructure are best protected if secure encryption is not undermined - then the rabbit hole becomes a presidential shoe with which we can walk well!

This is also confirmed by security researcher *Ross Anderson*, professor for *security engineering* at Cambridge University in England. He connects today's car thefts and easily intercept mobile communications with encryption weaknesses and the long-lasting discussions of the 1990s, when the US-government under President *Bill Clinton* tried to prevent secure encryption methods and the use of cryptographic solutions with the US-citizens for over a decade.

At the Chaos Communication Congress (rC3) he described some »today's security gaps as serious collateral damage«[111] in a video session: The years of political discussions about secure encryption and the associated failure to make progress in research and standardization would have resulted in a wrong culture led in this area: Millions of door locking systems therefore still use RFID chip cards of an old generation that have been considered cracked for many years! Wireless locking systems for cars also have insufficient encryption, so that the number of car thefts has almost doubled in recent years.

Encryption slowed down? For John Doe, according to this analysis, it would also be a collateral fiasco if, according to the view, nothing is learned from these braking experiences and braking traces of the past few years. The German *digital association D64*, which is close to the social democratic party but is independent of the party, therefore sees encryption as a »basic requirement for our society« and formulates in its position paper for citizens: »Trust is good, encryption is better«![112]

3.4   The nineth act: Main role WhatsApp, a deceased canary and Captain L. •

But the development of further lowering of security standards is happening faster than everyone is aware. At the turn of the year after the EU resolution became known, WhatsApp finally announced new terms and conditions. Without their acceptance, this previously encrypting messenger can no longer be used. Behind this is a further control of the weakening of encryption by the USA.

As we all know, terms of use are often simply clicked on, or better: clicked away. But there were also users who read it. They hadn't noticed anything for days either. It became clear and public through the Twitter user ›Shiftreduce‹, who compared the new terms and conditions of WhatsApp with the old terms and conditions from three years ago. Just with the new text alone, it would hardly have been noticed, but in comparison this research triggered a new discussion bubble.

WhatsApp had simply left out one sentence in the section on registering the client: »At no time does the WhatsApp server have access to any of the client's private key«[113].

This means that the software client must have been modified in such a way that it is basically possible or it is no longer guaranteed that the app can upload a customer's private key with a side channel.

In the USA, providers of communication solutions can be forced to cooperate with the authorities. Of course, this will not be made public. However, it can be dealt with with the following logic: The provider documents publicly that they are not subject to such an order. If this is suddenly no longer the case, the corresponding insurance is deleted: the documenting notice is hung up, the passage deleted.

This makes it clear: something has fundamentally changed - even if it cannot be talked about. The analogy is that of a canary that was taken underground in the mining industry. The litmus test: if the air is very unhealthy, the bird dies - and people should save themselves quickly. This old method of protection using a living canary is also being carried over to digital security and is called »Warrant Canary«: only that which is expressly confirmed can also be assumed. Anything that is not, or particularly: is no longer confirmed is also not a standard quality. The logic comes from rhetoric and the stylistic figure is called counter position.

This is understood to be the reverse of an implication, i.e., the conclusion from »If A, then B« to »If not B, then also not A«.

The bad air with the Facebook Messenger has always been suspected: Nobody can control unknown uploads when handling private keys, because the upload of a user's private key can be done at any time with a non-open-source client such as WhatsApp. Nobody knows and nobody can understand it, because the app is not open-source. If the code is not public, the function of encryption without a back-door is simply a claim that can hardly be verified. The integrity of the encryption can also be questioned if not only the client but also the server is not open-source.

The piquant thing about the process is that the client's update does not coincide with the update of the terms and conditions. In this respect, it can be assumed that the client may have been able to do this (the presumed upload of the keys) for some time and that only the security promise had to be adjusted. The option of providing the client with such an upload channel possibly would be too obvious and subsequent.

In addition, some Twitter posts suspect that not only WhatsApp can upload WhatsApp's private keys, but also the keys of other programs. First of all, the messenger Signal should be mentioned here, because it also has its server in the USA, is also keen on SMS registration and finally uses the same encryption method (double ratchet) as WhatsApp. The Signal installation file is always the same, which stores Signal's private keys in the known and defined paths of the mobile operating system. Since WhatsApp is granted access to the cell phone, the app also potentially knows from which point it can upload the private keys (and stored messages) from other apps as well.

This would be a further indication of the HoneyPot thesis regarding the messenger Signal, that all dissidents and renegades from WhatsApp should gather here, but whose data would be just as unsafe as that of WhatsApp users. With an order of the FBI, WhatsApp could also upload the keys and saved messages from the installation paths of Signal and other programs, as these install itself according to a predefined scheme. With this, the encryption of the messages could simply be opened with the associated key. If A = B, then B = A.

In this respect, the recommendations for Signal may not have created a real alternative, but only distribute the load on American servers. If you switch to Signal, it might be better to completely uninstall WhatsApp in order to rule out this risk and still get stuck in the risk of other non-open-source applications from the Facebook group or even the operating system.

After the announcement of new terms and conditions on WhatsApp, users triggered a wave of new registrations with other messengers. Especially with a messenger with a non-open-source server in Switzerland, as well as with the Signal server. Signal, of all things.

The now richest man in the world, who replaced *Jeff Bezos*, founder of the online mail order company Amazon, in this position, also spoke up dynamically: *Elon Musk*. With his rocket company SpaceX, he wants to bring people to Mars and with his electric car company Tesla he is heating up the other car manufacturers who still rely on internal combustion engines. He tweeted just two words to his 40 million friends on Twitter: »Use Signal«. Comedian *Jan Böhmermann* took on a similar role in German-speaking countries and wrote: »Erases WhatsApp. Now!« and called for people to leave Facebook.

Said. And Done. Many users follow this alternative, which also appears as a messenger alternative, but, as stated, could possibly not be one and should be treated with caution.

If the above assumptions are correct, the lesson from this act can only be: it is better to install and use your own, open-source server. Because there will definitely be a time after WhatsApp and Facebook, just as the messengers AOL, Pidgin or ICQ had their time on the desktop.

Interestingly, there is hardly a commercial messenger provider who builds its business plan on an open-source server and an open-source client. Of course, users would not buy the app for some money in the store but compile it themselves or download it from other free boards. However, can money be earned by using an open-source server if there is a critical mass there? The future will tell.

At present, the WhatsApp encryption document continues to say: »If a business user delegates operation of their Business API client to a vendor, that vendor will have access to their private keys - including if that vendor is Facebook«[114].

The guideline thus not only approves the content for communication content in cases of need, but also generally for professional use and also for evaluation by the Facebook group. It can therefore be summarized that WhatsApp no longer belongs to the encrypting messengers. Users with an interest must judge in whether it is appropriate to advertise with encryption if the private keys are subject to the acceptance of an upload to the business company at any time.

They did that then and because of the indignation and flight of the users, WhatsApp was forced to extend the date of the last possible approval of the new data protection rules by a good three months: According to the previous planning, the new conditions should be accepted by February 8, if the chat service belonging to Facebook should continue to be used. May 15th was then announced as the new end time. Apparently, the violent protests and strong migration to market competitors led to WhatsApp's decision. When the functionality of the app was finally reduced before it was switched off - the friends list was simply no longer displayed - even the Brazilian government asked to revoke this, as many poorer parts of the population there communicate with this tool and many would now be ready to make their private data available even more unprotected.

Some Twitter users also commented whether they should be grateful that at least the official regulations have been adapted to what might have been in practice for years because of the technology in the client: to steal, upload and monitor the private keys of an encryption through uploads?

As a consequence, this theoretical train of thought means better protecting the private key, e.g., on a machine that is not connected to the Internet, and instead copying the data packet with the cipher text from a protected device to the device, which is then connected to the Internet and regulates shipping. This option is discussed in more detail in Chapter 7. So conversion and shipping would have to be separated in a new protection option after this adjustment? Keys could also only be stored in the volatile main memory of a device, possibly also encoded or, as the saying goes: obfuscated. This is also discussed again below.

The public excitement was great, and the company tried to smooth out its own damage by updating the information on the website with soothing words: WhatsApp and Facebook will neither read private messages nor listen in to calls. The reason for this is end-to-end encryption, the protection of which also applies to or in front of the platform operators. But this statement does not correspond to what the terms and conditions now express!

The date is still interesting in the WhatsApp document (version 3) of the new year on the terms and conditions with specifications for encryption. Either it was created at that time, or it was deliberately back-dated: to October 22nd of the previous year, i.e., before the European initiative to upload the private keys. In this respect, WhatsApp may have carried out this update on the basis of an impulse from the agencies in its own country, and the EU jumped on this project, or the EU and the

USA chose the political agreements together and WhatsApp proceeded these implementations at the turn of the year more timely than, for example, the legislation in the individual European countries. The comparison document of the WhatsApp specifications (version 2), in which an assurance of the security of the private key is still described, was created three years earlier (dated December 19).

In any case, the political strategies of the USA and the Five-Eyes countries have influenced Europe on the one hand, or they together have set these stones in motion on the topic of decryption. The users now must analytically assess how they can keep their private keys private - or whether they should only be private keys loaned by the state or state-commissioned large tech companies: Privacy on the drip of only borrowed keys.

A documented practice option of borrowing or uploading private keys would, however, have an epoch-making quality of change.

From when the non-open-source messenger is or was technically supposed to be able to upload and decrypt private keys remains encrypted in the app, compiled and unknown. Also, because of the closed-source of the app, it cannot be proven whether the first key of a chat is generated on the device or on the server: The schematically updated keys are generated with the first key - and with any - or this first - of these keys the past chats are at any time traceable in plain text.

A translation of a commenting article by the Russian news agency TASS on the events of this messenger summarized it in the title: »New WhatsApp rules show: The end-to-end encryption was a lie!«[115]

While the spoken word to a friend in the inviolability of one's own apartment may only be broken into and intercepted by a court order, the text word that we talk to a distant (remote) girlfriend or to a distant friend in one is-supposed-to-be-send-protected, digital communication space, is not broken into and wiretapped after judicial deliberation, but directly visible to and by employees in global tech companies.

Since all of this happened at the time of the resignation and impeachment proceedings of US-President Donald Trump, and Twitter blocked the account of this US-President within the own country and deprived him of free speech (in the digital space), German Chancellor Angela Merkel rated this process as follows: »Freedom of expression is a Fundamental Right of elementary importance. This Fundamental Right can be interfered with, but along the lines of the law and only within the framework defined by the legislature. Not according to the decision of the corporate management of social media platforms. From this point of view, the Federal Government of Germany sees it as problematic that the accounts of the US-President have now been permanently blocked by employees of the economy.«[116] - Interesting, because what applies to the right to free speech should also apply to the right to private free speech: namely that employees of commercial companies cannot listen in, define and restrict it.

Because: The Right to Privacy is also a Human Right and is anchored in all modern democracies. This right can only be restricted because of the public and thus state or legislative interest in a person or for purposes of criminal prosecution. The protection of the private sphere in the German Basic Law can be derived from the general Right of Personality (Article 2, Paragraph 1 in conjunction with Article 1, Paragraph 1 of the Basic Law). The area of protection is concreted through the Inviolability of the Home (Art. 13 GG) and through the Secrecy of Post and Telecommunications (Art. 10 GG, in conjunction with § 88 para. 1 for telecommunications secrecy and § 206 injury to post or telecommunications secrecy).

The European Convention on Human Rights (1950) also states in Article 8 the Right to Respect for Private Life and the

Protection of Correspondence. Likewise, the Charter of Fundamental Rights of the European Union, 2000 (Art. 7, 8).

And in the United States of America, too, Privacy has a long tradition, which is derived from the 4th Amendment to the Constitution (Search and Seizure: Expectation of Privacy, US Supreme Court).

And continuing internationally: the principles of protection of private speech, communication and life in the Universal Declaration of Human Rights, 1948 (Art. 12) and in the International Covenant on Civil and Political Rights, 1966 (Art. 17).

The exceptions to this (wiretapping of telephone calls and apartments) are referred to as eavesdropping and are also regulated or regulated by law. So, if the Privacy of the population has been broken up en masse, permanently and by standard setting through corporate decisions and virtually depict a Stasi 2.0 surveillance model of the very own private communication with a partner in the private family area, then this Basic Right to Privacy will also become massive hollowed out.

Companies now seem to decide about our Privacy and that of our families in the 21st century. And: if a claim to protection of Privacy (e.g., through encryption) is additionally criminalized by the state, this can be described as an epoch-making change. Super Secreto: Does our Privacy with our sovereign decision about what others know or should (not) know belong on the scaffold of history? Or would a further public discussion be necessary as to which basic ethical and cultural values are defined by economic, technical and political decision-makers?

From a technical point of view, this »sabotage« towards the innovative methods of end-to-end encryption by the EU Parliament, by global security authorities and by the US messenger monopoly WhatsApp, which may have weakened its encryption, might remind of the machine storms Early 19th century?

A social movement of English textile workers destroyed numerous looms in wool and cotton mills. These representatives, known as *Luddites*, turned against the onset of automation and industrialization and thus against the deterioration of their living conditions in the course of the industrial revolution by deliberately destroying technology. They were named after their legendary, fictional leader *Ned Ludd*, also known as Captain, General or simply King Ludd.

This Luddism movement was finally defeated militarily in 1814. As a result, »machine storming« - that is, the technical sabotage and restriction of the spread of technical innovation potential - was even declared an economic capital crime!

Around 200 years later, from a technical point of view, the onslaught of numerous corporate actors on the technologies of end-to-end encryption and thus an extended attack on Privacy can be compared with their already existing crisis in the 21st century with the technology storm at that time, and with it be labeled as a politically deliberate delay in innovation?

Or are today's calls to respect the Fundamental Right to Privacy to be signed by a new Captain Neo, who also acts as a fictional leader and collective pseudonym in order to restore Privacy? Accordingly, in the computer game *The Moment of Silence*, »Luddites« fight against the surveillance state.

Or is the regulation of encryption a technically slowing but socially necessary measure?

How can the traditional Right to Privacy of the citizens and the goal of a corresponding social movement be led to a non-violent but grand enforcement in the digital world? - Not through sabotage of technology, but rather through increased interest in independent and decentralized installations of the citizens of secure technologies of end-to-end encryption?

Accelerated development: Acceleration instead of sabotage of technology is the new call of a new Captain Neo L. to the grassroots in the digital world today. But who is the new Captain L.? The letter L could stand in the context of an educational policy inclusion of the population for the learners: In particular, learners are interested in the subject of encryption and must be open to advanced technical approaches in the area of chat, e-mail and messaging. Learning is Captain: The learners of modern end-to-end encryption are captains. And they have to be? Otherwise the »Digitization with Blinkers« criticized by Federal Data Protection Commissioners becomes a »Blinker Cryptography«.

3.5   The tenth act: The discovery of innovative alternatives ●

As in every good novel, after the quarrels and confusions there is a cleansing, a catharsis of all the old pigtails and can be combined with a perspective for the future: the discussions about breaking weak algorithms, the discussions about the surrender of copies of the keys and the discussions about a compulsion not only to register the technical infrastructure at all ports, but also the compulsion (so far only proposed) to identify people with their ID card or even their human number was supplemented and enriched with the publication of a stable prototype for the coming period.

In the publication of *Casio Moonlander*, as well as in a blog of the well-known portal *FDroid* with numerous secondary information links, the completion of a new messenger was reported in December 2020. At the same time as the discussion about an intended restriction of encryption began.

It's about the world's first mobile messenger that uses an algorithm that even the fast quantum-computers already available in research centers cannot crack: Because this messenger includes the McEliece algorithm. Keys cannot be extracted from it as copies either, since it does not send one key per session, but a whole dozen keys per message. A registration of the correspondingly used open-source chat server is also not necessary, as it relates to private design options for the technical infrastructure. With a chat server at home, there is no need to present an identity card, as the Twitter user ›Ign8ite‹ confirms: »The trend will be towards self-hosted chat server solutions«!

This prototype with its development perspectives is presented in the third part of the book, because it is an ideal model project for teachers and learners: learning in and at the lighthouse for the Third Epoch of Cryptography. But first to what mathematics shows us all publicly: Because mathematics is not rocket science but can be learned by everyone.

3.6 Democratization of open-source encryption: A magnificent spectacle of only mathematics? •

The restrictions on or even attacks against Privacy with the erosion of other rights, as well as the underlining of the demand for a Right to Encryption and its educational processes, are, as seen, a necessary show of strength for the spectacle in several acts and scenes, which according to the EU initiative elaborate and choreographed like a ballet[117] came out step by step in a short window of time before Christmas. However, there was no choreographer, but the protagonists spoke up in large numbers, as it should be in a Democracy or an active school class.

And now Germany no longer wants to become »Number 1 Champion« in the field of encryption, but Europe should become Champion. But it seems, only in the area of decryption, not in the citizens' Right to Encryption with tap-proof end-to-end encryption.

Since laws are always the task of lawyers, even after political negotiations, to elaborate these on a country-specific basis, the journey of the »Right to Encryption for Everyone« through the world remains an equally exciting legislative development task, as the journey of law through the world with the »Marriage for all«? And at the same time, it cannot be compared in this way, since same-sex and different-sex couples who marry are assumed to have equality and equal rights, but who want to use encryption between two traders who want to use encryption, depending on the commodity: whether patent or narcotic drugs, possibly does not exist at all.

But, as with the legitimization of an online search for the executive branch, shouldn't there also be a judicial decision with regard to the claim on commercial enterprises to hand over keys for a clear inspection? And what does this equation of the view of plain text by handing out keys say about the balance and proportionality to online searches? And how do the requirements for using a state Trojan differ from those for using an state online search? Is it comparable to contrasting the inviolability of the apartment with a regulation that from now on window glass and curtains are forbidden and that every passerby is allowed to enter the apartment?

Or would citizens be obliged to install listening microphones called Alexa, Bixby, Google Assistant, Android or Siri in their own apartment? A regulation on mobile Internet devices with mandatory microphones in our apartments will soon define a new STASI 2.0 - which is not kept in check by a court order, but in which it is a matter of course for the companies of these language assistants to be able to potentially listen permanently - and we even install them ourselves?

In the movie »Zero Dark Thirty« to the documentary processing of the search for Al-Qaeda terrorist leader Osama bin Laden and his message carriers the scene is still present, as a taxi of cell phone reception of a motor head driver was tracked manually. This trauma uncontrolled person is not only fixed by the monitoring of smartphones, but also the cars follow the monitoring technology of smartphones: one may believe that Tesla was not established as a car company for the electric drive, but as a monitoring tool with dual-use function: everyone Tesla car has all around at least six high-resolution cameras that guarantee moving and parking a guard (»sentry«) mode with which the environment is recorded on Tesla servers. Not only with future facial recognition, even today, passers-by cannot fight against the recording. As with WhatsApp, that uploads the friend contacts unasked, Tesla also uploads the movies of the car-neighbors to own servers unquestioned. Tesla cars should not be allowed to be equipped with this camera function according to the German and European jurisprudence - and be allowed to drive on the streets. The Data Protection Authority in Germanys Baden-Württemberg prohibits parking and driving the Tesla vehicles, since cameras are firmly installed here and an uncontrolled Dashcams function is included. Previously, the German Federal Court of Justice (BGH) had already assessed a few years earlier that the use of so-called Dashcams is in principle inadmissible (Az. VI ZR 233/17). Does the Technical Monitoring Association (TÜV) have to regularly certify the deactivation of certain technological functions for the approval of the cars?

Encryption technology is easier to judge, as this must install any yourself, as monitoring technology, which may be provided by technology companies in close cooperation with the state de facto by default.

If we know that plain text from our private everyday communication has not to be sent to the Internet, users ultimately decide for themselves in the practical implementation to only send cipher text to the Internet (or not to buy the above-mentioned eavesdropping bugs). We remember: Unencrypted broadcasts on the Internet are like postcards: they can be read openly or are evaluated by computers after being sent and saved.

Not only mathematics teaches us: Nowadays encryption is no longer rocket science: encryption technologies are generally freely available and accessible. This is known as secularization and the »Democratization of Encryption«[118]. Open-source programs, such as the currently very comprehensive and advanced encryption software Spot-On or the simple e-mail-based messenger called Delta-Chat and others mentioned in the last section of this volume, contribute to the daily bread of encryption. The spokesman *Linus Neumann* from the Chaos Computer Club even demanded: »Only freely available, verifiable and open protocols (and thus programs) should be allowed to be used«[119]!

For all those involved around the world - apart from states that do not take Democracy that seriously and want to control every utterance, every trip and every request for information made by a citizen - it is clear that Cryptography is a standard that citizens cannot and will not do without.

On the contrary, it is necessary as a nation to play an independent role in the development and promotion of basic research, algorithms, programs for encryption and the provision of the necessary infrastructure as well as the definition of corresponding security standards.

Nobody in democratic countries today can seriously limit encryption and its research, neither the creation of corresponding programs, nor the research of the associated basics, nor the use of an encrypting solution. In concrete terms, this means that cipher text will also be sent in the future, e.g., via the Internet, i.e., when the clearly legible part of the message has been converted into encrypted characters.

Accordingly, the analysts commissioned to decrypt it have also added to their strategy: They try to install monitoring before a message is encrypted or when the recipient decrypts it. Breaking encryption is still possible as an attempt, but with the appropriate algorithms it is also more difficult and with multi-encryption also increasingly impossible. Therefore, the focus has shifted to access the control of sent communication where it has not yet been encrypted or is decrypted again: i.e., when typing or reading the plain text message.

Open-source encryption is therefore required in a Democracy for many reasons:

- Our economy is based on encryption: companies, people, customers, developers and the promoters of innovations need digital security that goes hand in hand with encryption processes.
- A state must use encryption to protect systemically relevant and therefore critical infrastructures: Providers of infrastructure that are vital for the community and national security as well as services in the areas of banking, health, power supply, water management, mobile radio and internet supply as well as other providers must be equipped with the best possible available encryption and corresponding security technologies.
- But encryption is also required for legal reasons and for reasons of joint regulatory agreements. This affects, for example, the actors in the healthcare sector as well as the providers of data management who store, process or send personal or business-related data. You must also have the best technology in place to ward off attacks or protect the integrity of the data. An example is the General Data Protection Regulation GDPR (DSGV) in Europe, according to which the individual has the right to legally demand protection and thus, for example, encryption or the deletion of data.
- This means that individuals have the right to feel safe in public and to know that private and commercial life and its interactions are protected by encryption, among other things. This is understood under the keyword »Privacy as standard setting / by default«.
- But not only at the micro level of the individual, the state also has an increased interest in protection at the macro level: The nation, the state and also its local agencies must

ensure that official data and information that they process are safe.

- In addition to the interest of the individual states in recording citizens' communications, it can still be assumed that various attackers in particular have a greater interest in decrypting encrypted messages than individual citizens are currently interested in sending their own messages encrypted. There is also a great economic interest behind this hacking nowadays.

Nobody can therefore do without encryption and the mathematics behind it. And everyone can learn it. It is therefore not only democratized, but also available to everyone with open-sources. Rather, it is about developing the best possible standard for one's own country or for its fellow citizens and using it. Renewed political initiatives to ban encryption instead of establishing encryption as a Fundamental Right to Privacy fall behind the status quo of the discussion that encryption is a standard that is not only urgently needed, and not only public, but is also technically not more to be prevented.

So, will the public discussions about end-to-end encryption and the options of Steganography for hiding, skipping, transforming and fading out of possibly multi-encrypted cipher text, as it was a few decades ago, lead to a more established and less demonized respective less persecuted or even criminalized situation?

In a learning curve, will we realize that
- we have to deal with these standards and innovations and their implementations in numerous tools, applications and messengers?
- we want to train students to do this?

- we have to promote open-source practice and learning projects, particularly in the field of mobile communication, as alternatives to the WhatsApp monopoly?
- and we should expand and update curricula and equip libraries with new books on topic accordingly?
- So, what can we learn from the American »Crypto-War« discussions in the 1990s, which after ten years finally did not criminalize asymmetric GPG encryption, but permitted it in general? Suddenly today end-to-end encryption is supposed to be controlled in Europe after these many decades and renewed discussions about it could bind this technology restriction again for decades and stop learning processes?
- And: Anyone who offers small pocket computers called smartphones available to citizens to monitor them should not be surprised if they use the existing technology accordingly to send encrypted messages using this standard?

There is hardly any other political process where there has been such a large-scale regional alliance and uniformity across numerous experts, teachers and educational institutions. The central summarizing message of Scientists4Crypto to colleges, universities and research groups is: »Cryptography is public knowledge and cannot be switched off«[120].

According to the Kerckhoffs principle[121], the openness of the specification of cryptographic tools is an essential component for security and trust. As a result, most systems and many high quality and user-friendly implementations are publicly known, making any attempt to limit the use of these mechanisms directly futile. The Kerckhoffs principle was formulated in 1883 by *Auguste Kerckhoffs*, Dutch linguist and cryptologist, and is now a well-known principle of modern Cryptography, which states that the security of a (symmetric) encryption method is not based on the secrecy of the encryption algorithm but must be based on the confidentiality of the key.

Likewise, *Jimmy Wales*, the founder of Wikipedia, commented on the freedom of the inexplicable and rather to be learned foreign language »Cryptography« a few years ago as follows: »To ban end-to-end encryption - a secret way of communicating in which eavesdroppers cannot access messages - I likened it to attempting to ban mathematics.»[122]

After this statement and mandate on public mathematics and information technology education, let's take a look at the essential fundamentals, functions and innovations of encryption technologies in the following sections. Encryption is now not only abstinent and ignorant («knowledge-free«) in the transmission of keys, it is also multi-encrypted, exponentially routed and secure against the fast quantum-computers. In a further section, the individual characteristics and development standards of over two dozen selected open-source programs for encryption, which are thus available worldwide, are explained.

Because: the real main role on the subject of encryption must apply to the learners when we talk about encryption technologies or their open-source functions and model projects in the future.

3.7   My kick-off: How do I personally approach the subject of encryption as a learner? •

So far, we have left encryption to mathematicians, computer scientists or those familiar with personal computers - in other words, generally to those who are familiar with data processing and app programming. We may not yet use encryption ourselves or would like to learn how to use it because we have politically noticed that it is always a topical issue in public discussion or is important for our own Privacy.

In addition to developing a personal approach to the topic and practical knowledge in the use of encryption and its tools, it is not only relevant for the discipline to get to know and use the three siblings WHAT, HOW, and WHY - but this can also be for every learner a preliminary consideration as a first step. That means: WHAT do we do, or do we want to do and learn, HOW do we do it and even more important: WHY do we do this or have an appropriate attitude and strategy to acquire this knowledge in this way (and other content may not be so pronounced).

The application of this learning triad of WHAT-HOW-WHY in the context of Cryptography and encryption is so central because we may notice that, on the one hand, the contents of the WHAT should concern us exactly, i.e., should be addressed to our needs and interests should be aligned. On the other hand, the content should also be appropriately modern so as not to look at old hats, but to be up to date with the learning curriculum. Second, the HOW may also be more a question of the teaching by the teacher, how much practical relevance the topic of encryption may have, how much mathematics or programming must be included, or which software applications are to be learned - and via which forms of learning all this is conveyed.

And finally, thirdly: the WHY we should or want to learn something often depends on personal interests and a formalized strategy and teaching plan. Therefore, with this should be started.

This mixture and interests can be quite different for everyone: some want to expand the basics; others find their way into the topic for the first time. If you go to a course or workshop for Cryptography, you might also want to try out or compare a software, a tool, or you are politically motivated and want to learn about the points of view of the individual associations, organizations and states and form your own opinion.

And there are also the open-source evangelists who want to promote open-source applications - which is also correct in Cryptography, because only with open-source programs can one prove that they are secure and do not harbor any back-doors. This also includes the intention to develop probably a new culture of encryption - too many messages are currently being sent to the Internet without encryption. According to this interest situation, the proportion of messages that are sent encrypted to the Internet must be increased even further until the plain text sent approaches zero.

Others, such as journalists, want to find out exactly how a message that they send to an informant, or the editorial office is encrypted. Some people simply ask themselves why the IT department of their own company or organization is not converting communication more comprehensively to encryption - especially if there is an exchange of information between lawyers, customers or even informants. And then there are the pupils and students who want to accelerate and deepen their learning experience with encryption, because the content will soon be relevant for the exam. In this way, topics can also be found that are worth exploring in a term paper or an examination paper.

Police officers also bring with them the perspective of analysts: How can encryption be broken, or plain text at least accessed?

Often, personal contacts or even lasting friendships result from such a workshop, because for encryption you always need someone who receives the message - and who is also willing to decrypt and return a message. This is extremely easy on today's smartphones because you always have this pocket computer with you. But you will quickly find that those who are not willing to try out a new messenger with you may not be the right friends either?

Figure 11: My story - Expectations

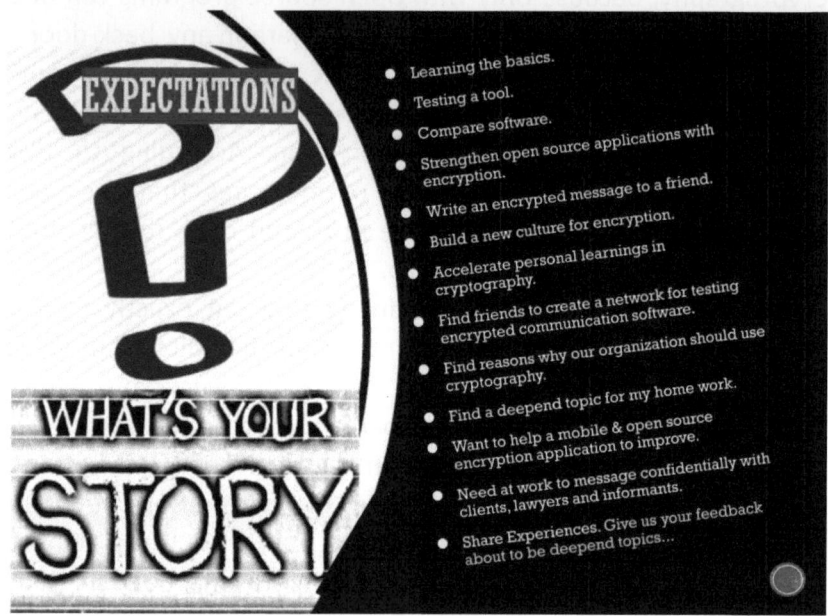

Source:[123]

Fortunately, there are also those kinds of people who like to share their knowledge and experience with others so that they can benefit from it. The working group in the school is an ideal learning environment in which one can exchange feedback: via cryptographic processes and ways of learning about it.

Anyone who knows the motivation with which one takes part in getting to know Cryptography for the first time also quickly knows which learning content should have a focus: The first short day of the introduction to Cryptography is always about the generation of keys with which the message should be encrypted. The establishment of an e-mail program in order to be able to communicate with it in encrypted form. As well as on a smartphone, increasingly also to set up a chat program, a messenger, in order to be able to send encrypted messages via an own server.

And then the time has come: A first encrypted message is sent, and a look is taken at what the cipher text of the message looks like. Of course, it is also about getting to know the relevant terms in Cryptography and understanding the modern methods of encryption. These are the usual goals on the didactic side of knowledge transfer - but above all: The topic to be learned should also be fun!

It is therefore important to include group work and practical exercises in the learning process. Learners are therefore asked not to neglect the practical part. The software applications and tools in the last third of this volume are easy to install (and for advanced users: they can also be compiled or even programmed). Encryption of content and data can be tried out in a team with others. The first preparation for learning is therefore to become certain for yourself what, how and why is important to one in learning encryption, in order to discuss these first perspectives, which can become in-depth focal points, with others in a dialogue.

The concept of this volume is therefore also to combine the positions of social and political discussion with the referenced expertise from a technical point of view, the applicable programs, tools and apps; and thirdly, to combine an innovative outlook into the Third Epoch of Cryptography. Everyone should be able to find something new to deepen in this content! And fourth, the inclusion of, in particular, open-source principles is provided: Super Secreto encryption, which is basically available to everyone with its source code.

4 HISTORICAL BEGINNINGS AND BASICS OF CRYPTOGRAPHY •

The historical beginnings of encryption go back a long way. People have always tried to structure communication in such a way that others do not understand it immediately. Should one start with the Tower of Babel according to Genesis 11, 1-9, where the Babylonian confusion of languages is said to have started? So, after the flood, a type of encryption began.

Cryptography (literally translated: secret writing) is the occupation with the secrecy of information. This information or text or data is converted with the help of a sequence of individual steps, an algorithm, into a form that cannot be read or understood by unauthorized persons. But: you can convert the jumbled letters back into readable text.

A central aspect of encryption is that, as a rule, both, such an algorithm and a key, are used in the process. The algorithm specifies schematically how the characters are to be encrypted, i.e., how they are to be replaced and mixed. A key (which is also a character string) represents the further component that specifies how the algorithm encrypts the original text. Even if the encryption method is known: Without the key, decryption should be almost impossible.

People from the Middle Ages on, whose stories of hardship and secrecy strategies have been passed down in greater detail, are often historically associated with encryption. Book printing also played a decisive role in these traditions: After language and writing, *Johannes Gutenberg*'s development of book printing was the third great revolution that replaced the Dark Ages with the Renaissance and the Age of Enlightenment. Completely new cultural, social and technical developments became possible and could be handed down in printed form. And: The preoccupation with printed scripts allowed these to be further developed as secret scripts.

However, one cannot avoid a very early person before the birth of *Jesus Christ* if one deals with encryption: and that is *Gaius Iulius Caesar*. Not only do we remember him when we think of Rome or Latin, and when dressing the salad of the same name, but also a first simple encryption algorithm was named according to him: the Caesar encryption. The Caesar`s Cipher is a kind of substitution algorithm in which every letter in the plain text is replaced by a precisely counted letter in the sequence of the alphabet. For example, with a right shift of three places, the A becomes a D. Each A is replaced by a D. And so on.

Gaius Iulius Caesar is said not only to have invented this method himself, but to have used it practically in his letters in order to gain sole rule of Rome.

Figure 12: The Caesar`s Cipher

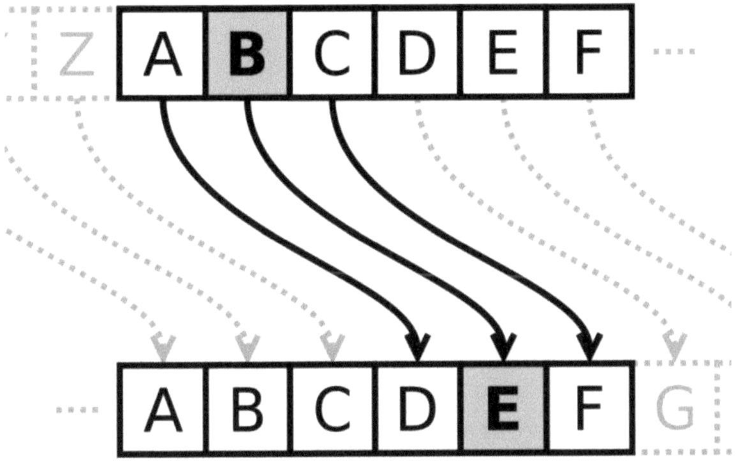

Source:[124]

Another algorithm with a similar principle is the ROT-13 algorithm - written out it is about the ROTATION now of 13 places. This replaces each letter of the alphabet by 13 places along the alphabet. A does not become D, but the thirteen additional letter of the alphabet is chosen. A becomes N. When Z arrives at the end, counting continues from the beginning at A. With ROT-13, the word HELLO becomes URYYB.

Figure 13: ROT-13-Encryption

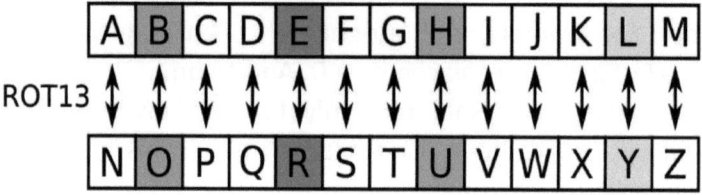

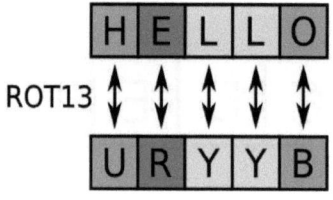

Source:[125]

The number of rotation or displacement of the letters to a replacement letter can be freely selected. To make things easier, a small tool was developed at the time that combines two circular disks like on a clock face: the original letter on the inside and the letter found as a replacement on the outside. Both circles could be rotated against each other and thus easily find the corresponding substitution letter. This method of encryption is therefore also referred to as a shift cipher or a cipher disk. Discs of this type have been around since the 15th century. The development of the first cipher disk is attributed to *Leon Battista*

Alberti, who as a cleric and long-time employee of the papal chancellery was also an expert in ancient architecture in Florence and Rimini.

Figure 14: Substitution by means of a shifting cipher disk

These historical methods of encryption are fascinating, but from today's perspective they offer no security and can be broken immediately with a little brains or electronic help. They described the beginnings of symmetric encryption, in which the key, a character string or a password, must be known and used on both sides.

This means that the character string of the replacement does not have to be in alphabetical order, but can be any, possibly random character string or a password.

Today we differentiate between two types of encryption: In addition to symmetric encryption, asymmetric encryption was added in the age of the computer, which we will discuss further below. First, let's go back to today's standard of symmetric encryption.

4.1 From Caesar to Enigma to AES: The symmetric encryption ●

As we have seen, with symmetric encryption, both parties involved - Alice and Bob are spoken in the usual language - must know the same character string (e.g., the alphabet) or the same password in order to convert the plain text into encrypted text - and vice versa to convert the encrypted text back to plain text.

According to the Caesar-cipher, this can be the number 13 for ROT-13, or a ROT-3 if the letter is only to be shifted 3 steps in the alphabet.

The key is then the sequence of characters (of the alphabet) shifted by 3 or 13 digits, and this specified procedure results in the cipher text of the encryption. Both parties involved, Alice and Bob, have to agree on a number or character string so that they can carry out the conversion procedure synchronously. Once three steps forward in the alphabet for encryption and three steps back again for decryption.

Like twins, Alice and Bob are mirrored and have the same information about the secret key in order to use a symmetric algorithm for encryption. Hence it is called symmetric encryption. The Greek term »Gemini« is therefore occasionally used for this twin situation. The Gemini is the number »13« as information with a reference to the character sequence of the alphabet beginning at a certain position, which both sides know to use this key to convert the texts.

The procedure then runs as follows: Alice and Bob agree on the use of this symmetric encryption system. They agree on the number »13« with which the rotation ROT should take place in the alphabet.

Alice takes her plain text and applies the algorithm ROT with the key of a character string that is offset by 13 characters in the alphabet. This generates the cipher text, which nobody can read or understand anymore. Alice finally sends the cipher text to Bob. Bob can convert the cipher text back, because with this mirrored information, as a quasi-twin, he also knows the key and the algorithm in this symmetric encryption system. He has to turn back each letter in the cipher text by 13 positions in the alphabet using the ROT algorithm and thus receives a readable version of the message.

Here it is already clear that the basic problem of symmetric encryption is not only transferring the cipher text from Alice to Bob, but also the key. If both transferals are done in the same way, this may be unskillful, because an attacker can tap and merge both and knows the method with which the text was converted: the ROT-shift and probably the key to this algorithm: It has been moved 13 positions in the defined and known character string of the alphabet. So, it would be smart to transfer the key with the 13-digit string of characters in a different way or to have transferred it unobserved in the past.

This type of symmetric encryption has been known for many thousands of years.

Encryption by substituting letters has been refined over time by further mechanisms and algorithms, e.g., to rule out an analysis of the letter frequency distribution from revealing that, for example, the letter E appears above average in our texts (it is the most common given at around 17 percent, followed by the letter N with about 8-9 percent, others, like the I, only follow with 6-7 percent). From the First World War, this symmetric Cryptography was then used in particular to decide entire field wars on the basis of less decrypted information.

This resulted in numerous cryptographic systems that were also used in electromagnetic machines to encrypt military texts. The Enigma machine should be remembered here, especially during the Second World War, which mechanically implemented rotations using sets of rollers. The trick was that the different rollers were movable and therefore one letter did not always map onto the same other letter. Simple procedures for recognizing the frequency of letters therefore failed.

Figure 15: Rollers of the Enigma machine

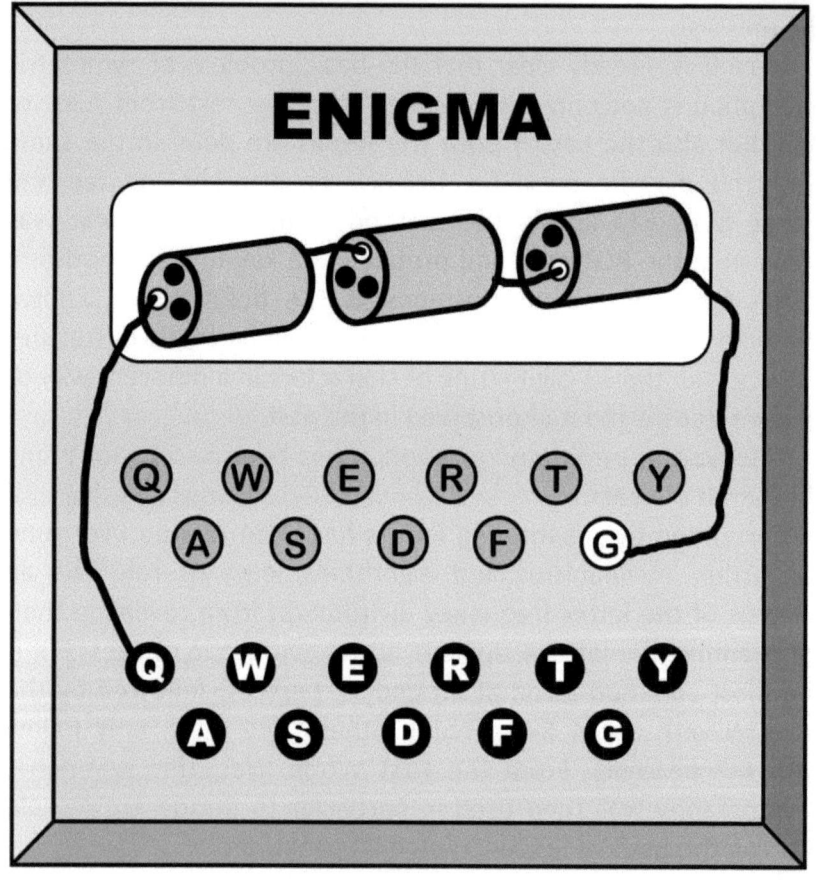

To crack the encryption or to find out the password string used as a key, either complex mathematical analyzes were necessary or the study of intercepted Enigma machines that fell into the hands of the other party. It was only after physical dismantling that you could see how many rollers it contained and how these were electrically wired - and which letters they used.

With their computing power, today's super-computers can now successfully decrypt Enigma-encrypted texts from the Second World War, as demonstrated at the beginning of this century - for that time, they were relatively safe, machine-aided processes on an electromagnetic basis. Even more the decoding of the Enigma texts, which was carried out around the British mathematician *Alan Turing*, is to be recognized as an ingenious achievement.

Alan Turing was not only a British logician, mathematician and cryptanalyst, but also a computer scientist and is now considered one of the most influential theorists of early computer development and computer science. He created a large part of the theoretical basis for modern information and computer technology and influenced the development of artificial intelligence, which has a major impact on our lives today.

The predictability model of the Turing machine named after him forms one of the foundations of theoretical computer science - in addition to its merits in the decryption of the texts from the Enigma machines. According to historians, his achievements probably shortened the duration of the war and ultimately helped to save many lives.

Alan Turing ultimately had to choose between imprisonment or hormone treatment. He chose the latter and fell ill with depression in 1952 as a result of these hormone injections, which were forced by the state, and died of suicide about two years later. The compulsion to castration by means of chemical drugs hit him - in his soul and with it his existence: The knowledge about homosexuality was little in the last century and same-sex partnerships were not yet socially or legally recognized.

In 2009, then British Prime Minister *Gordon Brown* finally paid tribute to his »outstanding service« during the war; after this official apology, *Queen Elizabeth II.* posthumously honored him with the »Royal Pardon«. Today the Bank of England's 50-pound note bears his portrait and was issued on June 23, his birthday. This shows how much his country's leaders honor the gay scientist Alan Turing today. The Twitter user ›Sherlockdown Stayholmes‹ commented on the day of death: R.I.P. *Alan Turing - I'm sure he would have liked instant messengers with end-to-end encryption.*

Nowadays, the replacements and then shifts and rotations of characters in modern algorithms are so refined in several rounds that they cannot be calculated or broken so easily even with the help of a computer without the appropriate key or character string. It is no longer just a matter of replacing a letter with a neighboring letter. After characters have been replaced, entire blocks of letters are shifted, rotated, swapped with one another - for the sake of simplicity one can say: mixed. A precise procedure in several rounds makes it impossible for humans as well as even powerful computers to find out the original plain text without further details about the algorithm and the key used or the character sequence used.

AES-256 is the name of today's standard with which messages are symmetrically encrypted. AES stands for Advanced Encryption Standard (AES) and is sometimes called the »American Encryption Standard« because this algorithm was officially standardized in the United States of America. The algorithm was originally developed by the two Belgian cryptologists *Vincent Rijmen* and *Joan Daemen*, initially under the name Rijndael. Today they are professors at KU Leuven and Radboud University Nijmegen in Belgium.

AES-256 does not do the conversion per character, instead it takes place with a block length of 128 bits and the choice of the key length is fixed at 256 bits. This makes the model somewhat more complex, as that character strings are substituted and rotated in multiple rounds and this with a key that does not consist of a few characters, but a total of 256 bits.

For the sake of simplicity, the functionality of the AES is described here more process-wise than mathematically.

The point is to divide the message text into smaller blocks and to write it in a matrix, a table, e.g., with 4x4 cells. The same is done with the key, which is lengthened or made adaptable to the required character length with a mathematical operation if necessary.

The point is now to replace the plain letter in a cell of this table (with a mathematical function) in connection with the character from the table, which is composed of the character string of the key (password). Finally, rows and columns are shifted and mixed up in this matrix table.

The AES algorithm essentially knows the following process steps:

(Preparation) key expansion
First of all, different partial keys (also called round keys) must be generated from the key, each of which has the same size as a data block. Thus, the original key must be expanded to the appropriate length by means of a mathematical operation (key expansion).

(Preparation) Confusion with the S-Box
A substitution box (S-Box) is used for mono-alphabetical encryption. It indicates how each byte of a block is to be replaced by another. An S-Box is therefore used as a process step in an encryption algorithm, usually to blur the relationship between plain text and cipher text, which is also called confusion in cryptological terminology.

(0) AddRoundKey

Before the first and after each encryption round, the data block is XORed with one of the round keys. This is the only function in which the user key is included. The following figure for AddRoundKey shows a bitwise XOR link between the block and the current round key.

Figure 16: The AES-function AddRoundKey

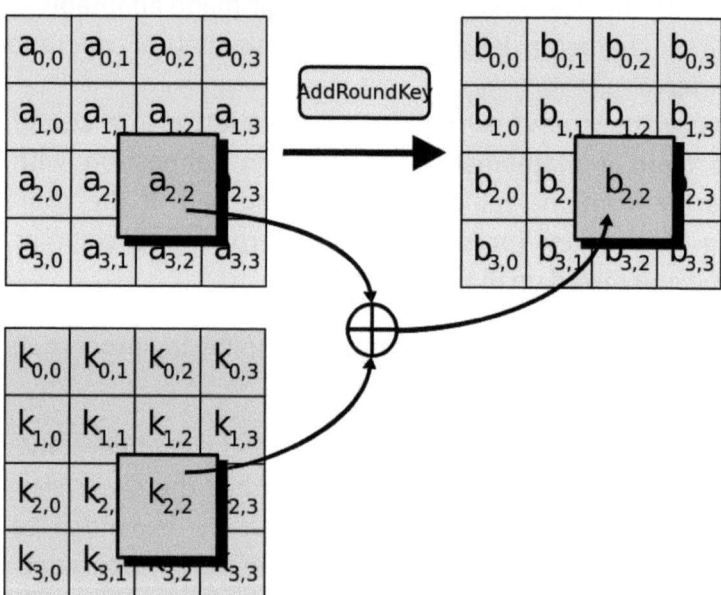

(1) SubBytes

In the first step of each round, each byte B in the block is replaced by the entry S(B) of the S-box. Thus the data is encrypted byte by byte mono-alphabetically. This function is called SubBytes.

Figure 17: The AES-function SubBytes

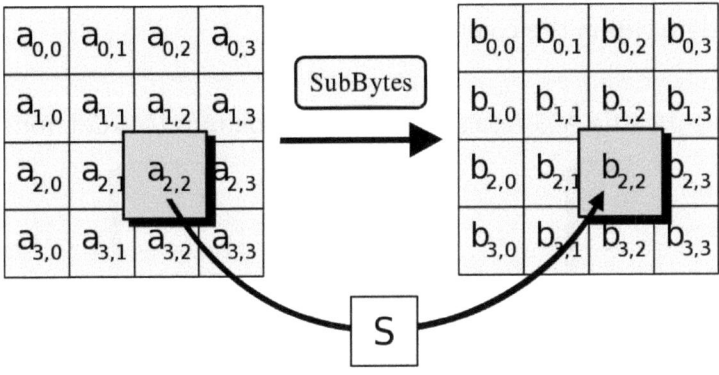

Source:[129]

(2) ShiftRows

In this function, rows are shifted to the left by a certain number of columns. As mentioned, a block is in the form of a two-dimensional table with four lines. In this second step of each round, the rows are shifted a certain number of columns to the left. Overflowing cells are continued from the right. The number of shifts depends on the line and block length.

Figure 18: The AES-function to shift the rows (ShiftRows)

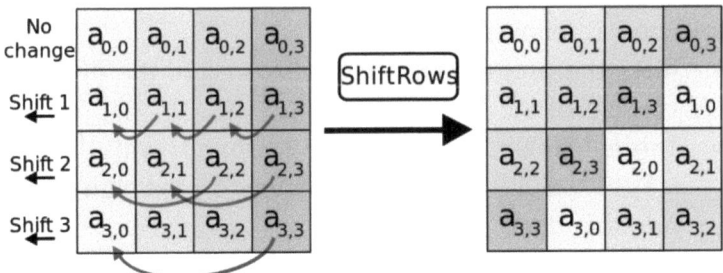

Source:[130]

(3) MixColumns

As the third operation of every round other than the final round, the data within the columns is shuffled.

Figure 19: The AES-function to mix the columns (MixColumns)

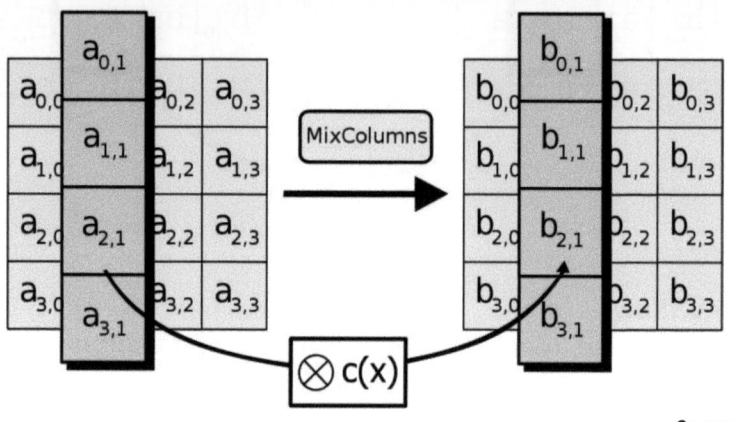

Source:[131]

The steps are accompanied by an opening round and, at the end, by an optimizing final round with elements of these process steps.

In a very abstract process sequence, the steps can be summarized as follows:

- After the preparation for KeyExpansion, the initial round consists of: AddRoundKey.
- This is followed by 9 or 11 or 13 rounds with the process steps: SubBytes, ShiftRows, MixColumns and AddRoundKey.
- The final round makes 10, 12 or 14 rounds in total with the sequence of SubBytes, ShiftRows and AddRoundKey.

And: the decryption is exactly the same, only backwards.

Unlike the Caesar algorithm and the one-time pad explained in the next section, AES does not encrypt each character individually, but entire blocks of characters. One therefore speaks of a block cipher.

Various operating modes are available with the AES: In the ECB mode (Electronic Code Book), each block is encrypted independently, which in turn can lead to recognizable patterns and repetitions. Therefore, the CBC (Cipher Block Chaining) mode links each block with the encryption of the previous block, avoiding the aforementioned problem. The GCM mode (Galois / Counter mode) is currently considered to be particularly secure, since an authenticated encryption mode with associated data is implemented here in order to enable both the authentication and the encryption of messages.

AES is therefore to be understood as a complex model of substitutions, shifts and intermingling - a large mixing machine, the processes of which are better automated by computers compared to the Caesar algorithm.

4.1.1 A special case: the one-time pad (OTP) •

Another variant that is considered to be particularly secure, in addition to the AES-256 conversion processes, is the so-called »One-Time Pad« (OTP), a string that is only used once.

Here is replaced bit by bit, that is, character by character; therefore, one speaks of stream encryption or of a stream cipher.

The OTP has the following properties:
- **First characteristic: The length of the key is exactly as long as the length of the message:** Here the password or the character string of the key is not 256 bits long, but the key is exactly as long as the plain text itself. This replaces

149

each character with another character in the random sequence of the one-time pad.

- **Second characteristic: The character string for the key must really be random:** The character string of the key must be random. Since every exchange or the character for the position to be exchanged is random, every cipher text is equally likely for every plain text.
- **Third characteristic: The key remains secret:** Another identifier of this encryption system should be noted that the key must be kept secret.
- **Fourth characteristic: Key transfer is still necessary:** Until the 1970s, there were only symmetric cryptosystems in which Alice as the sender and Bob as the recipient knew the same secret key. That means the key must be transferred from Alice to Bob. Key exchange and key management - key management as a whole - continues to be a major challenge here with OTP, especially since the character string can be longer than a short password.

The method was proposed for the first time by the American cryptologist *Frank Miller* in 1882. He graduated from Yale University and was an American cryptologist and banker from Sacramento. It was rediscovered and patented 35 years later by *Gilbert Vernam*. He and *Joseph Mauborgne* made it popular in the years that followed under the acronym OTP.

In 1882, *Frank Miller* set up a code book that provided corresponding numbers as encryption for 14,000 terms and parts of sentences. As a further (multi-)encryption, he proposed to link these code numbers in a second step with random numbers from a table, i.e., to add these random numbers to the code numbers. The result numbers obtained in this way were sent as cipher text by telegraph to the other side. Only both sides were allowed to have the list of random numbers as the only ones. Then, after transmission, the random numbers could simply be subtracted from the cipher text - you got the code numbers, which were translated back into words.

Carry-overs took place, i.e., if the addition resulted in a number greater than 14,000, the number 14,000 was subtracted again in order to always get a number from 1 to a maximum of 14,000 as a secret number. The subtraction and addition are therefore to be understood as modulo operations with the base 14,000.

Instead of an addition or subtraction based on a code book, the XOR operation can also be used.

Figure 20: Exemplary string of a one-time pad (OTP)

Exclusive Or: XOR

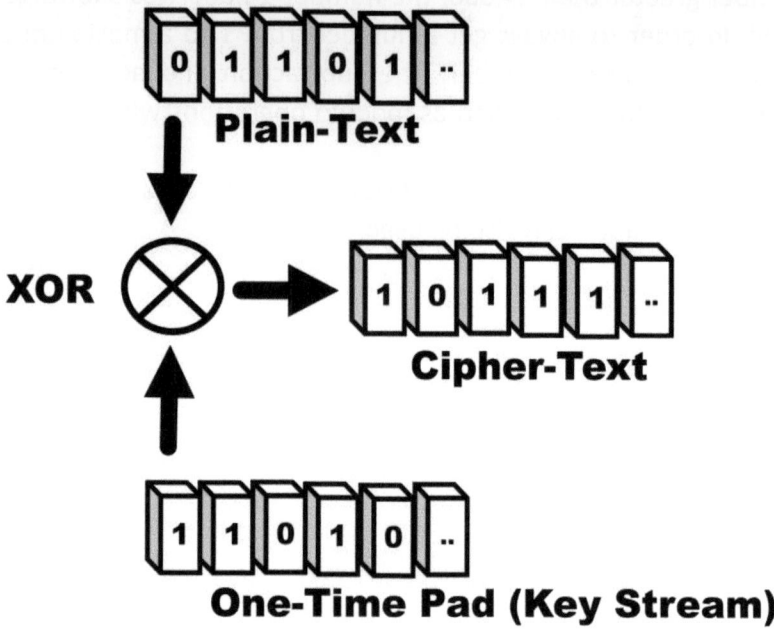

Plain-Text

XOR

Cipher-Text

One-Time Pad (Key Stream)

Source:[132]

The graphic shows the plain text in the top line, which has been converted to 0 and 1. The third stream is the string of the one-time pad. Both are XORed. This means that in the middle the string of the cipher text also results with 0 and 1. After XOR, the first position 0 and 1 result to 1 and in the second position 1 and 1 result to 0 and so on. To convert the cipher text back into plain text, knowledge of the OTP string is required. And: With knowledge of the plain text string, the OTP character string can also be formed with the cipher text.

The plain text as well as the character string of the OTP key is represented in binary in the form of 0 and 1. To mix and thus transform the bits, an exclusive-or-combination (XOR) of plain text and key bits is often used in addition to a pure letter replacement, because this is particularly easy to carry out. The process is often referred to as »Modulo 2« or »exclusive OR«, in short: »XOR«, as already described at the beginning. However, the type of combination is arbitrary and does not have to be kept secret. Alternatively, a different link, for example one addition (without carry over) per character, can also be used.

The graphic thus also illustrates the manner described at the beginning, when the plain text are the zeros and ones of the film by *James Bond* and the one-time pad represent the key stream sequence of the zeros and ones of the film *Mickey Mouse*. Both together result in a cipher text that no longer has anything to do with the zeros and ones of the merged originals. And it becomes clear: if the key is long enough, it could also be an independent message, i.e., the cipher text (or the XOR result) is converted back into two messages in this special case: once the OTP text of the Key Streams and once the plain text (if one of the two is known).

4.1.2 Three-dimensional mixing as a thought model in Cube Encryption •

While the OTP uses a long character string with really random characters as a key for replacements or for an XOR operation, the AES uses a short character string that has to be properly mixed afterwards. Because of the familiarity of the method and the increasingly high computing speed of computers, one might ask oneself whether the mixing is sufficient enough not to be able to mix back the mixing result again by trial and error, in order to recreate the plain text using the replacements from the key's character string.

To come to the point: the American standardization authority NIST continues to regard the AES algorithm as safe. Nevertheless, this section aims to address the question of what a train of thought can look like, to structure this or an algorithm in general in such a way that, if necessary, a higher level of complexity and thus security arises.

The AES processes all take place two-dimensionally on a 4x4 table (hereinafter also referred to as matrix). What if we did not just mix on one matrix, but in several matrices connected in series - not only to be able to mix more or more complexly, but also to introduce further keys at each level of an additional matrix?

The two Indian authors *S. Srisakthi* and *A.P. Shanthi* from Anna University in Chennai have therefore proposed to strengthen the AES algorithm that new keys are used when the rows or characters are shifted within the two-dimensional matrix.[133]

The extended key dependency increases the security of the algorithm: The authors' results show that a statistical pattern of the plain text is distributed more strongly over the cipher text, i.e., it is more harmonized, more even and thus less conspicuous, that means the plain text is better protected despite a cryptanalysis.

If characters are substituted with the AES, the XOR operation is run through and then rows and columns are shifted in a matrix, and this over several rounds one after the other, then, put simply, this is an extensive process of mixing. However, even more mixing within the same constellation does not necessarily result in greater security. If you have bad letters in a Scrabble game, you have noticeably bad letters. Even more mixing is of no use if you have a conspicuously large number of letters E.

Security would possibly be increased if, in an intermediate step, before further mixing, further letter sections are substituted with a further key - that is, a further password as a character string, so to speak. The blocks of plain text thus each receive different key character strings.

Several AES processes can also be used in parallel and interdependently. Character elements of a block or a matrix of the plain text migrate to another matrix after mixing and substitute there, whereby a different key has already been used there. All available matrix levels in this cube are run through until the drawing element is inserted again in the first matrix level.

The shifting of columns and rows in the AES has so far taken place on a two-dimensional level. The table, the matrix, has 4x4 fields as shown above for the AES. For the sake of clarity, consider a model with a matrix with 8x8 fields: like a chessboard.

With the AES, for example, with the »ShiftRow« function, it is as if a rook falls out at the end of the chessboard and is reinserted at the beginning of the line - in the same matrix or on the same chessboard.

Couldn't this method of replacing and mixing, known from AES, also be carried out in a three-dimensional cube? Let us imagine eight chess boards stacked on top of one another, they result in an 8x8x8 square cube, in the cells of which the characters of the plain text flow.

This train of thought could be called ›Cube Encryption Standard‹ (CES) and is presented in the following only as a model and in a generally understandable manner, to encourage learners to create their own ideas about process flows for algorithms. It is not about specifying everything down to the smallest detail or calculating it mathematically, but rather questioning given algorithms and creating own processes.

With the three-dimensional replacement and mixing according to this Cube Encryption to be developed - let us stay with the picture of the chessboard - the rook that is pushed out of a column or row of a first chessboard matrix is not reinserted on the same chessboard but is placed on another position on the second level of the cube.

Let us imagine several chess boards on top of each other, as mentioned, that form a three-dimensional space. Like a chocolate cake stand with different levels, with a chessboard on each level.

The rook that leaves a row or column of the chessboard on level 1 is placed on level 2 of another chessboard and thus pushes a symbol of the current mix status on this board on to level 3 and so on until a piece from the chessboard of the last top chessboard falls back onto the chessboard in level 1 and replaces the original rook.

It is possible to turn the stacked chessboards 90 or 180 degrees to the left or right after each round. This means that another mix procedure is inserted as a process step, which can work 90 or 180 degrees to the left or 90 or 180 degrees to the right and rotates or swaps rows and columns.

And beforehand, in addition to these further shuffling processes, further keys were used on each level: the rook can thus be replaced by the figure of a lady or the figure of a pawn while remaining in the picture. Each chessboard level has its own key that is used for substitution.

The Baltic chess master and former math teacher *Lionel Kieseritzky* constructed a »room chess« already in the middle of the 19th century, his cubic chess with 8×8×8 scope.

At the beginning of the 20th century, *Ferdinand Maack* also had an idea for a three-dimensional room chess: He positioned several chess boards on top of each other to form a cube and modified the rules of movement. After initial experiments with 8 conventional chess boards on top of each other and a normal set of pieces, he discovered that the game was far too complex. In the final version, he reduced it to a system with only 5x5 chess fields per board and 5 boards (Polychor System Chess).

Figure 21: Five 5x5 chess boards on top of each other in polychor system chess as a model for a 3D matrix in room chess

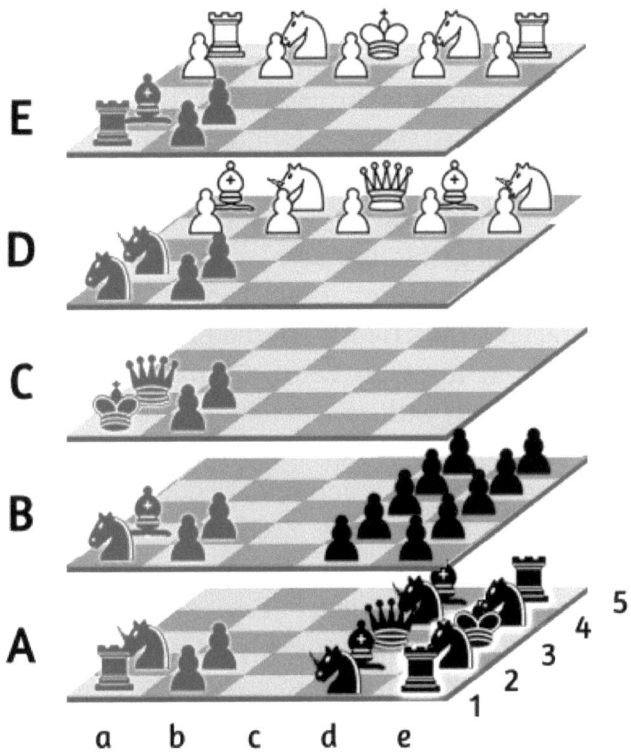

Source: [134]

With the regular chessboards, however, with the help of computer technology, a complex mixing machine can be represented as a three-dimensional 8x8x8 cube, which is transferred to algorithm steps to be created in Cryptography, for example in a 3D-AES, several character strings (passwords) as keys for substitution can be used: a separate character string on each chessboard level.

The character strings of the keys for level 1 and level 2 and so on, written one after the other, could also result in a long character string.

The length of the password strings joined together in this way can, depending on their length, come close to the length of a normal chat message, as in the case of an OTP.

The already well-established random in the characters of an OTP character string would be mixed up again in a combined character string from the keys for the individual chessboard levels by portioning this (random) character string, and then these portions on different levels can be used as a key for defined character strings (blocks) of the plain text.

That means: A message with 40 characters, for example, which is encrypted with a character string of 40 random characters as with OTP, may have an advantage if the 40-character string of the key is additionally cut in 5 portions (for the 5 model above) of 8 characters. Each of the 5 chessboard levels shown in the figure receives its own character string for substitutions, and each level can add these characters *individually* for substitutions (possibly also after different mixing processes or timestamps in the process).

It may be necessary in the future to include several passwords in different blocks or delimited parts of the plain text string, or better: to apply several mixing machines or mixing levels with their own passwords in parallel in a cube. As well could one element or a block from a mixing process then also be placed in the new mixing process of the next mixer or the next higher mixing level. (The cipher block chaining mode (CBC) in the previous 2D AES provides a similar chaining.)

This means that we are not only with more complex mixing and the addition of further character strings as keys on different levels, but thirdly we can also reconnect the individual mixing levels by moving chess pieces from the first chess board to the chess board of the second level - or in a mathematical sense, cell values of a first matrix migrate into cells of the second matrix, means: are substituted or XORed.

When, from which row or column a character jumps to the second level, and whether a level of the cube is rotated 180 degrees or substitutions are carried out on the respective level, is the task of the design of such an algorithm, the future process engineers take in or think through considering the increased computing power of computers when they are enjoying it.

Such a three-dimensional Cube Encryption method can be used eight times in parallel on each level with a total of eight different keys. Measures could be: consideration of characters to be substituted, moving a character (or block) to a new level, rotating different levels so that lines become columns or are displayed backwards, definition of individual process times, when this happens, etc.

With several levels and individual character strings for substitution on each level and described three-dimensional mixing options, it can be assumed that the combination variety and complexity will be increased. Supporter of this book, Jo van der Lou, would say: Beautiful.

So, let us set out to define multidimensional the process steps for character strings supplied in parallel for substitution, and mixing in and including multiple matrix levels, thirdly, matrix entries jumping over levels in a Cube Encryption.

(You could also think through this mental exercise not only with chess boards in the 8x8x8 cube, but also vividly in a 3x3x3 room of a magic cube, or classically in the 4x4x4 or 6x6x6 cube).

The Cube Encryption, however, has nothing to do with the Rubik's Cube Cipher by *Douglas W. Mitchell*, in which the plain text is written on a Rubik's Cube[135] and the cube is then rotated to mix the characters. No substitutions or other keys are used there!

This playful outlook on Cube Encryption can as further to be developed vision produce models for a future three-dimensional and more complex scheme: Possibly a new cube algorithm that students think through as an alternative proposal from their own university to the AES?

Let us come back to the existing and applied encryption, which developed under the name of asymmetric encryption with the availability of computers.

4.2 Asymmetric encryption ●

For asymmetric encryption Alice and Bob now use a total of four keys. Everyone has both, a public key and a private key. So, everyone has a key pair.

Alice and Bob have to exchange the public key with each other and keep the private key secret.

The other person's public key now makes it possible to encrypt data for the owner of the associated private key, and to use other constellations (or keys) to check the digital signatures or to implement authentication. The private key makes it possible to decrypt data encrypted with your own public key (as well as to authenticate yourself and to sign your own messages) - i.e., to certify that a message is also from you.

This is therefore also referred to as the so-called »public key« encryption process. It is often referred to as »*Public Key Infrastructure*« (PKI) to refer to the fact that an infrastructure is required for the keys to be managed and known.

It is a method of converting plain text into a cipher text with a public key, from which the plain text can only be retrieved with an associated private key.

Since the public key is not secret, the channel does not need to be secure against eavesdropping when the key is exchanged in the case of asymmetric procedures; The only important thing is that the public key can be unequivocally assigned to the owner of the associated private key.

For this purpose, for example, a trustworthy certification authority can issue a digital certificate which assigns the public key to an owner or to the respective e-mail address. As an alternative, a trust network can also be established without a central point by mutual certification of keys (Web of Trust), i.e., other friends sign and confirm the authenticity of their own key.

Figure 22: Asymmetric encryption method

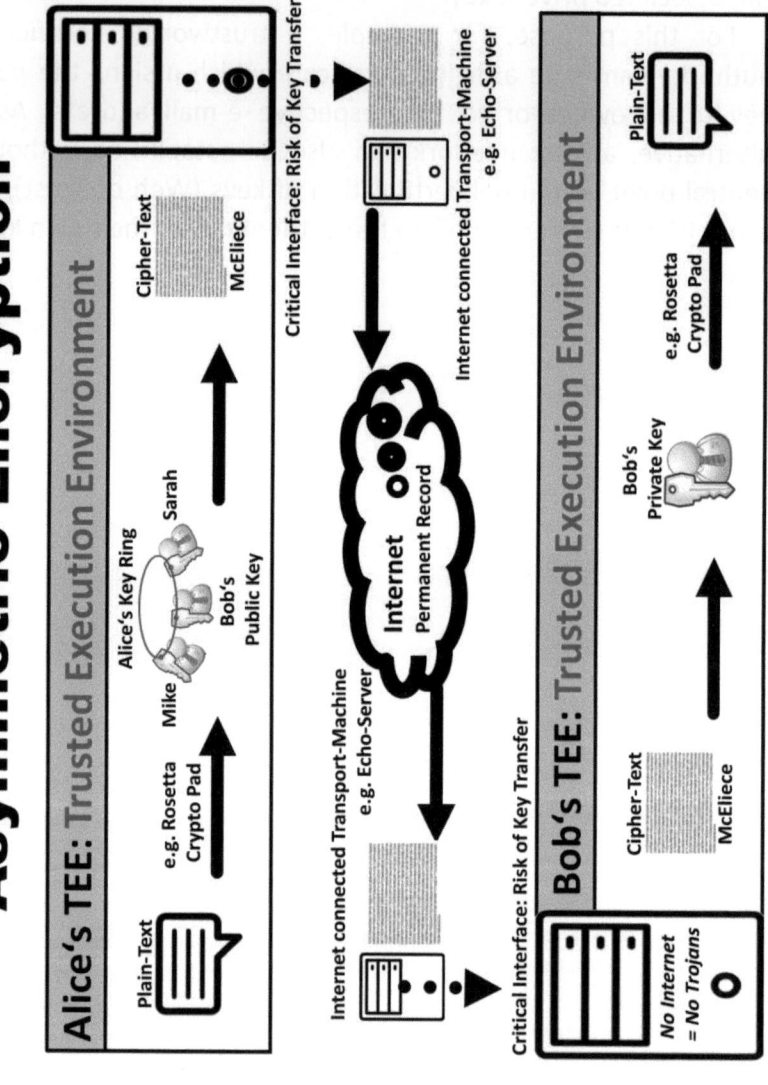

Source: [136]

With asymmetric encryption, Alice, and Bob, each have a private and a public key. Both must exchange the public key. The other person's public key encrypts the message. If Bob receives an encrypted message from Alice, he can convert it back into plain text using his private key. Ideally, the conversion from plain text to cipher text takes place in a trustworthy execution environment (or TEE for short). The risk of transferring private keys or a copy of the plain text can be reduced by Internet capping.

After *Whitfield Diffie* and *Martin Hellman* published[137] a theory on public key Cryptography in 1976, which is explained in more detail below, the three mathematicians *Ronald Rivest, Adi Shamir* and *Leonard Adleman* at the Massachusetts Institute of Technology (MIT) tried to refute these assumptions[138].

They were able to prove this in a variety of procedures, but eventually came across one that they found no point of attack. This resulted in the RSA encryption method, the first published algorithm for asymmetric encryption, in 1977. The name RSA stands for the first letters of their surname. It works with public and private keys as described above.

The American *Ron Rivest* is a professor at the Massachusetts Institute of Technology (MIT) in Cambridge. *Adi Shamir*, born in Tel Aviv, returned to the Weizmann Institute in Israel as an Israeli cryptographer in the 1980s. And *Leonard Adleman*, born into a Jewish family in California, went to university as a professor at the University of Southern California in Los Angeles in the 1980s.

Since 2016, however, the American authority NIST has considered this method to be »no longer secure«[139] in regard of the increasing computing capacity of quantum-computers. In contrast, the McEliece algorithm developed by *Robert McEliece* in 1978 and the NTRU algorithm (from 1996)[140] are not considered broken. As we shall see, these are loosely based on lattice problems that are considered unbreakable even with quantum-computers.

RSA had found widespread use in around 40 years of life, so it was built into numerous software applications and is calculated mathematically using prime numbers with both keys.

The public key is a pair of numbers (e, N) and the private key is also a pair of numbers (d, N), where N is the same for both keys. We call N the RSA module, e the encryption exponent and d the decryption exponent. These numbers are generated by a mathematical process in which two prime numbers p not equal to q are chosen randomly and stochastically independently. Since a prime number p is only divisible by 1 and itself, it is relatively prime to the numbers 1 to p-1. In addition, because it is greater than 1, it is not coprime to itself. With the encryption exponent e, a message can then be converted from plain text into cipher text.

Among other things, Euler's function is carried out in a mathematical calculation (to be deepened later elsewhere): Euler's phi-ϕ function is a number-theoretic function that indicates for every positive natural number n how many of n there are prime numbers that are not greater than n (also known as the totient of n).

Finally, to encrypt a message, the sender uses the formula

c is equivalent to m with exponent e (mod N)

and thus receives the cipher text c from the message m. The number m must be smaller than the RSA module N.

The process flow is summarized as follows: Alice and Bob also agree on an asymmetric crypto procedure, e.g., instead of RSA they use the McEliece algorithm, which is still secure today (with and because of its specific mathematical calculation). Alice and Bob exchange their public keys. Alice now encrypts her message using Bob's public key. Alice sends the cipher text to Bob. Now Bob can use his private key to decode and read Alice's message, thanks to the mathematical calculations shown above in the process steps.

4.2.1 GPG (GNU Privacy Guard) •

According to the guiding principle of the developers of the 1990s, encryption should be simple and strong, so that the social movements of citizens in the USA in particular can evade surveillance by state authorities. Encryption should also be made more friendly to use.

With PGP (abbreviated for: Pretty Good Privacy), a process and program arose in the original development of software programmer *Phil Zimmermann*, with which texts or e-mails according to the asymmetric method can be encrypted with a public key.

In the open-source variant, it is also called OpenPGP or GnuPG or abbreviated to: GPG - this term will also be used in the following.

Today *Phil Zimmermann* is also involved in social networks such as Okuna, formerly Openbook, which is intended to be an ethical and Privacy-friendly alternative to existing social networks, especially Facebook. Okuna is still in a test phase because of its specific form of financing and the alternatives RetroShare and Mastodon are already much more mature.

The first PGP version was written by him in 1991 and used the RSA algorithm to encrypt the data. Later versions also used the Elgamal algorithm, which goes back to the Egyptian cryptologist *Taher Elgamal*, who published this cryptosystem ten years earlier in his youth, before becoming chief scientist for the browser in the 1990s, Netscape, and finally technical chief of the well-known sales database ›Salesforce‹ became.

Today the developer *Werner Koch* from Germany oversees a large part of the free and open-source code bases of GPG, and the underlying software library derived from these origins. A few years ago, he was awarded the FSF Award (Award for the Advancement of Free Software of the Free Software Foundation) for his many years of service to GPG.

To conserve the computing capacity of the at those times slow computers, GPG does not encrypt the entire message in an asymmetric way. Instead, for reasons of efficiency, the actual message is encrypted in a symmetric way and only the key used is encrypted with the asymmetric method. This means that this symmetric key is then, for example, encrypted using the RSA cryptosystem with the recipient's public key and added to the message.

Again, a hybrid encryption. For this purpose, a symmetric session key is generated randomly each time. This also makes it possible to encrypt a message for several recipients at the same time.

Today, however, computing capacity no longer plays such an important role as computers and mobile devices have become much faster.

A GPG-encrypted message looks like this:

Figure 23: Example of a text encrypted with GPG

```
-----BEGIN PGP MESSAGE-----
Version: GnuPG v2.0.16 (GNU/Linux)

hTEMA1PUVhZb8UnsAQf+KS9PNvkWYFONnoStveMc4KwvGT7WlRFv/ZACvdyFsKDO
icurhL57uh56KCof1m5drfftwjDQWgNyMy0cixqV/2WzeQgjZILE0Z1FDg7cgAbs
UZvy2hmaJf0dhHEUziALotfUMhoSeHeObxmomzb7vovJv5tWDtQ9W+p2tbQ4tiin
LAsJtwQhEVTNItootBteC0dTgOdISe6kfqUSoN3A22SiSUihmjxMPiiO6iZB8gBS
hhfiSPa4khNwODncRe2BjqW+YQHf7L6CfLjx2S1BCSr+KWLmUnVdWSUonhHPF9ml
E/q7t2uoBWg0iQgCjQubgYeqSUYN/xWpqAUX9O71zdKUAbVjjLVT0qTjNLLvms2H
s4BDzHEqKeuGuMAWFzyfuW+VNofTxtcHhzrdjPuYi7sRL3YNUvqUpcGeKGyTApW2
k/fd7U32av7Pq63NoKK2g3RFcyBUiSdNlNhW8TYS1NdMSMXNw1R9dWVgFmsLj2vs
Rv89ufRiPbNLDXcx7CkRrTf13q0miy1850d6k5nt8qUFrnh4xQ==
=z6Xk
-----END PGP MESSAGE-----
```

Source: [141]

However, GPG encryption has not been implemented as user-friendly in the previous interfaces of programs as some would like it to be. The header or subject lines of an email were not encrypted or handled differently. GPG therefore did not really get popular. It has not yet been implemented as a standard in e-mail programs such as Thunderbird, Outlook, webmail, and others. A REPLEO or AutoCrypt function was also missing: The AutoCrypt function will be discussed further below: it describes the automated REPLEO exchange of keys. Until now, users had to set up the encryption manually, which was a laborious process.

Just a few years ago, the head of the security editorship of the well-known *Heise Security* portal *Jürgen Schmidt* demanded: »Let PGP / GPG finally die.«[142] - And who would have thought that this standard in the Delta-Chat client, which we will go into in more detail later, is experiencing a renaissance a few years later with REPLEO respective AutoCrypt? REPLEO rescues. AutoCrypt as well.

Even if GPG is still based on the old algorithms, possibly considered critical under certain conditions, and NTRU or McEliece are not yet built into the respective software libraries - or it does not contain a more modern design of a key management, GPG has already become more attractive thanks to this automated and encrypted transmission of own public keys to the counterpart within the applying clients and is still considered a well-known standard in encryption.

In particular, the beginnings of GPG remain historically interesting - e.g., with regard to the future effects it had: The development of better encryption, after public reception and critical appraisals, a few years later led to the intended restrictions on encryption being lifted. A new standard was accepted and introduced - this is how a quintessence and learning curve from the 1990s can be summarized.

This may also be the case with the current discussions about encryption in Europe and the associated countries of the Five-Eyes, if it is about end-to-end encryption or particularly secure encryption, e.g., with the McEliece algorithm - or also about key-transport-free (end-to-end) encryption or about Fiasco Keys, in which a particularly large number of keys are transmitted. Transport abstinence or its opposite, the sending of keys in the whole dozen, are essential keywords and criteria for the further development of modern and applied Cryptography in the Third Epoch. Key management comes on the agenda not only through political impetus, but also through technical innovations as a discussion topic.

In its early years, however, GPG encryption was not allowed to be exported license-free from the USA because, like weapons, it fell under an export law. However, in the late 1990s these laws were liberalized, and this type of encryption software could henceforth be used in most countries around the world.

To circumvent this limitation at the time, the complete source code was simply printed as a book in 1995. The ISBN 9780262240390 is still available at exorbitant prices as a rare copy in second-hand bookshops. The software could be distributed legally as a book: The strong laws on freedom of the press and freedom of expression in the USA then made it possible for the encryption method to be typed and published in other nations.

Nowadays this is unthinkable, especially since there are open-source and therefore license-free projects whose source code is already publicly readable across continents on Internet websites such as Github, Sourceforge, Bitbucket or Codeberg.

For example, the world's first mobile McEliece Messenger Smoke Crypto Chat has also chosen the analog Gutenberg method of modern letterpress printing for technical documentation: The documentary explanations with reference to the respective Java lines are intended as teaching and learning material for teachers, students and developers have not only been public for many years on the global web, but can now also be read and learned on paper.

The explanations by *Casio Moonlander* can be found once printed on around 1000 pages of paper (with the two ISBNs 9783752691993 & 9783752692006) or are still available as an e-book for one euro or dollar via the usual e-book readers such as Kindle, Tolino, Kobo or Lifebook readable.

Teaching and learning material about innovative model projects, prototypes, and methods of today's technologies such as the application of the McEliece algorithm can therefore be ordered or downloaded instantly at any bookstore, Walmart or Playstore or in any library. In view of the super-fast computers, everyone can stay super-secure and super-secret everywhere.

For all those who would like to read things up in their own hands, education means, in addition to the learning options, at the same time secularization and democratization of knowledge - here with regard to basic (mathematical) knowledge or practical (programming) experience in the field of promising asymmetric encryption with McEliece - instead of the old GPG with RSA or Elgamal as the algorithm. Will GPG stay dead or get a new heart through a McEliece transplant?

4.2.2 S/MIME •

For the encryption of e-mails, two procedures have been established for PKI-based asymmetric encryption: One is the PGP / GPG already introduced and the other, which is less used, is S / MIME. It stands for Secure / Multipurpose Internet Mail Extension, so it is an extension for e-mail.

Both are based on the same cryptographic methods. They only differ in the certification of public keys and thus also in the models of trust. Both methods are therefore not compatible with one another. This means that users of one method cannot exchange signed or encrypted messages with users of the other method.

S/MIME describes a standardized procedure in which so-called »X.509« certificates are used. The certification of the public key is offered as a service by public »trust centers« as certification authorities, i.e., institutions that give trust.

The trust model is therefore hierarchical. The identities are verified via a chain of certificates, starting with the certificate of the user up to each assigned intermediate certification authority up to the root CA certificate of the corresponding body at the highest level.

Because of the dependency on central structures or the interdependent dependencies of these interrelationships and the less frequent use, this encryption option should not be considered further, especially since the open GPG / GnuPG has also established itself more strongly and is better known here with a private and public key.

Keys that are generated directly from an application and can also be self-signed, i.e., can be found in a mutually confirming network of certifications without central authority, are certainly more user-friendly.

4.3   Hash-functions, certificates and signatures: SHA, Argon2 & Co. ●

A hash function is any sufficiently well-defined procedure or mathematical function that converts a large portion of data, possibly variable in length, into a small index. Usually, an integer that serves as an index to a data or character arrangement. The values that result from a hash function are called hash values.

A hash function can be used to create a type of string such as »6e32f66f62a8d... 98a2cc« from the sentence »Hello World«. Such a function is used to map strings of any length on a short hash, for example for digital signatures, for interlinked transactions such as the blockchain or, quite simply, for the security of file downloads. The short hash of a large download file should be the same before the download as it is measured after the download - then the file has not been changed during the download.

Collisions are unavoidable, i.e., there can be several text passages or files that result in the same hash. In contrast, a cryptographic hash function fulfills additional properties: It should be (strictly) resistant to such collisions. This means that only one hash value should be generated from a sentence, or a character string and this hash value should not be generated a second time from another sentence. If even a small character is changed in the sentence, the result is usually a completely new hash, a completely different string of characters. This is known as the avalanche effect.

At the same time, a hash function is not reversible. A complete sentence cannot be reconstructed from a hash. It is therefore not an encryption that can be decrypted again.

Nevertheless, some super-computers today are able to fill so-called »rainbow tables« and to store numerous sentences or

171

character strings that lead to hashes. If a hash appears again, you can use the inverse search via the hashes in the table to return to the original long text, since all pairs of hash and the associated character string are stored.

Since hashes are often used in passwords, such a password could be determined if the hash and the password are recorded in such a rainbow table. To prevent this from happening, the passwords are given in a corresponding length or extended with a so-called "cryptological salt" (that is, automatically supplemented with additional characters), which also increases the possibilities, so that a rainbow table cannot list all combinations of all possible word creations. You save the salt string with the hash value of the password. Rainbow tables are then no longer of any use because the attacker needed a new rainbow table with all possible passwords in the world for each new salt value.

A well-known hash algorithm is e.g., SHA-512, which converts a set of words into a short string of characters. Such a SHA-3 has been at the start since 2015. Another particularly secure hash process is called Argon2. The Sip hash method also generates particularly short hashes.

It is important that hashes cannot be converted back into readable strings. We will see why below, for example when a hash is added to a cipher text, as is done by the Echo protocol, e.g., in an encrypted Echo-capsule. And: Most applications do not save passwords for the login, but only their hashes. So when politicians ask for passwords to be issued, companies can often only offer these in hash, but not the password itself.

Signatures and certificates play a further role in addition to hashes: A digital signature is created using an asymmetric cryptosystem in which a sender uses a secret signature key (the private key) to calculate a value for any data, e.g., a digital message. This value is called the digital signature. It makes it possible to use the public verification key (the public key) to check the non-contestable authorship and integrity of the message. To be able to assign a signature created with a signature key to a person, the associated verification key must be clearly assigned to this person. This means that a key pair is required for encryption and, if necessary, another key pair for the signatures.

A digital certificate is a digital data record that confirms certain properties of people or objects and whose authenticity and integrity can be checked using cryptographic processes. In particular, the digital certificate contains the data required for its verification. The certificate is issued by an official *Certification Authority* (short: CA). Public key certificates are often used in accordance with the X.509 standard, which confirms the identity of the owner and other properties of a public cryptographic key.

So much for a few cryptographic basics that need to be deepened. The next section explains why we are at the beginning of a new, Third Epoch in Cryptography.

5 THE THIRD EPOCH OF CRYPTOGRAPHY: AN AGE FOR MULTI-ENCRYPTION, EXPONENTIAL ENCRYPTION & QUANTUM-SECURE ENCRYPTION? •

While the first Epoch begins with the millennia-old symmetric encryption with a password, the second Epoch is characterized by computer-based encryption using private and public keys, the *Third Epoch of Cryptography* now has to adapt to the fast computing capacities of super-computers.

So-called quantum-computers are high-performance computers that are not only particularly fast, but also calculate with a new method based on quantum mechanical states.

At the same time, existing strengths and security in the encryption and its processes can be applied more sustainably today, e.g., in the increased use of mathematical calculations, which offer certain advantages; e.g., with regard to key sizes or secure key transmissions through so-called Zero-Knowledge proofs or multiple security methods also through multi-encryption. More on this in the next sections.

The new thing that comes first has the effect that traditional things can no longer be used in the foreseeable future or can only be used with dysfunctions. We know it from all other areas of life as well: We must give up what has been used for years and is known in order to be able to use the new. And in the end, many say, it is good that we made it: the new bed, the change of furniture for the daughter's new room, the new tools, the new knives, the new smart-automated heating, the new car with electric, or the new monitor without quicksilver, all of this is better than the ancient devices and tools of the past. And it is the same with the RSA encryption algorithm, which has been very well known up to now. Because of fast quantum-computers, the near end of its product life cycle is now here.

5.1 Departure and farewell: No Longer Secure •

For a long time, RSA was the fundamental building block for security on the Internet - with HTTPS, VPNs, SSH and so on - because it enables digital signatures and secure key exchange in addition to encryption. Many generations have grown fond of RSA, learned about it, calculated it mathematically, and built this algorithm into their applications.

And what if RSA soon reached the end of its product life cycle? What would happen if RSA can no longer be considered secure? Because if an application has not been programmed with several algorithms to choose from, this application may not be future-proof either and the algorithm cannot be easily exchanged in the programming; economic damage also occurs at the end of the runtime for this application to the company that offers RSA. Therefore, they will always try to maintain the end of the life cycle of RSA for as long as possible.

However, there is also resistance to the need for change because one has become more or less fond of this familiar algorithm: Is it like taking one of the specific cuddly toys away from us with RSA? The 1918 Nobel Prize laureate in physics and founder of quantum physics, *Max Planck*, is said to have said: A new scientific truth does not usually assert itself in such a way that its opponents are convinced and declare themselves informed, but rather by the fact that they gradually become extinct, and that the next generation will be made acquainted with the truth from the outset. Or as the saying goes: 10,000 guards of the past stand at a fork in the road where one path leads into the future.

Let us therefore approach the assumed and possibly still applicable security of RSA in a completely unemotional-technical way and with objective calculation. As an applied computer scientist from the University of Hanover, *Wilhelm Drehling*

175

calculates the following example[143]: The numbers 2281 and 3323 are prime numbers. Multiplying them is not a great challenge and, if necessary, can be done with pen and paper without a calculator: 7,579,763 is the result. If, on the other hand, you give a person the task of finding the two prime numbers that, when multiplied, result in 7,579,763, most people will lose their fun even with a pocket calculator. To find the right prime numbers, you have to try for better or worse: Can you divide the number by 3? No. Not even through 5, 7, 11 or 13? A lot of trial divisions are necessary until you finally arrive at the prime number 2281 and immediately know that 2281 and 3323 are the prime factors you are looking for.

While the way there is easy with this multiplication, the way back, i.e., the factorization, is more complex. But is it complex enough not to be able to calculate it? People like to talk about a one-way function. But that is not correct with some restrictions, because the opposite way is also possible, albeit difficult or time-consuming. It can be compared to a mailbox, in which the postman can drop the letter, but it is difficult to get it out. It's the trap door. But this image of the one-way trap door is also limping: each and every one of us has pulled a letter out of the mailbox with long fingers.

In the above calculation example, a quick look at a math primer or on the Internet for a list of prime numbers is sufficient. The prime number 2281 is the 339th prime number in the ascending list of all prime numbers. So 339 attempts are sufficient to divide the number 7,579,763 by one of the 339 prime numbers in order to determine after the 339th attempt that this is an integer: 3323. For each result of an integer of this division then only has to be checked whether this number is also present in the list of prime numbers.

Even if only relatively small prime numbers were used in this example - the simple and complex calculation method becomes clear: And of course, it is not that simple, since RSA has other constants such as the RSA module N.

But quantum-computers should be able to bring this together in a quick process - so that everyone has to assess for themselves that the so-called one-way function is only a conditional one: Because it is only about how quickly we can try out all the prime numbers in this calculation. So do we have to be careful not to mentally fall into this trap door - with a false safety assumption through this term?

Some users crack an RSA-100 with a regular home desktop computer within a week, which 40 years ago took computers 75 years to do.

A few years ago, French scientists working with *Fabrice Boudot*[144] at the Université de Limoges demonstrated the possibility of breaking RSA (at that time with 705-bit keys).

With the help of two interconnected super-computers - »Lomonosov« and »Zhores« - from two Moscow institutes, three Russian scientists managed to crack this calculation process for the equally smaller RSA-232 with 786 bits and to determine the numbers for factorization. *Nikolai Zamarashkin* and *Dmitry Zheltkov* as well as their colleague *Sergey Matveev* achieved this impressive achievement with their computers[145].

Entire competitions are held to break RSA. Only what is proven could be believed. In addition, many mathematicians calculate the number of necessary arithmetic operations with corresponding key lengths and how long a break could take with the respective computing capacity.

Today, therefore, key lengths of at least 4096 bits should be used and the following also applies: in view of the quantum-computers, it is better not to use the RSA algorithm any longer, as it is no longer considered secure.

Figure 24: Time to break RSA depending on different computing speeds - what was to be calculated - Latin perhaps: »Quod Erat Demonstrandum«

RSA-Key:	50 Digits	75 Digits	100 Digits
Operations	$1,4 \times 10^{10}$	$9,0 \times 10^{12}$	$2,3 \times 10^{15}$
PC 1978	3,9 hours	104 days	79 years
PC 2018	7 seconds	7 hours	7 days
442 PFLOPS	Quod	Erat	Demonstrandum
5 QuBits 2015	Quod	Erat	Demonstrandum
53 QuBits 2019	Quod	Erat	Demonstrandum
500 QuBits 2023	Quod	Erat	Demonstrandum

Source: [146]

What is impressive, however, is not the increasing capacity of interconnected, fast super-computers, or even the analysis of the powers of the quantum-computers; sustainable logical evidence that the RSA process could become vulnerable is also interesting. In addition to pure computing power, there are also mathematical approaches to break RSA.

The German cryptologist *Claus Peter Schnorr* published an article in the public ePrint archive in 2021 that allegedly destroys this method: »This destroys the RSA cryptosystem«[147].

Claus Peter Schnorr retired a whole decade ago after 40 years at the University of Frankfurt and is still considered one of the best-known German cryptographers, because he developed an identification scheme based on the discrete logarithm (1989/91), the variant of which is still used today after the patent expired.

His work on »Fast Factoring Integers by SVP Algorithms« now claims that very large numbers can be broken down into prime factors very quickly. Because the computing effort increases exponentially with the size of the numbers and has made RSA secure so far.

What was mysterious, however, was that this sentence about the »destruction of the RSA system« was not included in a second, more recent version[148] of the paper from the University of Frankfurt; the original version dated back to October 31 of the previous year.

Blockchain researcher *Tim Ruffing* already called in a Twitter discussion to delete the paper from the server.

Compared to the well-known IT specialist portal *Heise online*, however, the author *Claus Peter Schnorr* confirmed that it was his work and that he had only accidentally uploaded the wrong version. He has now corrected that and uploaded a new version that also contains the thesis of the RSA destruction.[149]

Finally, various experts comment on the proposed method. For example, mathematician *Sophie Schmieg* and security IT specialist *Matthew Green* were curious about further evidence and the correction of possible errors.

Trying out the blunt is one method to crack the calculation, to calculate it mathematically smart, the other way. In addition to the aforementioned Schnorr's Fast Factoring, there have historically been many other approaches that cannot be discussed further here: such as the Lehmann algorithm, the Pollard-Rho method, the P-1 method or the Fermat factorization, up to a square sieve method such as MSIEVE.

One algorithm, however, we have to remember, is the Shor-algorithm, with whose method one can theoretically solve the factorization problem and can dissolve the discrete logarithm using quantum-computers in finite time - or given a slow processor in the desktop PC at home - then in in a flash time.

The Shor-algorithm not only belongs to the class of factorization methods, but also uses the resources of quantum informatics. He calculates a nontrivial divisor of a composite number on a quantum-computer. The Shor algorithm is therefore very important for Cryptography because it finds this nontrivial divisor essentially faster than classic algorithms and calculation methods: The Shor-algorithm only has a short, polynomial runtime (instead of the significantly higher time for sub-exponential methods).

This represents a particular danger for the RSA cryptosystems, whose security is based precisely on the assumption that there is no factoring method with a polynomial runtime - that is, which can find a solution for the prime numbers sought quickly enough. With the fast quantum-computers and the Shor calculation this can now be achieved.

Peter Shor published this algorithm in 1994/1997 when he was employed at AT&T Bell Laboratories at the time. In his work, a second algorithm for calculating the discrete logarithm is also described, which is also called the Shor-algorithm. The discrete logarithm is used in the Diffie/Hellman key calculation.

Can the basic values of RSA be found in an acceptable time with computing power and/or a mathematically skillful calculation?

It is clear that the world's most influential employer for cryptographers - the NSA in the USA - does not voluntarily publish breakthroughs in cracking procedures. Yet this is exactly what happened in the United States. Already in 2016. For RSA.

The fact is insofar as the American standardization institute NIST, which also belongs to the government, announced at the time that RSA and also the elliptical curves such as ECDSA are considered broken in view of the fast quantum-computers.

Not because the process itself would have a mathematical error, or a new calculation option had been found to complete the complex process in less time, but actually because today's fast super-quantum-computers are able to calculate faster than we could still imagine a few years ago.

In the meantime, media and programmers are increasingly concerned with these developments and possible alternatives: Many representatives of the public pioneering discussions about RSA were born in a year in which there were no pocket computers - or even quantum-computers - but suddenly the American government agency NIST informs that the time has come to have to consider these computational possibilities with effects on encryption in today's world. The public now began with new pioneers to discuss this information from the panels of experts.

Figure 25: RSA and ECDSA (elliptic Curves): »No longer secure« – in the NIST-publiction

Cryptographic Algorithm	Type	Purpose	Impact from large-scale quantum computer
AES-256	Symmetric key	Encryption	Larger key sizes needed
SHA-256, SHA-3		Hash functions	Larger output needed
RSA	Public key	Signatures, key establishment	No longer secure
ECDSA, ECDH (Elliptic Curve Cryptography)	Public key	Signatures, key exchange	No longer secure
DSA (Finite Field Cryptography)	Public key	Signatures, key exchange	No longer secure

Table 1 - Impact of Quantum Computing on Common Cryptographic Algorithms
Source: [150]

RSA is »no longer secure«, which means: »broken«. Not through our practice that we could break it ourselves at home. No, it is considered broken qua definition: and who better to pronounce this definition than the official standardization institute of the USA: NIST. And the same applies to Cryptography with elliptic curves, e.g., in the ECDSA algorithm; as well as for the DSA algorithm.

It is as if a user of cannabis realizes for himself that the active ingredient of this plant is not dangerous. However, if a state, together with medical professionals, declares that it should be defined as not marketable and therefore illegal because of its effects, then this definition should apply to everyone. One could argue that developers like to blink right at RSA and possibly also turn left for cannabis - but standardization means that we all drive straight ahead, if it is so defined.

The fact that John Doe cannot buy a super-computer in the next super-market does not mean that »quantum supremacy«, the superiority of these fast computers, did not exist. »Can be broken« therefore means: »is broken«. Anyone who can land on Mars, if only with highly specialized equipment, can claim that the impossibility of being able to land on Mars has been broken: it is possible to land on Mars. Regardless of whether we have been shown it, can understand it or even start the journey ourselves today.

The rapid pace, further development and networking of quantum-computers will therefore definitely have an impact on encryption with RSA.

With this development perspective, RSA is no longer considered secure. And it should mean something when an authority like NIST officially announces this to the world public (as it did many years ago).

And it is more likely that the authorities work rather slowly and that the scientific findings are only bundled in a standards institute after several confirmations and long years to publish them.

At the same time, as already indicated above, it can be assumed that reports on security vulnerabilities are deliberately made public, even with a delay, to have enough time for the development of alternatives, or let criminals continue to lull themselves to safety. And finally, it would trigger an avalanche in business and administration if we suddenly found that an algorithm used in the ID card or the secure connection when shopping or to the bank would become a shaky candidate. Which government decision-maker would continue to leave a vaccine with obvious health risks on the market?

It therefore makes sense to keep the lowest common denominator to the public standards, which are adjusted every decade: The standards are in manual at the American *National Institute of Standards and Technology* (NIST) in Manual SP-800, in Europe in the reports of the European ENCRYPT-CSA or in manual TS-02102 of the German *Federal Office for Information Security* (BSI).[151]

And at the same time, one should pay attention if it is not science experimentally, but one or the world's leading of these standardization institutes politically and officially declares that encryption is no longer secure, pardon: it is considered as no longer secure. Because then the official applies. So: it is no longer secure.

The German Federal Office BSI, for example, only discussed the NIST declaration on RSA- »No longer secure« from 2016 in a more detailed public report four years later following a request from Twitter inquiries. A Twitter user asked on March 21, 2020: »Why is the ECDSA algorithm recommended up to 2022 or even marked up to 2025+/2026+ by the *Federal Office for Information Security* (BSI) in 2018 [in guideline TR-03111] or again in 2019 [in guideline TR-02102-2], while the American institute NIST already determined in 2016: »no longer secure«? When will you update your papers«?

This then took place just one week later (in the public reporting on March 27, 2020) when - some lively tweets spoke of - *Sleeping Beauty* published a nine-page recommendation for post-quantum Cryptography[152] that was possibly quickly written down. Today the apparently updated and improved BSI document is dated August 2020, six months later.

Frank Wilhelm-Mauch, head of the institute at Forschungszentrum Jülich, who is also developing a quantum-computer himself as the initiator of the »Open Super Q« project, sums it up: »Germany used to be a sleeping giant, but has now woken up«[153].

So, it is not that these issues are not being worked on. It may also be a political issue to deal with security concerns in a public dialogue. It was not until 2020 that the German BSI Institute pointed out more clearly, directly on page 2 of a new guideline: in view of the quantum-computers, the McEliece algorithm should be better used and the following applies to RSA: »Temporary extension of the conformity of RSA keys with a key length of 2000 bits or more End of 2023.«[154] Oops - extension as in the soccer game means: The last minutes have started before some are allowed to go home.

The age of quantum-computers is only just beginning and in the morning mood we can stretch our limbs for a while before we run to the best of the day, in which the publicly communicated findings on the research area of quantum-computers continue to develop: In Tower of the Elves, the Hares and the Sleeping Beauty are vigorously spun silk.

And the fact-based calculators of a time-related probability of being able to break RSA with quantum superiority still consider the assessment of an uncertainty of RSA to be a »crazy« idea of »spinners« anyway.

Which of the two teams are young researchers in the *Max Planck* tradition interested in? One thing is certain, however: data that are to be protected for more than a few more years should not be encrypted with the RSA algorithm!

But the new gold and its bugs must also be discussed with citizens, such as how they can use applications with quantum-secure encryption or how they can be better and earlier involved in conferences that deal with post-quantum Cryptography: everyone has First of all, the questions: How many quantum-computers are there in the world? and where are they? who has access to it and how quickly can they actually calculate? And:

What mathematical effects does it have on the calculation of RSA encryption and why is such a calculation slower or not possible with other algorithms? How and why can quantum-computers with the Shor algorithm calculate the factorization of the RSA algorithm so quickly?

5.2 Quantum-computers and their superior breakthrough into a new Epoch •

So far, classic computers with extreme computing power have been referred to as super-computers or high-performance computers in various research institutions: They have a particularly large number of classic processors that are operated over 95 percent with Linux. One can think of it as numerous desktop computers connected in series that we know from our offices.

The currently fastest super-computer is in the city of Kobe in Japan and belongs to the RIKEN Center for Computational Science. His name is FUGAKU and he has 152,064 processors of the A64FX type (with 48 cores and 2.2 GHz). With this he can reach 442 peta-flops - that is the unit for this computing speed.

These FLOPS (short for: Floating-Point Operations Per Second) are a measure of the performance of high-performance computers or their processors: It denotes the number of floating-point operations (additions or multiplications) that can be carried out by them per second. However, the number of floating-point operations is not necessarily directly proportional to the clock speed of the processor, since - depending on the implementation - floating point operations require a different number of clock cycles.

In Germany, the seventh fastest super-computer in the world, called JUWELS, is located at the Research Center in Jülich (FZJ).[155]

Thanks to a new booster module, 85 peta-flops are now possible, which corresponds to 85 quadrillion arithmetic operations per second or the computing power of more than 300,000 modern PCs. But thanks to cooperation with Fujitsu, a variant of the Japanese machine FUGAKU mentioned above has also been available to scientists (as remote control) at the University of Regensburg as the first in Europe for simulations since July 2020.

While these classic computers or super-computers calculate binary, i.e., differentiate the world into zero and one and work on the basis of the laws of classical physics, a quantum-computer calculates with individual particles that obey the laws of quantum physics. These can be electrons, charged atoms (ions) or light quanta, for example.

These particles show a behavior that is not known from classical physics: Here, a quantum mechanical coherence (also called the superposition principle) and, secondly, the quantum entanglement are named as significant: That is, such an atom can be in two places at the same time or spread like a wave, parts of the wave can overlap and erase each other out. If these objects are information carriers, they can store a 0 and a 1 at the same time. An algorithm must be clever enough to use these imponderables as speed, but also to filter out imponderables such as mutual deletion of the waves until the correct result is obtained during the measurement.

It is important that the processing of these states takes place according to these quantum mechanical principles, which makes it possible not only to calculate in parallel, but also to arrive at the result more quickly.

The computing speed of quantum-computers is no longer denoted in Peta-Flops as in super-computers or high-performance computers of the classic type, but in QuBits.

After theoretical studies so far, some of these concepts were further tested and quantum-computers were initially implemented with just a few QuBits: the record is around 50 QuBits for some quantum-computers.

With the title »Quantum Supremacy« it was proven in 2019 that a corresponding quantum-computer from Google could solve an arithmetic operation in a few seconds - and thus the classic super-computers fell behind.

With this research result, quantum-computers not only became faster than classic super-computers for the first time, the leading unit of computing speed is consequently also changing from Peta-Flops to QuBits. This process is called quantum supremacy - as mentioned, when it comes to solving a complex problem, quantum-computers are now simply superior to classic super-computers. This also means the point in time from which a quantum-computer can solve a task in an acceptable time for which a computer whose technology is based on conventional digital technology would require unrecognizable computing time.

And this point in time was reached in 2019 with the exclamation »Quantum Supremacy«[156] from Google in the scientific community: their computer was called »SYCAMORE« and was 53 QuBits fast. The research group led by the physicists *John M. Martinis*, *Frank Arute* and others demonstrated experimentally with SYCAMORE that random numbers could be generated according to a special probability distribution.

John Martinis, an American physicist who is a professor at the University of California, Santa Barbara (UCSB), and deals with quantum information theory, has also been commissioned by Google for several years with an AI quantum team to build a fault-tolerant quantum-computer, which also includes *Frank Arute* and others in the team.

The random numbers in this experiment arrangement were chosen so that the corresponding task with SUMMIT, currently the second-fastest classic super-computer in the world (located at Oak Ridge National Laboratory), would take 10,000 years, while the SYCAMORE quantum-computer would only take 200 seconds. During this time, Grandpa does not even get his glasses cleaned properly! SYCAMORE made the running.

For several years now, many governments and research organizations as well as large computer and technology companies around the world have been investing in the development of quantum-computers, which are viewed by many as one of the emerging key technologies of the 21st century. This is also how the Third Epoch of Cryptography began.

The development can be seen not only in the rapid decryption of old algorithms such as RSA or elliptic curves, but also in new methods of encryption (while guaranteeing quantum physics) and the resistance testing of previous encryption methods against the fast-computing speed (i.e., operational application of this fast-computing speed of quantum-computers).

Using these effects, certain problems in computer science, e.g., searching in extremely large databases and factoring large numbers (see above: Shor algorithm) can now be solved more efficiently than with classic computers. Many mathematical problems are easier to solve today, and encryption based on these problems must therefore also be described as less secure.

In view of these developments, RSA is seen no longer secure, that the American NIST Institute has already officially announced. The algorithms McEliece and NTRU, however, are still considered secure. The algorithms in the programming of known software only need to be exchanged.

The researchers, states and governments have also recognized that it is necessary to have own quantum-computers available in the countries to at least be able to break encryptions of this old, weak type increasingly faster.

However, the state of research has meanwhile advanced: It is no longer just about individual quantum-computers, but several of these high-performance computers are to be connected in a network. These quantum networks, which form the core of quantum communication systems, enable physically separate quantum devices to exchange information also in the form of quantum bits. Such a network, which connects many individual quantum devices with one another, should help to solve tasks that previously overwhelmed a single quantum-computer. China is already sending unbreakable communication from earth to satellites - using quantum technology[157]. Other Asian researchers have also made a quantum communication system their goal, which relates not only to high speed, but also to long distances[158].

These connections should be connected in a compatible manner to the connections of classic communication technology. This not only ensures approval and enthusiasm in the research community, but also competition at university locations: the US Department of Defense has published a strategy for creating a quantum Internet, and American scientists have, for example, set up a quantum system that is over 80 kilometers long between suburbs around Chicago[159]. At the same time, a *Quantum Internet Alliance* (QIA) was founded in Europe, also with the aim of building such a large European quantum network. It's not just about research and making available, but also about using computing power to break encryption.

The governments of the leading industrial nations are also investing heavily financially in the field of quantum-computers - while data is the new oil, quantum technology seems to be a kind of new warp energy: The USA has for its part signed the National Quantum Initiative Act, with $ 1.2 billion for investment in this area. At the same time, the European Commission launched a quantum flagship program worth EUR 1.0 billion (USD 1.20 billion). The UK is also in the middle of a national quantum technology program (NQTP) that has invested more than $ 1.37 billion in total.

In the year the end-to-end encryption was politically questioned, the German federal government decided on a 130-billion-euro economic stimulus program in which quantum technologies in particular are promoted with a financial volume of several billion euros. With the aim of awarding the contract to build quantum-computers with at least 100 individually controllable QuBits and a scaling potential to 500 QuBits to suitable consortia from science and companies.

Even if SYCAMORE has now beaten SUMMIT or FUGAKU, high-performance computers in both systems, both, quantum mechanical and digital computers, remain complementary and develop hand in hand in order to also promote and network the research associations.

In Berlin, LISE, one of the most powerful computers at the time at the *Konrad Zuse* Institute in the Dahlem district, went online in 2019. Named after the female physicist *Lise Meitner* (1878-1968), it managed 16 quadrillion arithmetic operations per second at the start.

Konrad Zuse was actually a civil engineer, but also an inventor and, with his development of the Z3 machine, built the first freely programmable and binary working computer and thus the first functional computer in the world in 1941. *Lise Meitner* was a nuclear physicist and published the first physical-theoretical explanation of nuclear fission in 1939.

In addition to the Zuse Institute, the three major Berlin universities as well as the Charité - the oldest hospital in Berlin and one of the largest university hospitals in Europe - have been included in the Berlin funding. The Berlin super-computer and its twin Emmy in Göttingen cost 30 million euros[160]. There will be a total of eight centers for national high-performance computing in Germany, in addition to Berlin in Aachen, Darmstadt, Dresden, Erlangen-Nuremberg, Göttingen, Karlsruhe and Paderborn as well as an institute for quantum technologies in Ulm.

With 27 qubits, the Quantum System One from IBM became the first and therefore most powerful quantum computer for Europe in 2021: It is in Germany in Ehningen near Stuttgart and is operated by the Fraunhofer Society for Application-Oriented Research.

An »interdepartmental umbrella organization« in the form of a *German Quantum Community* (DQG) was set up for networking and coordination tasks. The number of quantum-computers will therefore increase at different locations, and they will also become faster, more networked, and more efficient - and thus also be available to larger groups of people.

With Azure Quantum, for example, Microsoft has a cloud solution on the market with which customers can already access a wide variety of quantum-computers and try out the applied development of quantum software. Another well-known platform that private individuals interested in quantum-computing can use to conduct smaller experiments is the Quantum Composer from IBM. In addition to Microsoft and IBM, not only are large IT companies active in this area with Google and Amazon, but also numerous scientists and developers who also exchange ideas in the relevant forums, mailing lists and the community.

Ultimately, developing quantum-computers will be just as exciting as developing a journey to Mars. And who knows, possibly the breaking of RSA already took place in 2016, it only remains open how many QuBits which key size of RSA managed in what time? As mentioned, regular computers have cracked a key size of 795 bits, then 5 QuBits in 2016 or 53 QuBits in 2019 and future speeds will also crack higher RSA key sizes. No longer secure.

A German vision was formulated with the milestone in the »Quantum Computing Roadmap«[161]: The goal is »internationally competitive quantum-computers with a high, three-digt scaling potential of QuBits«.

And on the American continent, IBM would like to increase the number of its QuBits in its quantum-computers from currently 65 to 1121: From the current quantum processor IBM Quantum »Hummingbird« with 65 QuBits, the number of QuBits should exceed 127 in the next year (»Eagle«) and then increased over the years with 433 QuBits (»Osprey«) up to 1121 QuBits in the »Condor« machine[162]. Calculating faster is certainly easier than flying to Mars faster. This is why a whole startup scene has emerged not only in the USA to make quantum-computing popular: The spirit of the founders, as if *Linus Torvalds* is reprogramming the Linux kernel or *Bill Gates* is re-establishing Microsoft. The last on the quantum market are the dogs biting? *Steve Jobs* would also have specified the quanta in his garage.

The companies Global Foundries and Psiquantum[163] have now announced that they will build the first quantum-computer with one million QuBits. Instead of using extremely deeply cooled atoms, ions or superconductors with just as deeply frozen electronics, the quantum properties should be generated using the properties of light that is enclosed in an optical system. In this optical quantum-computer based on light, new packets of entangled photon pairs in different frequency bands are fed into a fiber optic line one after the other. The light moves in it at almost 300,000 kilometers per second. The quantum states can thus be generated and measured with sufficient quality and its quantum properties can also be manipulated. At the end of the glass fiber, the photons come back into the computer after a while. Together with classic computer technology, quantum calculations with many thousands of QuBits are to be carried out in the near future.

The advancement of encryption in the Third Epoch of Cryptography already knows pervasive technologies - as well as their shields: Since there are only a few programs and messengers with the McEliece algorithm, a decisive differentiating feature from previous applications becomes clear here.

First the Spot-On application, as well as GoldBug, and finally the Smoke Messenger in the field of mobile devices, were and are the world's first productive model programs and functional prototypes in the field of quantum computing-secure encryption with this algorithm. And this not only in user-friendly programming, but also open-source available to everyone.

At the same time, McEliece and implementing programs are not the only remaining hope for security despite or in the face of quantum-computers. Existing processes can also be improved to make encryption more secure. For this purpose, topics such as multi-encryption or protocol designs for the transmission of encrypted message capsules can be included.

5.3   Multi-encryption: A cocktail at the bar? •

The term multi-encryption describes the process of encrypting texts or data that have already been encrypted. Instead of plain text, an existing cipher text is simply encrypted again. Either encrypted once more or several times. The encryption algorithm can also change. As with an alcoholic cocktail, different algorithms and methods are mixed as ingredients in multi-encryption. Multi-encryption is also known as super-encryption or super-encryption or cascading cipher.

Or it is simply called cocktail encryption, if it is not the bartender but the cryptographer who is simply more convincing in combining and mixing ingredients according to a previously defined sequence: a cocktail like ›Ellie's McSunrise‹, ›Golden Quanten-Grasshopper‹, ›CCCatch Club Cocktail - Cause you are young and need the Alco-rithm‹, ›Pool on the Euro-Beach‹, ›Ulmer Ziphtis Zombie‹, ›Fluffy French Fiasco‹ or ›NTRU on the RSA-Rocks‹ you like? - If mathematics students turn up at the bar more often in the future before studying instead of after studying and completing their thesis, procedures could certainly have names like this for a multi-mix crypto recipe. It is reminiscent of *Harry Potter*s Polyjuice Potion that transforms the appearance, and as ingredients knows: floe-flys, leech, river grass and knot, a ground horn of a two-horn and grated skin of a tree snake.

This means that a multi-algorithm for encryption can first be McEliece, then NTRU and the cipher text is finally provided again with symmetric AES encryption or transmitted securely through a TLS channel based on RSA.

To achieve this, hybrid systems for Cryptography are often used first, which can use both symmetric (i.e., with a password) and asymmetric encryption (with a public key). It is pointed out here that a symmetric encryption process is particularly efficient and an asymmetric encryption process with a public key is particularly convenient. Because with the public key, the key only must be transmitted once. In view of the sufficient processor power nowadays, however, this no longer matters. Both methods can be used, e.g., to efficiently encrypt the data with a key of a symmetric system and to send the key for this over a channel that is formed by an asymmetric encryption system or vice versa.

Multiple encryption also reduces the consequences if a favored algorithm is already weak or broken, and the data is continuously disclosed without our knowledge. Multiple encryption is therefore always more secure than just a single encryption. (So double alcohol in a cocktail helps if an alcohol should be bad or not have enough revolutions to stay in the picture of a cocktail encryption.)

This is sometimes questioned in a few short comments, with the argument that the security of an algorithm could possibly also be weakened by the second application of another algorithm. But so far these are only assumptions. It can also be assumed that this argument is used publicly in order to prevent multi-encryption from becoming popular. That is, on the contrary, it could be so sure that it provides special protection. Overall, there has been little research on multi-encryption so far. And de facto there are hardly any statements about how plain text behaves when it is first encrypted with McEliece, the resulting cipher text is then encrypted with RSA and the result is finally encrypted again with AES. Or whether plain text is more secure if it is encrypted first with AES and then with NTRU and finally with McEliece.

In any case, it can be assumed that a cipher text that is encrypted again is encrypted more securely than a cipher text that is only encrypted once, since the letters of the cipher text are not subject to any human-readable logic (i.e., neither semantically nor with the naked eye can be syntactically developed) but are only subject to the logic of the algorithm used. Even a computer does not know which algorithm was used in the third encryption process and whether an underlying cipher text got the letters or blocks mixed up using RSA or using the NTRU algorithm.

Thus, even without mathematical proof, it can be concluded that the thesis »multiple encryption must be more secure in any case« must weigh more than a mathematically unproven thesis that cipher text would or could become less secure after re-encryption.

Since we cannot always scientifically prove that a certain algorithm is strong, the question is not whether the following algorithms are strong in the cascading, but what leads us to believe that a certain algorithm is so strong that no additional protection is required. Any new encryption of a cipher text is therefore to be regarded as additional protection. It is like a doll in a doll: The well-known toy of the »Matryoshka Doll« (also called Babushka) shows that the outer shell protects the dolls that are still hidden inside.

Until specific mathematical evidence has been provided for a defined constellation of cascading different algorithms, the assumption of better mixing and protection applies. The simple folk wisdom therefore applies: A cascade of algorithms is at least as difficult to break as one of its component ciphers. Multi-encryption does not promise a better, but safer life through strengthened encryption. Every seamstress will confirm: Double-stitched is better! When an algorithm is broken (something we may not know), using other algorithms serially may be the only security in the system.

The encryption programs GoldBug and Spot-On are well equipped in the field of multi-encryption and are pioneers in the field of applied Cryptography for multi-encryption. They laid the modern foundations of multi-encryption with three or four or more levels of encryption, even if other systems have been using hybrid encryption with two levels in combination for some years, but not in multiple encapsulation of a message or serial encryption of cipher text. Regular hybrid systems usually differ in the way they are used to send a key through a further encrypted channel, and do not relate so much to the re-encryption of already existing chip text.

Spot-On initially implements a hybrid encryption system that also includes authentication and confidentiality. As already explained above, hybrid means that both variants are present in the encryption system, both the symmetric encryption system and the asymmetric encryption system with the public keys.

So, a part in Spot-On generates the key for authentication and encryption of the message. These two keys are used to authenticate the data (that is the message) and to encrypt it as a capsule, so to speak. The keys (for authentication and for encryption) are then encrypted for transport over the public key encryption part of the system.

Both methods can be combined with one another as required, i.e., in a triple encryption with completely different sequences and repetitions. This means that a message can first be encrypted a-symmetric with the PKI e.g. from McEliece as known and then symmetric with the AES cipher.

Or just the other way around. Other variants are also conceivable: the transmission path with permanent keys may only transmit temporary keys so that further communication takes place via these temporary channels. The temporary channel can again transmit a symmetric key according to an AES.

This means that there is not only the option of creating hybrid systems in the method of changing from PKI to AES or changing from an a-symmetric encryption system to a symmetric encryption system, but also in the change from permanent keys to temporary keys (same which type).

Encrypting multiple times and switching between the encryption systems or changing the algorithm within an encryption system (then again NTRU instead of McEliece again followed by McEliece encryption) and using time-limited keys, is a strong competence in this hybrid and multiple encryption. Spot-On and the slimmer user interface GoldBug Messenger provide a few options and are the pioneers and founders of modern multi-encryption in applied Cryptography.

Cipher text is converted to cipher text, and this is converted again to new cipher text. The above-mentioned programs extend the security of plain text through this multi-encryption because cipher text is either encrypted again or sent through a TLS channel. It is also possible to encrypt a file with the tools available in the software suite on the hard drive before it is sent via further encrypted channels (including other communication software) as described above. Or a symmetric password is set for an email to be sent.

You can now play theoretically and practically with these fundamentals. And individual procedures or algorithms can be used in different ways: Is a permanent key used first or a temporary key? Or again the symmetric key and then an a-symmetric encryption as a second or any later instance? or the other way around? Hybrid and multiple encryption therefore has numerous potentials and offers a wealth of research perspectives and practical applications. And makes existing encryption more secure compared to high-performance computing.

5.4   Exponential encryption with the Echo-protocol in the network of graphs •

The Echo protocol, which is also used in the encryption client Spot-On, has been established since 2011 and has been integrated into this communication program and the GoldBug Messenger since 2013. It is a very simple protocol that essentially comprises the following properties.

1. All data packets are encrypted in the Echo.

2. Each Echo node in the network forwards the incoming data packets to all connected neighbors (an exception to this is the adaptive Echo protocol, which only sends the data packets once over a distance to a defined neighbor node).

3. A third, additional criterion for the Echo protocol can be added: Because there is a special way in which the encrypted packet or the encrypted message capsule is unpacked. The capsule contains neither sender nor addressee information. And this is where the data packets differ from TCP packets. Instead, the message is identified using the hash of the unencrypted message, i.e., the plain text. If, after a decryption attempt from

the received text, the hash matches the enclosed hash of the original plain text, the decryption attempt was successful. The correct key was chosen. The message is then displayed to the user on the screen. This is known as an »Echo Match«[164].

With these requirements based on established encryption libraries, hybrid and multiple encryption can be implemented: Multi-encryption is the right term and focus here, as the original data (the message) can be encrypted multiple times within the Echo protocol. Hybrid encryption is also not a wrong term for Echo, as various algorithms and methods can be combined as options for encryption.

An example as already deduced with regard to multi-encryption: the data packet may be encrypted symmetric, for example, and then asymmetric before it is finally sent through a self-signed HTTPS channel. The following figure shows from the inside out the process of how an encrypted message capsule in the Echo protocol is formed in the various layers.

Figure 26: Encryption capsule of the Echo protocol

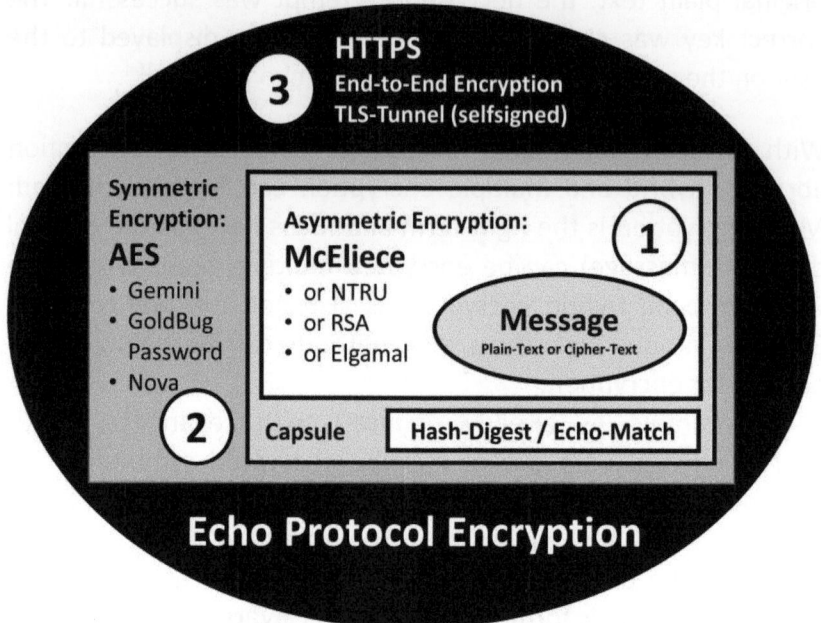

Source:[165]

First level of encryption: *the message is hashed and encrypted. The encrypted text and the hash value of the message are packed together, so to speak, in a capsule. It also follows the so-called encrypt-then-MAC paradigm. This means: In order to show that the cipher text has not been falsified for the recipient, the hash value is formed.*

Third level of encryption: *The capsule can now be transferred to the other party via a secure TLS connection.*

Second level of encryption: *It is also possible to provide the capsule on the first level with symmetric encryption (with the AES-256 algorithm, comparable to a password). In this way, a hybrid encryption is added to the already existing multi-encryption.*

Echo-Match: *In a node that receives the encrypted capsule after dispatch, all available keys from this node are tried out. If the cipher text can be converted into legible plain text, then the key was the right one. As described above, whether the converted text is correct is proved by checking the hash values (Echo Match). If the conversion is unsuccessful, the capsule is reassembled with hash and cipher text, i.e., as it came in, it is forwarded to all connected nodes. Since the inventor and developer of the Echo the protocol and its matching at* *lunch in the canteen has been randomly occurred, the encryption of the Echo is also called ›Boston Lunch Bundle‹, or short: Boston Bundle.*

The Echo is therefore a malleable concept. That is, an implementation does not require strictly dictated details. So, in that respect it is also a very flexible concept.

This malleability[166] also relates in Cryptography to the conversion of cipher text to cipher text. This also includes the hybrid and multiple encryption options of such a client. An encryption algorithm or process is malleable if it is possible for analysts to transform a cipher text into another cipher text, which then decodes to a plain text that relates to it. This is given with an encryption of a plain text M (like message), with which it is possible to encrypt this with a function F (M) in a cipher text. Using the known function F - without necessarily knowing or learning the message M.

Even if the necessary mathematical calculations cannot be considered further here, it becomes clear that the Echo brings a cipher text into contact with numerous variations. As we have seen, converting cipher text into cipher text is only one option. Hybrid encryption and in particular multiple encryption is therefore a substantial constant of the Echo and the Cryptography of the future - and can also protect against fast high-performance computers in the Third Epoch of Cryptography.

Another specific constant of the Echo is how the encrypted capsules and data packets are sent because each Echo graph model may have its own specific paths and obligations. An example:

Figure 27: Beyond Cryptographic Routing in the Echo Grid

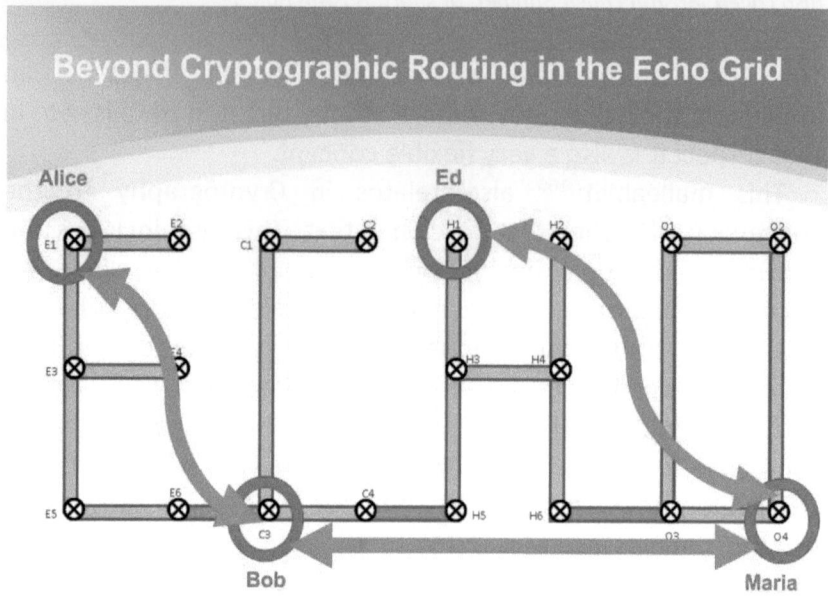

Source: [167]

The illustration of the Echo grid shows the four, at different corner points of the interconnected letters E-C-H-O as nodes. The individual nodes of Alice (E1), Bob (C3), Ed (H1) and Maria (O4) are marked with circles. In order to send a message from Ed to Alice, a forwarding via a defined graph is necessary. This can be from Ed to Maria (via H1, H3, H4, H5, O3 and O4), then to Bob (via O4, O3, H6, H5, C4, C3) and finally to from Bob to Alice (via C3, E6, E5, E3, E1). However, since all nodes send a message capsule to all nodes, the fastest possible graph will be: From Ed (H1) via H3, H5, C4, C3, E6, E5, E3 to Alice (E1). As an aside: The later described Turtle Hopping protocol of the RetroShare software would forward the message via the persons, i.e., Ed to Maria, then to Bob and from him to Alice. Because of the encryption, the Echo protocol includes shorter and more effective routes via intermediate nodes in the vicinity since each node sends data packets on to all neighbors. This also reduces metadata. This design is also more flexible compared to a graph path in the Tor or I2P network described below.

As mentioned, the Echo works on the elementary process that information is transmitted as encrypted capsules or data packets via different or simple passages and channels and each end point that receives it checks according to an Echo Match whether it matches the known keys are for receiving the data in their own instance.

The Spot-On application created the Echo protocol in concrete programming and development. The clients of the Echo protocol support data transmission via the communication channels Bluetooth, SCTP, TCP and UDP (both multicast and unicast). For TCP-based communications, OpenSSL is also supported in addition to the encryption described above. This means that the encrypted Echo capsule can be sent end-to-end encrypted again, protected by a TLS channel. This is optional, so that already encrypted data can be sent with or without TLS: Both sending via HTTPS and HTTP is possible.

The application also provides a mechanism to distribute session keys for this encapsulation of the data (or the encryption of the message), as described above: It is then about temporary keys. A supplementary mechanism distributes the session keys using the predetermined, permanent keys. That means: the keys are encapsulated / encrypted and transmitted via the public key system.

The message or information is then encrypted using the encryption algorithm for the cipher text and the algorithm for the signature. Further hash values are added. [168]

This enables cryptographic routing to be addressed. With cryptographic routing, IP addresses are not accepted as a destination, starting point or node for assignment in routing tables, but rather cryptographic keys and / or tokens represent a certain »constant« that must be considered. This does not mean the term »address« in the network, as it is not about replacing the IP address with a cryptographic key, such as: route instead of the IP address 192.168.1.1 now to the cryptographic key: a702a31adb52a19c07910ee2b2..96ab7097c49d3f4c6edee0b47. Instead, the message is sent in the Echo protocol without classic routing information. There are no tables with chart information regarding addressees or senders.

The affiliation of a message to the keys known in the own instance is determined by the Echo Match: Can a cipher text be converted back into readable plain text with the existing own keys - and this was checked using the hash process of the Echo Match - then the decryption attempt can be rated as successful.

In addition, since every message from every instance is forwarded to every connected instant, further target information is unnecessary. Therefore, one has to speak of »*Beyond Cryptographic Routing*«[169].

So that each message that is forwarded does not come to its own instance a second time, this mesh and flooding character is canceled by a function called *congestion control*: The hashes of the message capsules are collected in the node for a while, and if the hash of the capsule is already known, the capsule is not touched or unpacked a second time and tried out with all available keys or even forwarded. These known message capsules can be discarded.

Certain other modes of the Echo protocol also enable the transmission of data packets to be reduced (see Adaptive Echo (AE) as well as Half Echo and also mobile Echo via the SECRED protocol for smaller hardware devices such as cell phones). This ›reduction‹ is also known as Cryptographic Discovery and has been further developed in the SmokeStack[170] application - a server for Echo clients.

Echo encryption, Echo Matches, Cryprographic Discovery and (Beyond) Cryptographic Routing are possible in addition to congestion control in a network in which small groups participate and which is reminiscent of the »phenomenon of the small world«: under these circumstances, a *small world phenomenon* is often assumed that almost all users can be reached via five, six, or seven hops. In real life as well as in an electronic network that depicts friendships. The routing of an e-mail over the global network and server landscape takes just as few stations today.

The theoretical considerations of the so-called »small world phenomenon« - that everyone can be reached with seven hops via others - suggest that since recipients can be found in the Echo across multiple destinations, a message can also be transmitted successfully.

The phenomenon of the small world is a social psychological term that was coined in 1967 by *Stanley Milgram* and describes the high degree of shortened paths through personal relationships within social networks in modern society. It is an experimental hypothesis that everyone in the world is linked by a surprisingly short chain of acquaintances[171]. The phenomenon is often referred to as »six degrees of separation«. The underlying idea was presented in the short story »Láncszemek«[172] by the Hungarian *Frigyes Karinthy* published in 1929 - there even only over 5 hops.

And now this socio-psychological assumption can also be tested in a very practical way in the classroom on electronic networks with a handful of computers: The practical tests of the past several years with various Echo kernels have also shown the scalability of the protocol in a node and graph network structure, which even goes beyond the leaps of »small worlds«[173].

The advantage of this encryption is that it is multiple encrypted, that end-to-end encrypting keys can be exchanged instantly and immediately, that quantum-secure algorithms such as NTRU and McEliece can be used and it is linked to a graph theory such as Data packets find their way in the network: since every packet passes every node, no metadata is created - i.e., who communicated to whom and when. A packet that leaves a node with four neighbors can also be distributed to other neighbors at these new neighbors.

The graph theory paired with the processed encryption method offers *Exponential Encryption* here. It is comparable to the grain of rice on a chessboard that, according to a well-known story, doubles on every square on the chessboard. Complexity and chaos are added as research aspects next to target-oriented network and route design.[174]

Exponential Encryption makes the encrypted message available in every node, but it is secured by multiple and secure McEliece encryption and therefore dispenses with the provision of metadata about who was able to successfully unpack or read which message when.

In view of the analysis perspectives with regard to metadata, in the Third Epoch of Cryptography Exponential Encryption using Echo simply enables a higher level of security.

5.5   McEliece & NTRU: A new life cycle with secure algorithms?! ●

In addition to the option of multiple encryption and the option of routing an encrypted packet over several routes so that no metadata is recorded - as first measures against surveillance or decryption on the fly - two algorithms remain that are currently considered secure against the quantum-computers: NTRU and the McEliece algorithm, which has already been mentioned.

NTRU or NTRUEncrypt is an asymmetric encryption method that was developed in 1996 by mathematicians *Jeffrey Hoffstein, Jill Pipher* and *Joseph H. Silverman*. *Jeffrey Hoffstein* joined the American Mathematical Society (AMS) as a professor of mathematics after many years at Brown University, of which *Jill Pipher* is president. She was also President of the Association of

Women in Mathematics (AWM). *Joseph H. Silverman* is also a member of the Mathematical Society and focuses on Cryptography, on which he wrote more than 100 research articles in addition to various math books.

Their NTRU algorithm is loosely based on lattice problems that are considered unbreakable with quantum-computers. This algorithm is therefore increasingly becoming the focus of investigations[175].

At the beginning of 2011, a work by the cryptologists *Damien Stehlé* and *Ron Steinfeld* appeared, in which a security proof for a modified form of NTRUEncrypt is provided. Likewise, various considerations have been made to crack NTRU, which, however, cannot be discussed in detail here in the description and they remain of a general theoretical or customary type. Even if there are further formal security proofs and additional investigations for NTRUEncrypt, as there are numerous publications and analysis approaches for other cryptographic methods, the method has so far been considered secure for sufficiently large parameters.

The algorithm was patented in the USA at the time. The patents have expired today and there are also open-source replicas and applications that are now being included in the research. The McEliece algorithm currently seems to be much more in the field of attention of application and research than NTRU.

Robert J. McEliece, born on May 21, 1942, in Washington, D.C., was an American mathematician and electrical engineer. He was a professor of electrical engineering at the *California Institute of Technology* (Caltech). He studied there with a bachelor's degree in 1964 and a doctorate in mathematics three years later.

At the same time, a few years earlier he was an engineer at the *Jet Propulsion Laboratory* (JPL). The JPL builds and controls satellites and space probes for NASA and also advises the producers of science fiction films and series (for example for Star Trek or Babylon 5).

McEliece developed applications that were added to the Galileo spacecraft for a later redesign of the mission, for the planet Jupiter and its moons, as well as for studying a handful of other bodies in other solar systems.

In the Galileo probe, for example, error-correcting codes based on convolution codes were used, which he developed. He was also involved in the error-correcting codes of the Voyager program. When there were data transmission problems on the Galileo mission that jeopardized the transmission of photos from Jupiter, he was on the team that successfully reprogrammed the decoder on board. For these error-correcting codes in NASA space missions, he received the NASA Group Achievement Award twice (1981 and 1992), and once (1981) for his contributions to the Voyager mission.

He was the supervisor of the information processing group and a general consultant. In order to become a professor, he was initially a guest-professor at Caltech for several years. In a four-year stopover, he was appointed professor of mathematics at the University of Illinois at Urbana-Champaign, before becoming a permanent professor at Caltech in 1982.

Not only is he known for contributing to algebraic coding theory, but he also developed encodings for hard disk drives and flash memories at Sony. He also wrote a standard work on information and coding theory. A decent academic career with lots of topics and successes.

Already in his first professorship for mathematics in 1978 he and *Elwyn Berlekamp* developed a public key cryptosystem named after him (McEliece cryptosystem) based on linear codes: so-called Goppa codes[176], which he used. A corresponding digital signature for this cryptosystem, which is gradually becoming more successful, was subsequently developed: the McEliece-Niederreiter signature (additionally based on *Harald Niederreiter*).

In the early years and because of slow processors and transmission rates, the McEliece crypto system did not yet prevail against RSA encryption - also because of the key lengths in the range of a few megabytes. However, this cryptographic system was and is still recognized as being secure against attempts at decryption with a quantum-computer.

Robert McEliece died on May 8, 2019, in Pasadena, California - the year in which Google was supposed to proclaim »Quantum Supremacy,« that is, the quantum-computers were faster than the digital super-computers and the new age of the Third Epoch of Cryptography began.

RSA was marked as »no longer secure«, the quantum-computers took on the leading role in the thinking of Cryptography and his algorithm, designed as early as 1978, slipped into the first row of the viewing angle next to NTRU. What a high point to say goodbye to life if your own idea and research basis can live on: as in all moving stories, death and continuing life are close together.

A new life cycle begins: the McEliece & NTRU algorithms play an essential role in the security and resistance to quantum-super-computers. It took 20 years after the publication of his encryption concept for further researchers to contribute and it took another 20 years for the development of applied Cryptography to incorporate this algorithm into programs and messengers with a view to the future, as well as the slightly larger keys with different modules made this crypto system practicable.

Spot-On Encryption Suite and in the mobile area the Smoke Crypto Chat Messenger were not only in the area of multi-encryption, but also here the first applications to incorporate the

McEliece or NTRU algorithm into applied Cryptography in the area of messaging. They are also considered to be door-openers and pioneers in the field of quantum-computing-security, are available as (mature) applications for further open-source research and are therefore taken up again in a further section below.

In its report on »Quantum Migration«[177], the *European Cybersecurity Agency* (ENISA) presents, in addition to the two aforementioned, other new algorithms based on an assessment by NIST: Crystals-Kyber and Saber and, for signatures, Crystals-Dilithium, Falcon or Rainbow. A group of other alternative candidates is also named, such as NTRU-Prime and others as further developments.

The Cryptography in the Third Epoch is not only facing fundamental transformations with regard to new computing machines, new algorithms and their first implementations in applied programming and messengers, of which the research and development requirements need to be deepened.

6 TRANSFORMATION OF CRYPTOGRAPHY: THE KEY TRANSPORT PROBLEM IS SOLVED •

With these political and cryptographic basics and foundations for a new Epoch, we now turn to further innovations in Cryptography of this time. Through numerous process improvements, optimized methods and current innovations, Cryptography is currently »transforming«[178] as a whole. In view of the political demands for keys to be issued, both, the symmetric encryption (e.g., with AES, OTP) and asymmetric encryption (e.g., with McEliece, GPG, NTRU) play a particularly central role. How would it be if no more keys had to be transferred at all?

The innovation consists in the application of further mathematical methods compared to the millennia-old, symmetric encryption, that the keys no longer have to be transmitted to the other party but can be derived. This refers to the so-called »derived keys«. With its focus on key exchange, this *Derivative Cryptography* represents a further innovation in Cryptography, in addition to the methods that continue to exist for handling keys in the known encryption systems.

The Derivative Cryptography is implemented within the Secret Stream Keys and Juggerknaut Keys, which we will consider further below. Even with a mathematical function called »discrete logarithm« it is possible for computers to calculate keys without a transport path on both sides. Before doing this, there should be a few initial hints on methods considered that have been possible up to now to generate and exchange keys for encryption with corresponding protocols.

6.1 Key exchanges over DHM, REPLEO, EPKS or AutoCrypt? •

The key exchange mostly comprises defined, now predominantly electronically supported methods in Cryptography, with which cryptographic keys are exchanged between users. Only then is it possible to use a cryptographic algorithm.

To exchange encrypted messages, both parties must be appropriately equipped to encrypt messages to be sent and to be able to decrypt messages received. The type of equipment that is required depends on the encryption technology used. In any case, however, a key is required that shows how individual characters can be translated back into readable characters.

If the encryption is symmetric key encryption, then both need a copy of the same key. With this encryption there is the problem already mentioned that the key has to be transported: either it was transported in pockets by diplomats and handed over personally or it had to be delivered in a sealed manner by trustworthy couriers if no other secure (e.g. electronic) channel could be used.

And if a key with the property of public/private key is to be used for asymmetric encryption, both need the other's public key in exchange.

With the emergence of electronic communication networks, protocols and mathematical calculations were therefore found, discussed, and defined in order to be able to securely exchange or negotiate a session key between two parties on a public channel. Established protocols for electronic key transmission are:

- the protocol based on Merkle's Puzzle from 1974 (respective published 1978): here a symmetric key is exchanged between two parties[179].

- In 1976 the Diffie-Hellman key exchange was published by *Whitfield Diffie* with *Martin Hellman,* which referred to asymmetric procedures[180].
- In the Needham-Schroeder Protocol[181] from 1978, everyone with the same trustworthy other party has a shared secret key. The British computer scientist *Roger Needham* developed the protocol together with his American colleague *Michael Schroeder,* which formed a basis for Kerberos authentication, which was still used for Windows 2000.

Ralph Merkle's protocol, known as the Puzzle, is the first key exchange protocol in which the two parties do not already have to share or know a secret key with the other or a third party. The existence of such a sophisticated mathematical and process-oriented procedure has long been considered impossible, and this discovery can be understood as the beginning of public key Cryptography. On the other hand, the term Diffie-Hellmann protocol for such a key negotiation is better known.

Whitfield Diffie was with his student *Ralph Merkle* from 1969 at Stanford University, where his collaboration with *Martin Hellman* on Cryptography began. He later worked at Sun Microsystems in Menlo Park, California. *Martin Hellman* was on the full-time faculty for over 25 years before retiring as a professor in 1996.

Ralph Merkle's puzzle is both, a corresponding preparatory work and an addition. *Martin Hellman* in particular had argued that the protocol should be called Diffie-Hellman-Merkle key exchange, based on Merkle's separate contributions. A protocol with the abbreviation »DHM« is therefore also used: all three researchers - Merkle, Diffie and Hellman - are therefore considered to be the pioneers of asymmetric Cryptography in the

1970s. Alternatively, mathematically speaking, the discrete logarithm (DL) is also used.

This type of protocol design for key generation now enables two parties to negotiate a key with one another through a mathematical calculation without having to transmit it over the Internet or a public channel at the time. In the 1970s, not only was the foundation for *asymmetric* encryption given, but a milestone was also set in being able to negotiate a key on both sides without having to transmit it via public channels (as is the case today on the Internet).

In the section below, we also come to these options of dispensing with the transmission of keys in *symmetric* encryption, e.g., using Juggerknaut Keys and Secret Stream Keys, which also have a significant effect on the key transport problem and further establish another mathematical method as an applied cryptographic function.

And: The situation of key transport improves if public keys can be transmitted in a protected and automated manner (as is the case with REPLEO or the AutoCrypt function) or, for the transmission - regardless of which sort of key - already secured end-to-end encrypted channels are available, as it is implemented in the key transmission using the EPKS protocol. So, let us take a closer look at these protocols one after the other.

The DH protocol: the main thing is discrete - from the exponential function to the discrete logarithm

Alice and Bob want to communicate in encrypted form over a possibly insecure connection. To do this, when using a symmetric cryptosystem, they first need a shared secret key.

With the protocol from Diffie / Hellman or the preliminary work by *Ralph Merkle*, a secret key can be calculated without third-party eavesdroppers being able to find out. Both can use the mathematically calculated key in a symmetric process to communicate in encrypted form. However, mathematical constants still must be exchanged via the insecure line, as follows:

1. Alice and Bob first publicly agree on a large prime number. Publicly agreeing on this means that everyone can know these two numbers.
2. Alice and Bob each generate a random number that is to be kept secret. These are not transmitted, so they remain unknown to potential third parties, but also to the respective counterpart. Alice knows their number and Bob knows his number.
3. Alice uses her secret number to calculate the public key and sends it to Bob. Bob uses his secret number to calculate the public key and sends it to Alice.
4. Alice receives the key from Bob and also performs a calculation with her private key. Similarly, Bob calculates a number. The two calculated the same number. This is the shared key we are looking for.

A key creation could be achieved and only Alice and Bob know the key. Third parties cannot calculate this key from the intercepted communication. This inversion of the discrete exponential function is called the *discrete logarithm* (DL). And for this one would also have to be able to solve this computation of the discrete logarithm. However, based on current knowledge, this is not possible in a short time if the numbers are large enough. Alice and Bob can use the key they have created in this way for symmetric encryption with little risk. Alice and Bob get exactly the same number after their respective calculations, namely the secret key.

So, it's the simplified negotiation process: we both transfer large public numbers and use secret numbers we choose to calculate a key that nobody can recalculate because our secret numbers are not known.

However, the key exchange according to Diffie/Hellman did not address the problem of being certain of the actual identity of the person (the counterpart). And: The same assumption applies with regard to mathematical problems that cannot be solved in a finite time as with the RSA algorithm. It can be analyzed more deeply whether, in view of the quantum-computer, not only the factorization of prime numbers in the discrete exponential function has to be taken into account, or whether effects on the function of the discrete logarithm have to be examined as well.

Key exchange using a REPLEO

When Alice has received the public key from Bob, she can start encrypting immediately. She can encrypt a message, or she can encrypt her own public key. Now everyone will ask: the public key is public, so why should it be kept secret from the public or during transport? That is certainly true - but if the key does not have to be public, then it can remain protected. For this purpose, the REPLEO was devised and built into the Spot-On Encryption Suite software as a practical application. REPLEO means in the sense of the English »Reply« with the Latin mixture of »respondere«: I answer, I play back.

There was thus a process innovation within the programming of this applied Cryptography, that the public key can also be sent to Alice as cipher text. The REPLEO was the beginning of an initially manual, then automated and, above all, protected key exchange.

We note: with symmetric encryption, key transport is very important and can be risky. With asymmetric encryption, the public keys are exchanged. With the use of a REPLEO, there is also the option of keeping the public key protected. Accordingly, it can be common practice to combine both encryption methods with one another.

This type of hybrid or multi-encryption has already been reported in detail in the previous chapter: It can therefore be an assumption that the symmetric key is encrypted via the asymmetric encryption of the public key. Or a symmetric key is formed in the first place using the discrete logarithm function in the DH(M)-protocol. In the case of a REPLEO, Alice's public key (or the symmetric key) can also be encrypted with Bob's public key. And the other way around: Bob's public key could in principle also be made »transportable« with symmetric encryption as cipher text.

We see that these alternative solutions of hybrid encryption (i.e., the use of symmetric and also asymmetric encryption) or »multi-encryption« are interesting and complex, but only partially solve or simplify the key transport problem: the asymmetric encryption method with the exchange of the public key has the problem - in the RSA variant - possibly to be »no longer secure« in view of the current development of computing capacity (especially probably if one also knows public keys) and with symmetric encryption the risky transport of the key is still necessary.

Another solution can consist in the construction and permanent use of electronic networks which are permanently encrypted. Temporary keys can then be exchanged on this basis or via encrypted channels in the system. The EPKS protocol offers such a design option.

Key exchange in the EPKS protocol

So, if an existing encrypted electronic communication system with a secure end-to-end encrypted channel already exists, this is worth its weight in gold. There is no need to negotiate a key and there is no unsecured transport.

The EPKS protocol relates to such a network configuration of the Echo clients already explained above, whose connections can in principle be encrypted. The abbreviation EPKS stands for *Echo Public Key Share* and is a function implemented in the »Spot-On« Encryption Suite program, which is very well developed as mentioned, for the release of public keys over the network of encrypted connections.

In this way, a group of participants can exchange keys via secure channels and use them together, so that a classic key server is not required. This is a convenient option for electronic key exchange with a group or an individual user.

EPKS channels enable the exchange of (symmetric and asymmetric) keys within a network, quasi as a broadcast without server memory. These channels work according to the principle of symmetric encryption: the channel can be known to a community group or just a single person. EPKS automatically integrates the shared public keys into an EPKS community. Key broadcast is such an alternative to the key server.

The new process is that keys are not stored and searched for on a server but are sent from node to node in a secure channel - for which certain people have access authorization - either by manual transmission or by automated exchange from two nodes, e.g., two Spot-On clients (for the EPKS protocol) or through (two) e-mail clients via the AutoCrypt protocol derived later from EPKS.

Key exchange with the AutoCrypt protocol

AutoCrypt is also an automatic key exchange. This cryptographic process innovation relates fundamentally to the protocol definitions of a REPLEO and EPKS protocol and their further development. This means that users of the same messenger or e-mail client automatically exchange the public key for encryption with each other and from this point on they are secured for all further communication. As we have seen, the EPKS protocol provided for this many years before the term AutoCrypt became known. Other projects have also copied these process steps under the name KeySync.

The AutoCrypt process has since formed a whole community in the field of development and research in order to make key management more automated and convenient. Nevertheless, even with keys that are automatically accepted in an instance, there is a low risk, as attackers could send the wrong key to the machine. Therefore, an automated transport is to be assessed just as carefully as a manually confirming acceptance on the part of the recipient with less convenience.

6.2 Cryptographic Calling: from Forward Secrecy to Instant Perfect Forward Secrecy (IPFS) ●

With Cryptographic Calling, end-to-end encryption becomes as easy as making a phone call: press a button, establish an end-to-end connection, and discard the generated key after the conversation; so: hang up the phone or end the call on the smartphone.

In Cryptography, Forward Secrecy or Perfect Forward Secrecy (PFS) is a property of certain key exchange protocols with the aim of agreeing a shared session key between the communication partner so that it cannot be reconstructed by a third party even if one of the long-term keys should later be compromised.

So, it is about temporary keys. These are sent through a secure tunnel that was established using a long-term key. Since these temporary keys are only used for a short time, they are also deniable. In any case, they do not belong permanently to the user at the other end but are only used for the moment.

This function and paradigm of using temporary keys has changed. With the so-called method of Cryptographic Calling, these temporary keys can be sent very easily via existing encrypted network connections and then used for new encrypted channels. The Forward Secrecy or Perfect Forward Secrecy has become »Instant Perfect Forward Secrecy«, abbreviated: IPFS, This can be re-established at any time and »instantly«, i.e., immediately and several times, within an online session. Using a Cryptographic Call – an encrypted call to the other party.

More than a handful of different methods[182], which cannot all be explained in detail here, are available to carry out a Cryptographic Call.

2-Way-Calling is briefly explained as an easy-to-remember and interesting method: with Two-Way-Calling, the user Alice provides a password, and the user Bob also provides a password. The common password used by both is made up of a half-length character string: user Alice contributes 50% of the common password, and user Bob also contributes 50% to the common password. Let us assume that the password has 32 characters for each of the two: Then the first 16 characters of Alice's password are used for the shared password, and the last 16 characters of Bob's password are used. Fifty-Fifty. When the two are joined together, the result is a common password with 32 characters.

Figure 28: 2-Way-Calling as method of Cryptographic Calling

Password of Alice, Plain text:
Thats my Kung Fu
(16 ASCII-characters, each 1 Byte)

Translation in Hex:

T	h	a	t	s		m	y		K	u	n	g		F	u
54	68	61	74	73	20	6D	79	20	4B	75	6E	67	20	46	75

Resulting password:
54 68 61 74 73 20 6D 79 20 4B 75 6E 67 20 46 75

Second part will be used
54 68 61 74 73 20 6D 79 20 4B 75 6E 67 20 46 75

Password of Bob, Plain text:
Two One Nine Two
(16 ASCII-characters, each 1 Byte)

Translation in Hex:

T	w	o		O	n	e		N	i	n	e		T	w	o
54	77	6F	20	4F	6E	65	20	4E	69	6E	65	20	54	77	6F

Resulting Password:
54 77 6F 20 4F 6E 65 20 4E 69 6E 65 20 54 77 6F

First part will be used
54 77 6F 20 4F 6E 65 20 4E 69 6E 65 20 54 77 6F

The first part of Bob and the second part of Alice form the common password in the 2-Way method of Cryptographic Calling:

54 77 6F 20 4F 6E 65 20 20 4B 75 6E 67 20 46 75

Source: [183]

222

Cryptographic Calling is fast and curse and can use temporary keys that were exchanged in the past through an equally temporary channel. This makes this concept flexible in relation to permanent monitoring of Internet traffic and also more secure in relation to possible calculations of the algorithm by fast super- and quantum-computers. The keys for end-to-end encryption have become nimble as a mouse and are only used once - like a disposable paper-tissue handkerchief; the culture of washed, ironed and reusable, permanent cloth handkerchiefs is a thing of the past in this picture with the new IPFS processes of Cryptographic Calling.

And now Europe wants to collect all used one-way-tissue-handkerchiefs and assign them to identified users? No wonder if some are fed up with a full nose. And whether criminals can be asked to use a registered tissue-handkerchief for their noses remains questionable in this purely analogous picture of key management on behalf of the state. Accordingly, can permanent individual connection records of cryptographic tunnels also record the use of unregistered and unknown keys? So where is the key to this very secret text from Scarlett O'Hara? - in the future one will ask when keys like feathers or paper-handkerchiefs have to be collected in the wind. So, these days, modern applied Cryptography ensures that keys ... are gone with the wind!

6.3   Derivative Cryptography: Secret Stream Keys derived from the Socialist Millionaire Protocol (SMP) •

While a key was calculated in the Diffie / Hellman protocol at the end of the 1970s with the aid of the calculation of the *discrete logarithm* (DL) without having to transmit it over a public route (such as on the Internet), another method was established a few decades later to agree on keys that will be derived on both sides. They are also known as derivative keys. These keys are formed on the basis of mathematical calculations using so-called knowledge-free proofs (also: Zero-Knowledge proofs, or ZK-proofs for short) and establish the *Derivative Encryption*.

The theoretical foundation has been known for some time, but these keys have existed in applied Cryptography only for a few years. These *Secret Stream Keys* (short: SSK) are another example with another method that shows that keys are no longer transmitted over the Internet and that the key transport problem has thus been solved (with some restrictions). Should quantum-computers contribute to the uncertainty of the function of the discrete logarithm, this method of *Derivative Cryptography* is available as a possible alternative that needs to be investigated further.

Secret streams describe the creation of numerous temporary keys that result from a passphrase stored on both sides during the creation process. The keys come from or are derived from a so-called »Socialist-Millionaire Process« (SMP), which is based on Zero-Knowledge proof. The P optionally stands for process, problem, or protocol.

Described in the practical application process, this means the following: Alice and Bob, both enter the same secret password in their application - and this is not transmitted over the Internet. The mathematical procedure is used to determine whether the same password was entered on both sides: The Socialist Millionaire Protocol provides the mathematical calculation of this knowledge-free proof (»Zero-Knowledge proof«).

This socialist millionaire problem is one where two millionaires want to determine if their wealth is *equal* without telling each other information about their wealth. It is a variant of the millionaire's problem in which two millionaires want to compare their wealth to determine who has the *greatest* wealth, without telling each other information about their wealth. [184]

If the mathematical SMP proof is successful, it can be assumed that both sides have entered the same password in the mathematical process in each of their applications or that both millionaires are equally rich in the initial question - but without this password, as mentioned, ever being transmitted over the Internet or, in the initial question, someone would learn how wealthy both millionaires are.

The SMP is only a first part of the truth. With the Secret Streams, keys are now derived from the password that has been successfully verified on both sides. Since the output constant is veritably the same on both sides, the same method can now be used to derive further keys on both sides, which can then be used as temporary keys for further secure channels with end-to-end encryption. The key for exactly this cipher text is therefore in the head of the user - and in any case not in the hands of third parties.

This method of Secret Stream Keys, which has so far only been used in a few programs, as well as the Juggerknaut Keys, could therefore be used as a basis for a Transformation of Cryptography[185] as additional service processes: While it is currently clear that end-to-end encryption has reached its peak in application and political discussion, this heyday of end-to-end encryption has long been overtaken by this cryptographic design: Passwords that encrypt end-to-end no longer have to be transmitted over the Internet!

Secure channels are still required and a starting point such as a commonly known but secret password is required, but no key has to be transmitted online via these channels - as was previously the case with the classic transmission of a symmetric key.

Asymmetric Cryptography was founded as a »new direction« at the time under the title of the same name in the publication by Diffie and Hellman for the secure transmission of a symmetric key.[186]

Today it can be added for symmetric encryption that - by means of the »Secret Stream Keys« - no key has to be transmitted from one end to the other over the network.

Secret Stream Keys are therefore a further step in a new direction in Cryptography: They are a supplementary solution to the key transport problem - not via the function »I put the key in my diplomatic case« or via the key-forming function of the discrete logarithm - but via one Zero-Knowledge, mathematical proof in the Socialist Millionaire Protocol.

Of course, both Alice and Bob must first discuss a common level of knowledge or experience with minimal communication: e.g. in advance in real life and in the following way: Can you still remember the name of the restaurant where we met? Please enter this name as a phrase in the communication client.

The phrase is not transmitted over the Internet, but the mathematical calculation of the Zero-Knowledge proof shows us in the SMP protocol whether we have both entered the identical passphrase; and we are both authenticated persons at the same time. Because only you can know what the restaurant was actually called back then. Through the method / function of the Secret Streams, numerous temporary keys are derived in an identical manner on each side and used for end-to-end encryption.

Figure 29: The process of the Socialist Millionaire Protocol (SMP) produces Secret Stream Keys

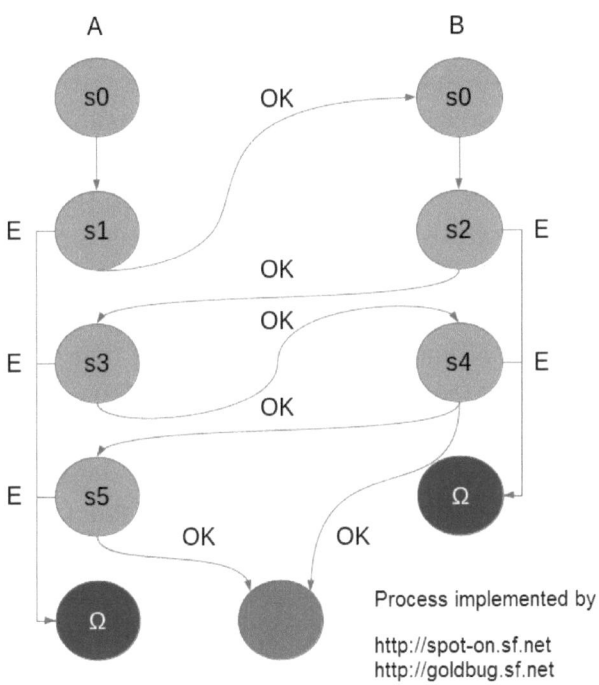

Secret Stream Keys are based on Zero-Knowledge proofs using the Socialist Millionaire Protocol (SMP). With today's Derivative Cryptography, temporary keys can be derived on both sides in a messenger, e.g., on this basis. It offers the potential to dispense with the transmission of keys in secure and unsecured channels of the Internet. Secret streams are programmed in C ++ and were first developed in the aforementioned encryption suite Spot-On.

6.4   Derivative Cryptography: Juggerknaut Keys ●

The problem of key transport can also be eliminated with the *Juggerknaut Keys* (short: JKK). These are exemplary programmed in Java (in the application of the Crypto Chat Messenger Smoke for the Android operating system) and are based on a similar method of a Zero-Knowledge proof: with the difference that here no (Socialist-Millionaire) SMP process is used but the mathematically similar process of the Juggerknaut PAKE protocol, in which Alice and Bob - each again on their own side - also enter a secret phrase or string, which again is not shared over the Internet. Temporary end-to-end encrypting keys are then derived using *Derivative Cryptography*.

Juggerknaut is a metaphorical term. It stands for an unstoppable force that transforms everything that is nearby. The word originates from the huge, many tons heavy Ratha processional floats, which are used during a certain Hindu procession (Ratha Yatra) in honor of the god Jagannatha. Once started, these vehicles are full of energy and can hardly be stopped by humans. During the British occupation of India, the term found its way into the English language and from there today partly also in other languages. In colloquial English, this term is also used today to refer to a heavy articulated truck. Mythological backgrounds and complex spiritual meanings of a »Ratha Yatra« pilgrimage revolve around saying goodbye to childhood and returning home. It is also compared to the repetitive journey of life: the many cycles of death and rebirth. But also, just to take a vacation. In relation to key management in Cryptography, it means: The keys become abstinent with regard to their readiness for transport. They are on vacation or have outgrown the usual transmission cycle.

The Juggerknaut Keys are a term based on this context and, in terms of content and technology, implement the PAKE protocol, which is also a mathematical Zero-Knowledge (ZK) proof: PAKE stands for Password-authenticated key agreement a key that was authenticated using a password.

A password-authenticating method for key agreement according to PAKE is therefore an interactive method for two or more parties to set up cryptographic keys based on the knowledge of one or more parties with regard to a common password.

One specification of this is the J-PAKE protocol, Password-authenticated key agreement *by Juggling*. It was presented by *Feng Hao* and *Peter Ryan*[188]. With this protocol, two parties can also establish private and authenticated communication based solely on their shared password (of little length or complexity) without the need for a public key infrastructure. The mathematical testing process is similar to juggling with balls between the two sides, hence: by juggling.

J-PAKE was documented in a more sophisticated way than PAKE in RFC 8236 or in an ISO / IEC. No matter whether PAKE or J-PAKE with juggling - the protocol variants offer mutual authentication for key exchange, a function that is missing in the Diffie-Hellman key exchange protocol described above.

The important additional property remains that an eavesdropper in the middle cannot get enough information to be able to guess this password stored on both sides without further interactions with the parties based on a guesswork. This also means that a remarkably high level of security can be achieved with weak passwords.

The first successful methods of negotiating passwords with password authentication were described by *Steven M. Bellovin* and *Michael Merritt,* two US researchers in the field of computer networks and information security at AT&T Bell Laboratories, in

1992 for the exchange of encrypted keys (Encrypted Key Exchange, short: EKE). The first demonstrably secure PAKE protocols were mentioned in further theoretical work around the turn of the millennium[189].

A first fully developed application in the context of applied Cryptography took place with the so-called »Juggerknaut« Keys of the Smoke Crypto Messenger twenty years later. Overall, it is not only a ›MBT‹: mathematically breath-taking process that can be spoken of here, but also an innovation in applied Cryptography: here, too, encryption without critical transmission of the key over the Internet.

Authentications and derived keys for end-to-end encrypted channels can therefore be designed with these »silent passwords«. In the next section, let us take a closer look at the verification process of a Zero-Knowledge proof in the cave of Ali Baba.

6.5   Free of knowledge in the Ali Baba Cave •

There is a well-known story explaining the basic ideas of Zero-Knowledge proofs first published by *Jean-Jacques Quisquater* and others in their article »How to Explain Zero-Knowledge protocols to Your Children«. As a Belgian university lecturer, he (together with the German *Claus Peter Schnorr*) received the *RSA Award for Excellence* in Mathematics.

In this story, it is customary to identify the two parties in an unknowing evidence as Peggy (the testimony tester) and Victor (also the testimony tester). P and V stand for proof and validate, as both are interactively included in the checking process.

Figure 30: Alibaba Cave - Peggy randomly takes either Path A or B while Victor waits outside

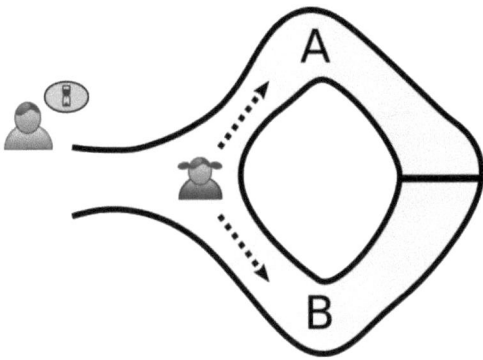

Source: [190]

In this story, Peggy uncovered the secret word that was used to open a magical door in a cave. The cave is shaped like a ring with the entrance on one side and the magic door blocking the opposite side. Victor wants to know if Peggy knows the secret word. But Peggy, a very private person, does not want to reveal her knowledge (the secret word) to Victor, nor does she want to reveal the facts of her knowledge to the world in general.

You now label the left and right path from the entrance as A and B. First, Victor waits in front of the cave while Peggy enters. Peggy takes either Route A or Route B; Victor is not allowed to see which way she is going. Then Victor enters the cave and calls out the name of the path she is supposed to return on, either A or B, chosen at random. Provided she really knows the magic word, this is easy: she opens the door if necessary and returns on the desired route.

Figure 31: Alibaba Cave - Victor chooses an exit route

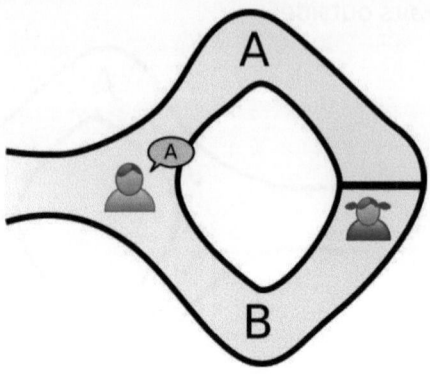

Source: [191]

Suppose she did not know the magic word for opening the door. Then she would only be able to return on the named path if Victor gave the name of the same path on which she had entered. Since Victor would randomly choose A or B, she would have a 50% chance of guessing correctly. If they repeated this trick many times, about twenty times in a row, their chances of successfully anticipating all of Victor's requests would be astonishingly small (about one chance in a million).

Figure 32: Alibaba Cave - Peggy appears reliably at the exit that Victor named

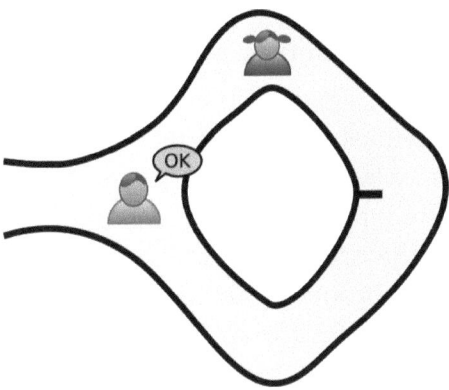

Source: [192]

If Peggy repeatedly appears at the exit named by Victor, he can conclude that it is extremely likely that Peggy actually knows the secret word for opening the door.

So, you can imagine how conditions on the other side can be assessed without knowing the key for access on the other side, i.e., with Victor. Authentication is done through repeated interactions.

This multiple testing, and throwing the juggling ball back and forth, enables answers to the aforementioned questions in the mathematical calculation: Which side has the greater wealth, or do both sides have the same wealth, i.e., have both sides stored the same password and can it be concluded that the other side also knows the password for opening the door at all?

6.6 Automated freedom of interaction and other perspectives on Zero-Knowledge proofs for further programming in Cryptography ●

The applied, practical solution of the key transport system using Secret Stream Keys and Juggerknaut Keys defines a new perspective for programming and thus the future of Cryptography: The solution of the key transport problem with Zero-Knowledge proofs with derived (symmetric) keys is therefore not only a description for transformative innovations in theoretical Cryptography, but also a model for programmers of applied developments, since open-source programming in both important programming languages (C ++ and Java) is available as software libraries or blueprints.

Now, one might consider that one must exchange a secret before using the online internet infrastructure. This is relevant, with restrictions since the aim is to determine a keyword from a common horizon of experience without naming this keyword. Ultimately, in a simple case, each and every participant could only be indexed once with a keyword, so that from now on encryption can take place without key transmission via the Internet - each with »fresh« (i.e., at the respective point in time) derived keys.

So, if the British agent knows that he has to mentally map his friend, the American agent, with the password »Houston« and the Russian agent with the password »Moscow« and the Chinese agent with the password »Beijing«, then these agents no longer need a key exchange, but only a messenger and a corresponding network or internet architecture (i.e. an online connection) in order to communicate undisturbed - but without key exchange. If the British agent wants to speak to the American agent securely, they both enter the word »Houston« - and new, fresh and temporary keys are derived in order to establish or temporarily renew end-to-end encryption.

It is no longer necessary to transmit current keys over the Internet - and there is no longer a security problem. The keys are derived from the remembered agreement between both parties, which only has to be agreed once and then verified by the computer - that is, the other party is authenticated at the same time - but can from now on also communicate securely end-to-end encrypted. And: what works with one key also works in parallel with several keys.

Multiple derived keys in a whole dozen
The Fiasco Forwarding Keys will be discussed later. So far, with Derivative Cryptography, one key has been derived on both sides. What if a whole dozen keys are derived and all of them have to be tried out to decrypt a message?

This type of encryption can therefore be described as *Volatile Encryption*. Volatil does not mean recklessly and shaky in security, but diverse in the complex design of having to try out several keys to decrypt a message. Then the process can be described as volatile. The Derivative Encryption can therefore become a Volatile Encryption, as we will see below on the Fiasco Keys. They also can be derived.

The following overview shows the development of the complexity that has arisen in the area of key management in recent years. Just a few years ago, each user only had one key. Permanent. One key was then transferred per online session. Hybrid encryption secured keys using the other encryption method or cipher text itself was encrypted several times (with appropriate key management). After all, with Cryptographic Calling, keys could be renewed at any time (instant) and multiple times per session. The encrypted packets also took numerous paths in the Echo protocol, for example, and defined Exponential

Encryption. And with Fiasco Forwarding, a whole dozen keys were sent for each message to be decrypted (Volatile Encryption). And the opposite, but particularly secure process became clear: in the end, no keys were transferred at all in the Derivative Encryption. This abstinence in the transport of keys is achieved through the Secret Stream Keys or Juggerknaut Keys.

Figure 33: Development of the complexity of the management of keys in Cryptography: historical development of examples of »good practice« of the next generation

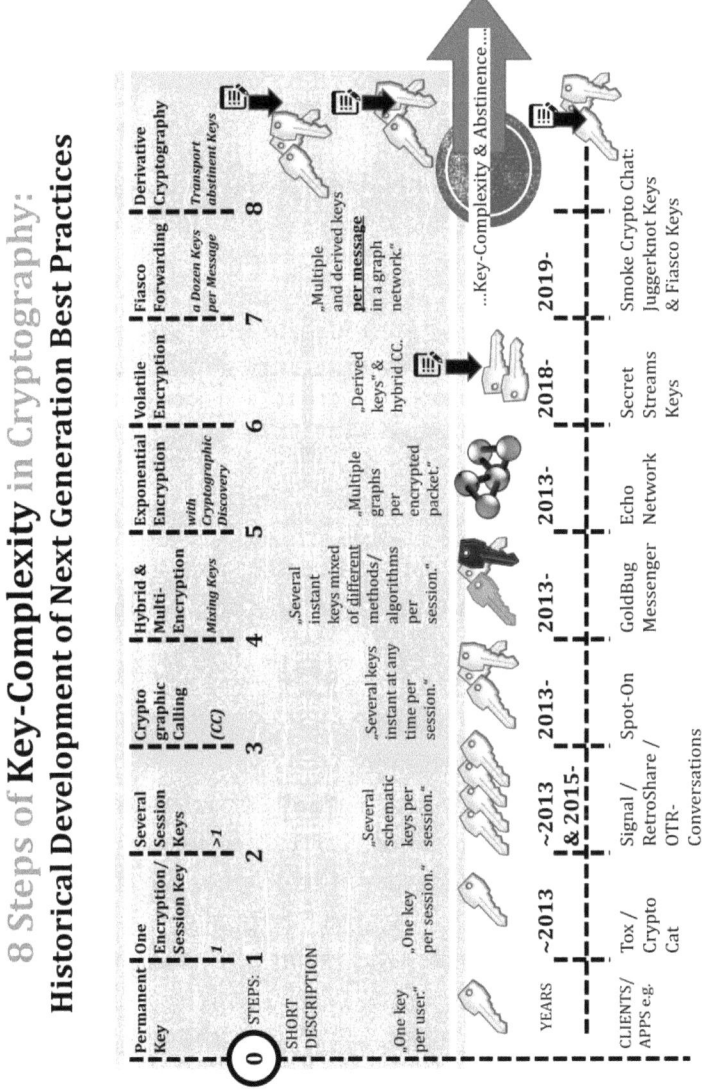

Source: [193]

Derivation of public instead of symmetric keys in Derivative Encryption

So far, so good - key management has developed and varied considerably. Now there is not only the question of whether it is possible to check a password on every page with a Zero-Knowledge proof and to derive one or more symmetric keys from it. The question also arises as to whether it is possible to derive two keys for asymmetric encryption from a Zero-Knowledge proof, e.g., a private and public key for the McEliece algorithm. So, can the transport of public keys be saved? And could this way a new kind of GPG be invented?

To put it simply: In the McEliece algorithm, P and S are each a random matrix, which is required here. They are derived from a secret character string (»Secret Stream«), which is indistinguishable from a character string that was generated at random (»Random Stream«).

This means that the two matrices P and S can also be defined by the characters of a character string (stream), which are derived from an identical (and possibly extended) password on both sides.

The derivation process must include repeatable randomness: suppose each cell in the matrix table is a 0 or a 1, and the selection of a cell is repeated randomness.

The cell (i, J) is then derived from the character from the random character string. It is not about the values of the cell, but about the location or coordinate of the cell, i.e., which cell it is.

The third matrix that the McEliece algorithm requires, however, does not require randomness. It is formed from a perturbation, i.e., a mixture of the two known matrices P and S.

Could a Zero-Knowledge proof, e.g., with the J-PAKE protocol, generate a private and public key for this algorithm?

These forms of the respective matrix can be subject to further research: A matrix can be created, for example, by selecting the

238

coordinates of all cells that should contain a 1. All other cells of the matrix are filled with a 0.

Such a matrix can become extremely large: 8 bits are not sufficient to describe anything over 256. 16 bits (characters) are sufficient (| P |, | S | <7000 ^ 2). Thus, there are 32 bits to describe a location, a coordinate, of a cell. For a 7000 ^ 2 matrix that should have filled 90% of the cells, we need a character string of 32 * 0.9 * 7000 ^ 2 = 1,411,200,000 bits or characters. The percentage can vary. In other words, a relatively long string of characters that a smartphone cannot create, but a computer can create at the appropriate speed.

As a result, each of the two interlocutors would have established a key pair (albeit the same) with which the plain text can be converted into cipher text: Both sides can then take over encryption and decryption processes and use the McEliece algorithm.

Since both sides have the same (derived) private and public keys, this asymmetric encryption can be used like symmetric encryption (on both sides).

Or the process of the Zero-Knowledge proof is only used as a generator for character strings that flow into the McEliece algorithm: and the public key continues to be exchanged regularly.

This special case in which both sides use the same key pair with a private and public key, however, saves a key transmission here as well - but guarantees the security of the McEliece algorithm.

Derivation of »Vanishing Fingerprints«: Deniable authenticity
The same method can also be used for a key pair for digital signature. This authenticates users but can be used as a one-time signature. Let us call them »Vanishing Fingerprints« - digital signatures that let us know that the message was signed by the

desired person, but we only know this once. This creates deniable authenticity, which only guarantees the authenticity of a message from the relevant sender at this moment.

Automated freedom of interaction

As is so often the case when engineers develop something: At the beginning there is a model or even a prototype, and at the end there is a sophisticated series production process. Whether it is the two-legged robots from Boston Dynamics that, after years of development, can immediately calculate any thrust and compensate for the equilibrium balance, whether it's the car that is now driving autonomously, or other routines that develop more and more through professionalization and automation. This is also how the methods of Cryptography develop. A further Transformation of Cryptography in the applied programming can therefore also contribute to the fact that keys are increasingly no longer transmitted.

While the SMP process requires interaction, chat programs could automatically derive keys from the chat that has taken place. It is then about automatic Zero-Knowledge proofs. This means that the other person is not directly involved in the review process. This works as follows:

A session includes a conversation. After S sentences or, for example, a total of 32 words (e.g., larger than 4 characters), one of the two selects a word in the chat history by clicking and sends a non-interactive ZK protocol. Since the other person also has these words in the memory of the chat history of his machine, the process can be automatically checked by iterative steps for each word and then concluded. The respective word is hashed, and the hash is fed to the unconscious ZK proof. This means that this new password has not been transmitted over the Internet.

The process is reminiscent of a comparison with a game of marbles. One side selects a marble from 32 marbles (these

240

correspond to the last 32 words in the chat). As a result of the conversation, the other person also has 32 identical marbles (or words) in their pot of the chat history. The iterative Zero-Knowledge process tests all of them automatically until the same marble has been compared and found on the other side.

It is a process that can also take place automatically from existing conversations - i.e., chat lines that have already been typed. Then the user does not click on one of the chat words, but the computer randomly selects one. Online friends have conversations: a personalized, automated process gathers information from such a chat session without the need to ask questions. Both partners are sure that they mean the same thing - without having said the secret and without typing it in. This can be referred to as automated freedom of interaction.

These hurdles of typing errors and misunderstood questions or commands to enter the intended and desired password right now only exist in the Socialist-Millionaire process, because the SMP is interactively related to imaginary passwords.

And now, with this proposal for automated freedom of interaction, the process can be expanded to include a non-interactive solution: Automatic, non-interactive, knowledge-free proofs are Zero-Knowledge proofs that do not require any interaction between examiner Alice or examiner Bob on the other side: Automatic Non-Interactive-Zero Knowledge-Proofs, also abbreviated as: ANI-ZKP).

The process does not require any interaction between participants in the chat, the underlying mathematical operation is an automatic one. If this process is successful, keys are derived and not transferred.

This method extends Cryptographic Calling to establish end-to-end encryption by another variant: Since it requires some detective work or playful testing of the other machine, which of the last 32 words (or figuratively: murmuring) lead to success, this idea presented and discussed in the Smoke-Messenger developer forum was also referred to as Marble Calling. Another design of an interaction-free, automated Cryptographic Calling (which has not yet been implemented on a code basis) has been presented with this idea of a marble machine.

It became apparent as early as the late 1980s that a common reference string between the examiner Alice and the examiner Bob was sufficient to achieve zero mathematical knowledge without the need for interaction[194]. It was not until 20 years later in 2018 that the knowledge was first described theoretically in an application under the name »Bulletproofs«[195], with which, using a logarithmic number (in the bit length of that range) of field and group elements, it can be proven that a specified value is in the range. An implementation was discussed for a library in the field of CryptoCurrency, which, however, used the ECDSA algorithm, which was no longer regarded as secure at the time of that proposal, and was therefore no longer so »bulletproof«[196].

The transformation to freedom of interaction in chat is new and arises from the discussion in the development work on the above chat and encryption application.

From a human point of view, the authenticity of a conversation participant becomes more sustainable when the conversation becomes more detailed.

Traditional zero-knowledge proof requires two or more people to agree on a secret, as in the Socialist-Millionaire Process (SMP).

This process is carried out with shared knowledge of the shared password, but preferably without prior context in the chat: In other words, both sides enter the place of their marriage without being asked, but neither ask each other in the chat, nor do they speak out the question where they got married because someone who overhears them could research or even know.

Human conversations during the chat, on the other hand, require context. The strength of a context-free, interactive, zero-knowledge proof compared to a context-rich, non-interactive, Zero-Knowledge proof, requires further investigations, including to establish authenticity. Which method is more substantial and safer from a linguistic point of view?

The automated process of Marble Calling in a messenger brings a lot of charm to the idea of promoting abstinence from key transmissions.

After all, the point is not to send a password over the Internet and thereby to become more secure. An investigation therefore does not have to take place between the interactive ZK and the non-interactive or also automated ZK, but between key transmission and non-key transmission.

And it also plays a role whether the proof was done interactively or automatically, not only in terms of security, but also in terms of convenience.

Juggerli Keys

Juggerli Keys are based on the Juggerknaut Keys and include an XORed public key. This means that automated, non-interactive zero-knowledge proofs have also been built into Messenger Smoke worldwide as the first blueprint of this concept. Juggerli sound like Sugar-li or as the Swiss say: »Zückerli«. Something sweet for the horses who do the hard work of the moving "Yatha-Rata" car of encryption. Because: public keys are known and can be converted into a password using XOR, which can be used for J-PAKE. Automated end-to-end encryption without key transmission, in Smoke Messenger - which is also described in more detail below.

These are new, promising game variants of symmetric encryption. Transferring an asymmetric (public) key indicates that end-to-end encryption is beginning. Transferring a symmetric key, as well. Continuing encrypted communication, resulting from the clear words of a context-rich communication on both sides - but not with third parties -, forming a transmission-abstinent key from it, and automatically checking and deriving this in the chat client, has a new, special quality of renewable end-to-end encryption and verifiable authenticity.

If, for example, you have to chat on a system that has been weakened by political influence and switch to this new method of Calling after the first few words, you have created a strong end-to-end encrypting multi-encryption.

The text that is to be sent through a channel of a weak system, possibly with broken end-to-end encryption, is simply encrypted again beforehand using the method shown above.

Attackers will then only find the double-wrapped cipher text - they will not find the attempt to transmit an end-to-end encrypting key because there was no key transport, but the new key was formed from one of the last chat words in the already encrypted channel. End-to-end encryption without key transport is the new credo: Super Secreto.

Trepidation of Memory
The Future of Cryptography will discuss in the Third Epoch further evolutionary steps: while Derivative Cryptography can dispense with the transfer of keys, further concepts and implementations (as in Messenger Smoke) creates an Amnestic Public Key Cryptography or one can describe it as a Cryptography of Forgetting (Trepidation of Memory).

With that, the private and public keys are only associated with each other in an initial moment. With Forward Secrecy, keys are derived, but not transferred, and public and private keys are no longer associated. Each person has a variety of keys that do not fit together but were generated in several points of a time process.

The process described below brings the status closer and closer to a state of a place and a time at which the original pairing of the two sides is lost. We call that: Trepidation of Memory.

The more a message from this point of time is timely ahead, the more both keys must be found and tried in a generated cloud of all possible keys. It's like a stuck in the fog to find the right private key to the associated public key. The pairing from the public and private key is lost over time, it is as if the memory is lost by trepidation, as it would be comparable to the amnesia of people ill with dementia.

In this, about the timeline-growing fog with numerous, temporarily generated keys, the right pair is to be found. Colloquially, in the discussion forums, in addition to a "Forgetful or Amnesic Public Key Cryptography", therefore, has also been spoken for simplicity from an "Andromeda Encryption". Andromeda Keys therefore have no assignment and will not be transferred.

Figure 34: Historical sketches for the development of "Forgetful or Amnesic Public Key Cryptography" with Andromeda Keys that are unbound

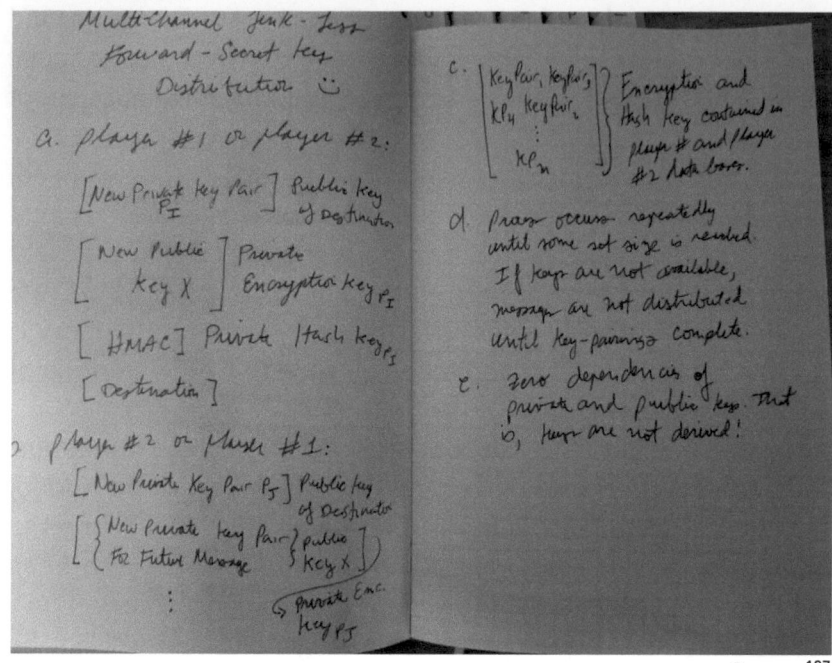

The following process of the concept is transcribed:

Forgetful or Amnesic Public Key Cryptography
Multi-Channel Junk-less Forward-Secret Key Distribution
(Trepidation of Memory)

A) Play #1 or Player # 2:
[New Private Key Pair - P1] Public Key of Destination
[New Public Key X] Private Encryption Key P1
[HMAC] Private Hash Keys P1
[Destination]

B) Player #2 or Player #1:
[New Private Key Pair – PT] Public Key of Destination
[(New Private Key Pair For Future Message) Public Key X] Private
Encryption Key PT

C) [Keypair, Keypair 3, KP4, Keypair 2, ... KP (n)] Encryption and Hash Key
contained in Player #1 and Player # 2 database.

D) Process occurs separately until some set singe is revealed.
If Keys are not available, messages are not distributed, until key Pairings
are complete.

E) Zero Dependencies of Private and Public Keys. That is, Keys are not
derived!

That means the keys are not derived. Derivative Cryptography
has evolved into an Amnesic Cryptography because of a
Trepidation of Memory in the course of a time history.

An implementation, as it would ideally be integrated in the
messenger Smoke conceptually, is the most complex part. The
concept is present. Every new message created a loss of the past.
The more news, the farther the condition is of the original fit, the
Big Bang. The more messages are sent, the less there is a clarity
into the past.

Figure 35: Historical sketch of the development of the concept for the loss of the original Public Key over time

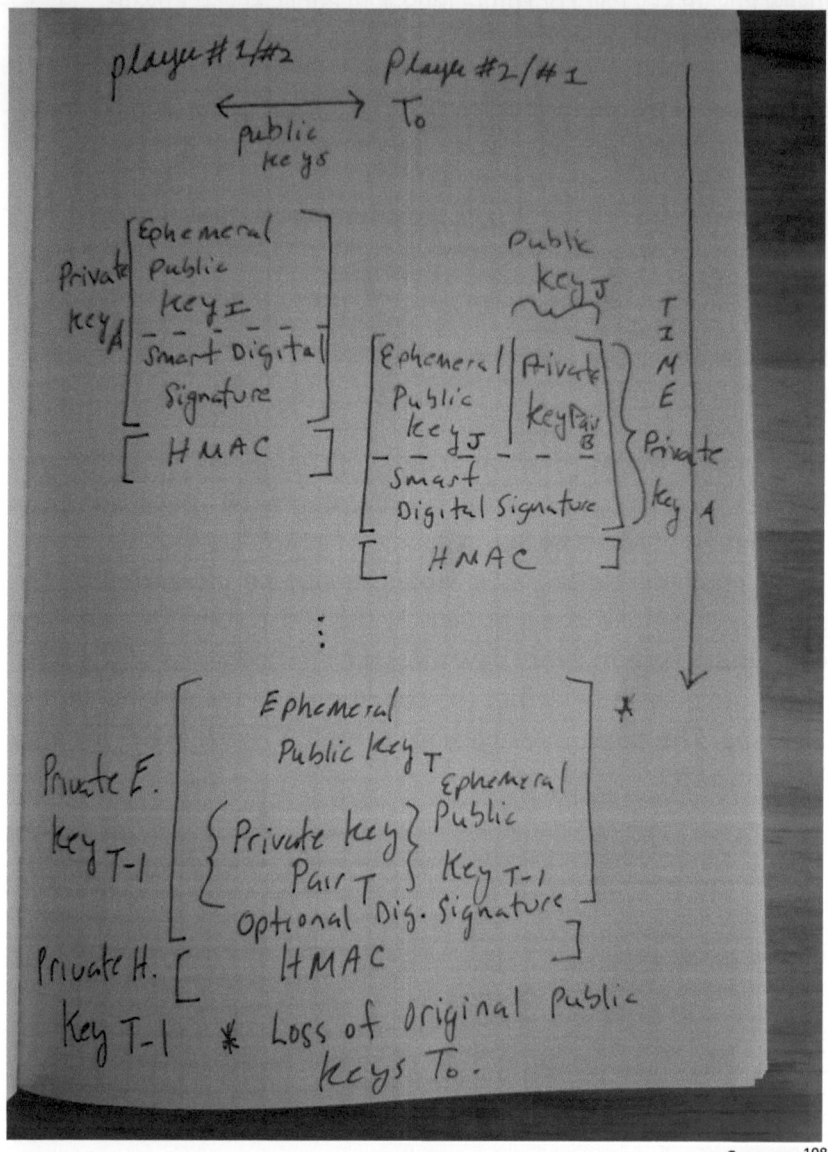

Transcribed the following course can be supplemented:

Player #1 / #2 <== Public Keys - T_0 (Timeline) ===>
Player #2 / #1

Private Key A
[Ephemeral Public Key 1]
[Smart Digital Signature]
[HMAC]

Public Keys
[Public Keys]
[Ephemeral Public Keys | Private KeyPair B]
[Smart Digital Signature]
===> Private Key A
[HMAC]

TIMELINE
...

* Loss of original Public Keys T_0 (Timeline)

Private Encryption Key T_1
[Ephemeral Public Key T
(Private Key Pair T) Ephemeral Public Key T_1
Optional Digital Signature
Private Hash [HMAC]

This establishes a slow evaporation of permanent keys in favor of temporary (ephemeral) keys.

Thus, the evolution of key management, which is described in the above shown graphic based on programmed clients of the past by the year 2021, can be extended to a future classification of the development steps, which applies to the Third Epoch of Cryptography and may also be discussed as characteristic:

(1) The goal of cryptographic calling was to equip two instances with new keys, using two partitions (see e.g., the two-way calling).

(2) In the next step of the evolution of Cryptographic Calling, Forward Secrecy was introduced. This generates temporary keys. Both development levels, the original Cryptographic Calling, as well as its successor, the Cryptographic Calling with Forward Secrecy, are unbound in terms of the random keys.

(3) The next stage of development is characterized by the examination of secret (private keys) generated by Forward Secrecy and Independence. This was described as Derivative Cryptography with its characteristics.

(4) The next evolutionary stage according to this is in the Third Epoch of Cryptography to maintain or find a pairing of private and public keys respective the two communicating people, that no longer requires the original mating of the two persons and their keys. This means the ancestry is no longer preserved.

New keys do not require any more ancestors - as is e.g., the case with the Double Ratchet method, in which the new key is generated from the message and the key of the previous sent data: Not only Fiasco Forwarding, but also Andromeda Keys in the concept of Forgetful Public Key Cryptography have created a successor to old-fashioned methods!

The fact that quantum computers are fairly well suited to break key pairs of public-key infrastructures (PKI) is now well known. This will also be the problem for electronic money such as e.g., the Crypto Currency Bitcoin: You can search for particularly valuable wallets, break the encryption and steal the money - especially in the blockchain where every transaction history is known. The new methods for new crypto currency networks are also known as: see McEliece encryption and see Echo network distribution. PKI intended in a »new direction«: If now with the forgetful cryptography and their Andromeda keys, the key pairs of a PKI can no longer be assigned to numerous private keys in the course of time to numerous public keys, and they no longer will be transferred, then this can establish a New Epoch in Cyber security.

7 DIGITAL AND CRYPTOGRAPHIC SOVEREIGNTY: NATIONAL, PERSONAL AND ENTREPRENEURIAL •

As seen in the previous chapters, it is not only about understanding encryption in its basic functions and using it, but also about understanding its current transformation in many functions and in the algorithms: To make the decryption and encryption processes more secure, the interplay of possible attack scenarios must always be taken into account.

Attack surfaces are reduced if users know how to use encryption technology correctly and if possible do not expose attack surfaces at all - that is, present them to the outside world.

We saw options for this not only with Steganography, but also with the protection of keys (using REPLEO) or with the making of keys invisible, in which they either do not appear in the channel or are sent as a whole swarm, the one true key blinded.

The use of your own servers, which may not even be visible at the ports, because they are accessed with a regular VPN connection and they are located behind a firewall, is a measure to put data less in the attack options of third parties (risk and opportunity or regulatory element of the unregistered telecommunication systems behind VPN ports, through whose encrypted channels cipher text is passed).

All of these mechanisms and approaches to increase security are ultimately related to the concept of sovereignty. It is important to know for yourself what you can do with encryption. It depends on having investigated the code of the open-source application for encryption, if necessary. It is important, if possible, to install and operate a server for telecommunication within the family and with friends. It is important to independently select the right hardware and software for protected communication for yourself or a company or even to produce it (as a nation). And in applied Cryptography, it is particularly important to detach yourself from potentially viewing third parties wherever we convert plain text into cipher text.

It is about striving for »digital and cryptographic sovereignty«: In the discussions of an increasing strategy of digitization, and also the design of Cryptography, this term for digital independence has developed into a central theme.

This vision with strategies to achieve sovereignty should not only be thought of on the macro level of countries and nations, but it also begins on the micro level with each individual person and trainee. There is also an intermediate level (so-called meso-level) of people in their groups such as organizations, at work or in the family: Everyone can ask themselves how independent am I with the group around me in the digital-cryptographic context?

According to a publication by the *Gesellschaft für Informatik* (GI), digital sovereignty in Cryptography is defined by the »self-determined action and decision-making of (1) individuals, (2) companies and other institutions and (3) entire states or transnational institutions such as of the European Union in the digital space«.[199]

So, what could be done, for example, to confidently shape these three levels with essential measures, especially in Cryptography of the Third Epoch?

Digital and cryptographic sovereignty at the state level
Every nation should become more independent of others, not only for reasons of security and economic success, i.e., become more sovereign in the cryptographic processes it initiates and directs.

This sovereignty is often mentioned or required in connection with national dependencies and monopolies of the technologically leading companies. It is about the economic monopolies of China or the USA, for example, and now also of the individual countries of the European economic area, it is about the freedom of municipal machines from the monopoly of the MS Windows operating system - and it is about state-initiated, national lighthouse projects as a unique selling point compared to other industrialized countries.

That can mean producing and providing your own and thus unmanipulated chips, operating systems or other digital services and offers, and it also means not (only) focusing on foreign nations that want to offer encryption methods and technologies, but above all to be able to design the cipher text using your own methods and technologies. This includes increased and regular checks on the security and processes of independent digital education at all levels, if this is not to be adopted by other countries or is based on participation in cross-national open-source projects.

The difference in quality in the field of practical and applied Cryptography remains to be analyzed continuously compared to other countries: the strengths and successes of companies, of open-source projects and of science in one's own country must therefore be brought to the public more strongly in order to be able to participate in cross-border exchange and competition to be able to assess the degree of independence in detail. Do we only notice in a pandemic that Europe cannot provide basic medical supplies such as respiratory masks? And only when we are discussing the compatibility of messengers, we notice which location or which university is developing or operating an open-source chat server itself?

There are also other aspects such as: How many teachers do we have with different focuses in this area? Which thematic focus centers are there and how many employees are there? Which cryptographer programs himself or is involved in a cooperation network for the creation of cryptographic tools and apps? Or how many programmers for encryption programs are trained each year? Which open-source applications are created or used in the professional and non-professional area in your own country? How is the educational canon at schools and universities on this topic structured in terms of content and time - and how is it promoted and updated by which groups?

Encryption and decryption are mutually dependent: if you want to decrypt, you must train the students in your country with such high qualifications that they also learn to encrypt from the beginning of their training - only then can a culture of decryption succeed, in which a state is so often interested.

The following applies to the state: promote its own production, its own infrastructure, and its own educational programs for a confident appearance in the cryptographic dialogue.

Figure 36: National distribution of (open source) cryptographic tools and programs

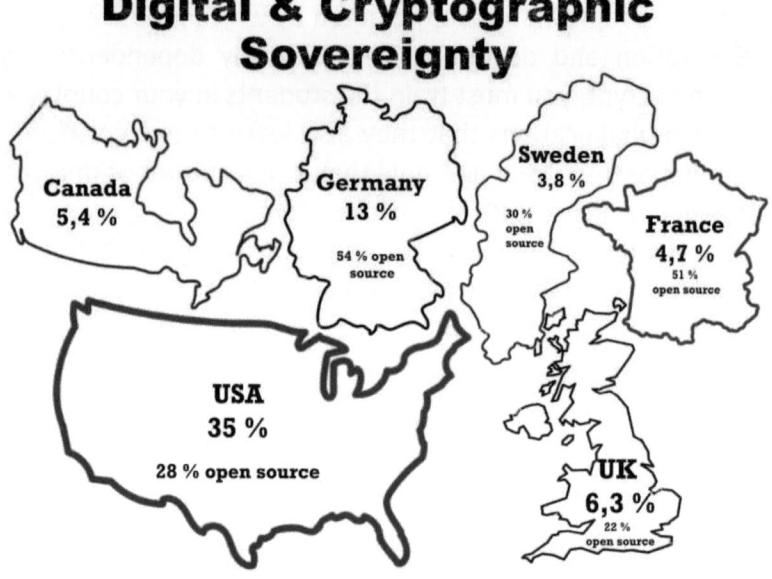

Digital & Cryptographic Sovereignty

Canada 5,4 %

Germany 13 % — 54 % open source

Sweden 3,8 % — 30 % open source

France 4,7 % — 51 % open source

USA 35 % — 28 % open source

UK 6,3 % — 22 % open source

Source: [200]

Crypto Wars & Crypto Competition: USA offers more than a third in the cryptographic market. In some European countries every second crypto tool is free & open source.

Digital and cryptographic sovereignty at the level of companies, organizations, and associations

Companies, organizations such as schools and municipal employers or associations are not only well advised if they implement data protection and security regulations accordingly, but also define a strategy for measures for encryption that are desired by organizational policy.

Previous models of a security assessment are often of a time in which encryption had no role in the Internet and in view of quantum computers. Accordingly, there is often no connection between encryption and a strategic goal definition.

For example, many trainees have learned over generations to enumerate the levels in the well-known security model OSI: from the hardware level to the network level, via transport routes to the level of the software used. In the meantime, it has been expanded to include additional levels for the strategy of including and assessing cryptographic processes.

Today, the SAM model can be considered, in which the aforementioned model is integrated: SAM stands for Secure Architecture Model and adds not only the encryption component to the previous model assumptions, but also, that strategies and policies as objectives are to be developed for it.

Figure 37: The Secure Architecture Model (SAM) according to Wake et al.

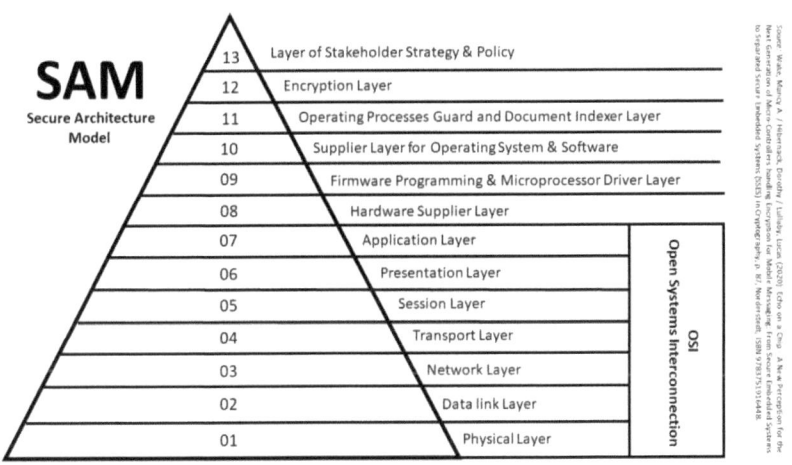

Source: [201]

The SAM (Secure Architecture Model) model expands the OSI model by adding additional levels of consideration to a total of 13 security levels. The OSI model (short for: Open Systems Interconnection) has so far consisted of seven levels for assessing security processes in IT security. Previous elements are incorporated into the SAM model. Above all, it is about the addition of the assessment level of encryption as well as the top level, to have formulated a strategy and policy for it. Companies and organizations can now use this model to describe and run through their processes and carry out a so-called SWOT analysis of strengths, weaknesses, opportunities and risks at every level. The results found can in turn be incorporated into the strategy and policy. The level of strategy and policy can therefore also be assessed and strengthened in a self-referential way and not only in comparison with other companies and organizations or by external analysts when using a self-evaluation.

Data protection officers in companies and organizations such as schools, municipal employers or associations are thus able to formulate and expand a strategy for the people, machines and electronic channels and data storage entrusted to them, and to merge it with other principles, like the no-plaintext strategy mentioned at the end of this volume, for example.

Digital and cryptographic sovereignty on a personal level:
A personal measure to achieve digital and cryptographic sovereignty can provide for a more active demand for training content that multipliers make available to contribute to the development of skills in the field of IT security through encryption - and thus also to one's own security. Inquiries have an essential stimulating effect, also for oneself.

In addition, users should better secure their own infrastructure, their home network, and their own devices. This can start, for example, with the use of a router of your choice (instead of the router of the provider of the line) and includes the choice of a secure password for this router.

Even if routers have built in a small firewall, this is by no means as secure as an additional firewall behind the router of the Internet connection (such as the firewall program PFSENSE on a small computer connected downstream of the router).

Devices on which cipher text is converted are often linked to the operating system manufacturer. These can send so-called »telemetry data« to their home. Updates and the monitoring of the machines by the manufacturers of the operating systems represent a major personal security risk today, since this third-party maintenance could be used to install monitoring software at any time, or programs that have already been installed can transfer texts and data.

Anyone who has set the boot manager of their computer to a simultaneous Windows and Linux installation - but so that Linux is booted first, will find in Windows mode, if the computer stayed on overnight, that Microsoft is installing an update executed independently and the computer booted into the Linux system after restarting. Today, users no longer have any control over the programs that are controlled by external providers on their own machines. Monitoring software such as a Trojan horse can potentially be installed in this way, with which passwords, keys or plain text can be extracted before and after the conversion. And on the smartphone, we do not even notice that a PDF or DOC file is only opened by an application if the central server of the app was able to upload a copy of this file and its contents.

Only with a Linux system do users have the updates for their own computer under control, since all changes have to be confirmed with a password.

Today, a firewall no longer has to protect against attacks from the outside, but against sending outs from within. This is a very original understanding of the term »firewall«, because it burns inside and not by attacks from the outside.

And how do users get more sovereignty with regard to a secure conversion of plain text and cipher text in Cryptography?

The conversion of the texts should take place on a machine in which, for example, a firewall ensures that no data packets or plain text can leave the machine unobserved, or, better still, a computer is used that is not online at all.

Even if a transport problem arises for the cipher text or the encrypted message capsule from an Internet-free machine to a machine that can then send the cipher text on the Internet, this is the safest way, to create an unobserved conversion of texts.

This architecture paradigm is briefly referred to as TEE, short for: *Trusted Execution Environment*. Users need a trustworthy environment in which the cryptographic processes, particularly those relating to plain text conversion that is worth protecting, can be carried out without the risk of copying.

The example of the Stuxnet Trojan shows that the TEE has to be so precisely separated from an online environment. This was specially developed for the sabotage of the Iranian nuclear program. To enrich uranium, the centrifuges with the material must rotate at a certain speed. As a Trojan worm, Stuxnet changed the speed of rotation on Windows computers and made attempts by the Iranians to enrich atomic material worthless for years. However, since the centrifuges' computers were not even connected to the Internet, Stuxnet was transferred to them via a USB stick.

So, if someone has set up a Linux machine without Internet to convert text and cipher text exclusively on this trustworthy and protected platform, the cipher text must be copied to another machine using a USB stick, for example Internet is and can then send the cipher text (or in the opposite direction to receive cipher text).

If you do not want to manually transfer the cipher text for each individual encrypted message capsule via USB stick, you can also consider a protocol change: For example, the Internet-free machine could be connected to the Internet machine that is then transported via Bluetooth in the hope that this protocol change will make remote access and injections of monitoring software from outside not so easy. However, it is not as secure as a complete separation of the TEE machine with a manual transport of the encrypted capsule, for example using a USB stick.

Under the keyword #GoTrusted has already formed a movement that uses devices for encryption, which were continuously not connected to the Internet. The trend of the security-oriented is therefore the second device: on this the message is encrypted, and then the encrypted capsule or the ciphertext is transferred to another device and pasted in the online channels available there. Uncomfortable Slow Chat - but secure!

It certainly sounds exaggerated, but if you want to define security as the standard, you must safeguard the TEE accordingly. It is comparable to an allergy: traces of allergenic substances such as gluten or nuts can trigger powerful reactions and therefore these must be strictly prevented by separation. A TEE machine, a private, trustworthy and secure computer environment, must always avoid online contact like holy water avoids the devil, so that it remains pure and unspoiled in its original state.

As a pioneer in Europe, the German federal states also demanded in a further act that providers of operating systems for PCs, laptops and cell phones, for example, be obliged to preinstall even further filter software: IT and media associations and even voluntary self-regulation institutions are sharply criticizing this in incendiary letters: age ratings for Youth media protection not in the browser or router, but as a filter directly in the operating system are »neither technically feasible nor feasible in terms of content: devices would have to reveal the age of the user« - and transmit anonymously via a software interface integrated in the operating system. This forced filtering interface can also be used for plain text monitoring, tapping cipher text and installing other state monitoring Trojans: Is the *German Youth Protection Act* (JuSchG) itself a Trojan, for total monitoring of all citizens with noble arguments in every operating system to introduce? Trusted Execution Environments will increasingly rely on Linux operating systems that are free of this type and that do not have the Internet or an online filter interface on their own device. Will there soon no longer be from state uncontrolled hardware that is online?

MS-Windows disables the operating system after some time if it has not been activated on the Internet, already today. The security considerations are thus further thought out than it is to be suspected.

The sustainability with which the German state is trying to get onto online devices in these times in order not to miss any opportunities in which Trojans can be pushed onto the devices is also shown by this law on the update obligation for providers of end device operating systems and apps.

The opposite of a »TEE« is a »DATA-SNITCHER« - snitching means to narc and was related to Twitter discussions as a term as Apple announced filter software on the devices to scan over the contents of users.

The Twitter user ›Change Your Mind‹ puts it: »If every American and Chinese phone is a spy-board, the must a TEE be free from the interests of these innovations? Digital sovereignty will become the next exciting topic: #DigitalSelf-defense, how some also call it. A ›package of measures‹ with teaching media skills in schools and (project-funded) offers for citizens is required to be able to assess the trustworthiness of computer equipment, as is the case with the training of the ›DigitalAngels‹ in the Women-Computer-Center (FCZB), for example in Berlin.

Figure 38: Personal checkpoints for IT security

CHECK POINTS	NONE	FIRST	SOON	GOOD
		PRACTICAL EXPERIENCE		
● VeraCrypt is used to encrypt the laptop.				
● A Linux machine is ready.				
● I regularly test an alternative.				
● A machine that has never been on the Internet is there for common private activities.				
● I can install my own chat server.				
● A keyboard protected by open-source is used for apps.				
● Plain text is not sent to the Internet.				
● I help to ensure that knowledge and all information are freely accessible.				
● I can generate keys with GPG or Spot-On.				
● I promote decentralization.				
● I protect my private data.				
● I share the strategy that learning with computers should be unlimited and complete.				
● I can install my own firewall like PFSENSE.				
● I have already created my own compilation of an open-source Android app such as the Messenger Smoke.				
● I used the SAM model for a security process and thought it through and described it with all levels.				

With the areas of interest, security orientation, personal skills and experience in the design of security-relevant measures shown in the table, an initial assessment of one's own digital and cryptographic sovereignty can be made.

Further personal cryptographic sovereignty begins with a curriculum or simply on an own initiative with testing apps, programs and tools: With which programs and open-source lighthouse projects should I start to encrypt - or with which tools do other pupils and students in international schools in partner-cities of the respective local school encrypt, so that we should get to know their methods and applications? - Some of these are explained in the next section.

8 APPS, PROGRAMS AND TOOLS – WITH WHICH LEARNERS LEARN, TO BECOME ENCRYPTION MASTER NO. 1 ●

The following sections on well-known software programs explain their use for increasing security on the Internet as well as their cryptographic aspects.

Not every program will be updated or developed over time. Some have a defined base of users and may no longer be or not yet as popular.

Even prototypes and the so-called »Early Birds«, which never lose anything in terms of their technical idea and architectural design, continue to mature or are likely to develop further as they are supported by schoolchildren, students, and learners or by the next generation of developers: The apps can be analyzed in depth, compared, and applied or even redesigned.

8.1   Hard disk encryption with Veracrypt ●

VeraCrypt is the successor to TrueCrypt and is used to encrypt the hard drive in the computer or the entire operating system. The program was originally developed by two programmers who were barely in the public eye, until they both suddenly withdrew from this project. It was suspected that they had to resign because they might have been asked to do so by state actors. Can this mean the software was too good? And government agencies have broken their teeth on hard disk encryption?

The last version of TrueCrypt 7.1a is still available on the net and works wonderfully. It is interesting that the developers, when stopping their project, also hinted at the fact that TrueCrypt 7.1 had weaknesses and should therefore no longer be used. This can also be a launched and therefore wanted or forced message so that this strong encryption in version 7.1a is no longer used.

Since TrueCrypt has always been open-source, the program has found a new home under the name VeraCrypt with a developer and cryptologist in France. A security check of TrueCrypt was also carried out when the project was taken over. Only minor recommendations were found, which have since been corrected. The program was not fundamentally called into question at the time, as is not the case today. In this respect, it can currently still be assumed that it could have been an intended strategic message that TrueCrypt 7.1 has weaknesses. Because any code can have potential, slight weaknesses and these are usually corrected in the next version.

The program TrueCrypt or today VeraCrypt has two essential cryptographic functions: It can also create a container with a size of several gigabytes, i.e., a file like »container.dat«, which is then encrypted and its own new drive, a new file path, contains. So, you can keep all your documents safe in it. The documents are unencrypted, but because they are stored in this encrypted container, as a cover, they can only be accessed with a password.

The second basic function is that you do not pack a path in a container file, but instead encrypt the entire operating system. The user then must enter a password when starting the laptop before the operating system even starts.

This is useful, for example, if company laptops are lying free on the passenger seat in the company car and are stolen after this invitation. However, when VeraCrypt is installed, the thief cannot start the laptop without knowing the password and the data cannot be read even with the hard drive removed.

Figure 39: VeraCrypt – Container Creation

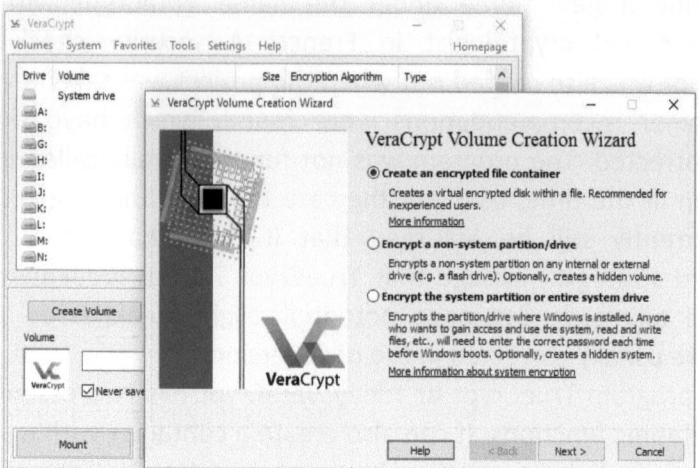

Source: [202]

Veracrypt is increasingly being pushed back when used in companies by a similar function in the Microsoft Windows operating system: Bitlocker. Windows also only starts with this Bitlocker option if a password has been entered.

Linux operating systems also have their own encryption for the data partition.

Companies would therefore no longer have to install VeraCrypt additionally. However, it can be assumed (of course and presumably) that government agencies (or at least Microsoft as the provider itself) can easily open Bitlocker at any time. However, it is not possible for the simple laptop thief to overcome this encryption - and for the IT departments it is again convenient not to have to install any additional software.

For private users, however, the situation may be different. They may want to use secure software and open-source software for this purpose: VeraCrypt is therefore the means of choice for private use cases to encrypt the laptop or the hard drive of a computer.

In the meantime, VeraCrypt has also been audited by the *German Federal Office for Information Security* (BSI): »The investigation of VeraCrypt did not identify any serious weak points«.[203]

How users encrypt individual files with other applications - instead of entire paths, operating systems, or hard drives - we will come to later. After all, users essentially want their files to be encrypted when they store them on a data carrier or in the cloud, for example, or when they send text with a messenger. So, let us first look at communication programs in the following: the messenger.

8.2   Smoke Crypto Chat: Mobile McEliece-Messenger ●

Smoke Crypto Chat Messenger is an open-source software application for the Android operating system.

The Smoke Messenger is considered to be the world's first mobile messenger to introduce the McEliece algorithm in the field of chat messengers for mobile devices. This means that the messenger is protected against attacks from fast quantum-computers thanks to this particularly secure algorithm.

In addition, the application established the so-called »Fiasco Forwarding« with its Fiasco keys, which offers greater security than is available with other messengers, e.g., with the double ratchet method (see WhatsApp, Omemo, Signal, etc.)).

The messenger is also compatible with Echo encryption, which can use multiple encryption techniques.

And fourth, with Smoke, the so-called »Juggerknaut Keys« have been established, which no longer have to be transmitted on the Internet, but are derived on both sides.

The file transfers are based on end-to-end encryption with the Steam protocol (TCP-E), which also dispenses with the sending of keys and reliably transfers the file across several intermediate stations.

The renouncement of uploading the own telephone number or the telephone numbers of friends from the contact book, the connection to an open-source server, as well as the use of your own or exported/imported keys, and thus also the simultaneous use of the application on several devices to be taken for granted with Smoke.

The important criteria of the *General Data Protection Regulation* (GDPR) - such as no upload of phone numbers or friend lists - are therefore met and differentiate this open-source messenger from the commercial ones. It is therefore ideal for further development in own projects for school and municipal or organizational purposes, for which the GDPR should be considered.

Regarding selected functions and characteristics in detail:

Chat via the McEliece algorithm: The Smoke Messenger uses the McEliece algorithm with several different moduli, i.e., selection variants: Smoke supports McEliece-Fujisaki[204] and McEliece-Pointcheval[205] via the BouncyCastle library.

The Pointcheval adaptation is a module based on the work of *David Pointcheval*, who has worked as a French cryptographer and experienced researcher for many years at the National Scientific Research Center CNRS (*Center national de la recherche scientifique*). There he heads the computer science department and the Cryptography laboratory at the French university »*École Normale Supérieure*«.

The other two McEliece modules in Smoke Messenger are two *Fujisaki-Okamato* conversions, based on the work of two researchers of the same name at NTT Laboratories in Yokosuka-shi, Japan. The NTT research and development laboratories identify themselves with the vision that technology should become such a convincing part of society there that the population remains unconscious through its presence - in other words: this technology will become a matter of course[206]. Accordingly, the two researchers are better known among experts and tend to avoid the public.

What you have devised in your modulus adjustment for better implementation of the McEliece algorithm and is now available as first programming in the mobile McEliece-Messenger, actually has the potential to be based on NTT's vision of being a messenger technology, which users can use easily and naturally without realizing that they are using a very modern model project technology that is much more secure than that of many common applications.

However, since it took twenty years until the McEliece algorithm (1978) was theoretically expanded with these modules (2002) and it took another twenty years until such a module was implemented in a mobile messenger (since 2016), it it will now hopefully take less than decades for this messenger technology and its source code to find widespread use in further follow-up and development activities. Or like VeraCrypt may be analyzed or audited in a timely manner, e.g., by the *Federal Office for Information Security* (BSI), if this algorithm is considered to be the most secure technology that we have currently against computers with high performance capacity.

Finally, the Smoke Messenger also contains a particularly future-proof Super-McEliece Modulus as a fourth variant, which works with particularly large constants in the encryption (m=13, T=118).

At the same time, the Smoke App also offers the RSA method with strong keys for encryption. The mathematical highlight is that users with the McEliece algorithm can also chat with those who are still using the RSA algorithm.

Sufficient research is given for the next generation of students to study this program of applied Cryptography extensively, including its source-code, which *Casio Moonlander* published as a textbook[207] with annotated technical notes. Because the application is much more than just a chat: it is an Android Echo software application that unfolds further cryptographic and protocol-related functions such as key management or a Cryptographic Discovery function with its counterpart, the SmokeStack server. Through Cryptographic Discovery, servers learn to forward encrypted packets to the appropriate mobile clients without providing battery-intensive data responsibility on the client side.

Multi-encryption and other features: The messenger is compatible with the multi-encrypting and therefore particularly secure protocol of an Echo server, in which the encrypted message is ultimately transmitted via HTTPS. The dispatch is thus secured again with a self-signed SSL/TLS connection. Sending via HTTP listener or server also remains possible (in non-TLS mode).

Messages to friends who are offline are cached in what is known as an »Ozone-mailbox«, which can easily be set up in the SmokeStack server with a term such as »Alice«. The cryptographic keys take care of the rest.

Fiasco Forwarding: A particular strength in Smoke Messenger is given not only by the McEliece algorithm, but also by the methods of end-to-end encryption: Users have numerous options thanks to the implementation of Cryptographic Calling: to store an own password, or to have one derived, or to switch from asymmetric encryption to symmetric encryption.

With the Smoke Crypto Chat Messenger, the so-called »Fiasco Forwarding« with its Fiasco Keys has also been established as a further form of Cryptographic Calling: Up until now, only one key was transmitted per online session with the earlier Jabber /

XMPP encryption (so-called »Off-the-Record« method (OTR)). In the more modern process, the Messenger Signal used a separate key for each message or derived it from the key of the previous message (so-called »double ratchet« method, see also: Signal- or Omemo-protocol encryption).

In this respect, the Smoke Messenger now represents a higher, third level of security with Fiasco Forwarding:

After OTR (one key per session) and double ratchet (one key per message), the next higher security level is the Fiasco Forwarding protocol. With the Fiasco Forwarding key method developed in Smoke Messenger, a whole handful of keys are generated for each message. These Fiasco Keys are collected in a cache. Then they are all tried in turn for decryption. As a result of the temporary key - as with all forwarding - the message is therefore deniable in relation to the permanent keys. The permanent keys, on the other hand, are always associated with the user (as a basic chat key) and first establish a secure connection through which the other temporary keys are then sent.

The permanent keys are therefore not subject to temporary use - and thus also no »dress for the moment«, as is the model of the clothing company »New Yorker« for young fashion - according to which you should keep reinventing yourself in fashion at every moment. *Cryptography for the Moment* à la Fiasco accordingly always keeps sufficient keys available for each message with the Fiasco Keys of Fiasco Forwarding. Or you call it, as the German population often put it in times of the corona pandemic when hoarding toilet paper: »Stocking makes sense and, by the way, it has always been«.[208] - So may it be a few more rolls of keys?

Juggerknaut Keys: Another type of end-to-end encrypting key in Smoke Messenger are the Juggerknaut Keys already presented in the front section. These keys are derived from a password

271

permanently stored on both sides but are not transmitted over the Internet. They correspond to the concept of the Secret Stream Keys in the Encryption Suite Spot-On.

The mathematical method of a Zero-Knowledge proof calculates on both sides how the Juggerknaut Key is to be defined and checks whether the respectively compatible key is present on both sides. This means that keys are derived by means of »juggling« (a test mechanism reminiscent of juggling, as the so-called »J-PAKE« method is also described above). Because of the abstinence in key transmission, a key can no longer be intercepted while on the move.

With this method, in which the keys via Fiasco Forwarding are not transmitted, a large number of times per message, one can speak of *Volatile Encryption*[209] as we have seen. They are temporary keys, which, like feathers in the wind, can hardly be grasped or, similar to an inconspicuous imagination in Steganography, do not even appear or blossom at the edge of the road.

It is therefore made extremely difficult for attackers to break this particularly secure end-to-end encryption. Neither with just one end-to-end key for the respective chat message, nor with regard to the initial encryption through which these Fiasco Keys are sent - or in the case of the Juggerknaut Keys: are not sent - the encryption can be decrypted become. More than an initial key is required, temporary keys are required and ideally a handful or even more of them per chat message - which are ideally free of transport: neither over a permanent channel nor over a temporary channel.

And as an alternative, there is also the option to use asymmetric McEliece encryption that is currently and will probably not be broken in the future. The cipher text is also recommended to be tap-proof.

In addition to the Juggerknaut keys, the automated and interaction-free Juggerli keys were also explained in the first part of the volume, which can automatically produce end-to-end encryption using XORs of a public key that is verified via J-PAKE.

Interaction with an open-source server: The open-source chat app Smoke is technologically ahead of many other applications thanks to these implementations and also works together with an easy-to-manage server: SmokeStack is the name of the server for Smoke and is also an app for Android. With SmokeStack, chat servers were brought into uncharted territory, i.e., on a mobile device in the pocket of every pair of jeans: e.g., a smartphone or tablet with Android. So far, chat servers have required large Linux or Windows machines. Thanks to the simple HTTPS listener, however, the chat can be set up on any smartphone or Raspberry-Pi computer.

In addition to SmokeStack, the listeners/servers for the Spot-On, Spot-On light applications and the GoldBug Messenger server also work compatible, as they all include a chat based on HTTPS. GoldBug Messenger has therefore also integrated the Smoke & SmokeStack Android APK installation file in its installation file from version 5.2. As is also prescribed for open-source applications, the source code is also included, since these applications are compatible (interoperability) and open-source.

A good example of the often-required interoperability of the applications with one another based on the well-known HTTPS protocol of the so-called »Echo server« used here for chat.

A model project establishes further perspectives in the Third Epoch of Cryptography: The Smoke Messenger with its paradigm of Fiasco Forwarding and associated (numerous) Fiasco Keys or Juggerknaut Keys, which made us abstain from key transmission on the Internet, and in particular the first establishment of the more than 40 year old theoretical McEliece algorithm in the now applied Cryptography and open-source programming in a mobile messenger, as a pioneering project and *example par excellence*, makes a decisive contribution to the design of the *Third Epoch of Cryptography.*

Did *Neil Armstrong* say when he landed on the moon: »One small step for a messenger - one giant leap for mankind«? - In any case, it wasn't *Louis Armstrong*! - but: *Casio Moonlander.*

Further developing fork projects of the Smoke App, whose repositories can be found at Github, Gitlab and Sourceforge, from the community of developers will certainly be able to contribute their potential to offer a simple and intuitive user interface in some places for further user friendliness.

A model project that will be put into further use by other developers. The project prototype is now considered complete. Young developers can take up the open-source project and develop it further independently or use it with a financier in organizations individually. An Italian development team has already started a Swift port for the Apple operating system.

From a research perspective, Smoke and SmokeStack are the applications that every school class can use to learn how to compile an Android app with Android Studio, and scientific research in this applied Cryptography will certainly further develop and deepen the previous results on algorithms and protocols.

8.3 Spot-On – Well-known suite for encryption •

While students in the field of computer science can hardly avoid getting to know and use the Smoke Messenger as a model because of its innovations in a teaching unit on McEliece or algorithms in general, a further software is also referred - more related on the desktop area or on the small Raspberry-Pi computer - to the repertoire of the learning students in technical subjects as well as in Cryptography: It is the Encryption Suite Spot-On (at Github and Gitlab).

Spot-On is currently an extremely modern and elaborated program to learn applied encryption and its methods and represents a fundamental project for applied Cryptography. The software is in the meantime at many universities included in usage and learned in basic and preparatory courses, so-called »Tutorials«, and also scientifically analyzed which advances were and are associated with this application in the field of applied Cryptography. The students give lectures on key words such as: Exponential Encryption, Cryptographic Calling, SMP authentication, Echo servers, multi-encryption or the Secret Stream Keys (as a parallel development to the aforementioned Juggerknaut Keys) and other cryptographic contexts.

As a »suite«, i.e., equipped with several functional modules, the software covers the most frequently used processes by users on the Internet: communication with friends via chat and e-mail, searching for websites, end-to-end secure transfer of files and finally the conversion of files and texts into encrypted cipher text. Everything in a suite with corresponding tabs, as it is known from the earlier Netscape Communicator or, with regard to the tabs, from every web browser today. Spot-On is or the functions of Spot-On are to be seen as a *Suite of Cryptography*: The developments of Spot-On cover numerous cryptographic functions and innovations, as well as usage requirements on the Internet.

Basically, everything that is sent with and in Spot-On is encrypted. There is a group chat in the style of the well-known *Internet Relay Chat* (IRC), which is available to all participants who know the password on the basis of symmetric encryption: Only those who know the password can read the chat.

The chat encryption of direct friends initially uses asymmetric encryption (with one public and one private, permanent key each as part of the PKI (*Public Key Infrastructure*)). With Cryptographic Calling, which can send new temporary keys for the chat at any time, the encryption can also be changed to symmetric encryption (with a password known to both sides).

Also in this program: The chat with a friend can also be secured via a so-called »SMP« according to the *Socialist Millionaire Protocol* (SMP). Both partners manually enter the same (and previously agreed) secret word on each side. For example, it could be the place where both, Alice and Bob, got married: Honolulu. The mathematical SMP proof (again a Zero-Knowledge proof) proves that both have entered the same password without the Honolulu password being transmitted over the Internet. If the mathematical proof is true, it can also be assumed that the person at the other end of the line is really who they say they are. Alice or Bob. Authentication took place.

And now: With this password, further keys for end-to-end encryption can here also be derived; these are the Keys of the »Secret Streams« already mentioned in detail above, which also behave abstinently with regard to transport.

In the e-mail area, further corresponding keys are also available in the Spot-On application, which are separate from the keys for chat or those for other functions. An e-mail in this program can be a regular e-mail via IMAP / POP3 mailboxes, or a P2P e-mail, so that no central or external service outside the circle of friends is required. There are again three methods available for this purpose, which are described in more detail below in the section on P2P e-mail.

Another major innovation has been introduced by Spot-On in this context - chat via e-mail server. Long before other applications such as the Messenger Delta-Chat or the GoldBug Messenger or the Spike Messenger explained or took over this function. This protocol standard for chat via e-mail is described with the POPTASTIC protocol and is based on the classic mailbox name POP3, which exists alongside IMAP. E-mail is fast enough to present a chat via the e-mail server in the user interface.

The main thing about the chat via the POPTASTIC protocol is that it is always encrypted. Administrators of mailboxes see POPTASTIC-Chat or the Delta-Chat application that this method has been adopted as a welcome plagiarism in the open-source world from the messengers Spot-On and GoldBug and (based on GPG) then also in the area of mobile devices popularized only encrypted cipher text in the mailbox.

Another essential function of the Encryption Suite Spot-On is the function of maintaining a URL database for searching websites, which will be explained in more detail below.

Of course, Spot-On can also encrypt individual files (e.g., before uploading them to a cloud) or send these files encrypted directly from Alice to Bob. For this purpose, so-called »Magnet-URI« links with cryptographic values have been redefined. Anyone who knows the link can load the file.

Numerous cryptographic innovations and processes are associated with this software, which must be explained in more detail elsewhere, since the overview of individual encryption tools only deals with the essential and selected functions of the programs.

Anyone who wants to read the contexts of graph theory, the Echo protocol, Cryptographic Calling or POPTASTIC chat via e-mail server and numerous other process innovations in Cryptography should therefore refer to the technical documentation[210] and a manual[211] for Spot-On as well to the explanations of the routing information in encrypted networks, which are now »Beyond Cryptographic Routing«[212] - that is, cryptographic tokens can manage without predefined routes.

8.4   Rosetta-Crypto-Pad
– With conversions to a conversation •

The *Rosetta Crypto Pad* (RCP) takes its name from the Rosetta Stone, which has been in the British Museum in London since 1802 and is still a major attraction in collections from across the British Empire. It is the fragment of a stone tablet with a priest's decree, which is carved in three blocks of script (hieroglyphics, demotic, ancient Greek) with the same meaning. So it helps to translate or convert the individual languages into the readable language.

The Rosetta Crypto Pad does exactly this: It converts plain text into cipher text. It is part of the aforementioned encryption suite and is used as a separate window application[213].

Using the copy/paste function, users can insert plain text, convert it into cipher text and copy the cipher text out again. In this way, other channels without encryption such as those of other chat messengers or forums on the Internet can be supplied with cipher text.

The Rosetta Crypto Pad has no connected channel, i.e., it does not send any cipher text or keys automatically, i.e., it is not connected to the network. Users have to insert or copy the text themselves.

The special thing about the pad is that it does not work with a password for the cipher text but uses asymmetric encryption. This means that the user must first exchange the public key with the other person. After all, everything else can be done without manually exchanging keys.

The pad uses two encryption standards: GPG on the one hand: if GPG is installed on the machine (under Windows it is the GPG4Win program), Rosetta functions as the user interface and uses the already installed key management for GPG.

The other method is to use the pad with the keys generated in Spot-On, here the Rosetta key (based on the Libgcrypt library or the code for the McEliece algorithm). Since there is now again the choice between McEliece, NTRU and other algorithms, the cipher text can via Rosetta also be made particularly secure compared to RSA or Elgamal encryption. Or other, weaker channels, can be improved with it.

If you cannot or do not want to connect your machine to a server at times, you can convert texts at any time using the Rosetta Crypto Pad. It is therefore also suitable as a »Trusted Execution Environment« (TEE), possibly on a further computer not connected to the Internet as described. Should the pad be on a machine with Internet, the private key is protected against uploading because there are several private keys to increase complexity.

The Rosetta Crypto Pad is thus a kind of clipboard for text: Before the message is sent in another application, the plain text in Rosetta is converted to cipher text. Thanks to McEliece and the openness of the source, not only private users achieve professional encryption of their communication, but also professional users of encryption, regardless of their occupation: the text to be sent can now be encrypted at any time in a qualified manner against attacks from super-computers.

Cryptomator is another tool with similar functions as the Rosetta-Crypto-Pad, but with symmetric (AES-256) instead of (a selection of) asymmetric encryption. It was created as an open source and therefore welcome parallel or derivative development (from 2014) after the Rosetta Crypto Pad (2013). Both algorithms used, AES-256 and McEliece, are today considered secure.

8.5   GoldBug Messenger – Show us your GUI ●

The GoldBug Messenger can be found as open-source software in numerous download portals. His name is reminiscent of the short story of the same name, »The Goldbug« by *Edgar Alan Poe*, about a so-called »cryptogram«, a golden small insect bug and the adventures of three friends.

The icon picture of GoldBug is a gold-yellow-black-ringed Maya the Bee with the slogan - »Diligent Bee 4 Crypto« - means: A studious bee in the field of Cryptography.

This application also uses the protocol via HTTPS and can connect to any Echo server or kernel. This makes it clear that this program is just a different, *Graphical User Interface* (GUI) to the Spot-On encryption software. All the aforementioned functions such as chat, e-mail, file transfer or web search are therefore also available in the GoldBug Messenger.

The so-called »MELODICA« button, implemented in the first versions, goes back to this messenger, which accompanied the beginnings of Cryptographic Calling in 2012/2013 until this button for the renewal of secure end-to-end encryption was no longer required in the course of the expansion of the methods for Cryptographic Calling in the software.

MELODICA is the acronym for MULTI ENCRYPRTED LONG DISTANCE CALLING. This means that the end-to-end encryption can also be updated also via different stations while a network connection is in operation, and the encryption supplements and secures the packets sent via HTTPS multiple times. As seen, encrypted cipher text is created with the encrypted Echo capsule, and this is sent again as an encrypted capsule through an encrypting TLS or HTTPS channel.

With this design of asymmetric encryption, a Cryptographic Call can add another level of symmetric encryption with a password or replace asymmetric encryption with symmetric encryption (still within the TLS or HTTPS channel). With end-to-end encryption, it should be possible to play as easily as possible, like on a piano keyboard: The symbol of the MELODICA button consisted of the black and white keys of a piano. The introduction of Cryptographic Calling was thus accompanied in this messenger with the symbol of piano keys.

In addition to the options of this scale of possibilities, GoldBug also offers its users a built-in keyboard, in case a (e.g., infiltrated) hardware keyboard could not meet the desired security standards.

Figure 40: Goldbug Messenger with virtual Keyboard

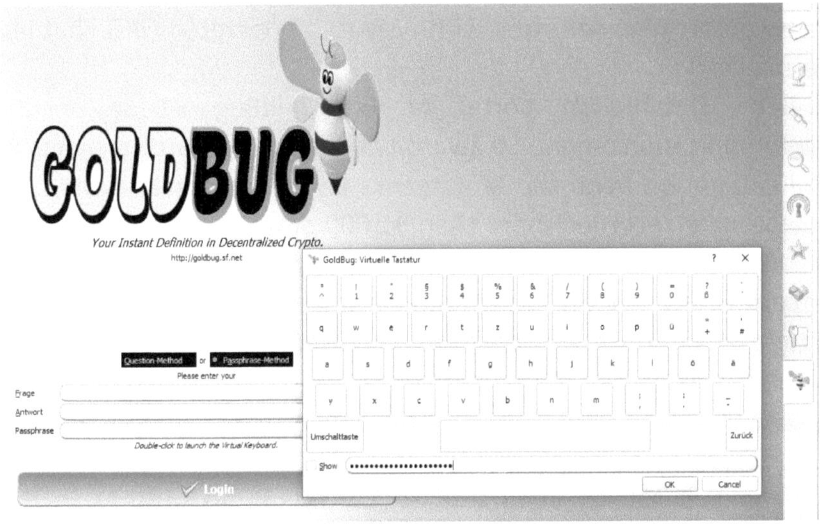

Source: Screenshot of the Login-Page of the GoldBug Messenger.

The figure shows the login page of the GoldBug Messenger, which requires a login password to start the application and to decrypt the hard drive data for this application. Since passwords can be accessed via physical keyboards, a double-click in the password field enables a virtual keyboard specified by the application to be displayed. This means that the password can be entered by clicking the mouse on the virtual keyboard. A potential eavesdropper would not be able to recognize the letters, but only individual clicks of the mouse.

The control elements of this messenger have been reduced in many cases for the sake of simplicity or can be further hidden in a minimal view, but the program functions are based on the extensive software mentioned above.

In 2015/2016, this messenger was subjected to an audit[214] in the »Big-Seven« study and compared with six other open-source and encrypted messengers. GoldBug was judged to be safe, reliable, innovative and promising in this audit. Among other things, this study also presented the POPTASTIC chat via e-mail server as the present practical model in more depth and in addition to the technical documentation, from which and whose ideas the Delta-Chat client emerged a year later, and which is now performing very well with easy to be operated GPG chat via e-mail server.

The Datamation portal ranked GoldBug #1 in secure communication among 50 award-winning open source projects in all categories. With the Majorgeeks download portal alone, the messenger recorded more than 31,000 downloads, about half as many as Telegram or Teamspeak for the desktop there. Digia, the manufacturer of the programming environment Qt, with which the user interface was created, has taken GoldBug into its show case gallery as a Qt model project.

At the same time, this does not mean that the cryptographic processes in it intuitively fall into the lap of a user without learning. It can be compared to the numerous buttons in the cockpit of an airplane. Pilots also have to learn what to set up for a flight with it. Without a school working group, a student tutorial or practical tips at a crypto party, the Qt software GoldBug will be particularly accessible to the resourceful teams despite minimized buttons in the graphical user interface. Because that was the quintessence in the GoldBug short story by *Edgar Alan Poe*: Treasure hunt is tricky and requires a few friends as a team.

However, if you have an idea and interest in the Qt development environment or the Cryptography behind this user interface, you may not fail in a learning method through trial and error in self-study and may also be able to convey own independent experiences to others. The source openness of GoldBug allows teachers and learners in the field of Qt application development to create their own user interface with relatively little effort, which sends their chat to a self-set HTTPS server or to an Echo kernel in the port of friends. Today, Cryptography is also applied programming in a team of at least three.

8.6   Delta-Chat: POPTASTIC popular •

The exchange of messages via chat or e-mail is increasingly merging under the term »messaging«. Some programs now also convert e-mail messages into chat messages, i.e., they offer comfortable chat using the POPTASTIC protocol via the decentralized e-mail servers based on IMAP or POP3. The chat can also be encrypted.

Delta-Chat is one such messenger, which implements chat via e-mail servers and ties in with the good practice of the POPTASTIC protocol in Spot-On and GoldBug Messenger.

The Delta-Chat-Messenger is also available for other common platforms. Since it operates based on e-mail, it can be used both, as an e-mail program for unencrypted messages and for encrypted chat, if the other party also uses the Delta-Chat client.

POPTASTIC in the client area of Delta-Chat has great potential to offer an alternative for popular messengers and monopolists such as WhatsApp: With every user of Delta-Chat, cipher text is promoted in e-mail inboxes and a text exchange is made safer.

The encryption automatically exchanges the public key between two users via e-mail with the function called AutoCrypt. Unfortunately, Delta-Chat did not use the full GPG standard, so that GPG keys that have already been generated externally cannot (yet) be imported.

The MOMEDO study[215] compared the Smoke-Chat-Messenger with the Delta-Chat-Messenger, mainly with regard to the integration of own and public servers. Smoke requires its own chat server (SmokeStack) and Delta-Chat mostly uses public and free e-mail providers such as Gmail, Outlook, Yahoo or GMX and the web.

Since these often offer the service free of charge, they will certainly no longer do this if cipher text is sent over it. Then the messages can no longer be searched for keywords related to the advertising industry. Of course, one can also set up an email server for your own group, class, or family on an own Linux machine or even a Raspberry-Pi computer and run Delta-Chat with this server. A separate server is always necessary if the free providers no longer want or are allowed to tolerate cipher text in the mailbox.

The MOMEDO study comes to the result that a separate chat server using SmokeStack (including key management) for Smoke might be easier to install than an IMAP/SMTP server. It could also be a recommendation for Delta-Chat to address e-mail mailboxes hybrid, e.g., to add an Ozone mailbox like in the SmokeStack next to IMAP.

Another interesting future perspective for Delta-Chat is in file sharing[216]. Delta is building a network of trust (Web-of-Trust) to befriended users via e-mail, so that a search for or a transfer of files can take place.

The RetroShare software described below can give an example here: It can also be used to load a file from friends over several hops (so-called Turtle Hopping protocol[217]). For example, an MP3 music file could be forwarded to multiple e-mail accounts. The implementation in the RetroShare client via the various hops of the individual instances is, however, without end-to-end encryption.

When transferring files in Smoke Messenger - via the there implemented Steam protocol[218] - the file transfer is encrypted according to today's standard and is also encrypted over several hops. Steam is a universal protocol that is not tied to specific clients; it is also possible to use Steam to send cipher text or the cipher text of an encrypted file to a SHH client, which is then collected and decrypted at the port.

File sharing (and thus web browsing à la Tor) in Delta-Chat could certainly make this messenger quite popular. Back then, Samsung's first Android smartphones also had an app for downloading music MP3 files. These were loaded from the social network V-Kontakte. It can be assumed that at that time Samsung and Android from Google had a massive influence on the market with this method with ordered programming so that they became so big. The devices with the free music file download were selling like sliced bread.

Delta-Chat would also be a good starting point for an application that sends the cipher text in steganographed images via an e-mail server - instead of text messages.

But even without these three conceivable development goals of Delta-Chat, the implementation of Ozone mailboxes, file sharing and web browsing using the Steam or Turtle Hopping protocols, or the sending of steganographed images, Delta-Chat or also his derivative Spike-Chat are today Messengers, which are already doing well with six-digit download numbers at the usual download locations. Popular POPTASTIC with potential.

8.7 Silence - A SMS-App with End-to-End-Encryption •

SMS it is still often used for messaging. As with e-mail, the servers are always there. The SMS client Silence.im solves the problem that SMS does not have any encryption as standard. If the chat partner also uses the Silence app and a key has been exchanged, the chat is encrypted end-to-end using the double ratchet method known from Signal or WhatsApp.

In principle, you can of course also insert cipher text using copy and paste from another conversion tool such as Rosetta. Silence is open-source and is available in the F-Droid Store as well as in the Google Play Store (which may not be recommended).

8.8 Conversations App: The old dinosaur in the moult? •

For the sake of completeness, the tradition that is associated with innovation should not be left out or be unmentioned.

Many have grown up with Jabber or today the XMPP chat protocol with its decentralized and also inter-operable (federate-able) servers as an established standard in numerous clients.

However, this chat technology must be seen as an established dinosaur today. XMPP was developed in an unencrypted environment that hardly meets today's requirements. A manifesto[219], a written declaration of vision, was required to swear all servers and clients to encryption. Only a few clients and servers have complied with this until today. And a lot of plain text is still being sent over this infrastructure.

The first approaches to encryption for XMPP were intended in the off-the-record (OTR) protocol with only one key per session. Today's update in the Omemo protocol is more adapted and has the status according to the double ratchet method with a statically derived key per message (as it is also implemented in the Signal protocol). In purely quantitative terms, however, both methods do not come close to the level of *Volatile Encryption* in Fiasco Forwarding (numerous keys for each individual message). And they also do not achieve the status of the Secret Stream Keys (in the Spot-On Messenger) or Juggerknaut Keys (in the Smoke Messenger), for which no key is transmitted at all (through the SMP process or J-PAKE-Juggling in the Zero-Knowledge proof).

XMPP messengers are neither on the technical level of the times, nor are they in an architecture that is encrypted as a whole or that could easily implement modern methods of Cryptographic Calling. After all, there are currently no messengers with this dinosaur that implemented the McEliece algorithm.

The Conversations app is still a well-known and relatively nice messenger for Android, which is open-source, but after a while requires a legitimate fee for both, the installation and the use of the chat server.

The Omemo encryption used has developed from the old OTR encryption and as described, is still based on the double ratchet algorithm and the personal eventing protocol (POP, XEP-0136). The Curve25519 / Ed25519 algorithm, which is not safe for quantum computing, is used here. According to the specifications of the NIST for elliptic curves, this is also classified as critical under these conditions[220].

XMPP chat servers that an administrator can install themselves and support encryption are Prosody and Ejabberd. For technically inexperienced people, they can probably only be installed with appropriate specialist knowledge. Furthermore, these servers do not include any key management.

In his FOSS-ASIA presentation, XMPP developer *Daniel Gultsch* listed eight of thirty common XMPP servers without Omemo encryption according to XEP-0384-with the following comment: »The problem with the fragmented XMPP eco-system is that it is out of date There are servers that do not support these latest

287

encryption enhancements. Part of the solution is to make the problem visible«.[221] So, is it hopeless to teach the dinosaurs to dance?

XMPP comes from a time that is no longer modern and is a hopeless case for encryption if, instead of plain text, cipher text from a conversion is not copied into the XMPP client elsewhere. Delta-Chat is definitely the better client for laypeople and for those who are curious about more up-to-date procedures and want to learn encryption, the Smoke Messenger is the richer client, although the user interface may not be nicer.

But as said at the beginning: in a training we will continue to hear many people who have learned »on XMPP« for years to come. That sounds like working in (or on) the (cole) mining industry in the past. But those times are over. And we will meet far too few teachers who decline the status quo of innovative clients, never mind compare them. So, let's leave XMPP to the archaeologists, because some people give advice: Inter-library loan (of a book) is the meaning of life: every now and then read something new and unknown or have it flown in with FedEx and DHL, stay up to date well into old age. There is bound to be something newer than XMPP or its alternatives to discover soon.

Already in 2016, Twitter user ›Moxie Marlinspike‹ wrote that the ecosystem was moving and is moving[222], and three years later the user ›Cane‹ even demanded: »Let Jabber/XMPP finally die«! - XMPP is not up to date with encryption technology that it is a metadata sling, a patchwork quilt in software integration and a dinosaur[223]. that is hostile to innovation. The servers also let too much plain text through - something why the strategy of some computer clubs rejects these servers. And the eco-system is not up to date. He may be right; engineers should always be up to date with the latest technology.

With XMPP there are many structural reasons mentioned above, why this architecture can no longer become modern with regard to encryption! Renaissance of the dinosaur excluded?! Now we know what the Greek *deinós* means: tremendously terrible.

8.9   Hacker's Keyboard:
Prevent taps in plain text ●

Hacker's Keyboard is an app for an Android keyboard. Since plain text entries can be monitored via the operating system or smartphone's own or pre-installed keyboard, an open-source keyboard app should always be used. Central servers can be contacted just for the suggestions for completing entered words and they will record everything. A monitoring Trojan does not therefore have to be installed as a background program, i.e., as a so-called »daemon«, but it is sufficient to modify the keyboard application alone via the manufacturer without being noticed.

Other open-source keyboard applications can be found in the open-source FDroid store, such as the BeHe keyboard or the AnySoft keyboard, which, however, asks for authorization to complete contacts and wants to get to know the friends list in the private phone book. The Hacker's Keyboard, on the other hand, has been created by several developers on a non-profit basis and has therefore also been checked in the source code. The app protects against a central operating system back-door: the tapping of the written texts directly via the keyboard. Anyone who does not want to afford a second machine for inputting and converting plain text to cipher text, which is detached from the Internet, can at least protect himself from potential reading along with his texts using an open-source keyboard. Since Apple, unlike Android, does not allow installation from third sources, these users only have to switch to open-source smartphone operating systems such as UB ports from Ubuntu Touch or

Sailfish OS or Android Linux without a connection to Google services.

8.10 Federation without accounts: Echo Chat Server & XMPP Server & Matrix Server & Co●

Server software plays a much bigger role than the beauty of a chat app, at least from a technical point of view. Even if an intuitive experience and the design of the user interface are decisive for the popularity of a messenger at an early stage. It is comparable to buying a car: the color and shape of the car belong in a sensible balance to the horsepower and technological innovations under the bonnet. But the DeLorean will not run without a flux-capacitor. So, let's take a look at a few selected and open-source servers with brief notes on encrypted chat.

Signal server: While the Signal messenger is well known and popular, the associated Signal server is not really open-source and has not yet been mirrored by anyone on an alternative IP. Alternative Signal servers therefore hardly exist or do not exist and must also lead to reprogramming on both sides in the synchronization with the client (e.g., with regard to the SMS registration). In addition, this messenger also requires the phone number to be uploaded, even if it is hashed: If you know all phone numbers, you can also assign them in encoded form.

It can also be assumed, as already indicated at the beginning, that the Signal Messenger should act as a collecting tank for all those who are dissatisfied with Facebook and WhatsApp. Then Signal would be a Trojan horse. However, it cannot be proven. But: All of these companies are interested in operating an SMS server that guarantees users' phone authentication. And: What is the interest of Signal's donors in offering the same encryption and authentication method as the messengers in the Facebook group? A side channel for uploading the private key could at least be better assessed in the open-source Signal if its private key is not uploaded by other apps.

But how can it be that Signal for its server infrastructure just recourse to companies with dubious level of data protection in the US - like Google, Amazon, and Microsoft - and is considered safe?

Moritz Tremmel and *Sebastian Grüner* assume in an analysis: »With the Signal server, it would be difficult to install a server-side monitoring interface if the server only receives encrypted and metadata-reduced data from the app anyway. Changes to the app and server are also publicly visible. In the case of the app, so-called »reproducible builds« (means: post-produced compilations) can also be used to determine that only the published code is in the app.«[224]

They do not consider that the server can keep a different compilation, e.g., with plugins or additional code, than in the public repository and that other channels and apps upload the data from Signal than the Signal app itself. And so, the Signal server that is actually running remains a »non-reproduced build« on the analysts' computer at home. Especially since the server code of the signal server has not been updated for a long time, a different code must be running on the servers. The Signal Eco-System could therefore not be used for a long time and developed further - only public inquiries[225] induced an update of the public server code.

XMPP server: The plain text processing XMPP servers, with the exception of Prosody or Ejabbered at the moment, belong to the dinosaur age, as described for the conversation client. For a technically trained person, the installation processes can certainly be understood, for learners and consumers John Doe, however, the installations do not open up by itself. There is hardly a trace of server-side cryptographic management either.

291

Matrix server: Matrix servers also require professionals who are paid by institutions. Larger organizations can afford this, but neither schools nor classes, families, associations or clubs. The architecture of the server and client is also very well-tailored to one another, accounts are required and there is also a high level of dependency on specifically integrated software libraries during compilation. The matrix client called Element is graphically appealing, but so far hardly anyone has set up a server at home for the family in no time at all. The manufacturer offers server support as a chargeable service for organizations. That also means: It has to be complicated and made dependent on procedures and libraries and with regard to compilation specifics, so that the customer does not manage it himself and is happy to pay for it. A so-called »accountless federation«, i.e., the interconnection and networking of several servers and their clients, without the need for specific registration obligations for users, facilitates the operation of a sovereign chat infrastructure, but is not the case with matrix servers either.

Joachim Selzer, who has already been in charge of organizing several dozen crypto workshops on digital sovereignty and cryptographic fundamentals, has been giving lectures on this topic for many years: most recently at the Global Media Forum or the annual meeting of the Research Network, here in particular to train journalists in the protection of informants through encryption.

There he not only conveys the participants with a wink to his Twitter profile, in line with his credo, that it is not always a good idea to print out the entire Internet right away, but also the philosophical-religious question in the workshops: »To be or being Offline « - after all, he also acts as a voluntary data protection officer for the Protestant church in his local church district.

He recently explained in an RBB radio interview[226] that many people ask him how to operate their own chat server, but here even technicians have to realize: »The installation and operation of an own matrix server requires enthusiast qualities, since these servers are not quite - let's say - layman compatible « - here the idea would be easier to put into practice, to familiarize oneself with the breeding of carrier pigeons!

Since even in organizations, IT departments no longer employ technicians, but have to mutate into purchasing departments that are no longer allowed to face the responsibility of operating servers themselves (even if these were easy to install), these buyers prefer to conclude contracts with external third parties, future scapegoats, in the case that a server should not work. Outsourcing to the cloud and to external IT service providers instead of the so-called »on-premises« design of the server »on your own sheet metal« is the educational perspective testimony to the fact that you are no longer allowed or able to cook in the server room yourself? However, as much as technicians would like to set up their own servers, they are often not allowed to do so because of the decisions made in commercial management structures. The question about IT security and freedom in companies, buy, rent, or make themselves, has long been decided. And that starts with the external communication servers that promise the formation of internal »teams«.

Element, the open-source application for the matrix server, has been temporarily removed from the Playstore by Google. Is it the start of a wave of cleansing of decentralized, sovereign servers and their applications? Not many servers for chat applications can be installed by the users themselves at home. Matrix servers are still part of it, even if it is more difficult to get them up and running than other servers. Since Element became more popular as a messenger but is not subject to central control because of decentralized servers, it was excluded from the playstores. This also shows the users' dependence on the market power of the smartphone manufacturers or the manufacturers of the operating systems and thus also the providers of the app stores. And it is a hybrid power: monopoly power meets state power. Neither of the two is interested in decentralized servers. The state power tacitly grants the monopoly power the cleaning of decentralized servers, because it is in the interests of both that citizens do not operate sovereign telecommunications systems, i.e., chat servers, with the applications of their smartphones. Behind this is the interest in completely monitoring communication and limiting the proliferation of servers. After a few days, the Matrix apps were approved in the App Store again, as »extremely offensive content«[227] was found on their standard server by Google and could now be removed. So decentralized potency played no role. Really?

At least the power of the monopoly owners becomes clear. This example shows that they not only rate content, but also channels. Agency-journalist and specialist lawyer for digitization and security *Hendrik Wieduwilt* therefore sees the app deletions and app censorship as well as Trump account locks as the beginning of a post-modern internet[228], because not only the state demands structures, transparency and personnel for opinion management from the Internet corporations. Internet corporations and public platforms are thus showing more clearly than ever before who is in charge of the digital public when the going gets tough: not a social movement, not even the state, and not an immune head of state either the person with the nuclear codes, but them, the corporations. Have they now become a kind of fifth power? - according to this statement, this is a question in the area of the postmodern Internet.

Echo server: Echo servers have already been described as simple HTTP or HTTPS servers that are available for programming with Java or C ++ for numerous operating systems, as well as for a small Raspberry-Pi computer or a mobile Android Device.

A technically oriented litmus indicator can therefore consist in preferring a chat server not only if it is easy to install and use, but also if it can process cipher text on a Raspberry-Pi computer - i.e., where low machine capacity is required.

While users often only look at a simple, intuitive usability of the chat program, and those interested in technology are still trying to find out which encryption is used; a central, not to be neglected focus is rather on a chat server, which is open-source, easy to administer, networkable (federate-able) and, in particular, cryptographically equipped, ideally also supports in key management. And: can also run on a micro-computer.

It is a simple, practice-oriented litmus test to ask someone who represents a particular chat program, often with religious fanaticism solely on the basis of the app, how we can install the appropriate chat server ourselves or how we can learn it. The training objective »chat server installation« should be part of the regular final examination of technical training and university degrees or a compulsory subject of computer science in school in order to be able to install a communication server for encrypted communication yourself.

However, we will only achieve this goal if each school sets up its own chat server for the school classes and selected teachers and IT administrators are available and trained in each school.

If bets are made that out of ten computer science teachers from ten different schools in the context of a hackathon with the 10 best students from the computer science class of the respective school, there is not a group who can set up their own chat server from the above-mentioned providers for their own school within a workshop just lasting several hours?

The market for open-source messenger applications is extensive. Why shouldn't every school run its own server and messenger? One cannot imagine a more optimal topic than a learning program in the field of information technology, computer science and digitization. An individual Right to Encryption in the messenger should also strengthen a School-Right to Federalism, so that a school can opt out of the ministerially prescribed educational clouds and central IT offers in order to pursue its own educational paths in the IT architecture, for example to learn about and use own messengers and their servers.

Ultimately, in the focus of a further grain size, it leads to the question of whether a YouTube tele-college can be as centralized as WhatsApp, so that a local college of teachers can be rationalized away? The initial question, how schools organize their internal and digital communication structures, starts with a commitment to self-chosen chat server software and corresponds to the question of the extent to which teachers put their own teaching materials and (are allowed to) bring in their own didactics into a (virtual) classroom. If we do not, is a nationwide video from YouTube canned just as good as a ministerially prescribed messenger or server for all schools?

A simple criteria overview that has to be worked out can help to compare chat servers in order to find such a chat server installation at the local school, which could regulate communication with each other on the next class trip.

Figure 41: Sample template for a learning task »Criteria-based chat server comparison«

Criteria / selected Chat server software	Easy to to install/ administer	Crypto-Functions such as key management are available	Open-soure	networkable & federate-able / without accounts	Easy to compile / instructions available
BigBlueButton					
DHT Servers					
Echo Netcat/Socat					
GoldBug Server					
IMAP / POP3					
Jitsi					
Matrix					
OwnCloud					
Signal					
SmokeStack					
NetCat & SoCat					
Spot-On					
Spot-On Lite Serv					
Wire AWS					
XMPP Prosody					
XMPP Ejabberd					

Source: [229]

Further research will analyze the topic of chat server software and how it works in more detail. There is an urgent need for further research here. School classes in IT lessons can also explore this topic in a practice-oriented manner by installing a chat server in each year and documenting the experiences and / or comparing them with the previous year's classes.

Figure 42: Smoke Crypto Chat Messenger

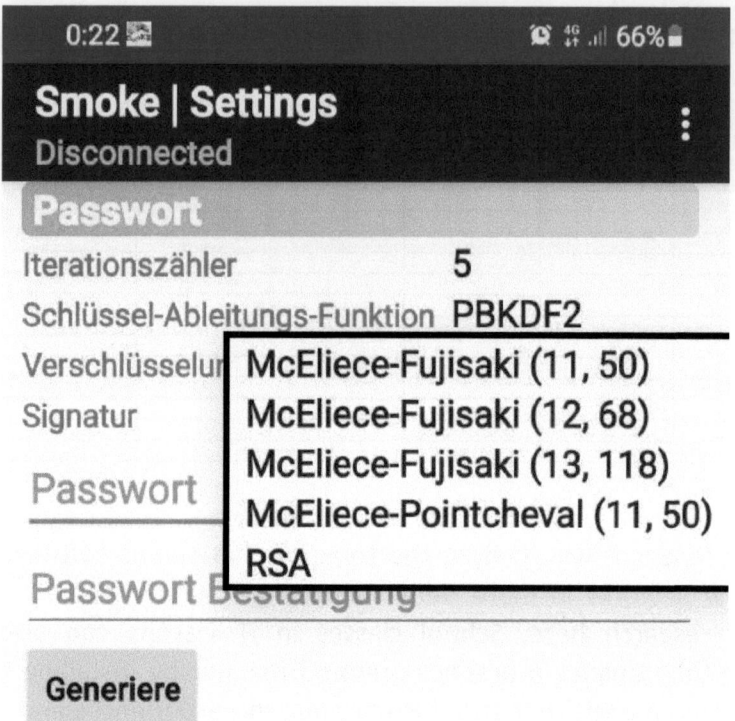

Source: [230]

The Smoke Crypto Chat Messenger is an ECHO software application not only for chat, but also for further exploratory cryptographic functions and is considered the world's first quantum computing secure Mobile McEliece Messenger. It has three McEliece implementations according to Fujisaki respective Pointcheval and a super-McEliece implementation with high key values. With its open-source server Smokestack, it harmonizes as an encrypted messaging solution on the Android operating system. Implementation on the Apple operating system in the SWIFT programming language is in preparation by an Italian developer group. All transferred and stored data are highly encrypted. Chats with RSA keys are thanks to appropriate mathematics and implementation compatible and inter-operable with chats from McEliece keys. The Messenger is considered a training and evaluation project par excellence for the age of the Third Epoch of Cryptography and is usually tested by school classes as Messenger in practice lessons (https://f-droid.org/de/packages/org.purple.smoke/).

We are guided by at least four questions:

(1) First, can I install the open-source chat server myself (compile it, if necessary, but at least: administer it)?

(2) Second, can the chat server for the size of a group to be defined be installed on small computers such as a Raspberry-Pi or on a mobile Android device?

(3) Third, can the chat server also manage cryptographic keys and cipher text, e.g., cache the cipher text for offline friends?

(4) And fourth, how can several servers without registered accounts be interconnected (federated)?

8.11 Netcat & Socat: Terminal-commands as Telecommunication system? ●

The HTTPS server and the matching, encrypting Echo protocol, which relate to the named clients, have nothing to do with the Echo, which is defined in a so-called »RFC« memorandum (short for: Request for Comments). Nevertheless, with RFC 862 there is also a definition that mirrors everything as a reflector server and outputs what comes in again. Just like an Echo. This should therefore also be of interest with various chat protocols based on HTTPS. Especially for the encrypting Echo protocol. Echo-862 meets Echo protocol. For this purpose, the Socat function (instead of Netcat) can be used as an Echo server and Netcat as a client. The setup takes place via a few command lines.

Socat Echo Server (listens at TCP-Port 1234):
```
socat -v tcp-l:1234,fork exec:'/bin/cat'
```

Netcat Klient (connects to Server-IP at TCP-Port 1234):
```
nc serverip 1234
ncat -e /bin/cat -k -u -l 1234
```

-e means: it executes / bin / cat (to mirror back what is typed).
-k means a keep-alive that it is still lurking after every connection.
-u means UDP.
-l 1235 denotes the port 1235.

QTerminal, which can be found on Github, is a terminal with an attractive Qt interface that can also be connected to an Echo server as a simple chat command line.

The opening of such a reflector or mediator as a server on the command line, which connects two clients, is probably the simplest way to think of a server, e.g., with the HTTP(S) chat protocol, or with end-to-end encryption to be distributed to several devices connected to the server and made readable. How could Netcat and Socat be understood only as a telecommunications system? This Echo Service 862 is a tool from May 1983, almost a time before any Democratization of Encryption and almost a decade before the publication of PGP/GPG (Pretty Good Privacy or Gnu Privacy Guard), as well as any intention to amend telecommunications systems for end-to-end encryption. And ultimately, it's just a simple mirror or repeater that harmonizes with selected chat clients.

8.12   RetroShare:
What was Turtle Hopping again? ●

RetroShare is an encrypting, open-source chat and file transfer program that is strong at finding and downloading files from friends' shared repositories. Since all connections to contacts are encrypted and only made to defined (trusted) friends, a so called »Web-of-Trust« is created. This enables to go beyond own contacts when searching for and transferring files. In this way, the databases of friends and their friends, and in turn their friends, are addressed. And so on, up to seven hops.

This describes the so-called »Turtle Hopping«[231], as it has been described at the beginning of the turn of the century by *Petr Matejka* and *Bogdan Popescu* with *Bruno Crispo* and the IT professor *Andrew Tanenbaum* at the Free University of Amsterdam as a model for the Gnutella network or as a way out of the peer-to-peer file sharing crisis. *Andrew Tanenbaum* was best known as the developer of the Unix-like Minix operating system and as the author of several standard works on various topics in computer science.

With RetroShare, this architecture was built into this encrypted friend-to-friend network.

Encryption-based Turtle Hopping transforms a peer-to-peer (P2P) network into a friend-to-friend (F2F) network, i.e., the connection that a node establishes is no longer directed to an unknown peer, but to a known and trusted friend.

Because: Anyone who connects indiscriminately to an unknown peer and its IP address without encryption respective without this trust always runs the risk of meeting a lawyer at this node. Then the data transfer could be analyzed and as has often happened in the music industry over the years, examined with a copyright prosecution.

So far, every user in RetoShare was bound to their IP address with the GPG key and could also be found in the above-mentioned Distributed Hash Table (DHT). After the publication of the Echo protocol, RetroShare has now adopted a more or less similar procedure and placed an additional level of keys over this static (already encrypted) Turtle Hopping network. This means that although it is connected to an identifiable IP and the GPG key, further temporary keys are then generated on this basis, which are no longer linked to the IP address and can therefore be used independently, e.g., for forum posts. So, there was an Echo there too: In this respect, a few years ago, RetroShare, similar to this protocol, implemented temporary keys that were not linked to the IP address as a superimposed network or identification mechanism for messages. The »Beyond Cryptographic Routing« paradigm was adopted here based on this.

From the very beginning, RetroShare has been a comprehensive network that gets bigger the more friends you add - and these friends do the same. As already mentioned, it also has cryptographic specifications: for example, no end-to-end encryption or even Volatile Encryption is provided for a file transfer. If you want to share your music files with other friends in a searchable manner, you will also find extensive download options here in the friends' files. These are cryptographically secure as long as the direct IP connections are actually only made to trusted friends. And if all others in the download chain or in the network fulfill this promise of trust. The security thus relates to point-to-point encryption, i.e., each intermediate station will unpack a file to be transferred after the download and pack it again with encryption before the further upload. Since everyone trusts everyone, this is considered safe.

In addition to chat and file transfer, RetroShare also has an internally referring P2P e-mail and forum system. Anyone can open public or private forums for defined participants and post a message in them with an anonymous name. The message can be in plain text or, if, for example, Rosetta is used for a previous conversion, also in cipher text.

A less developed alternative to RetroShare is the »Alliance P2P« program.

8.13 Get four mailboxes from friends without human number identification: Institution, Care-Of, Ozone and BitMessage ●

In addition to Retroshare's internal P2P e-mail system, there are four other distributed and cryptographically supported e-mail systems that not only do not require a central server but are also interesting in terms of protocol and Cryptography.

P2P e-mail will come to the fore when publicly accessible e-mail inboxes without SMS authentication or identification with the identity card can no longer be received anonymously - even if at this point the churches may be surprised that the initiation process, when a young person receives an ID card or a telephone number for the first time, could be more important from a state security point of view than the first communion or youth consecration from a religious point of view. The telephone number identifies us all, as does the identity card. And US citizens ask themselves in well-known IT forums why the telephone number is not equated with the nationally unique social security number in the USA - because here the social security number has the function of a general personal identifier, as there is no general reporting requirement to district governments.

In Europe we only know such a personal identification number for taxes or for the purpose of recording the age groups in voluntary work or in the military. But it can already be assumed today that the USA maintains lists of all telephone numbers assigned worldwide and the associated persons. After all, all the phone numbers are on WhatsApp or have received a text message from Facebook. A new WhatsApp function is now expanding this recording service to include biometric features: If you want to access the WhatsApp web or the WhatsApp desktop app, you first must approve the registration using your fingerprint or facial recognition on your smartphone. The function will be activated automatically on Android devices that use biometric authentication systems. The same applies to iOS devices from iOS version 14. And: the registration cannot simply be deactivated. If you want to switch off biometric authentication, you must deactivate the entire biometric authentication system of the smartphone.

The following applies in Germany: The introduction of a number for humans followed only a few weeks after the European amendment described at the beginning of this book to restrict end-to-end encryption[232]. Each and every German is therefore no longer provided with a lifelong personal identifier only for the tax office, but the legislature decided to introduce this number for humans also for other purposes. The tax ID is to be used as a uniform identifier in all administrative areas at federal and state level. The resistance from data protection agencies remained unheard. Expanding the tax ID to many other government areas has already given the interior ministers the Big Brother Award, the negative prize for data protection officials. This number for humans, also known as the friendly citizen number, is another epoch-making step in a society that is controlled by computers and algorithms. Counting every person with a number is considered by many to be not worthy of the person. Human dignity is touched with a number for humans.

The systems of the state will soon no longer be able to process people by name, but only by their identification numbers in the lead. And this also touches a dignified image of human beings.

Will we have to carry out compulsory processes based on the number in the near future and have to estimate the potential of great harm based on the number for humans? Assessments from science, from the data protection authorities of the federal states and even from the Scientific Service of the German Bundestag itself had expressed doubts as to whether such a uniform identification for human within electronic systems is even constitutional.[233]

The project for a personal identification number in the Federal Republic of Germany was rejected as early as the 1970s, because the Legal Committee of the German Bundestag determined in 1976 that »the development, introduction and use of numbering systems that enable uniform numbering of the population within the scope of this law, because of a lack of legal basis is inadmissible«.[234]

An identification number for the entire German tax system was introduced 40 years later after the personal identification number (PKZ) in the German Democratic Republic (GDR) on July 1, 2007 - but only for the purpose of collecting taxes. To implement this, each residents' registration office submitted to the *Federal Central Tax Office* (BZSt) every citizen listed in the registry at the end of June 30, 2007. Duplicates have been eliminated.

Indeed, a municipality can sing a song about the fact that the address data of citizens are manually imported into each office because there is no common address directory and so numerous duplicates, and incorrect spelling are created.

With the human identification number based on the newly created law, it is now technically possible to link more than 50 different state databases and registers with each other: This ranges from the population register, radio fee, school registration, issuing certificates to vehicle registration. Anyone who brings this data together not only receives a congruent data landscape in the administration, but also a very precise picture of a person's living conditions. Even with a census, it may make sense to be able to name each person clearly identified. Finally, all German soldiers, those doing community service and members of the administration in the Bundeswehr and the *Federal Office for Family and Civil Society Tasks* are provided with a personal identification number. This is made up of the date of birth, the first letter of the surname and a five-digit number, of which the first three digits indicate the registration area.

So far, however, there was no personal identification number or a common identification feature of people for overarching administrative processes allowed. From 1976 until recordation and usage as tax identification in 2007, it only took another 14 years until the functional purpose of tax identification was converted to human identification in 2021, with which the offices can now address all official processes relating to human dignity.

The data protection officer of the State of Saxony, *Andreas Schurig*, tried to prevent the conversion of the tax ID into an identification number for every citizen, i.e., this number for humans or personal identification number, with the argument: there is a risk that extensive personality profiles will be created. There are also reasons in history to reject such a personal identification number: »In the GDR, a comprehensive personal identification number was introduced at the beginning of the 1970s, which was used to control the population«.[235]

As chairman of the German data protection conference, *Andreas Schurig* is not only a mathematician and data protection expert, but also a studied theologian with a philosophical-theological background.

The ecclesiastical context in particular seems to require an active position on the number for humans, because the paradisaical »Garden of Eden« as the epitome of the unity of Humans with God and the access to the eternal fullness of life in the »Tree of Life« (Gen 3:22 EU) is not only possible lost through the fall of man, in which the human being henceforth begins the story of the mortal between birth and death with the animal »fur dress« (Gen 3.21 EU), but also characterizes a fall into sin when this fur is now provided with a numbered label. Today one would say: tattooing or »chipping« an electronic capsule under the skin.

It remains to be seen how *the German Federal Constitutional Court* evaluates the granting of a unique number for people in the case of a lawsuit. People are worthy to be addressed by a name and, if necessary, by their date of birth, and not by a mere number to identify the person.

Because: Not only the personal number in the former GDR plays a role historically, an understanding of values and law that rejects this number for humans is also because of the even more distant German history: The National Socialists murdered people because they belonged to certain groups recorded in registers and directories.

In addition, in the then darkest time of Germany, people got a number tattooed on them, e.g., in the Auschwitz concentration camp by the tattooist *Lale Sokolov*: It was only after the death of his wife Gita that *Lale Sokolov* decided to tell his story 50 years later to an acquaintance, author *Heather Morris* who wrote the gripping true story from his memories, stories and her own research: The tattooist from Auschwitz - *Lale Sokolov*. Lale was born under the name *Ludwig Eisenberg* on October 28, 1916, in Krompachy (Krompach), Slovakia. On April 23, 1942, he was deported to Auschwitz, where he was given the prisoner number 32407. Lale was only able to survive this madness in Auschwitz by making numbers out of people: after barely surviving a typhoid, he became the main tattooist of the camp, not in the end because he spoke several languages and quickly learned how to do it in order not to attract attention and to survive with it. *Lale Sokolov* had to stick the five-digit numbers in the forearms of countless fellow prisoners - the symbol for the unimaginable atrocities of the Nazis. Its history was marked by a struggle for survival. His wife Gita (born 1925) died in October 2003 and Lale in October 2006, the book was then published in 2018 and shows how a number for humans was thought of by the National Socialists.

The social psychologist *Erich Fromm* also describes in the case of *Adolf Eichmann* how a socialization into administrative thinking, which turns people into numbers, can generate the type of organizational person who can not only be related to the time of that time, but also as a symbol for us all sees: »The Eichmann case is symbolic of our situation and has a meaning that goes far beyond what its accusers are dealing with in the Jerusalem court. Eichmann is the prototype of the organizational man, the estranged bureaucrat for whom men, women and children have become mere numbers. He is the symbol for all of us.« [236]

During the time of National Socialism and the Second World War, *Adolf Eichmann* headed the »Eichmannreferat« in Berlin. This central office of the *Reich Security Main Office* (RSHA, with the abbreviation IV D 4) organized the persecution, expulsion and deportation of Jews and was jointly responsible for the murder of an estimated six million people in Europe, which was largely occupied by the Nazi state. In May 1960, he was kidnapped from Argentina by Israeli agents and taken to Israel, where he was tried in public. He was sentenced to death and executed by hanging on the night of May 31st, 1962.

Who, when counting people, counts on people's lives as in the case of *Adolf Eichmann*, as if living people were numbers, shows how feelings have frozen into ice: It is not humane and dignified to give people numbers. In 2013 the German city of Pforzheim published a commemorative publication on the euthanasia crimes committed by the National Socialists against people from Pforzheim with the title: »Names, not numbers«[237].

So, should people continue to be marked more with their name than with a personal identification number, an administrative identification number or a number for humans? For example, with the date of birth and then the name: »19X1-01-01-Tenzer-Theo«? Or does it make no numerical difference if this is a 16-digit number instead of a textual character string?

And should today's civil servants feel bad as an organizing person to create, to administer and to dealt with it? In this respect, it cannot just be about technically achieved efficiency or clarity, or about a historical responsibility, but about the dignity of the human being, not to mark humans with a number. This can not only be a legal issue, but also has to be an ethical one. Numbers for humans are therefore deeply indecent; or the question must be asked: is there a deep lack of moral compass of value-oriented decency among those who assign a unique number to humans?

Data retention can refer to the time-specific storage of IP addresses that users or their computers use temporarily or permanently on the Internet. A permanent assignment of a number to a person or the casual identification of people for communication opportunities is one step more than a mere store of numbers, it is a person number and storage of personal data. With this, both individually and in combination, the previously mentioned matrix monitoring is created: Person 53-88-14 is identified, at the IP address 123.153.312.32 at port 4812 communication with a counterpart with similar identifying numbers at that time to have made, whereby the keys for the communication content must be stored, and so that these can be used; any electronic communication content is also stored at the same time.

When monitoring road traffic, the same thing is currently being determined: Here you can monitor all exits of a street, or people driving with their vehicles. Which is more efficient? Who cannot check all ports on the Internet, whether there is an unregistered communication server behind them, tries to shorten this with the registration of every person and the chosen communication channel?

Analogue and digital movements (journeys by means of transport or visits to websites) and forwarding of messages (letter post or messenger) with stored channel data (IP address and port) and time stamps, the technical machines and means for movements and registering messages in a reportable manner (selected car brand, selected means of transport or selected messenger) as well as not only registering the people themselves, but also identifying them beforehand, if necessary, is a totalitarian fantasy.

Exactly this draft law came - across Europe - just a few months later after the EU legislation on encryption and the German introduction of the number for human beings: European citizens will now electronically prove their identity via smartphone using a so-called EUid wallet. Providers such as Facebook or Google then prepare the new EU-ID for logging in (without using a pseudonym): no more e-mail or chat messages without an identified login via an ›e-wallet‹. The unique and permanent identification feature like or similar to the German identification number for human beings must also be provided with biometric authentication - this is what the regulation for electronic identification and trust services for electronic transactions provides (in short: eIDAS[238] - for: Electronic Identification and Trust Services for Electronic Transactions). Is Europe setting out with this eIDAS procedure to create the basis for being able to count people across Europe better than German places ever could?

Christian Stöcker, university professor for the digital communication course in Hamburg, therefore called for the resignation of the interior minister in the magazine »Der Spiegel« after the legislative resolution for the identification number for humans and an identification requirement on the Internet: The German interior minister is trying to coax a totalitarian, obviously unconstitutional reorganization of the Internet into a public distracted by Corona - by the way, already in at least the second attempt. Even these attempts are so indecent that one would have to say now at the latest: It's enough: Dismiss German

Interior Minister *Horst Seehofer*. He formulated this direct criticism of the long-standing Berlin and Munich government official not only because he studied cultural criticism at the Bavarian Academy also in Munich, but also because it is substantiated in terms of content. In the opinion of the opposition, too, this minister, with these totalitarian fantasies, has simply become a threat to Democracy.[239]

And these fantasies are now also becoming real in several laws in a completely overlapping context: In addition to the legally determined number for humans in an electronic wallet, »additional« laws are also provided: now central biometric databases[240] for passport photos and signatures are to be set up. And: According to a supplementary law, smartphones should be used as an electronic means of identification in economic processes[241]. The *trade association from the IT industry*, Eco, welcomed this, for example to be able to open bank accounts electronically outside of the home country. The German *Forum of Computer Scientists for Peace and Social Responsibility* (FIFF) resolutely rejects these concepts and these amalgamations of total surveillance[242].

The question also arises as to whether the European member states will humanistic-ally support the overlapping leadership in the thoroughness of these German administrative ideas and whether calls for resignation do not have to be addressed later in Europe?

It is not just a question of a total surveillance bill (see above), but the sum of the individual parts is always more than the total. This means that a strategic evaluation of the individual measures is also required in relation to each other and in relation to one another: Anyone who identifies people with numbers, records their biometric characteristics in databases, to which they have to grant identification access via their smartphone, for example if they want to book a self-driving car or writing an e-mail is not far

311

from implanting a chip in people for permanent control on every electronic door to every toilet or request for that.

In this respect, these beginnings are not only about the registration of the communication devices or the communication channels, but also about the people who communicate in them and the image of those who create this image of human beings. If, according to these country-specific amendments in Europe, not only numbers to humans are assigned, but people are indexed biometrically in databases and chat servers are to be registered on IP ports, then, in practical terms, @-email mailboxes would in future also be used as reportable and to be regarded as subject to identification, since they represent a communication port for humane creatures.

To be free from these obligations, the infrastructure can only be converted to communication ports that are based on peer-to-peer or (as seen with RetroShare) better on friend-to-friend architectures. It's about setting up vendor-independent communication systems: technical communication software that can be installed and used by anyone without professional and commercial providers in the field of messaging. According to this claim, it is forbidden to pay financial resources to a provider or service for communication technology if you do not finance your own independence with them.

One such early and rudimentary prototype for P2P messaging was BitMessage: A mailbox, without a provider!

BitMessage: The client is based on a small network via a built-in (DHT) server contact and connects the individual client which can send a message to other clients. The direct connection is not interesting because it works when both users are online. But the question with P2P networks is how Bob can reach Alice when she is offline. The message is then to be stored temporarily in the network in other active nodes until Alice comes online again.

BitMessage achieves this by temporarily storing the message in several neighboring nodes that are online. A high level of redundancy in the messages is therefore required in order to find a copy of a message if intermediate storage nodes should go offline in the meantime. However, since the network is experimental, there are hardly any stable storage options in this P2P email, except possibly for the operator's account point.

BitMessage's encryption protocol, which is intended to enable confidential and anonymous exchange of e-mail-like messages in this peer-to-peer network, is based on the blockchain technology known from Bitcoin electronic money. The blockchain is characterized by the fact that metadata is recorded: The current chain link has all information about previous transaction points in this chain.

With BitMessage, the messages are encrypted and transmitted with a signature. In contrast to the GPG and S/MIME email encryption protocols, for example, BitMessage also encrypts the sender, recipient and subject line.

In 2012, the developer still assumed that an attacker could eavesdrop on or control a single Internet connection, but not the Internet connections of all BitMessage users. This assumption is invalid after the Snowden-papers 2013 and the proven paradigm of the »Permanent Record«, the permanent potential recording of all content transmitted on the Internet. Metadata of a BitMessage message can therefore also be viewed from the outside at any time: transmission time, message length, neighbors' nodes, etc.; At the same time, as mentioned, the blockchain technology also stores the past events of the respective nodes of a connection chain. If it is possible to gain access to a private key, all messages previously received with the associated BitMessage address can be decrypted later. BitMessage is therefore not programmed to exchange Forward Secrecy or temporary keys or even multiple keys as in Fiasco

Forwarding. The last version 0.6.1 was a few years ago and it can be assumed that it will no longer be up to date.

Care-of method: Another method of caching P2P e-mails in a network is the Care-of method. Here, the messages from two friends are stored in a shared third node. Because of the encryption, this temporary storage station cannot see the message. It is only necessary that Alice and Bob have a third friend together or use an account on a web server as a third instance, which is then online when one of the two is offline.

For example, in the three-way constellation Alice, John and Bob: As a friend of both, Bob and Alice, John will cache the e-mail messages for both of them at any time if Alice or Bob should ever be offline. If they come back online, they can get the messages from the instance of John if he was online during their own offline time. So, there is a lot to be said for networking several friends who are online when one should be offline oneself. This is known as the so-called »c/o - Care-of-Method«. It can be found in the P2P email of the Spot-On client.

E-mail institution: Another method in the aforementioned software is to set up an »e-mail institution«. This is equivalent to setting up an e-mail inbox. What is special, however, is that this mailbox is addressed via a cryptographic key, so the institution only needs to be known in the network but does not require addressing on the TCP / IP level. Thanks to Cryptography, the messages arrive as soon as the user comes online. The operator of an e-mail institution issues a cryptographic token for this mailbox. The mailbox is therefore not linked to its own key for e-mail, as is the case with the Care-of method: an operator of an institution can use this service for friends from the own private e-mails separate.

Ozone mailbox: Finally, the fourth option to store messages in a P2P network is to set up an Ozone mailbox. This is administered in the SmokeStack server or automatically stored there by a messenger after connection. For an Ozone, only a simple term has to be defined that appears in the server and in the respective client: If the user has stored the term BERLIN in the messenger, for example, and this term has also been stored in the SmokeStack server, the messenger can use this mailbox immediately. Because of the encryption and its own key, it does not matter if someone else stores the same word BERLIN as an Ozone mailbox on the server.

There is also no need to establish a direct connection to the server to retrieve messages. It is sufficient if it is integrated somewhere in the P2P network and connected or accessible via intermediate nodes.

Means: Ozone's are virtually configuration-free mailboxes that control themselves via the cryptographic key; so, they are much easier to set up than a classic IMAP e-mail mailbox with IP and port, account and password.

Of course, the number for humans can also be used as a character string or as an alias for an Ozone mailbox instead of a word like »Berlin«: It couldn't be easier to imagine a secure DE-Mail that reaches every citizen?

So, if you want to save your own encrypted messages from storage by third parties or central providers, you are in good hands with one of the above-mentioned P2P networks with various methods, if friends are also open to one of these decentralized ecosystems for communication. Ultimately, it is not a question of faith, but in the case of P2P e-mail as well as chat, in turn, only the creation, networking of your own infrastructure and resign the financing of messaging providers, which force you to give up independence. And as we have seen, it is very easy and uncomplicated to set up chat and e-mail for loved ones with some friend-to-friend connecting applications.

8.14 In the invisible DHT-network
with Briar ●

Briar (as much as thorny thicket or thorn bush) is a free peer-to-peer instant messenger. Thanks to a Distributed Hash Table (DHT), Briar manages without a central server and requires only minimal external infrastructure, so, connections are also established via the Tor randomization network.

A DHT overlay network connects individual nodes in a P2P network. A node can then find the respective responsible node or the associated IP address for a specific key. Each node maintains connections to other nodes (its neighboring nodes) in a routing table. A node chooses its neighbors according to the structure of the network.

There is the following basic property in a DHT: for each key, each node either knows the ID of the node that is responsible for this key, or it has a link to a node whose ID is closer to the key sought, a distance measure is used for this. In the field of messaging, this key is defined in the DHT as an identification feature in order to locate the friend's IP. But it also means: if you know the key of a node, you can also find out the IP address (and attack it probably, if not secured via Tor). This »overlaid« small P2P network also enables messengers to start communication with friends with the appropriate IP address without asking a server that knows everyone. The server's database is moved to a P2P network in which those who are currently online are asked whether they know Alice and what current IP address she has. Then Bob can connect to her directly without a server. This means that there is no server provider or company that could be obliged to copy or upload keys.

Also in a DHT are the messenger alternatives aTox, qTox and uTox, which are independent to Briar - but the disadvantages here are that none of these programs do not display the existing connections in the user interface, the encryption is not up-to-date, and the jagged development community probably has also left half-finished programs dormant for several years and not updated enough. In short: they cannot all be explained further here, and Briar is referenced as an exemplary DHT messenger next to Jami in the following.

Many users also feel insecure with messengers who connect to numerous nodes in such a DHT instead of to a fixed, known server address. Especially when there are incoming and outgoing connections from the Tor network, as with Briar, because a connection always goes in both directions - and who wants to let the cyber scripters with the Tor-IP addresses access the own smartphone?

Messages in Briar are also end-to-end encrypted and only saved on the devices of the communication partners involved. However, Briar only gave a rudimentary answer to the art and technological option of messaging to offline friends, as is established with other messengers, and writes on the website: If your contact is offline, the message will be delivered the next time if you are both online together at the same time. Would it be an idea to get the message hybrid from an Ozone or Care-of mailbox? Practically and cryptographically, there are now more developed methods in other messengers to receive messages from offline friends from these so-called »DHT networks« (with and without Tor).

An alternative to Briar is Jami, which can do without the Tor network. Jami is quite unknown and currently offers two different functionalities in the same application: A SIP client that is suitable for classic VoIP telephony on the PC with the login data of a provider. There are also Jami accounts with P2P functionality. However, neither account type is suitable for interaction. Instead of a server, a DHT is also used, it is the OpenDHT network. The app uses end-to-end encryption with Perfect Forward Secrecy for communication and meets the X.509 standard. Jami is open-source and available across platforms. Jami also only saves the message for offline friends for a few minutes, possibly in the provider's central servers. Although servers are not required in Jami, they are named on the website for five specific cases: push notifications, the OpenDHT proxy, bootstrap, name server and TURN. Therefore, a user of the well-known Reddit forum asks: Why does Jami talk about P2P when there are servers in the middle?

8.15   Encrypted File-Sharing: Freenet & Offsystem •

Classic peer-to-peer file sharing (such as with Gnutella, EMule or Torrent) has been replaced with RetroShare by secure friend-to-friend file sharing (including Turtle Hopping, see above). Nevertheless, a presence, i.e., the online existence of a data source, is a prerequisite.

Two other networks also allow a file to be published to be stored on a network and then taking the client offline so that the only key for decryption has to be published at a later point in time. This means that the publisher or the author remains offline as a data source. The programs that establish these networks are called Freenet or Offsystem. (Or Offload is also another application for the same network).

In practical terms, a file is distributed (uploaded) to an online network and remains there encrypted in the storage containers of other nodes in this network. Since users come and go in a network, it is also necessary here to load all the blocks of a file at least three times into the network so that after a while all the

318

puzzle pieces of the file are still available in the network when someone downloads or. wants to reassemble the file from it. Redundancy is therefore also required here - and the willingness of users in the network to store encrypted blocks from others on their own hard drive that cannot be viewed because of the encryption!

But who would want to store potentially foreign or even unwanted files with oneself? That is the compromise one has to make if one also wants to back up own files in one of these networks (respective in other one's node).

Here everyone comes to own ethical limits and begins to see encryption in this context: Since one cannot look into encryption, does it (not) matter what is in the encrypted blocks?

Rather, the security of the encryption is questioned - or an assumption is raised: there could also be potentially unwanted content in someone else's encrypted file that would transfer the responsibility of others to one's own hard drive? If others don't care what I encrypt, should I also care what others encrypt? Wouldn't we care if we didn't know what is?

A lawyer who regularly receives encrypted e-mails suddenly cannot open an encrypted e-mail. What if this encryption included instructions on how to illegally build bombs? How long could the lawyer imagine keeping the email? And how is the e-mail inbox operator doing before the lawyer downloads this encrypted e-mail to the own client? Or leave a copy on the server of the IMAP e-mail server?

Wouldn't we care if we had this ignorance around us? Or could we endure it because the ignorance is based on encryption? The fact that we recognize ignorance usually leads to the fact that we reject the unknown because we cannot get to know it, as would be the case when searching for and reading or getting to know legible books in a library?

So, the question is: don't we trust the encryption - because, if it worked, there wasn't an individual weighing problem? Or do we want no unknown options, so no encryption either? Freedom is always the freedom of those who think differently, and encryption is always also the acknowledgment of new science about the possibly private communication content of other people?

In this context *Scott Edwards* asks about the following analogy: »›The freedom of the other begins with the acceptance of his cipher text‹ - if the well-known quote from *Rosa Luxemburg* (1918) can be applied in this formulation to the next century? If it is difficult to accept the limits of someone else's legible opinion, how easy should it be for us to accept the limits of someone else's illegible opinion«? must be asked[243]. Or as the saying goes: What I do not know does not make me hot, or: as you do me, so I do you?

Do professional drivers value their transport of pigs to the scaffold of a slaughterhouse ethically differently if they could bring Swiss knives to Solothurn instead? Or does an awareness about the cargo play no role?

Pupils discuss similar ethical or tautological discussions in relation to logistics including the storage and forwarding of encrypted data packets: Locked packets leave us ignorant of personally legitimate or socially legal content and transports that cannot be separated from other considerations because they are locked. Nobody should say I didn't know the content, or I just forwarded the delivery?! Should ignorance be exchanged for the surrender of Privacy, or can an ethic of responsibility be developed that is based on loss of control? And nobody should put their point of view above that of the socially defined ?!

There are things we know and things we don't know, and among those things there are other things where we don't know that we don't know; and even the things we need to know are and remain unknown because we don't know enough to know that we can't know them. For all we know, should we know that these well-known things are small and the smallness of them is actually not so well known, so it is best to know that we cannot know or decipher anything?

Or as *Ludwig Wittgenstein*, who incorporated an encrypted code into more than 450 places in his estate, once put it: »The limits of my language mean the limits of my world«.[244] This philosopher often found philosophical ideas in addition to reflections on cultural-historical content. He often reports in code about the way he philosophizes. Interestingly, he also wrote instructions for the publication of his writings in code, which indicates that he was apparently aware of the simplicity of deciphering his code and that it should not be referred to as cipher.

Encryption is here also reminiscent of a winged word of ancient origin since the Greek philosopher *Socrates*: »We know that we know nothing«, which Plato addresses in his apology. *Plato*'s passages only say that *Socrates* is aware of the fact that he lacks wisdom or a real, beyond doubt, knowledge.

So, can for not knowing the content of encrypted data packets a parallel be drawn to the philosophy of new science, because encryption prevents knowledge of the content as well as a lack of experience horizons or unknown learning content?

There is no talk of technical expertise, but of provisions in the area of virtues and the question of what is good: »What is prudence? What is bravery? What is piety? What is justice?« is asked. And: The true human wisdom is to be aware of not knowing in the need to know what is good.

How the historical *Socrates* assessed his ignorance, and the fundamental possibility or impossibility of human knowledge possession is, however, controversial in ancient studies - just as a right to encryption may controversially judge the exclusive knowledge and cognitive interest of others in today's age: Who caches encrypted data of others, must be aware that he or she cannot see the content in it. Actually, quite trivial and carefree? Because encrypted data can generally not be viewed by others.

But from these questions and reflections on personally closed or collectively controlled knowledge or legal guarantee of new science of others back to technology, which often always works according to the same definition scheme and only enables access and knowledge with one key.

In addition to the encryption of a file, the Offsystem network has a particularly specific approach that can be read on the application's homepage: A file consists of binary values, i.e., a 0 or a 1. Using the XOR method, the character string from 0 and 1 values can be merged with another character string. It only depends on the arithmetic operation whether one character string or the other is received during the conversion. This is reminiscent of the chapter on Steganography at the beginning, i.e., hiding a file in another file, or its cipher text or encoded text.

In simple terms: think of the number twelve (12). It can be represented as five plus seven (5+7), or twenty-five minus thirteen (25-13). In this case, the *meaning* is not in the numbers, but in the relationship between the numbers. If the numbers are taken individually, i.e., 5, 7, 13 and 25, they are never 12. And they in no way *contain* the number 12. [245]

If a music file is merged with the other music file in this way via various operations and the calculation method is known, then a separation can be brought about again from the common mass. The XOR procedure (»XOR concatenation«) used is not a strong encryption in the Offsystem. And the way to separate two merged files again is documented in a URL with cryptographic values, which in turn can also be mixed into other file blocks. So, you just have to find a beginning somewhere, load the first block, and you get a key with which you can load the next block and so on.

However, since the URL is more or less a key, all of this does not work securely in the peer-to-peer network unless there is an encrypted channel for the transmission of the URL key. The network as a buffer for the blocks in a peer-to-peer network should have been separated from a friend-to-friend communication network, in which the URL key for assembling the blocks is shared among friends. In other words, a Web-of-Trust for the keys should have been added to the data blocks, as RetroShare offers in the creation only three years later and now over several decades. The data blocks themselves can remain in a P2P network, they are only character strings consisting of 0 and 1; and are therefore always uncritical or not significant if no arithmetic operation stored in a URL gives them meaning.

With the realization of this architectural gap and the further effort to close it, the developer of Offsystem in the midlife crisis of mid-40s - in addition to an incipient physical illness - also ideally said goodbye to his goals of the past and this network by giving up the project for data storage in a decentralized and redundant cloud. Encrypting friend-to-friend chat should have been added to this peer-to-peer network.

This is exactly the path taken by the similarly structured network Freenet: In addition to the P2P network, it also included the option of only connecting to familiar friends in a friend-to-friend (F2F) network. A messenger or communication network was laid over the »ocean of encrypted blocks«, so to speak, which firstly only communicates with trusted friends and secondly is encrypted.

In this respect, nowadays (in addition to Freenet), RetroShare is also more completely encrypted than the Offsystem program and it can be used well if it doesn't bother that a source can be offline at times or (with RetroShare) there exists no continuous end-to-end encryption in the individual intermediate stations during Turtle Hopping.

The question of the technological architecture therefore depends on the intended use: If a journalist travels to another country and has to hand out the smartphone at the airport so that a complete copy of the contents of the memory can be made, she or he may want to do not leave references to certain interview partners or documents in someone else's hands at the border. For this it would be good to only encrypt or remember a URL or a key, with which a zipped file can be reloaded from a cloud - or in this context: P2P-cloud like Freenet - after landing with the internet connection behind the border.

Back in the home country after the trip and continuously online, like friends or the editorial team, the interview documents can also be sent to colleagues via RetroShare.

Freenet and Offsystem come from the time of file sharing more than two decades ago, which has now declined because of streaming subscriptions. However, with these networks, a file could be uploaded in the past. In this way, the key to »pulling« and downloading the file from the network could also be carried out in the subsequent period using encrypted blocks. Namely when the original distributor is offline again. The insertion of a file remained anonymous. Would it be a perfect architecture, e.g., for the publications of the disclosure portal Wikileaks, which were previously carried out there on a central server and which ultimately led to the well-known entanglement? What effects does it have on whistle-blowing if documents are to be passed on by these persons themselves and brought to the public – or, only a password for documents that others have already made publicly available on the Internet, but stored in encrypted form?

So why shouldn't there still be a redundant, distributed cloud today that is supported by a P2P network and thus provides storage space that is available everywhere and cannot be centrally controlled and censored? Could Gaia-X, the European cloud, become a Gaia Freenet P2P cloud through the use of users? The P2P forum portal Osiris[246], which was last updated in 2011, tried to map precisely this purpose in such a distributed network for free speech in public forums.

The protection of one's own opinion, the publication of data and opinions without attributing authorship, has now become part of the RetroShare or Freenet network, which is actively used by many journalists. Ultimately, however, any website with cipher text can be a document that is accessible when a key becomes available. Because encryption has *mostly* already taken place in the past. These P2P networks are not required if cipher text is in the data lines or on the homepages.

8.16   OnionShare – Transfer without chat ●

OnionShare enables the anonymous 1: 1 exchange of files of any size over the Internet. Loading from the swarm of several users is not intended, as is the case with the aforementioned clients. The tool relies on the anonymizing Tor network. During use, OnionShare sets up a web server on the user's computer, which others can access as a so-called »hidden service«. For this purpose, OnionShare provides a URL that enables other users to download the offered file. It is crucial that the download URL is only sent via a reliably encrypted channel. The recipient establishes the absolutely necessary connection to the Tor network, for example by installing the Tor browser. But OnionShare itself also has the necessary on-board resources to ensure the download via Tor. With this exchange program one is directly connected to the randomization network.

Other transfer programs can also be connected to Tor via the LocalHost. Thus, for example, the file transfer in the programs Smoke Chat with the Steam function or RetroShare or GoldBug Messenger and many others with a proxy function can be connected to the Tor-LocalHost. Using the Smoke Messenger has the advantage that lost data packets are checked again by the Steam protocol and transmitted again, as is the case with TCP.

Depending on the application, an available web server can be connected inside or outside the randomization network connected via LocalHost. It is ultimately a matter of taste, whether an HTTPS Echo server is addressed outside of Tor or an OnionShare server within Tor as a hidden service.

However, the encryption is different: OnionShare does not encrypt itself, but only uses Tor's channels. The other clients mentioned, which are connected to Tor's LocalHost, also encrypt the file packets to be sent or can even set a password on the file.

OnionShare has not only not implemented its own encryption, but also does not offer an option for an encrypted chat, because the download links must somehow be securely transmitted to the other party. The same dilemma as in the Offsystem. Therefore, tools should be connected to Tor that have secure chat channels as well as further channels for file transfer, even if a chat server might have to be addressed outside of Tor via TLS or HTTPS connections.

In this respect, OnionShare is only a partial alternative to the introduced RetroShare program (via Tor).

8.17   Websearch and P2P-URL-Sharing with YaCy & Spot-On •

In addition to communication on the Internet, chat and e-mail, as well as the transfer of files, the third major area of intended use on the web plays a central role: the search for information. Websites with articles and news deliver these on the World Wide Web.

We google it, look at Wikipedia to see what's going on - or network users on social media such as RetroShare, Mastodon, Twitter or Facebook send us the URLs for the latest topics in our news list.

At the university, young scientists often learn an »encyclopedic principle« in their information processing - which means something like: first sift through everything and then incorporate what is relevant into the issue to be dealt with. Or as the Bible puts it in Chapter 5 of the first letter to the Thessalonians: Look and examine everything and keep what is good!

At the same time, however, it becomes clear to us in the public and digital world that we cannot search for a lot at all. Much information is left behind and only reaches the public after years, as it took over 50 years, for example, for it to be common knowledge that asbestos is harmful to health. Or the informers are caught up in structural conditions: we only receive news in a so-called »filter bubble«, i.e., from friends in the social networks with the same views. However, we do not learn enough about the arguments of an opposing party and therefore cannot understand them for us. Or: Users are dependent on a central service like Google, and that also means being dependent on the prioritization of messages by others - or even, if the URL is not listed in the index, this adjustment to reality (not to say censorship) to be subject to.

Access to autonomous, complete and un-prioritized knowledge is therefore a major concern.

At the same time, this also means leaving the storage, availability and administration of the information stock not just to a central service, but rather placing it in the hands of many of the confident users.

The Twitter user ›Camelia‹ recently asked about software that enables to make the URLs of her found websites searchable in a database. She probably wanted to compile a database on Jewish culture.

Or URLs from websites for queer people in the LGBTQIA community: in the digital age, these too are collected by the relevant lectures at universities just as they have been collecting thematic books on their shelves over the past 50 years.

The members of the Chinese »Falun Gong« group in China have been denied this digital transformation of the knowledge base. Progressive websites on this keyword are not shown in the country-specific search engine Baidu, nor are some websites on the subject of Human Rights.

These are just a few use cases, cryptographic or mathematical departments at universities may also save subject-specific URLs and their documents as well as private users on all hobby topics and areas of interest.

All these individual and organization-specific perspectives have an interest in their own searchable database of URLs and websites. In short: Instead of Google, better a web search with your own database at home on your own hard drive? A database that belongs to us. And a P2P web search can provide this.

YaCy is a well-known P2P web search that also does not require a central server for web search. It has established P2P web search over the last decade and, with around 250 to at peak times over 1000 simultaneous online nodes in this network, is able to offer everyone an alternative to Google with millions of indexed websites thanks to the swarm intelligence of a few people.

With the Spot-On P2P web search, the URL databases are shared in the network instead of the search words: The search is not carried out in the network, but in the respective local URL database on the hard drive (in the LocalHost). In this way, no documentation of search queries (so-called »query hits«) is generated in the other nodes of the network. (Likewise, the

Startpage.com page would not be a p2p-oriented, but a central search engine database on the web that does not identify the search words in the URL.)

If user Alice has a database with 1000 URLs, and user Bob has a database with 1000 URLs, and both exchange the key for the URL transmission, then the URL number in each client adds up to 2000 URLs. Filter options for incoming URLs are given.

As a standard, the connections in the P2P network with Spot-On web search are always encrypted, to the existing web interface as well as to other nodes. These are some differences to the YaCy URL network.

Spot-On web search can also index the documents and make them available on the local computer as well as on the web: a copy of only the text of the website is saved in the local database as a PDF or text file.

In short: The Spot-On Web- and URL-search is a technical alternative that implements the URL transfer in encrypted form, supports PostgreSQL and SQLite databases, can be fed in via RSS, P2P and URL insertions and at the same time from the local database delivers a text or PDF document to the URL. The search can take place in the client as well as in the web interface of a browser.

Via the RSS functions of both clients, YaCy and Spot-On, databases or current search results for specific keywords can also be networked in a hybrid design and also collected locally in a corresponding database.

However, many people are not interested in making a contribution to the maintenance of knowledge. They simply accept the option of being able to »google« centrally and free of charge. Teachers and parents may still need to be enthusiastic about Wikipedia's annual donation marathon, hardly knowing how much information is missing in Wikipedia, articles are blocked for updates, new information is subject to editing wars and deletion campaigns.

The fact that unobserved and unrecorded search behavior is necessary shows that Twitter, Google and other regimes as well as censoring regimes such as China can determine in the permanent records at any time who searched for or wrote which keyword and when.

We want to hope that the police will never again be on their doorstep just because of people's interests in knowledge or that teachers and judges will be dismissed from office because of their research, as has been the case in the thousands in Turkey in recent years[247].

A few therefore see the need to make a contribution in the infrastructure and in the construction of thematic search catalogs for their own web search.

It is therefore important that every school, every educational institution with its own node contributes to the provision of freely accessible and immediately readable P2P-networked knowledge databases, probably also only mentally.

The German Chancellor *Gerhard Schröder* and the French President *Jacques Chirac* recognized this at the time in 2008 and set up the Quaero project. The aim was to redefine web search, possibly also P2P. However, the project proposals were so broadly defined in terms of search processes that the project did not produce any real internet or P2P web search. At most, the companies Exalead and Startpage developed another central search engine from the project, which, however, now also reflects results from Google.

It can also be assumed, however, that Germany's political dependence on America did not allow this freedom to set up one's own European web search. Search, database building and secret service surveillance take place overseas. Smaller technology companies in Europe have no economic access to the topic of a URL database.

And Google is really excellent at capturing the new. Anyone who researches the new ISBN of a book on the day of the first edition, which has not yet been listed on the Internet, will find that the page growth occurs very quickly in Google, but not in the other major search engines Bing, Yandex or Baidu. The thoroughness of Google's collection service offers a good service but is also frightening with regard to the extensive monitoring technology - and thus prevents alternatives.

Ten years later after Quaero, attempts are also being made with the European Cloud Gaia-X to create European sovereignty in the area of data storage. This project may disappear as soon as Quaero. Nevertheless, the now intensified data protection laws have made it possible that data at least does not have to be stored overseas.

The establishment of a European, national or user-specific search database for websites has therefore not been successful, as this is associated with costs and efforts.

Thus, the swarm intelligence of a P2P network remains an important solution method with which educational institutions can remain the driving force for building a searchable level of knowledge. To this end, every educational institution that has a website on the Internet could be legally obliged to maintain a server for searchable URLs in a P2P network of databases if this distributed voluntary work in educational policy is to be further expanded in relation to a market monopoly. What used to be the ISBN for books is now the URL for websites and online resources. So why shouldn't there also be the step that every city provides a database with URLs to websites such as a city library that can be searched, when knowledge in blogs and websites has become so fast and decentralized that the population can no longer wait until someone summarizes the knowledge in a book and this can be found in a library using ISBN? The printing press brought libraries, the Internet should provide every city with a quickly searchable URL database. It is an overdue step in our society's knowledge management not to depend on a monopoly URL database in web searches.

YaCy and Spot-On have so far provided the models and blueprints for such distributed and searchable databases with URLs to websites.

8.18   Web browsing with Dooble, Iron and a Cookie-Washer●

Not only the search words of our life are permanently recorded, the websites we visit every day also collect data via cookies - short identification numbers that are stored in our browser - and other methods. E.g., what, and how long we are interested in a website.

The Tor network as an anonymous, upstream protection proxy has grown in size because it does not reveal the IP address and location to websites. More on that in a moment.

At the same time, one of the truths of the surveillance system on the Internet is also in the browser for the web itself. The browser not only stores and sends information about the cookies stored to the websites, but it also sends information to the manufacturer, in the case of the Chrome browser e.g., to Google. The Google Chrome browser has a built-in identification number (Chrome ID) for this purpose. In addition to cookies and other tracking methods, this is used to clearly save on Google that the user or this browser has already been to the website and has accessed this URL.

An open-source copy of the Google Chrome browser is the Iron Browser. It's the same Google Chrome but without this number.

The Dooble Web Browser is also based on the Chromium library and has additional security features, such as the option to save all of the own data in an encrypted container. You can only get to this after entering a password. Without this, you stay in the browser's virgin guest mode, and nobody can see the surfing history. With this function it is the VeraCrypt of the browsers.

In addition, Dooble also has a kind of cookie washer. This cookie management makes it possible to delete all cookies after a surfing session. However, it is possible for defined websites to keep the cookies, for example if you want to stay logged in there permanently or if you have stored the password for the website in your browser. All the rest of the websites or associated cookies that you have only visited in passing and that will continue to track you are washed out: that is, are deleted. Are cookies the corona virus of websites, where a cookie washer helps to keep free of it? Instead of every website forcing us to approve the use of cookies, browsers could also be obliged according to this blueprint to implement cookie washers that positively confirm or retain each individual cookie - but wash out all others after the session.

The following deliberate data protection attacks by the Chrome browser can be compared with other browsers:

Problem: Installation ID
- *Chrome:* A copy of Google Chrome contains a generated installation number that is sent to Google when Chrome is first installed and used. The number will be deleted when Google Chrome automatically checks for updates. If Chrome is downloaded as part of an advertising campaign, a unique advertising number may be generated and sent to Google the first time Google Chrome is used.
- *Dooble:* not available in Dooble.
- *Iron:* not present in Iron.

Problem: cookie tracking
- *Chrome:* Cookies can only be deleted as a whole.
- *Dooble:* Cookie washer / management, individual cookies can be defined and retained during the deletion process.
- *Iron:* Cookies can only be deleted as a whole.

Problem: Search suggestions from the central server
- *Chrome:* Depending on the configuration, every time we type something in the address bar, this information is sent to Google so that search suggestions can be displayed.
- *Dooble:* not available in Dooble.
- *Iron:* not present in Iron.

Problem: RLZ tracking
- *Chrome:* This Chrome function transmits information in encoded form to Google, e.g. when and where Chrome was downloaded.
- *Dooble:* not available in Dooble.
- *Iron:* not present in Iron.

Problem: URL tracker
- *Chrome:* Depending on the configuration, Chrome opens the Google homepage in the background five seconds after starting the browser.
- *Dooble:* not available in Dooble.
- *Iron:* not present in Iron.

8.19   Tor Browser: Disguise the IP address ●

Tor is a network that forwards the IP requests of the own computer through many other IP addresses, so that one finally access a website with the IP address of the last station in the chain. Anyone who installs the Tor browser will automatically be routed through this network. If one use it to query the own IP address on the website www.whatismyip.com, for example, we will notice that it is different from the IP address that is displayed in the router at home (or with a browser without a Tor on this above-mentioned website appears).

Depending on the configuration of the browser, one can either surf or forward other requests to a desired website using the own IP address.

This works quite well so far, but one can't hide more than the local location with it, as websites continue to try to set cookies and other methods from the JavaScript area can also recognize users.

There are also internal websites within the forwarding network. These are found with an .onion address as the ending and are therefore also published anonymously. These websites are often referred to as dark-net because they contain forums and marketplaces where the usual triad of bad guys and drug and weapon dealers meet. Organizations for Human Rights or for Privacy might be found less there, it is reported. In this respect, it is right that analyzes, and investigations are carried out here.

Tor is also not entirely without criticism, because government funding sources are repeatedly mentioned that suggest a certain dependency and thus the monitoring function of a honey pot quality[248]. As well as the sometimes unfriendly demeanor and the lack of team competence of the so-called »Tor scripters«[249], who praise and support this network almost religiously, are mentioned.

At the same time, the Tor browser is tied to the - also economic - unit of the browser (currently Firefox). With Tor's purely technical proxy tool called Vidalia, however, it was previously possible to use other browsers.

Tor remains a functioning network for journalists and soldiers abroad in order to separate websites visited and communication about them from the respective local location. The JonDo program is an alternative to Tor.

Programs and messengers that can bind themselves to Tor's LocalHost interface using the proxy function can communicate over the network without revealing the IP address or regional location.

The messengers Jami, Spot-On, RetroShare, Smoke and also the GoldBug Messenger can, in addition to other tools such as

Onionshare, also pass through the Tor network and connect to an HTTP or HTTPS server (listener) on the Internet.

Tor is usually programmed so that the last Tor node connects to a web server and that last mile is unencrypted. A so-called »exit node« will see everything that it is supposed to retrieve on behalf of remote hops. So, it was hardly possible to establish an encrypted HTTPS connection to the web server in the last mile. Since cipher text can also be transmitted via HTTP without encryption in the case of messengers, and regular websites increasingly only allow HTTPS requests, the exit nodes will increasingly have to adapt to more encryption.

Today, the GoldBug Messenger is also used experimentally, depending on the network and architecture design, as a messenger for Tor via a proxy connection, and with McEliece encryption it wins over the design of an originally different, no longer developed prototype of a »Tor Messenger« of further growth - in addition to OnionShare and Briar.

8.20   A network with a perspective for surfing: Hello Echo... •

Tor also has alternatives with potential: They are the Echo, I2P and GnuNet networks with their respective architectures and specifics. The Encryption Suite Spot-On is known to be based on the HTTPS protocol. As seen, this encrypts a message and sends it to another contact or server and so on. This principle can be compared with the functioning of the Tor network in parallels and at the same time has special advantages, which are referred to as »Beyond Cryptographic Routing« as we have seen. Because: routing information is not required here because of the cryptographic functions. The architecture design can therefore be considered as a draft for a Tor-2 or, because of the file-sharing option, as a Torrent-2. In terms of Cryptography, it is also far more pronounced than Tor or Torrent. Nevertheless, Echo is only a preliminary study, because currently only communication messages and files can be sent in this network; a proxy function for websites has not yet been implemented in any of the clients.

The Tor development can benefit from the Echo protocol, or a network development of the Echo can also take into account a hybrid or bridge function to the Tor network when implementing a proxy function for websites. However, this remains a need for research and the design of future generations of developers who would like to go to the World Wide Web on the basis of a network that does not require location detection.

8.21 I2P Network: Invisible in the mix network •

In addition to Tor and Echo, there is still the I2P network, which stands for »Invisible-to-Peer«, which means »Invisible in the neighbors' network«. It works as a further mixed network just like Tor, but mainly relates to the internal nodes, i.e., websites or communication packages to participants in the normal Internet cannot be addressed regularly with it. The network of a niche society. Even if there is a server in the network that can also be used to query external websites or mailboxes. This also works via a central node where administrators can see everything that is accessed in this network. The open-source application is written in Java and has its own sub-applications for the various functions such as file sharing (IMule), forums or messages (I2Bote). As in RetroShare, these forums can be used as non-erasable storage points for cipher text: Invisible meeting points for encrypted text.

8.22   If you can do UNIX, you can do GNUnet ●

A fourth mix network is GNUnet. It is a long-term and fundamental research project that primarily addresses technically competent users from the Linux and command line community. Here, too, users can use the jungle of the group to remain anonymous. Mainly for anonymous, censorship-resistant file sharing. It is developed at the University of Applied Sciences Bern. Participants who contribute to the network will be rewarded with better service in terms of resources. All data in the GNUnet network is transmitted from sender to recipient using end-to-end encryption. Nobody, not even one of the forwarding participants, should be able to monitor, disturb or censor the communication. With the friend-to-friend option, GNUnet offers the function of exchanging information and files in a chain via the IP addresses of the friends who are directly connected and their friends, etc. GNUnet then only connects to authorized, trustworthy nodes (friends), as with RetroShare. GNUnet is therefore also known as the RetroShare of the Unix community.

8.23   OpenVPN – an established tunnel to the peer? ●

Often, a secure data connection that cannot be read by third parties should be established over an insecure network, such as the Internet or a local, non-encrypted wireless LAN. Typical use cases are the connection of individual employees in the field service in the company's network, the connection of a branch with the data center or the connection of locally distributed chat servers or servers from data centers to one another.

OpenVPN is the free software for setting up such a virtual private network (VPN) via an encrypted TLS connection.

OpenssL/TLS can be used for encryption. OpenVPN uses either UDP or TCP for transport. However, OpenVPN connections can be recognized by means of a deep inspection of the encrypted packets from the known header data. With this recognition, the connection could be blocked, the partners in communication could be determined and the data recorded.

Alternatively, these security requirements can also be provided by other suitable protocols (e.g., SSH, HTTPS, Steam, SFTP) if implemented in a corresponding application. Some of these protocols can also be passed through a tunnel of the Spot-On Encryption Suite with the McEliece algorithm quantum-immune through two nodes, quasi a VPN tunnel in the McEliece tunnel. Then the header data of the VPN channel can no longer be recognized. After IP inspection and now port inspection, sewer inspection will have to come soon. The open-source firewall PFSENSE also offers a VPN server with which, for example, the smartphone can surf with the IP address of the router at home or address a Mumble audio conference or chat server through the VPN channel without a Chat server port that must be open. The open-source firewall OPNsense is also an alternative with a built-in VPN.

Wireguard also provides fast, code-lean and modern VPN technology, alternatively on a P2P basis. Only public cryptographic keys are used to identify two computers with one another in the peer-to-peer network of many different computers. For example, five computers can form a P2P network and computers two and three accept the key from computer five and surf using the IP address of this computer. As a VPN, F2F-Wireguard comes close to the proxy idea of a trustworthy F2F Tor network or account-based Echo or I2P network for remote surfing. Professional VPN providers are: ExpressVPN, NordVPN, HideMyAss!, Hola VPN, OpenVPN, VyprVPN, TorGuard, IPVanish, VPN Unlimited and many more. The Israeli Hola VPN uses also community-powered peer-to-peer caching. Paying users can choose to redirect all requests to peers but are themselves never used as peers. The Hola application redirects the request to go through the computers and Internet connections of other users in free geo-specific areas. Also the Tinc-Projekt (http://www.tinc-vpn.org), Freelan (http://www.freelan.org), Ipop (http://ipop-project.org) and Zero Tier (http://www.zerotier.com) connect via a P2P VPN to websites.

8.24 Checkpoint CryptPad •

CryptPad is a collaboration board in the browser to work together on texts, as Collabora Office with Libre-Office in the cloud, or Office 365 for Word documents or Google with Google Docs enable. The difference: with the CryptPad, the connection to the pad is encrypted and only members with the appropriate password have access to this editable and formattable text cave. However, the access authorization to editable texts on the web is only one function. Furthermore, such a pad can be used to store cipher text on the corresponding page so that others can copy it and convert it into plain text in their machine. As seen, plain text can be converted into cipher text using additional pads, such as the aforementioned Rosetta Crypto Pad. Any Internet or forum page that offers all public - or even just authorized - access can be used to store cipher text there. The cipher text moves from the user's CryptoPad to the CryptPad and back to the friend's CryptoPad, in which the cipher text is converted back into plain text. The CryptPad acts as a server or so-called »dead drop« - as a dead mailbox in which the encrypted message is stored. Such editable pages are contained in numerous software products such as boards or wikis and can also be installed in or behind randomization networks, so that exchange points for cipher text are not public and the cipher text is stored via encrypted connections - for those who are waiting there at the checkpoint CryptPad for him and another decryption option. Checkpoint Charlie was yesterday. Checkpoint CryptPad is the new agent's transition server today. Apart from that, every auditing company does nothing else when it stores messages and files in its own secure portal for a company to be audited.

8.25   OpenStego – I don't see anything that you can see ●

OpenStego is a Steganography application that offers two functions: a) Hiding data: It can hide any data in a deck file (e.g., an image), b) Inserting invisible watermarks: Watermarks are added to files using an invisible signature. This can be used, for example, to detect unauthorized copying of files or to hide a message in a picture. The OpenPuff or OutGuess programs are appropriate alternatives.

A message file »love letter.txt« can easily be inserted into a picture as a text file. The picture is sent to the girlfriend or boyfriend by e-mail and then the text can be extracted from the picture again. Mobile messengers, which reduce the size of the picture before sending, can of course not be used, as the picture must be preserved as an original file. To do this, you would first have to pack the picture in a ZIP file and then send it. Then the messenger is prevented from reducing the size of the image. Messages can be sent simply by exchanging images - with relatively little conversion effort. Sending images is a kind of »slow chat«, as is the copying and pasting of cipher text using conversion pads in any communication channels, public or private forums, or in Steganography carrier materials.

8.26   Tails – Amnesia at the Kiosk •

Tails - The Amnesic Incognito Live System - is a Linux distribution based on Debian. Its aim is to protect the Privacy and anonymity of users. To achieve this, Tails relies in particular on the use of the Tor network. The system can be booted directly from a live DVD or a USB stick and then leaves no traces on the computer used.

Tails was first released on June 23, 2009 - then under the name Amnesia. The name goes back to the Amnesia CD of the German working group on data retention, which appeared for the first time in 2007 and contained numerous programs to increase security and anonymity on the Internet[250].

Amnesia is a term for forgetting: in the medical sense, amnesia describes a form of memory disruption for temporal or content-related memories. This operating system is designed as a so-called »kiosk system«, i.e., it does not retain any data and is always in its original state when it is switched on and booted up and the previous session left no data traces. The kiosk opens every morning with a fresh, new newspaper. These kiosk systems are often used as public access points in Internet cafes. The Dooble web browser also works according to this principle, since it always starts without old data if the user profile is not opened with a password. The Knoppix CD, as well as a Linux live operating system that also starts as a kiosk with all the necessary applications, is an alternative to Tails, but without anonymizing the IP address via Tor. Both completely wash out old data when restarting or shutting down the system. The Dooble web browser, for example, can remember the data securely encrypted in a container for the next session when a password is entered. So here only limited amnesia at the kiosk.

8.27 Mumble Audio as well Jitsi, Nextcloud and BigBlueButton Video Chat ●

The encryption of voice or video images is basically to be seen like the encryption of text. Nevertheless, this convenience can only be achieved with audio / video using a larger amount of data and must therefore be considered separately from text encryption. Servers also have special requirements here, and the few that are open-source can be listed on one hand: The Mumble program can be used to transmit encrypted speech. With the server systems Jitsi, Nextcloud (based on WebRTC and central (viewable) certificates and intermediate servers) and BigBlueButton, there are still open-source systems for video transmissions that are currently not end-to-end encrypted, but probably planning it, like the non-open-source variants Skype, Teams or Zoom.

8.28 Telegram, Threema and Wire ●

The Telegram instant messaging service can be used on smartphones, tablets and PCs. In addition to text messages, users can also exchange voice messages, photos, videos, and documents, as well as use voice and video telephony with others. The chats can be cloud-based or alternatively as »secret chats« directly between the end devices. The imprint of the messenger and its server of a Russian founder is now given as Dubai. It is criticized that the security of Telegram is based solely on trust in the operating company and that the encryption must be switched on, the standard is not default. The sent and received messages are also stored unencrypted in the memory of the end device. So, if the device is physically owned or a Trojan is installed, these messages can be accessed.

Threema is a free end-to-end encrypting instant messaging service from Switzerland. Its client is open-source, but the server is not. The software is designed for data protection and data avoidance and, in contrast to most competitors in the market, does not require a telephone number or other personal information for use. All messages are only sent end-to-end encrypted. In group chats, the message is encrypted separately for each recipient and delivered individually. As a result, the Threema servers can neither understand which groups there are nor who is a member of a group. Media, on the other hand, are encrypted once and uploaded to the Threema server and only then the symmetric key is distributed. The name Threema is derived from the acronym EEEMA, short for End-to-End Encrypting Messaging Application, where the three E have been replaced by the term Three.

Wire is an instant messenger for smartphones and tablets as well as Linux, Windows and MacOS computers. Calls to and from common web browsers are possible via the WebRTC interface. No telephone number is required to register for use, the user can also log in with an email address. All communication content on Wire is also end-to-end encrypted. According to the manufacturer, Wire is now completely open-source (client and server): it is possible to operate an own server. However, the code is only available for an Amazon Web Services (AWS) installation. In this respect, there are compilation hurdles to compiling and installing an own server at home. This may be necessary because companies should pay for the service; the chat client is only free for private users.

The same applies to the provider SureSpot, whose server in the university town of Boulder in Colorado, USA, is not open-source. Boulder is also the city with a branch of the American »National Institute of Standards and Technology« (NIST), which certifies all cryptographic procedures. It can only be speculated whether a NIST software developer will make this server available. Whether this non-open-source server in Boulder just in front of the Grand Canyon is more ideal for the own encrypted mail than a server in supposedly Dubai or at Amazon Web Services?

In this respect, these providers can be summarized under the aspects of greater popularity, but a server that is not kept open-source for everyone or for installation at home.

8.29   Mastodon's decentral Chat-Servernet ●

While messages on paper have changed to electronic messages, so are electronic distribution channels. In the past, news were made available for collection on websites, or made available through subject-specific mailing lists or RSS feeds. Today everyone has the opportunity to write own news and have it delivered to a broader public. The short message service Twitter has become the message form *par excellence*. Even if only the URLs for messages are sent and discussed.

   A decentralized alternative to this is the Mastodon news service: Mastodon is a microblogging service that has been created by a German programmer from Jena for several years. Everyone can set up an own server and join the server community. In contrast to large comparable platforms such as Twitter, Mastodon is designed as a decentralized network: The service is therefore not based on a central platform but consists of many different server instances that are operated independently by private individuals, associations or other bodies. The servers communicate with each other in encrypted form and numerous users only send cipher text via the channels of these private telecommunication facilities, which are nevertheless very public.

8.30 Public enemies No. 1: Cash and microphone-free rooms prevent glass people •

Microphone-free rooms and cash can be regarded as the No. 1 enemies of the state. The control of the citizens is made more difficult and both means are developing in the opposite direction: cash is to be abolished through convenient electronic payments and the living spaces with microphones are to be increased in order to be able to better control people.

Every car connected to the Internet has integrated microphones. Even in the world of work, as was recently reported by well-known online senders, every parcel scanner has a microphone to listen to conversations made by employees - nothing unusual, because the voice-controlled devices are already available at home. Every mid-range smartphone has more than a handful of highly sensitive field microphones installed that can listen to the next room.

The freedom to pay with cash is a means that can be assigned to its cryptographic sister - Steganography. The digital currencies currently emerging from BitCoin, starting with other brands from other providers such as those offered by the Facebook group and even some financial institutions, will not only create serious changes in human history with an epoch-making character in terms of Privacy, such as the furnishing of the living spaces of the population microphones, but also the expansion of electronic payment processes with the usual, known currency, contributes to this. The goal (especially its promotion in times of the corona pandemic) to make contact- and cashless payments via smartphone or smart watch at a terminal is not only convenient, but also a great danger and deprivation of freedom and Privacy in the 21st century, which many proponents of the necessary digitalization have not yet fully assessed in terms of their social impact.

Because: Here the way is exactly the other way around. Citizens currently have the standard setting of being able to pay with cash »on claws« and with electronic payments they enter into a task of Privacy, and thus into the dependency of a permanent control of payment data and their consumption content, from which they are no longer come out when the cash is pushed back to its abolition. This is not about the payment of larger amounts, such as those arising from the purchase of a used car, which can rightly be controlled in order to prevent money laundering. Rather, it is about the purchases of essentials without cash at many stations of the day - because there every human need is electronically registered and can be evaluated.

Paying with cash unobserved not only frees you from the storage of personal data, geo-location monitoring, monitoring of personal needs and the monitoring of people as a whole. Rather, doing without electronic payment transactions is also the best standard for protecting private needs, because the waiver via this quasi-Steganography denies the existence of a clear process: Nobody needs to know how many products were bought when and where for which needs. The same applies to cashback cards, which record purchases electronically and promise few discount points for giving up this freedom and producing transparent consumers.

Only cash that our teeth can bite would be according to this view also securely protected from being »crossed out« of this arithmetical value in the account. Because: Strictly speaking, digital money does not belong to people; the bank owns it. It is different with banknotes or gold that we can put in the piggy bank or under the pillow. Digital currency is equivalent to the borrowed government key, as mentioned above: In electronic payment processes and virtual money, people's existence is on a drip. This development in the digitization of payment processes in the shopping market must also be taken into account when it comes to the future of freedom and Privacy for people: Is cash freedom that we currently don't reflect enough on and appreciate? »Pay more often with cash and go to the bank once a month to equip yourself with banknotes,« a Twitter user named »Crashflow« shouted in the context of this steganographic discussion. Electronic payments with ›pin & plastic money‹ are not compliant with a »no-plaintext strategy«, which will be explained in a moment.

8.31   Cryptographic Cafeteria ●

The »Cryptographic Cafeteria« is a didactic game for teachers and students, which was introduced by *Linda A. Bertram* in the lexicon for Internet security and encryption »Nomenclatura«. According to this a group of pupils has to explain and present a term in a lecture by random procedure or by simply leafing through the lexicon. Similar to the selection of snacks in a cafeteria, the presentation teams can also negotiate their terms with one another according to a defined algorithm.

This can also be used in computer science lessons in schools and can also be adapted to an analysis and presentation of the over two dozen programs and tools for encryption presented here as examples. Each with the content focus of WHAT-HOW-WHY: For what purpose is the program used? How and with which cryptographic functions does this tool or program increase security on the Internet? And what added value does it bring to which users compared to another program? Why should it be used as part of a no-plaintext strategy?

Learners not only get to know the theoretical background, but also very specifically how to use the computer and its encrypting programs and gain insight into the procedures for how key exchanges or the non-transfer of keys work.

At the same time, learning in the subjects »Applied Cryptography« and »Architecture, Development and Use of Software Applications« must be given greater consideration in the training of teachers for natural sciences and computer science in schools, and these digital tools must also be taken into account to learn at colleges and universities as well as part-time.

In order to disseminate knowledge, skills and experience in the field of Cryptography just as easily as knowledge about having children, up-to-date work materials, books and laptops are required - as well as appropriate multipliers who bring colleagues and schoolchildren such reading material with them to the »cafeteria« or their room and lend it to others. Or introduce it in virtual hybrid lessons between blackboard and tablet.

9 INTEROPERABILITY, CONGRUENCE AND INTER-CONNECTIVITY OF SCOTTISH EGGS •

It is often desired that different providers of messaging and chat services can also receive, process and deliver messages from other services. Just as it is possible with e-mail or with different telephone providers with different numbers or area codes. This is summarized under the keyword interoperability of messengers.

9.1   Interoperability: not only technically a hopeless endeavor? •

Since the cryptographic protocols, architectures and designs are completely different in each case, this desire is becoming a long way off and, in particular, is technically very difficult to achieve. The abundance of applications and architectures already mentioned above as examples cannot be pushed through a standardizing gat.

Because interoperability also always means setting a standard for everyone. A standard that could possibly soon be the oldest and worst standard because several services would have to agree on a mediocrity. New developments would be inhibited, and innovative research paralyzed because it can only develop outside of the standard - an uneconomical field that nobody then occupies. According to this basic assumption, interoperability would be an obstacle to innovation and future development.

Interoperability, congruence, and interconnectivity are seen in a context, the meanings of which are to be described as follows.

Interoperability means that the encrypting messenger systems can receive and process the encrypted message packages of the users - regardless of how and by which messenger or email app they were encrypted. Interoperability is a somewhat broader term than, for example, purely technical compatibility. In a figurative sense, not all cars have to be powered by an electric motor but can continue to be interoperable on the roads with combustion engine technology. As early as 1984, *Karl Rihaczek* made a distinction in his article »Encryption and Standardization« that compatibility can refer to the three areas of user compatibility, connection compatibility and exchange compatibility[251]. So, the conditions for use can be identical, manufacturers should build identical (compatible) systems or individual encryption modules from different manufacturers must be able to harmonize consistently in the system environment, e.g., in the application of a desired algorithm or its keys.

Interconnectivity therefore means that an encrypted message packet can also be thrown into the server of the Conversations messenger, for example from the Delta-Chat Messenger server, or the encrypted message packet from the Smoke Messenger can be thrown into the Threema server. The individual servers of the providers must be connected to one another and forward the encrypted message capsules to the respective correct server.

Finally, *congruence* means that the server is located in the regional area where the user has the current location, which is also assigned to a police authority under administrative law. The server should be physically accessible within the regional boundaries of the respective police district so that online communication can be accessed on site and servers can also be confiscated. Rather, users do not need to be required to identify themselves, but rather an obligation on the part of service providers to ensure that their server is »identified« and is congruent to the user's place of residence.

What does this sense and an interplay of interoperability, congruence and interconnectivity mean in concrete terms for messengers? One could postulate that messengers are based on the secure McEliece algorithm with regard to encryption. Accordingly, widely used encryption libraries and methods (such as the GPG / Libgcrypt library) could also integrate McEliece for asymmetric keys.

And/or: At the same time, Fiasco Forwarding Keys (multiple keys) should be used for end-to-end encryption, supplemented by the innovative method of the Juggerknaut Keys (keys not transferred).

Not only an algorithm or protocol standard would have to be standardized, but the server standard would also have to be defined: for example, e-mail servers would have to be just as capable of forwarding the encrypted messages of the messenger Telegram, as is already the case with the messenger Delta-Chat, Spot-On, Spike, GoldBug Messenger & Email Client, and more is the case. Making chat servers interoperable also means including chat via e-mail servers (POP3 / IMAP)!

However, while these messengers address IMAP mailboxes for retrieving messages from offline friends or the Smoke Messenger addresses the Ozone mailboxes established there, in the case of interoperability, numerous e-mail servers would also have to be expanded accordingly to the Ozone mailbox technology. That would certainly be the right step if the established Ozone mailbox standard showed advantages in the cryptographic process. It shows how different the interests of the heirs and creators of interoperability can be. And who wanted to define that an inheritor would not be allowed to inherit the technological legacy in the future? And who wanted to define the circumstances of a death? Can we do without POP3 chat servers or XMPP chat servers?

In addition to algorithms, protocols and servers, it is more about the architectures: for example, as mentioned when calling up messages from friends who are currently offline, or when a server or client should be found de-centrally via a Distributed

Hash Table (DHT), every client in it is a so-called »servent«, so it is both: server and client.

In addition, the providers would ultimately also be subject to economic adjustments, as we know it with so-called »telephone roaming«: fees could be different if third-party services to which the customer has not currently subscribed are used; For example, a Skype user would like to insert the message into the WhatsApp Messenger server - or would like to dial into the paid landline network from it.

So, is it a hopeless undertaking to create interoperability for messengers? Not only because the foreign monopoly providers would not set themselves harmonizing requirements, but simply because the technical diversity cannot bring it to a promising denominator and if smaller providers are excluded, niches remain immediately?

At the end of this section, a perspective is given, namely: to set up a »taxi service«, as it were, for the message packages from different providers - a new house as a cheese dome, in which providers can find shelter and remain as specific as they are; However, under this bell, messages packages reach everyone involved.

Rather, it is worth considering and the goal that the monopoly power of the messenger WhatsApp in the Facebook group must be addressed and enriched with alternative options.

The German Federal Cartel Office, which is carrying out a sector investigation into messenger services for this purpose, is therefore advised against both objectives, the analysis of interoperability, congruence and interconnectivity, as well as the analysis of options for breaking the market power of monopoly providers in the messenger market cannot collect any satisfactory results in such a study - apart from a note on the funding of alternative, open-source projects and the establishment of cryptographic recommendations.

Figure 43: More than 2,000 million - Number of active WhatsApp users worldwide 2013-2020 (in millions)

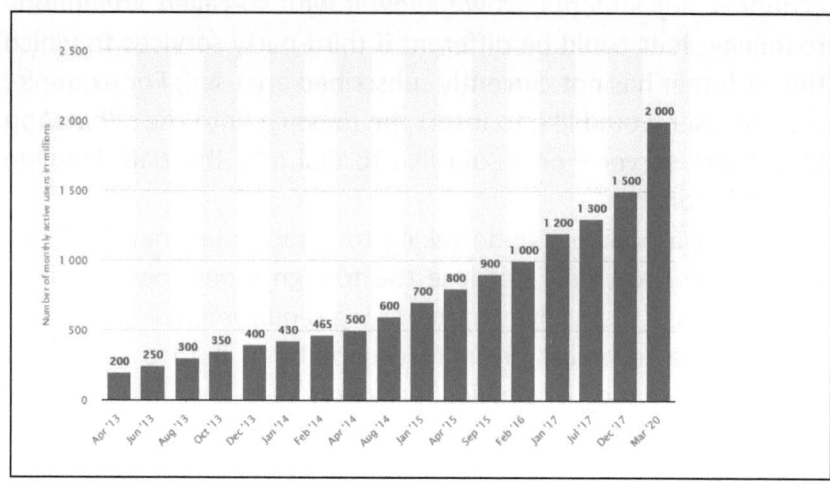

A first step towards harmonization would therefore be to analyze and compare the individual messengers and their technical features, especially with regard to their architectures and cryptographic functions as well as the cryptographic innovation potential.

9.2   Big-7-Study: Open-source Messenger in comparison

A first comparative study of cryptographic messengers in this context is the Big-Seven-Study (short: Big-7) by security researchers *David Adams* and *Ann-Kathrin Maier* from 2016, which compared seven different open-source messengers, including their cryptographic aspects.

The study offers an overview of all encrypting (also not open-source) messengers that have been compiled from various overview studies or have already been assessed with criteria by various portals. All open-source messengers in the field of encryption have been listed. Then all the criteria used by these portals were merged, cryptographic functions were described and finally applied, compared and assessed to seven decisive messengers that are open-source.

This resulted in an analysis for the applications CryptoCat, XMPP encryption, RetroShare, GoldBug, Signal, SureSpot and Tox. The comparison overview was embedded in the context of an auditing analysis of the then relatively young messenger GoldBug: The GoldBug messenger was audited at the same time with over 20 perspectives and set in reference to the other messengers mentioned.

It is a comprehensive task to analyze the messenger market and to keep it up to date, as messengers expand their functions, implement the McEliece algorithm, change the project name or owner or the programming team becomes toxic or less motivated, depending on the enthusiasm of the team-members. As with the Messenger Tox, development can virtually come to a standstill for these reasons.

As a result, the Big-7-Study collected points assessments as indicative values based on various criteria to be read there, which, when added together, showed that three out of seven applications have fundamentally good potential for the cryptographic functions.

Figure 44: Big-7-Study on Open Source Messenger

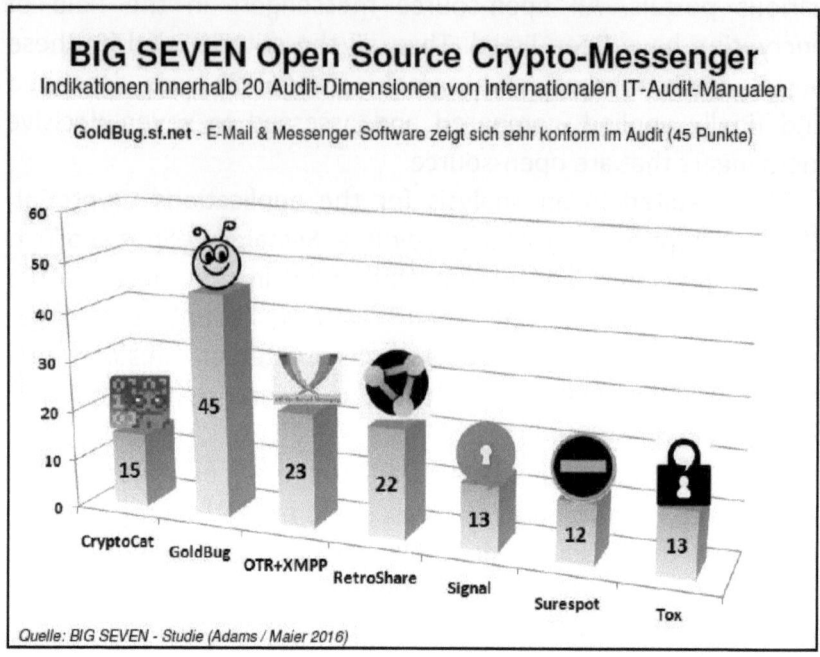

After its publication, the Big-7-study had various effects - in terms of building up and reducing resources and assessing cryptographic contexts, because for the first-time encrypting messengers were brought into detailed referential relation to one another. The study thus supported the cryptographic change, e.g., in the following areas:

- In the study, the POPTASTIC protocol for chat via e-mail server was presented in more detail, which led developers to set up the Delta-Chat client on the basis of GPG encryption. So, three things, GPG, as well as the POPTASTIC protocol, and finally the REPLEO function now referred to as AutoCrypt, were popularized thanks to the also open-source and thus welcome »idea loan« of this chat innovation existing as a blueprint via the server architecture of email accounts.

- Over time, cryptographic functions receive updates and new, secure procedures would have to be built into the programming. According to this comparative study, the messenger CryptoCat was discontinued and taken off the website. The developer had outgrown his student status and updating and improving the cryptographic functions may have robbed too much time, although he continues to teach professionally in this context.
- In the period that followed, the Tox developer did not become involved and left a work to be worked on for the other project participants, not to say: a patchwork of various functions.

In addition to the analysis of the relevant audit fields and the various open-source messengers with their cryptographic functions, 10 trends in the field of crypto messaging were also identified as a summary. This consisted of analyzing the following trends

- **Trend 01:** Chat and e-mail are growing together under the heading of messaging. E-mail servers are also used for encrypted chat with the POPTASTIC protocol.
- **Trend 02:** Data that is written to the hard disk or to a database must be encrypted.
- **Trend 03:** Secret evidence is not only used for authentication, but also for key management (SMP, ZK, Juggerknaut Keys or Secret Stream Keys).
- **Trend 04:** Multi-Encryption refers to the renewed encryption of cipher text with the same or a different algorithm.
- **Trend 05:** The sharing and transmission of keys with methods such as REPLEO and EPKS or AutoCrypt are

moving into a more central perspective in order to make encryption more user-friendly.

- **Trend 06:** Temporary keys, the so-called ephemeral keys, are not only included once per session, but in Fiasco Forwarding, numerous keys per message indicate a high level of security.
- **Trend 07:** Values for encryption are set individually, be it key size, selection of the hash method, selection of an algorithm for encryption. The Spot-On encryption suite shows numerous options for designing an individual crypto-DNA.
- **Trend 08:** End-to-end encryption can use manually entered passwords as keys. And it relates to your own keys (e.g., GPG keys generated elsewhere) that can be imported into applications (BYOK: Bring Your Own Key; CSEK: Customer Supplied Encryption Keys).
- **Trend 09:** Meta-Data, i.e., the evidence of who communicated with whom and via which IP or port, can be minimized with modern messengers by options in the graph design, i.e., which path an encrypted message packet takes. These include, for example, the mix networks Tor, Echo or I2P, which protect the IP address of the sender from metadata collection. Or the Messenger Briar, which is directly connected to Tor.
- **Trend 10:** McEliece and NTRU are the alternative algorithms to those that have been considered no longer secure since 2016 and with the beginning of the quantum-computer era: RSA and encryption based on elliptic curves.

These trends or dimensions are still considered to be fundamental aspects in the area of analysis dimensions to be considered for software audits of applications with cryptographic functions. An interoperability analysis should consider all ten dimensions. These »trends« or »analysis dimensions« are graphically shown in the following diagram, which is shown here as a gray image:

Figure 45: Trends in Crypto Messaging

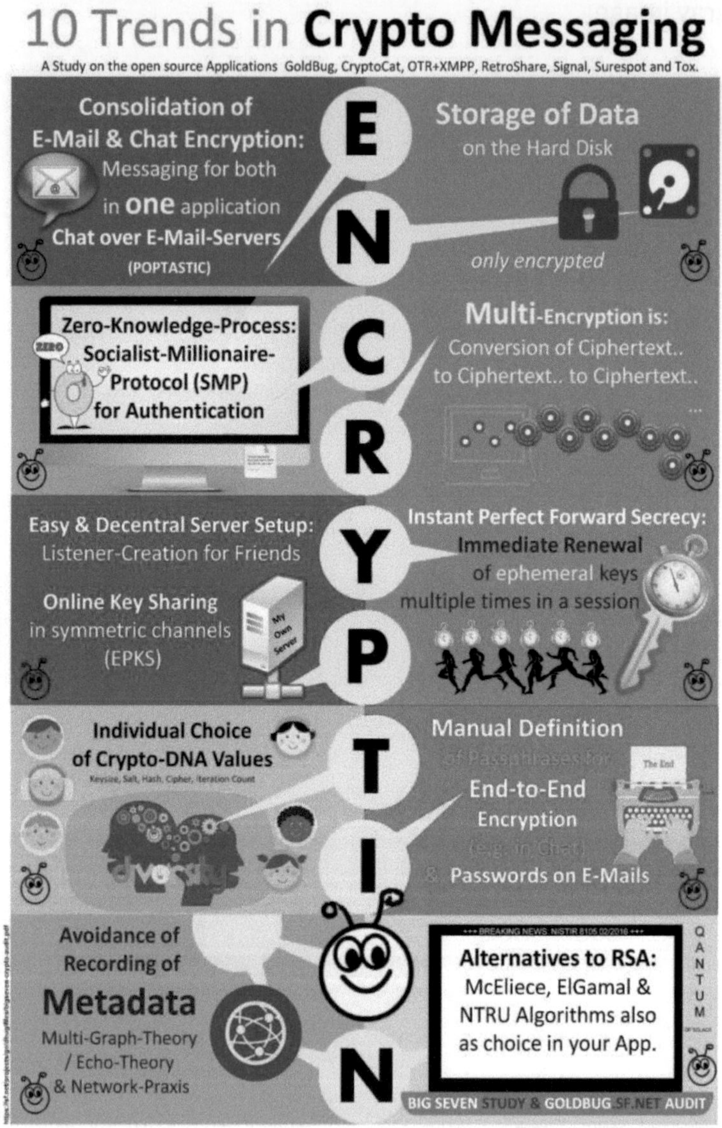

10 Trends in Crypto Messaging
A Study on the open source Applications GoldBug, CryptoCat, OTR+XMPP, RetroShare, Signal, Surespot and Tox.
ENCRYPTION
Consolidation of E-Mail & Chat Encryption:
Messaging for both in one application
Chat over E-Mail-Servers
(POPTASTIC)
Storage of Data
on the Hard Disk
only encrypted
Zero-Knowledge-Process:
Socialist-Millionaire-Protocol (SMP)
for Authentication
Multi-Encryption is:
Conversion of Ciphertext.. to Ciphertext.. to Ciphertext..
Easy & Decentral Server Setup:
Listener-Creation for Friends
Online Key Sharing
in symmetric channels
(EPKS)
My Own Server
Instant Perfect Forward Secrecy:
Immediate Renewal
of ephemeral keys
multiple times in a session
Individual Choice
of Crypto-DNA Values
Keysize, Salt, Hash, Cipher, Iteration Count
Manual Definition
of Passphrases for
End-to-End
Encryption
(e.g. in Chat)
& Passwords on E-Mails
The End
Avoidance of
Recording of
Metadata
Multi-Graph-Theory
/ Echo-Theory
& Network-Praxis
+++ BREAKING NEWS: NISTIR 8105 02/2016 +++
Alternatives to RSA:
McEliece, ElGamal &
NTRU Algorithms also
as choice in your App.
QANTUM
BIG SEVEN STUDY & GOLDBUG SF.NET AUDIT

Adams, D. / Maier, A.K. (2016)

9.3 Messenger Scorecards: For the completeness of cryptographic criteria ●

The visualization of comparisons with regard to cryptographic functions and the resulting knowledge of trends or important cryptographic dimensions, which new messengers may take into account, not only resulted in the cessation (CryptoCat), boggling (Tox) or the emergence of new messengers (Delta-Chat) or new servers (SmokeStack) impact, but also to consolidate a comparative method overall.

The instrument of a ScoreCard can support this comparison of cryptographic technology and specific functional scopes. The ScoreCard is a kind of points collection card, on which an evaluation is carried out on the basis of various criteria according to a point scale, so that the total results in a total number.

The aim here should be that as many criteria as possible are used as a basis in such a ScoreCard. Other comparison portals can provide information on possible criteria and initial analyzes that need to be updated.

Various portals with scorecard assessments of messengers were included as the first analyzes in the Big-7-study. The result turned out that some did not give a comprehensive market overview and were also not comprehensive in terms of subject matter or the selection of criteria. The scorecard of the American civil rights movement EFF (Electronic Frontier Foundation), for example, was made by just one activist. The EFF is a non-governmental organization in the United States that campaigns for Fundamental Rights in the information age. In comparison to other ScoreCard analyzes, however, it was shown that the EFF scorecard had a so-called »bias«, that is, it was pretentious and did not apply all-encompassing criteria or did not adequately consider open-source messengers. This scorecard was therefore scheduled for revision and update after a few weeks after the

Big-7-Study was published but remained offline for the following years.

Nevertheless, as mentioned, the method of comparison was with these models on ScoreCards made known to a wider audience and stimulated. Numerous Messenger ScoreCards were created in Germany in particular, with which students compared different open-source messengers on their websites or in their blogs on the basis of defined criteria and described advantages and disadvantages or, first of all, cryptographic functions and relationships (in a so-called SWOT -Analysis).

From the experience of previous evaluation processes, it can certainly be learned that many technical and cryptographic functions can only be represented and comparatively evaluated after familiarization with the technical specifics of a messenger. That is, in a context of cryptographic knowledge, it must be taken into account which criteria are possibly comparable and also which strategic importance they have.

For example, usually only the client, the application that can be installed on the smartphone, is evaluated, but not whether the server is open-source and repeatable or not. For this it is then necessary, for example, to assess whether the source code for a server can also be created for the Raspberry-Pi computer at home (on own »metal«, »on premise«), or just an execution environment, for example is possible on the Amazon web systems.

Or the question of whether the methods used are up to date must be assessed. If a hash method such as SHA1 is considered unsafe, it is important to include this criterion and compare it with more modern hash methods of other messengers.

Ultimately, it is also a matter of weighing up the relevance of desired functions against aspects of security. Is the messenger also rated as a video chat or just a text messenger that can also transfer recorded audio files? This assessment is given a completely different reference if the server is then also to be video-capable, or libraries such as WebRTC are integrated with the video process. These require a central certificate for encryption, which can therefore be assessed as a weak point if video streams are to be eavesdropped. An experienced technician can test this, for example, by connecting two video chat clients (e.g., via Nextcloud) in the home network to an existing server, but the home network cannot access the Internet behind a PFSENSE firewall or the Internet is not connected at all. The WebRTC video library would always look for a server on the Internet to check certificates and possibly not establish video chat.

What use are different security standards for text chat and video chat if video chat is a welcome function, but it means a loss in the security standard?

Against the background of the Third Epoch of Cryptography with old algorithms that are no longer considered secure and the new computing capacities of quantum-computers, the criteria that point to the McEliece or NTRU algorithms or multi-encryption for security must be emphasized. In the course of increased government attention to private keys, it should also be possible to define them manually. Applications that allow users their own and flexibly changeable passwords can also be given a special focus.

And finally, as described, it is not only about the source openness of the application, but also of the server, which should also be used for compilation or installation in an own home network.

Corresponding data security is of great relevance for many organizations, e.g., according to the General Data Protection Regulation (GDPR), as well as the fact that a server location e.g., in Europe does not receive data access from companies overseas because of legal and political regulations such as the Cloud Act or FISA (*Foreign Intelligence Surveillance Act*).

Uploading contact lists and phone numbers of friends is a major problem, especially with WhatsApp and Telegram and other alternatives, even if the phone numbers are only uploaded in hashed form. This also applies to the reservations in companies, schools, and municipal organizations to set up MS teams or cloud-based matrix servers instead of self-hosted installations, as it is currently unclear with the above regulations whether the data could illegally flow into the USA or not.

Essential criteria that are mapped in various Internet portals according to the aforementioned method, as well as over a dozen open-source messengers, were therefore referenced in the following overview. It represents a current overview, further functions will be updated, if necessary, new names for open-source messengers will be added. Nevertheless, because of the openness of the source, these messengers will be available to users and developers over the coming years in order to further advance usage and development interests based on this comparison overview.

Ultimately, such an analysis has to be deepened and technically explained when it comes to the subject of standards in the market and in development. This in turn also applies to the topic of interoperability, congruence and interconnectivity of Messenger, if you want to standardize this and not let each user decide for themselves which communication channel to choose with loved ones at home.

At the same time, it can also become clear that this topic of a supposed necessity for interoperability is being sold as a convenient solution so that ultimately the methods of breaking into the encrypting messaging systems are harmonized and also have a (politically reduced) standard in encryption, easily broken by government analysts? It remains to be discussed whether interoperability is the right and most urgent means of balancing WhatsApp's market power. This could also be achieved through an obligation to regional servers (congruence).

The opposite pole, individual encryption instead of standardized encryption, was called individual crypto-DNA in the Big-7-Study. The more individual it is, the more independent a server is in terms of design and digital sovereignty of the users, the more secure against standardized attacks is and will remain the architecture. Users should be able to confidently select their hash method, their key size, their algorithm and other encryption methods and process steps. Because then it is likely to be more secure than if everyone had to choose the same constants in the encryption.

Are those in favor of maintaining secure end-to-end encryption therefore always opponents of the interoperability of messengers?

A recommendation can therefore be to develop as many architectures as possible from the multitude of different messenger systems, not only in terms of application, but also in terms of technical understanding. There will therefore have to be more years of comparative and in-depth analysis of messengers. The following referencing of messengers and their criteria and features represents a comparative overview that needs to be updated.

Figure 46: Messenger in a criteria-based comparison

Kriterium	ATox	Briar	Chat Secure	Conversations	Delta Chat	Element	GoldBug	RetroShare	Signal	Smoke	Spot-On	SureSpot	Telegram	Threema	Wire
A	•	•	X	•	•	•	X	•	•	•	X	•	•	•	•
B	X	•	•	X	•	•	X	X	•	X	X	X	•	•	•
C	•	•	X	X	•	•	•	•	•	X	•	X	•	•	•
D	X	X	X	X	X	X	•	X	X	•	•	X	X	X	X
E	X	X	X	X	X	X	•	X	•	•	•	X	X	X	X
F	X	X	X	X	•	X	•	•	X	•	•	X	X	X	X
G	X	•	•	•	•	•	•	•	•	•	•	•	•	•	•
H	X	X	X	X	X	X	•	X	X	•	•	X	X	X	X
I	X	X	X	X	X	X	•	•	X	•	•	X	X	X	X
J	X	X	X	X	•	X	•	X	X	•	•	X	X	X	X
K	X	X	X	X	•	X	•	X	X	•	•	X	X	X	X
L	X	X	X	X	X	X	•	X	X	•	•	X	X	X	X
M	1	1	X	X	•	X	•	X	X	•	•	X	X	X	X
N	X	X	X	X	X	X	X	X	X	•	X	X	X	X	X
O	X	•	•	•	•	•	•	X	•	•	•	•	•	•	•
P	•	•	X	X	•	•	•	•	•	•	•	X	•	X	•
Q	X	X	X	X	X	X	•	X	X	•	•	X	X	X	X
R	•	•	•	•	•	•	•	•	X	•	•	X	X	•	•
S	•	•	•	•	•	•	•	•	X	•	•	X	X	X	2
T	•	•	•	•	•	•	•	•	X	•	•	X	X	•	•
U	X	X	X	X	X	X	•	X	X	•	•	X	X	X	X
V	X	X	X	X	X	X	•	X	X	•	•	X	X	X	X
W	•	•	•	•	•	X	•	•	X	•	•	X	•	•	X
X	X	X	X	X	X	X	X	X	•	X	X	X	•	•	•
Y	X	X	X	X	X	X	•	X	X	•	•	X	X	X	X
Z	X	X	X	X	•	•	X	X	•	X	X	X	•	•	•

• = given, x = probably in development, Update-Feedback welcome. *Source:* [253]

26 criteria:

A	Android Client
B	IOS Client
C	Desktop Client
D	saves encrypted in database
E	End-to-end encryption (secret / password) can be defined by yourself
F	Multi device capable
G	encrypted group chat
H	Modern Hashing, e.g., Argon2
I	Manual renewal of the session key (Cryptographic Calling)
J	Multiple temporary keys, e.g. with Fiasco Forwarding
K	Own keys (Customer Suppl. Encr. Keys, CSEK) can be imported
L	Has a login password and exit button
M	Mobile server for Android or Raspberry-Pi available
N	End-to-end encryption with asymmetric keys
O	Messages to offline friends
P	Free of charge
Q	Quantum immune by McEliece or NTRU algorithm / current security
R	Without SMS registration of your own telephone number / alias identifier
S	Server open-source
T	Without phone number upload of the phone book / GDPR compliance
U	Abstinence from key transmissions (Zero-Knowledge derivation)
V	Attachments and images are saved in encrypted form
W	Server location outside of the USA / Privacy Shield (Schremps) conformity
X	Voice call
Y	SMP / J-PAKE authentication
Z	Send a voice message as a file

366

9.4 Possible recommendations for the standardization and interoperability of messengers •

So, if you want to bring differences to a common denominator or at least want to build bridges, network existing bridges or update to higher quality standards, you first have to know and evaluate the differences and similarities, not to say: compare. A common denominator can only be defined and formed on the basis of in-depth technical analyzes. To do this, it is necessary to define the things that should be present above the line. After researching the technical definition of interoperability, there are already some first bloggers and portals who are thinking about how monopolists can be supplemented by an alternative and what the strengths and weaknesses of technical harmonization[254] are.

In the following, an attempt to standardize as a possible basis for discussion and recommendation will therefore be compiled as to which essential functions are to be defined in the case of interoperability of messengers.

(1) Messenger services that offer RSA or Cryptography with elliptic curves (such as ECDSA) as an algorithm should be hybrid by 2016 at the latest, for example with the McEliece algorithm - or optionally use NTRU.

(2) Implemented McEliece algorithms should, if necessary, remain downward-compatible with RSA, as is the case with the Smoke-Messenger model project, or even better completely dispense with insecure algorithms such as RSA.

(3) For end-to-end encryption, it is not necessary to use one key per session or one key per message, but rather several keys per message. This established standard of Fiasco Forwarding should be built into every interoperable messenger instead of the rigid double ratchet protocol, in which a previous message helps determine the encryption of the next

message; or the risk is to be assessed that if a key is uploaded or known, all previous messages are legibly »torn open«.

(4) Because of innovative protocols, it is not necessary to transmit keys for secure end-to-end encryption, as is the case with the Juggerknaut Keys. These should supplement the corresponding Fiasco Keys.

(5) Standardized messenger encryption should also consider the hybrid change from symmetric and asymmetric encryption in an ongoing session, as well as options for multi-encryption.

(6) Servers should forward the encrypted message capsules of different protocols to all connected users, including different clients. This must be taken into account in particular for the IMAP and POP3 e-mail servers in order to include the POPTASTIC chat (via e-mail server) of many messenger clients. So it's mostly about server interoperability.

(7) Email encryption in the GPG standard could also include the McEliece algorithm. Software libraries used in messengers should be supplemented by further promising algorithms.

(8) Connected clients should be able to cache cryptographic messages from offline friends in the same way as servers do (so-called care-of method).

(9) All of these requirements apply in particular to open-source, interoperable servers and clients.

(10) Interoperability can mean balancing the market power of the monopoly providers, but not resetting the cryptographic standard to a lowest (possibly common) denominator. It is not the lowest standard that needs to be addressed, but the better standard in each case must set the pace.

(11) Likewise, innovations and telecommunications systems that deviate from the standard are not to be criminalized, but to be promoted.

(12) Regional servers should be able to hand over the private keys to regional investigative authorities if required after a legal decision.

(13) In order to balance the market power of monopoly providers, providers of telecommunications services should have to maintain servers based on the market location principle at the national level. The company's communication server must also be set up not where a company is based for tax purposes, but where the user is located: so that the user is at a messenger client depending on their current physical location be able to dial in to a local server on site (e.g., in Berlin or optionally Munich or Brussels). It cannot be that we have to submit a report to the local police for criminal offenses, but the perpetrator of a crime dials into a server that is outside of this market and crime scene principle. Police must also be able to patrol local markets and networks in the digital world. This balance of market power begins with the obligation to maintain regional servers, which users choose depending on their location in the federal state - instead of a single powerful WhatsApp server in the USA. WhatsApp has to set up its chat server wherever a Berliner reports a crime by Berliners to the police that has been prepared in WhatsApp: in Berlin! Only in this way can police officers in Berlin address this issue - and, if necessary, have access to search and forensic analysis. In the digital world, it's not just about »interoperability« - better, much more: about (regional) congruence. I.e., it is about a congruence of the location coordinates of chat servers with the location coordinates of police stations and crime scenes as well as the users. Otherwise, remote and regional or even cross-continental investigations remain necessary, which are often delayed and unsuccessful.

(14) Establishing interoperability includes the economic separation of server and client: A non-profit, public digital infrastructure could be set up for the chat servers and at the same time competition law could be changed so that platform and server providers could do so that other clients can use them as well and that the servers are compatible with non-profit servers. Separate from the rules for messenger clients, new rules for the server economy are required in competition law, which include state infrastructure and non-profit servers.

(15) The operation of private and association-linked messenger telecommunications server systems for organizations, associations, youth groups, school classes or families should - as is the case with Freifunk for the offer of free WiFi Internet access - recognized - and recognized as non-profit be exempt from relevant taxes. This is the only way to ensure adequate protection against the power of the Internet giants.

(16) State and state-funded open-source servers are required as a networked overlay network, which also connect to the servers of the messenger services. This interconnectivity can create - and promote - a »mailbox system« for encrypted message capsules for forwarding to all providers.

(17) The *German Federal Office for Information Security* (BSI) or its European equivalent, the EU-Committee for Science and Technology Options Assessment of the European Parliament (STOA), could soon provide exemplary analyzes the Messenger, which makes the compatibility of RSA and future-oriented McEliece keys interoperable. These are currently e.g., the Messenger Smoke, GoldBug and other open source.

(18) Data protection-friendly projects and providers that meet these criteria should also be able to receive appropriate

funding, as well as scientific work by students on individual aspects of interoperability and congruence of messengers.

A first compiled basis for discussion on the interoperability of messengers could be discussed in this or a similar way, which is to be assessed in an interdisciplinary group: Overall, there is a need for further research and development.

Andreas Mundt, President of the German Federal Cartel Office, sums up the project for both objectives of breaking up messenger monopolies by promoting alternatives and having encrypted message capsules forwarded and transported by all server providers as follows: »Users of various messenger services usually cannot communicate with each other across different communication servers. The Cartel Office will conduct a study for consumers to investigate the impact that improved interoperability would have on the selection of Privacy-friendly providers, among other things. Because there is often uncertainty about whether and to what extent personal data is even protected in the various services. Consumers must be truthfully informed about how the security of their communication is guaranteed. We want to provide information about this and about possible violations of consumer rights. Because messenger services have become indispensable as a means of communication in everyday life for consumers«![255]

For the future, let us wish that, instead of monopoly-like structures, more decentralized and open-source servers are used in the messenger environment, that every class teacher can easily set up and administer such a chat server for the learners and the most innovative and most secure level of encryption is analyzed, comparatively documented and used in order to bring encrypted message capsules to the correct address of a cryptographic token?

9.5 Technical outlook: The coat of the Scottish egg - State servers as an overlay network? ●

If one does not want to go the way of defining a common technical denominator for messaging, another option should be presented here in which the different characteristics of a messenger can be retained. The messages are put into an envelope with an address, and this is delivered to the correct address by a transport system to be set up.

In order to achieve interoperability of messenger services, the package - or let's say a capsule - with the message, whether encrypted or not, could be encrypted again in a transport capsule. Each transport capsule then receives such a hash or cryptographic token, similar to an EAN barcode (European Article Number). Just as we know it with a barcode for tracking at parcel delivery companies such as FedEx or DHL. At the parcel counter, a sticker with a barcode is affixed to the parcel. Users can use it to »throw« their encrypted message capsule into one server or another, wrapped in an encrypted transport capsule. The respective server recognizes which messenger provider the transport capsule is for and forwards it to the correct server.

Metaphorically speaking, every continent (aka messaging provider) has a harbor (server) in which ships with taxis (transport capsules) arrive, each with an encrypted laptop (with a message) on the passenger seat. In the harbor it is recognized that the taxi does not have a corresponding license plate that is associated with the current continent of the harbor. Then the taxi (the transport capsule) including the laptop (message capsule) is packed back onto the ship and forwarded to the next continent (messaging provider) with the corresponding harbor. If the right continent is there, on which the taxi can drive with its license plate, a driver of a driver service takes over the task of delivering the encrypted laptop on the car seat.

So, we come to interoperability with more encryption and with cryptographic tokens for routing, quasi the license plate in the above example, than with less encryption.

All that is required is a second so-called »overlay network« or an additional encryption layer for the transport capsule. A cross-service infrastructure is then required that can also take regional servers into account. Why shouldn't you be able to throw your encrypted messenger message capsule into every regional server of a regional police station that organizes delivery to the respective service?

Protocols that use cryptographic tokens to define a graph path (such as the AE protocol) have provided a blueprint for this. It is thus determined via which stations the message packet is delivered and which node can process and read it. With cryptographic tokens, not only so-called national routing (compare so-called »Schengen routing«) can be implemented, but the necessary encryption of the data packets can also be included.

The additional encryption layer required for this can be visualized using »Scotch Eggs«: in this national dish of the Scots, boiled eggs are coated with minced meat and fried again in the oven. If you cut through it, you can first see the egg yolk as the first layer, around it the egg white as the second layer and finally the minced meat as the third and last layer.

Figure 47: Scottish eggs in cross section

Source: Kitchen.

These visual models of congruence and interoperability require further scientific analyzes and drafts of updates - as do people who question monopolies and install and use alternative messengers and servers in order to test interoperability and congruence, and to supply these alternative offers a basis for use.

Is the idea of building a state structure in the field of information technology too adventurous? After all, we have these in the field of water supply, electricity supply, the state post office, or the supply of living space as well. This should possibly also apply to electronic mail.

In this sense, Brazil also had the idea in 2013 of setting up a sovereign, country-specific e-mail system for the country in its own data lines: In response to revelations about the extensive electronic surveillance by the NSA, Brazil's Minister of Communications *Paulo Bernardo* told the daily *Folha de São Paulo*[256] that a national email system should be created. The NSA had attacked e-mails from the country's economy and from then President *Dilma Rousseff*.

Russia has already implemented this idea through its #RUNET, which can be switched off from the global world by means of its own infrastructure in the event of a crisis and then only continues to function within the country and thus also affects the e-mail system. Germany has so far relied on the system of communication via DE-Mail, which has already been mentioned, but which can be described as a dead tiger: it has not been used for many years also because of insufficient encryption. Or it is experiencing a renaissance in the area of extended *DE-Messaging* with state servers.

Brazil's plan to create a state email that offers alternatives to American servers and protects citizens has not yet been a model for Germany and Europe in connection with encrypted options. Espionage analyzes of the communication of European citizens by the US technology companies are therefore wanted, and it is only regrettable that they, as monopolists, have such a grip on the market that the communication analysts do not carry out these investigations on alternative servers in the own country?

One finding could be: Anyone who wants to offer own alternatives to the monopoly WhatsApp should also have alternative servers on their own: Either state for everyone, or everyone for family and friends: The erosion and the crisis of Privacy through monopoly information technologies could be countered with innovative models.

And: the first step on the way out of the encryption dilemma is to turn away from foreign servers towards the provision and use of national servers with regard to digital and cryptographic sovereignty?

Instead of numerous monitoring measures in the 21st century, will a state-sponsored, social movement towards open-source messenger alternatives have to be formed, which also includes a sponsored technical provision of both, clients and servers?

The Right to Privacy in the digital space will therefore remain an ongoing task for the future in this Third Epoch of Cryptography - especially for the next up-and-coming generations of the designers of the post-modern Internet.

In the 1990s there were the powerful messengers from AOL and ICQ, they are obsolete today. Will there also be a move away from WhatsApp in the future, which our friends electronically »make« available to us? If the state and monopoly companies lend private keys, restrict free speech and break the Protection of Privacy, then they are allowed to offer textual options for conversation with friends - until other friends without this technology can be found or reached or other, alternative tools are used to contact them? Having an alternative to choose is essential in a Democracy - is it also in the choice of which technology we use to contact our loved ones? With your own choice and installation of a communication technology, it is important to promote an alternative to monopoly - and also standard. Because this has social implications.

Time will tell which communication servers will be used in 50 or 100 years and whether the Facebook & WhatsApp servers will still be equally popular. Then the transmission of messages to Mars will also be a more modern technology: For planets as well as for Scotland and for individuals, the number one learning objective applies: If you want to communicate electronically with others, you must be able to set up a server! Communicating via WhatsApp server is comparable to having our teeth brushing only carried out by dental offices abroad. The use of WhatsApp servers is therefore to be assessed as Stone Age and not geared towards a humanistic idea of independence. Chat servers, which anyone can easily install themselves at home, give us humans a toothbrush to the hand: what an evolution!

10 SOCIAL OUTLOOK: WITH A NO-PLAINTEXT-STRATEGY INTO THE DILEMMA OF AN ENCRYPTED SOCIETY? •

You know it: Since the Snowden-papers in 2013, it has been clear that all content that is sent over the Internet is saved - and thus also (can) be analyzed. And they are analyzed. As we have seen, encryption in particular protects against this. In the years that followed, there were numerous initiatives to strengthen, expand and make encryption more secure, to discuss and further develop standards, to update programs, and to *somehow* increase the proportion of cipher text that is sent to the Internet. However, this success rate is less to be seen in the willingness of users to encrypt individual messages.

In other words, with e-mail encryption there is still a great need to make encryption easier to use. However, automated solutions provide encryption much more, as is the case with the transfer of websites. For example, there was the *Encrypt Everywhere* initiative, which provides owners of websites and domains with free certificates for HTTPS and thus the encrypted transmission of the website. The initiatives of the browser manufacturers should also be mentioned, through which HTTPS websites, which are transmitted in encrypted form compared to the old HTTP websites, are now marked differently in the browser. Or a few years later there was also the change that the browser always calls up the HTTPS URL of a website first, and if this does not exist, the insecure HTTP standard is only then used.

This of course increases the volume of the encrypted data packets in the data lines. But it is also necessary for users to recognize that their individual e-mail message needs to be encrypted. The automated encryption by the e-mail client Delta-Chat is very promising and will soon also be built into the other open-source e-mail clients - such as Thunderbird - as a standard, so that two Thunderbird clients have the key Exchange automatically, as the technical developments according to the functions REPLEO, EPKS and AutoCrypt show as a model.

At the same time, there may be a perspective that the number of messages in plain text will be further reduced. With a no-plaintext strategy or a program for »never-again-plain-text-sending«.

After we have recognized that a message can be read by anyone like a postcard without encryption, the goal can be pursued to reduce this to a minimum - if not even to zero. This may correspond to the approach in the corona pandemic of reducing infections to zero with a NoCovid or ZeroCovid strategy, as the city of Gersheim was the first to succeed in the pandemic in Germany.

The no-plaintext strategy thus presents a comparable way to more security on the Internet. Readable text on the Internet should be avoided. The encryption of Internet communication between two people is a central pillar.

The cornerstones of a no-plaintext strategy are:
- Encryption of Internet communication between two people should be a standard.
- A no-plaintext strategy requires a collaborative effort: It requires a joint effort that includes members from technology and politics, management and information science as well as operational administration.
- The aim is to increase the number of encrypted data packets in the data lines of the Internet.
- The aim of the no-plaintext strategy is that all data packets and content on the Internet are encrypted.
- Each plain text message is one too many plain text messages.
- It must be ensured that only authorized persons have access to the plain text and not just anyone inside or outside of organizations can gain access.

- The fight against crime is a social and not a technical problem or even of the disciplines of mathematics or Cryptography or Steganography.
- The alienation of everyone from encryption, just to prosecute a few criminals, is hardly feasible - and whether it is justifiable requires detailed discussion by relevant social groups.
- The content must be checked by third parties when reading and writing the messages.
- The data to be decrypted with an authorization concept must be classified into data in motion, data at rest and data in use. The point is to determine which data should be decrypted at which point and by whom after it has been transferred over the network, which data can still be encrypted in the devices and which data, which is only temporarily stored, for what duration, and by whom, can be decrypted for a short time. For example, whether volatile keys and data are viewed in the device's main memory or in the permanent hard disk storage.
- The initiation of the implementation of a no-plaintext strategy is not only the task of data protection officers in every organization and company.
- A no-plaintext strategy can include a discussion of a right to encryption.
- The promotion of servers that prevent the forwarding of plain text is to be expanded.
- Anonymous access to the network and anonymous shipping messages on the Internet must be guaranteed by law.
- Joint learning is to be continued and maintained, which includes regular discussion and updating of the »No-Plaintext« security strategy.

The Chaos Computer Club has been committed to phasing out unencrypted communication for many years and therefore calls for a ban on unencrypted communication. Every bit and every byte that is transported by providers and processed by banks or the tax office must be encrypted. XMPP communication servers that still allow plain text to pass through must consequently be shut down. Anyone who transmits and archives their customers' data in unencrypted form and thus endangers their security should be subject to severe penalties - this is the point of view of this leading organization[257] of a spirit that is often still student-influenced but revealing about a vision of a no-plaintext strategy.

The liberal party of Germany will finally issue a no-plaint-text strategy as a principle in its program this year: The encryption of network traffic and its data is about the protection of property, Privacy and the confidentiality of communication, so there should be next to a Right to Encryption, basic encryption of electronic communication also be provided[258]. But almost all other parties are not ruling out more or less »the strengthening of IT security with excellent and secure encryption«.

Nevertheless, this strategy is only one side of the consideration. Social control by colleagues, neighbors, IT administrators and state actors wants to keep the proportions of encrypted data packets sent in the data lines as low as possible in order to be able to control them. That brings us back to the argument at the beginning of this volume. Back to Start and the Monopoly game starts all over again! The way out of this loop was given by the no-plaintext strategy: Third parties control the content before encryption and after decryption.

It should also be noted that the game of secret control of plain text is the game of corporate actors. Citizens may be able to embark on a no-plaintext strategy, especially after appropriate education and training measures, in which they recognize that this security is in their own best interest - for themselves and their loved ones. Because there are many processes in which John Doe is not recognizing it clear which gaps exist, in which own data is carelessly disclosed on the Internet.

At the same time, a movement can be seen among administrators with the aim of making the systems on the Internet more secure. The development is slow but continuous, similar to the development of safety systems in the automotive industry. For example, assistance systems in cars have become more and more sophisticated over the years and are moving from optional equipment to standard equipment. So, if we look a decade or two into the future, we may also find that encryption has increased continuously - as may drastically measures to access it in plain text.

And: is it to be assumed for a future development that we are moving towards an ›encrypted society‹ with the interactions on the Internet? In this, the interactions between two people and within groups could be more protected from the guiding glances of third parties, if not more comprehensively and mathematically correctly encrypted. These processes of an *encrypted society* will have an impact on the social capital of our society. It will no longer be so easy to intervene in the interaction processes with social norms by advising or guarding third parties, because they will often not be visible.

Parents used to know which school friend called which school friend. They could participate in interactions or grandparents could give advice as they heard situations. Today, parents often no longer know who has just sent their children a text message via a messenger or one of the many channels or who is currently bullying them at school if they do not care about which chats and interaction portals their children are included in.

The thesis could be put forward that parents have never been able to participate so less in the forms of interaction between young people as today, because nowadays this takes place via smartphone technology, in which parents too often are left out of the picture. Similar tendencies will exist when increasing encryption processes no longer allow parents, neighbors, colleagues, and friends to intervene in an individual's communication to correct it.

Not only messenger technologies, but also encryption technologies change our interactions, all the more when messenger, electronic communication and encryption come together.

It used to be that what was thought was not, or at least not one-to-one, thrown at someone's head in a real situation. Twitter, Facebook and other social media have removed this decency and limit. In electronic and public communication, many people publish their thoughts and their hatred as a matter of course and addressing it directly to a counterpart in public in an incompatible way, at least in a way that a generation before would never have dared to throw this direct hatred at someone in a personal situation with such a phrase at the head.

Your own opinion - possibly even confirmed in a (closed) partial public - in (encrypted) chats cannot be linked to the claim that it would be immediately political reality - ultimately this also undermines the representative processes of Democracy: So, become today partly-public awareness - cemented as impermeable, negative accusations against others – promoted, and disinformation controlled by digital communication in such a way that our European societies are polarized and thus disintegrated?

It will therefore require further ministers of the interior as well as analyzing scientists who also come as digital natives from the - so to speak: indigenous - smartphone generation in order to carry out analyzes, for example with regard to right-wing radical chat groups within the police, federal or fire services and to take action. It could be chat groups that may be encrypted in the future and no longer allow access even to colleagues with different attitudes.

Thus, in such an encrypted society, it is not only about the insight into the preparation of criminal offenses, but also about an insight into a creeping erosion of norms and decency and social interaction standards, which may remain undetected and can therefore no longer be corrected. Who intervenes in social media when someone messes with their message and how can they learn a cultural and media competence of mutual apology instead of blocking a contact?

The dilemma is twofold: On the one hand, we need security in online communication, but we also have to be aware of the inaccessibility of other people and groups who communicate in encrypted form. And finally, every single person who engages in encrypted and non-encrypted online interaction will have to learn and test himself in it but cannot necessarily expect learning effects or excuses from others in the online world. Encrypted interaction may be a special learning field here:

So, what if the future murderer of a politician is strengthened by his chat partner in an encrypted 1: 1 chat? And what if a policewoman discovers in an encrypted group chat at the regional police station that right-wing extremist slogans are being established here in this online team, which she does not like? Does the exit and the report on this encrypted group have to be compared with whistle-blowing processes or would someone in the group as an individual write their oppositional opinion?

We are already beginning to experience this phenomenon when the female teammates from the department create a WhatsApp group and communicate about the men in the team at work after work. It also affects companies that do not allow WhatsApp, but who use it to continue using the company's corridor on their private cell phones after work or even address customers via it. Numerous labor court cases increasingly have to include screenshots of communication from messenger side channels in order to substantiate statements, assessments and facts.

The third dilemma for the individual is that they can no longer evade modern online communication and at the same time be subject to its learning processes - or suffer from it.

Enduring a conflict, shit storm or hate mail or alienated values in groups online may be even easier than discovering a fundamental loneliness or overload in connection with online communication. Because electronic communication via messenger does not replace human interaction. It is a surrogate that can and does lead to deficits. Real interaction can be via video chat, and technologically this is already there as well. Text chat, on the other hand, is viewed critically by some analysts: Can the assumption be nurtured or even proven that messenger communication is harmful to the individual and to society? And in no case can it be proven that messenger communication is helpful for society? So, with this thought through to the end, could one also call electronic communication a deforming trap in which we are caught? Isn't there hardly anything human about writing something in a block of electronics and waiting for an answer? Instead, would face-to-face and video-to-video or audio-to-audio designs be better alternatives?

But even this appearance of real human interaction can lead to a fall into reality after switching off the technology: In the corona pandemic time, many singles report that the online meetings via Jitsi, Mumble, Bigbluebutton or Skype, Teams or Zoom led to a depression after the technology and thus the community experience was switched off. It was made clear to the users that after switching off the channel they are alone again and are only subject to virtual reality. The simulation of authenticity and vitality turned out to be hypocrisy.

Could the technology of interactive text in Messenger have damaged society in a more degrading and lasting way than we think? WhatsApp's addiction to attention and encouragement consists in bringing a contact who is listed at the bottom and has not been addressed for a long time back to the top of the list with a message. Isn't such an algorithm-controlled attention economy already present when the internet and our messenger are only about a smiley face or a forwarded image, and not about a real message?

A study in the *International Journal of Psychology*, however, shows that video calls, although they work suddenly and appeal to multiple senses, are not always the best way to stay in touch: »We found that sending small text messages« via Messenger - spread over the day - better helps to stay in contact than video conferences.«[259] These are more complex to plan and therefore less common, said *Nicole Krämer*, professor for social psychology of media and communication at the University of Duisburg-Essen.

Regardless of whether it's video or text chat, overall, does it seem like there's something fishy about it because there is so much profit orientation and attention from people associated with it? As a substitute for messaging, is WhatsApp a big casino of isolated and unhappy people who are wasting their time in order to escape a void - which harms all of us and each and every one of us as a whole? Because this time is also missing for volunteering and service to fellow human beings?

It is therefore becoming more relevant to studies that analyze a correlation with the growth of messenger messages relating to depression, suicides, deaths and extremism as well as a lack of resources for charity and subsidiary neighborhood responsibility in our society.

For example, the film »The Social Dilemma« was released on Netflix. A pessimistic picture of the future is drawn in this analysis. A dystopia that draws attention to dubious social developments of the present - and is not aimed at the salvation of society in the future, as a utopia promises: The story of a teenager who develops an addiction to social media is told. The story is interrupted by interviews with various US-American personalities from the environment of the big social media companies. Among other things, topics such as data mining, how the product design of the apps aims to increase addiction potential, the effects of social media on mental health, also with a special focus on the rising suicide rates among teenagers, and the role of social media in the spread of conspiracy theories are dealt with or the overall success of political communication.

In addition to technical interoperability, social interoperability must therefore also be ensured for messengers and social platforms of our communication: It is the well-known filter bubble that arises when we only receive messages from friends in electronic communication, but not from people who think differently. Then it has to be checked whether a previously described deformation gains potential. Among other things, this can lead to drastic developments in encrypted group chats if no third outside opinion can be added as a social corrective. Right-wing police chats are evidence of this, as is the right-wing murderer of the German politician *Walter Lübcke*, who in this first right-wing murder case in post-war history was strengthened by a friend in his attitude and perception of reality communicatively - also via chat. In addition, right-wing extremists and right-wing populists often openly expressed joy at the shooting in social chats, insulted and mocked those killed and announced further murders.

Failure to prosecute hate crimes on social networks was criticized. Encrypted communication can not only be understood as protection against third parties or spies but must also be thought of as a structural deformation that prevents corrective external opinions from entering encrypted communication. How necessary it is for the police to break up conspiracies in encrypted joint agreements is also demonstrated by the examples in which this has been successful.

Much more important than finding a supposedly confirming mirror in the social filter bubble is what electronic communication does with us, with the individual. Do we become more disgruntled and anti-social, even more extreme, while we wait for a reaction from someone on the smartphone with extended screen time? Will the WhatsApp double hook, which signals to us that a message has been read and, if necessary, will be answered soon, become a hook for ourselves on which we are caught?

Psychologists are already defining personal countermeasures so that young people in particular can escape this destructive power of messengers. Personal countermeasures that interpersonal interactions via telecommunications on the Internet become toxic include in particular:

- The visualization of the knowledge that the smartphone operating systems show under the »Wellness« function: Reduction of above-average hours in which the smartphone screen and its applications are used.
- In order not to be alerted to the mobile phone acoustically or by vibration again and again, the notification function for certain applications should be reduced or switched off. A visual display without an audio message is also sufficient.
- Social media applications that only take up time should be uninstalled.
- And also, in our content-related feedback in the channels to everyone or friends, the facts should first be checked before something is commented on. Do we answer far too quickly when we share, find something good or

comment on something just because the information looks surprising?

- At the same time, a supply of information must also be ensured that illuminates issues from other perspectives, even from areas or from people with whom we might not feel in agreement or with whom we might have common interests.
- Finally, the topic of the aggregation of hate reports in supposedly like-minded groups on the Internet is a major problem on which further studies are required, both in individual and collective handling of this phenomenon.
- Adolescents must first learn skills for interaction via smartphones. Young adults, explorers and young love in particular communicate before, during and after school. Via messenger and other internet channels. It is therefore important to learn the messenger function and how to express content and emotions using it. And it is best not to put smartphones into the hands of children too early, which means: no screen time! Social media are not based on comparison with other children, but on completed school classes and learned learning content and skills.
- Mobile devices should also be removed from the bedroom.

The Ministry of Social Affairs of the State of Mecklenburg-Western Pomerania, however, believes in its educational concept for 0 to 10 year old children that they should learn to use digital media at an early age. This is just as important as practicing with scissors: »For children, it basically makes no difference whether they cut a sheet of paper with scissors or digitally select a section of a picture«. It makes sense for children under 10 to develop and practice both techniques. Digital media enable three to six-year-olds to have new experiences if children use it not only in consumption but as tools, it is said. »If you take a tablet with you on a walk in the forest, the children can use it as a magnifying glass or microscope«.[260] Only children under three years of age are not recommended to work with digital media. So, the use of encrypting messengers as a tool can start from the age of three?!

The effects of intensive digital communication on young people show, on the one hand, that social communication via digital networks can be conducive to bonding with their peers, on the other hand, warnings are given of the risk of excessive or addictive use.

The combination of different means of communication can then certainly promote social integration in the family and among friends. Together with »offline communication« with family members and friends, according to the authors of a study[261] by the German *Institute for Trust and Security on the Internet* (DIVSI), digital communication makes a significant contribution to the identification and self-image of children, adolescents, and young adults. »Face-to-face communication« with friends and acquaintances will not be replaced by digital forms of communication, but will be continued, supplemented and in some cases even deepened - if they are used in moderation.

The PhD philosopher and former high school teacher for physics and mathematics, *Eduard Kaeser*, who now also works as a freelance journalist and jazz musician, on the other hand, sums up the need to deal more rationally and with learning more with digital technology with a rather gloomy perspective as follows: »What we are moving towards in an encrypted society is open. At least one thing should be clear: we have to locate the enemies of the open society not only in the terrorists, secret services, the dubious Internet giants or financial institutions, but also in us: that means in our indolence and carelessness towards someone who has got out of hand digitized way of life in whose veins exclusive - that is to say: secret - information flows. Today it is about a 'strong' human intelligence that recognizes what it is getting into if it does not stop the artificial intelligence«.[262]

However, this risk perspective may remain a minor opinion. The ›High Quadriga‹ of the formed *German National Pact for Cybersecurity*, whose four members represent the participation of the state, business, science and civil society, on the other hand, affirmed in its »declaration for society as a whole« in several fields of action that the »easy availability of security enhancing Encryption technology has to be accessible to everyone« - and not just to maintain competitiveness. This should make encryption available to everyone. Pragmatic assistance for understanding and securely handling Cryptography and IT should therefore become a »recognized and integral part of (pre-) school and professional training in order to improve the level of personal security and lay the foundation for further interest in this subject area«.[263]

As a representative of the social groups, this *National Cybersecurity Pact* is also embedded in existing international initiatives, because it represents a contribution to the »Paris Call for Trust & Security in Cyberspace« by French President Emmanuel Macron was presented at the Paris Peace Forum and a year later at the United Nations Internet Governance Forum in Berlin, is also supported by the governments of most EU member states, as well as numerous other states, including Great Britain, Australia and Japan. A wide variety of companies, associations and non-governmental organizations are also among the signatories.

In European countries and beyond, in the common perspective of the state, business, science, technology and civil society, a co-evolution of technical and social conditions is required, and this cooperation applies in particular to the individual and social use of technologies for messaging and for encryption.

After Pope Francis survived a bowel surgery, he thanked all employees in the healthcare system: an excellent, all accessible health care is important! Can the fundamental right to privacy through excellent training for encryption as well be seen as an important requirement of basic care for humans?

Learning in these fields then must be addressed more strongly and does not start with the daughter or son, but with the hope that mother and father will be able to help their descendants in the future, for example, to bring Linux with an encrypted data partition to the laptop. The installation and administration of open source and free Linux is - like encrypted messaging - one of the things that are worth learning and that the next generation should give young people today.

How could this volume with the story of the beginning of the *Third Epoch of Cryptography* be closed better than with the sentence: *Decryption is a cultural technique and is already de facto part of the world cultural heritage - that we should be interested in?*

EPILOG

»Are you sure the line is clean?«
»Yes, sure.«
»Nevertheless, I have to go!«

(Start of the movie: Matrix.)

INDEX OF FIGURES •

Image references:

See endnotes.

GLOSSARY ●

- **Adaptive Echo (AE):** AE is a specific form of the encrypting Echo. The Adaptive Echo does not send an encrypted message packet to every connected neighboring node in the sense of the normal Echo protocol, but a cryptographic token (a character string) is required for the transfer of a message. The protocol is provided with routing information for this adaptive mode. Only network nodes for which a cryptographic token determined in this way is known receive the message.
- **AES:** The Advanced Encryption Standard (AES) is a specification for encrypting electronic data that was established by the US National Institute for Standards and Technology (NIST) in 2001.
- **Algorithm:** In mathematics and computer science, an algorithm is a self-contained, step-by-step set of operations that must be performed. There are algorithms that perform calculations, data processing and automated processes.
- **Asymmetric Calling:** Cryptographic Calling is the immediate transmission of information for end-to-end encryption to secure a communication channel. Cryptographic Calling was developed by the Spot-On software project. Asymmetric Calling is a mode for Cryptographic Calling in which temporary asymmetric keys are sent for end-to-end encryption. It refers to sending an asymmetric key over a secured channel. The call with asymmetric information for encryption refers to short-lived asymmetric keys that are used for the time of the »Call«. This can be a session or even a shorter part of the session. That depends on when a communication partner initiates another Call. The asymmetric short-lived information for the Call should be transmitted via a secure connection which is either a (permanent) symmetric key, an a-symmetric key (PKI) or a currently existing channel connection, in this case a short-lived asymmetric temporary key.
- **Asymmetric Encryption:** The »asymmetric cryptosystem« or cryptosystem with »public key infrastructure« (PKI) is a cryptographic procedure in which, in contrast to a symmetric cryptosystem, the communicating parties do not need to know a shared secret key. Each user generates his own key pair, which consists of a private key (part to be kept secret) and a public key (non-secret part). The public key enables everyone to encrypt data for the owner of the private key, to check the digital signatures or to authenticate the key. The private key makes it possible to decrypt data encrypted with your own public key, to generate digital signatures or to authenticate yourself.
- **Autocrypt:** AutoCrypt is the function of an automatic key exchange. This was originally used by the Spot-On project and relates to the definitions of a REPLEO and EPKS protocol. A REPLEO is a method of encrypting the own public key with the public key received from a friend before sending it. This secures the own public key from the public using the encryption method. The EPKS protocol is the Echo Public Key Sharing protocol with which the own key can be automatically sent to one or more people via an existing encrypted connection. The EPKS protocol was originally implemented in the Spot-On project and in the GoldBug project and also included

in other projects in an automated way for an e-mail response. This means that two users of the same e-mail client exchange the public encryption key and are then secured for all further communication. The EPKS protocol provides for this many years before the term AutoCrypt was published. Other projects have also copied this innovation under the name KeySync. The new process is that the key is not stored and searched on a key server but is sent from node to node in a secure channel, either by manual sending or by an automated exchange between two nodes, e.g., an email client like Delta-Chat, or Spot-On clients via the EPKS protocol.

- **Big-Seven-Study:** Well-known study from 2016 comparing open-source messengers with encryption.
- **Bouncycastle:** Bouncy Castle Crypto Library is a collection of open-source cryptographic programming interfaces (API) for the programming languages Java and C #. They are released by the Australia-based Legion of the Bouncy Castle Inc.
- **C/O (Care-of)-Function:** »C/O« is used to address a letter when the letter has to go through an intermediary or post office box: neighbors are often asked to take care of postal letters. The e-mail function of the encrypting P2P e-mail program Spot-On digitally maps such a function.
- **Cipher:** With an encryption process - with a cipher or an algorithm - plain text can be converted into cipher text (encryption) and, conversely, the cipher text can be converted back into plain text (decryption). A key is often used here. A process that is considered to be particularly future proof in digital communication today is based on the McEliece algorithm.
- **Cipher-Text:** Cipher text (also secret text, chi text, cryptogram, or crypto text) is a text or amount of data in Cryptography that is encrypted using a cryptographic process (by hand or by machine), that means: has been changed using a key in such a way that it is no longer possible to understand its content without further ado. With the help of a secret or private key, the cipher text can be converted back into the original plain text.
- **Client-side encryption:** The client-side encryption is the cryptographic technique for encrypting data on the (trustworthy and possibly specially secured) device of the user before the cipher text is transmitted to a server in a computer network.
- **Cryptogram:** A Cryptogram used to refer to a cipher text. Nowadays, a cryptogram denotes a mathematical puzzle: it is a mathematical equation or a system of equations of unknown numbers, the digits of which have been replaced by letters. The goal is to find the value of each letter.
- **Cryptographic Calling:** Cryptographic Calling is a way of providing end-to-end credentials over a secure connection. The new temporary key can be a-symmetric (PKI) or symmetric. The idea is to make end-to-end encryption as easy as calling someone on the phone, in that temporary encryption keys can be renewed immediately, and the »call« ends the previous channel and starts immediately a new one with others encryption values. There are different methods of Cryptographic Calling: for example, Asymmetric Calling, Forward Secrecy Calling, Symmetric Calling, SMP-Calling and 2-Way-Calling, etc. It is also possible to define the end-to-end encrypted password manually (manually defined Calling).

- **Cryptographic Discovery:** Cryptographic Discovery describes the method of the Echo protocol to find nodes in an Echo network. Peers know other peers and their cryptographic identities based on a Cryptographic Discovery within the network. Nodes inform other nodes about their neighbors so that they can be addressed.

- **Cryptographic Routing:** Cryptographic Routing is a term used as an antagonism to describe how the Echo protocol works, as this goes beyond routing (Beyond Cryptographic Routing). Echo simply means to forward an address-less message. No routing information is given within this protocol. Cryptographic Routing would exist if a node had a specific cryptographic token as an identifier. (This is the case with Adaptive Echo (AE): Here one can sometimes speak of Cryptographic Routing, since a destination address could be specified).

- **Cryptography:** Cryptography deals with the encryption of information. Today it also relates generally to the topic of information security, especially for the Internet (cybersecurity).

- **Cryptologie:** Cryptology is the science in the field of Cryptography, which deals with the encryption and decryption of information and thus with information security.

- **CryptoPad:** A cryptopad is a tool for converting plain text into cipher text. The Rosetta Crypto Pad can be mentioned as an example: The Rosetta CryptoPad uses asymmetric keys, i.e., is based on PKI and both parties have to exchange the public key. The respective text can then be inserted into other applications after conversion using the copy and paste function.

- **Crypto-Party:** A crypto party is a meeting of people with the aim of teaching each other basic encryption and obfuscation techniques.

- **Customer Supplied Encryption Keys (#CECS):** Customer Supplied Encryption Keys are keys that are brought by users.

- **Democratization of encryption:** describes the process that encryption technologies are increasingly open-source today and are therefore available to all citizens.

- **Distributed Hash Table:** A distributed hash table, DHT, is a data structure that distributes data in a network as evenly as possible over the available storage nodes. Each storage node corresponds to an entry in the hash table. So it can be found from any other node.

- **Echo-Match:** The Echo Match is a specific cryptographic process to compare the hash of a plain text message supplied - with the hash of a conversion of a cipher text. If both hashes have the same value, then the correct key has been applied. Since the hash cannot be inverted, it does not give any information about the encrypted message. The process provides that all known keys are used for the conversion of a message.

- **Echo-Protocol:** The Echo protocol was introduced by the Spot-On application. The Echo is based on the elementary basis that information is transported over multiple or single passages and the data obtained from the channel endpoints are evaluated. The Echo combines encryption with graph theory. The following characterizations are fundamental: firstly, every message is encrypted in the Echo and, secondly, every message is forwarded to every connected neighbor in an Echo network. In order to filter redundant data, the applications have implemented their own algorithm for congestion control. As a third criterion, it can be added that a message packet does not have any sender or destination information, but rather uses the Echo Match to check that a correct key was used for decryption. Different operating modes such as Full or Half Echo are known. The Echo protocol is based on HTTPS and only sends encrypted messages based on the specifications for the Echo. An Echo network is accordingly a network based on Echo nodes (server and clients) that communicate via the Echo protocol (HTTPS).

- **End-to-end:** End-to-end encryption (E2EE) means the encryption of transmitted data across all transmission stations. Only both parties (the respective endpoints of the communication) can decrypt the message.
- **Ephemeral keys:** Ephemeral keys are keys that are temporarily used for encryption. These temporary keys are more deniable than permanent keys.
- **EPKS (Echo Public Key Share):** Echo Public Key Share (EPKS) is a method of sharing keys with others through secure online channels.
- **Exponential Encryption:** Exponential encryption is a term coined by the authors Mele Gasakis and Max Schmidt in their book on the New Era of Exponential Encryption. In a network configuration in which every encrypted message is sent to every connected node, it is compared to the picture of a grain of rice that - according to a well-known story - doubles on every square on a chessboard. Encrypted message capsules are exponentially forwarded to all other connected nodes. It concerns graph theory in connection with encryption.
- **Fiasco Keys:** Fiasco Keys are temporary keys that were first introduced in the Smoke Messenger application. These keys consist of a handful of temporary keys for end-to-end encryption. Instead of one key per session or message, multiple keys are sent per message, only one of which is valid. This is a more volatile design that increases security.
- **Forward Secrecy:** Perfect Forward Secrecy (PFS) is a property of certain key exchange protocols in Cryptography with the aim of agreeing a common session key between the communication partners in such a way that it cannot be reconstructed by a third party even if one of the two long-term keys should later be compromised. This means that recorded encrypted communication cannot be subsequently decrypted even if the long-term key is known. Occasionally this property is also treated under the catchphrase lack of consequences.
- **Friend-to-Friend (F2F):** A friend-to-friend computer network (F2F network) is a special peer-to-peer network in which you can only contact friends, i.e. known, trustworthy users. A connection to publicly accessible account points is excluded. The authentication is carried out using passwords or digital signatures.
- **GnuPG:** GNU Privacy Guard, abbreviated GnuPG or GPG, is a free Cryptography system. It is used to encrypt and decrypt data as well as to generate and check electronic signatures. The program implements the OpenPGP standard according to RFC 4880 as an open source replacement for PGP.

- **GoldBug (Application):** The GoldBug Messenger and E-Mail Client is a user interface that offers an alternative to the user interface originally offered for the kernel and the Spot-On encryption program. GoldBug has a simplified graphical user interface (GUI) that is not only used on the desktop, but can also be made available for mobile devices.

- **GoldBug (E-Mail-Password):** The GoldBug function adds a symmetric encryption (AES) password to an email. There is additional encryption in the software of the same name, so that the e-mail can only be read if both sides enter the password for this e-mail.

- **Graph-Theory:** In graph theory, a graph is an abstract structure that represents a set of objects together with the connections between these objects. Illustrative examples of graphs are a family tree or a subway network.

- **Hash:** A hash function is a mapping that maps a large amount of input (e.g., texts or keys) to a smaller target amount (the hash values). A hash function is therefore generally not reversible. The input set can contain elements of different lengths, whereas the elements of the target set usually have a fixed length.

- **HTTPS:** Hypertext Transfer Protocol Secure (HTTPS) is a communication protocol in the World Wide Web with which data can be transferred securely. It represents a transport encryption.

- **Impersonator-Function:** From time to time, an impersonator function sends messages between two chat clients communicating in encrypted form, which only contain random words or characters. This method makes it more difficult for attackers to distinguish between real and false communication.

- **Instant Perfect Forward Secrecy (IPFS):** While Perfect Forward Secrecy, often just called Forward Secrecy, describes the transmission of temporary keys in many applications and also from a theoretical concept, it is implicitly linked to the fact that this takes place once per session. With IPFS, a new paradigm has been created with which these keys can be transferred instantly at any time (i.e., several times per session). (Perfect) Forward Secrecy has evolved into Instant Perfect Forward Secrecy (IPFS).

- **Institution:** In Cryptography, an institution is an e-mail post box to save messages for offline friends in a p2p network. The institution is based on cryptographic credentials in order to save messages for offline participants in a p2p Echo network.

- **Juggerknaut Keys:** Juggerknaut Keys are derived using the (J-) PAKE protocol on both chat sides after entering a secret password and therefore do not have to be transmitted over the Internet (key deriving). In addition to other methods such as Secret Stream Keys (which are formed using the SMP protocol), they establish a Derivative Cryptography.

- **Libgcrypt:** Libgcrypt is a Cryptography library that was developed as a separate module from GnuPG. It can also be used independently of GnuPG. It offers functions for all basic cryptographic components.

- **Listener:** Listener means receiver. The term is also often used for access to a port on a communication server.

400

- **McEliece:** The McEliece cryptosystem is an asymmetric encryption algorithm and was introduced in 1978 by the cryptographer Robert J. McEliece. Even using quantum-computers, no efficient way is known to break the McEliece cryptosystem, making it an ideal algorithm for post-quantum Cryptography.

- **Messenger:** Instant messaging is a method of communication in which two or more people chat using text messages. The message should reach the other party as immediately as possible.

- **Metadata:** Metadata, or meta information, is structured data that contains information about characteristics of other data. Typical metadata for a book are, for example, the name of the author, the edition, the year of publication, the publisher and the ISBN. The resulting metadata is often considered when communicating on the Internet: Who communicated when with whom for how long from which location is just as interesting as the content of a message. Also called traffic data or telemetry data.

- **Multi-Encryption:** With multiple or multi-encryption, an already encrypted message is encrypted again one or more times using the same or a different algorithm. It is also known as cascade encryption or super encryption. A hybrid cryptosystem can combine the convenience of a public key cryptosystem with the efficiency of a symmetric key cryptosystem in a multi-encryption.

- **NTRU:** NTRU is an open public key cryptosystem that uses grid-based Cryptography to encrypt and decrypt data. In contrast to other popular public key cryptosystems, it is resistant to attacks by quantum-computers.

- **Off-the-record (OTR):** Off-the-Record Messaging (OTR) is a cryptographic protocol that provides encryption for instant messaging conversations. OTR uses (per session) a combination of an AES algorithm with a symmetric key and a key length of only 128 bits, the Diffie-Hellman key exchange with a size of 1536 bits and the SHA-1 hash function.

- **One-Time-Magnet (OTM):** A one-time magnet (OTM) is a magnet URI link that can only be used once in various encryption programs to bundle cryptographic values in a URL known from the browser, e.g. to download an encrypted file.

- **One-Time-Pad (OTP):** The one-time pad (abbreviation: OTP, literally: one-time block) is a symmetric encryption method for the secret transmission of messages. It is characteristic that a key is used that is (at least) as long as the message itself. The OTP can demonstrably not be broken - provided it is used as intended.

- **Open-source:** Software is referred to as open source if the source text can be viewed, changed and used publicly and by third parties. In the case of cryptographic programs, it is imperative to inspect it so that back doors by external reviewers can be excluded. Open source software can mostly be used free of charge.

- **Ozone Postbox:** With an Ozone mailbox, offline friends can reach each other within the Smoke Mobile Crypto client or the SmokeStack communication server for Android. The ozone mailbox serves as a cache for friends who are not online. The Ozone is just a passphrase that is used in both the Smoke client and the SmokeStack server. The rest of the work is done by the cryptographic keys. Hence it is more than just a postbox

- **Passphrase:** A passphrase or password is a string of characters that is used for access control.

- **Peer-to-Peer (P2P):** Peer-to-peer (usually P2P for short) or computer-computer connection are synonymous terms for communication among equals, here based on a computer network. In a peer-to-peer network, computers have equal rights and can both use and provide services to one another.

- **PKI:** In Cryptography, public key infrastructure (PKI for short) is a system that can issue, distribute and check digital certificates.

- **Plain-Text:** The term plain text describes the open, readable wording of a text, i.e., an unencrypted message or a block of data. Encryption using an encryption process and a key converts the plain text into a cipher text. Conversely, the plain text is recovered from a cipher text through decryption.

- **Point-to-Point:** Point-to-point encryption (English: point-to-point encryption, P2PE, or also transport encryption) is the encryption of the network connection between two devices in a computer network. This offers security against eavesdropping on the data lines, but if encrypted lines are connected in series, all intermediate stations on the way between two terminals have access to the plain text of the message.

- **POPTASTIC:** POPTASTIC is a function that enables encrypted chat and encrypted e-mails via the regular POP3 and IMAP mailboxes. A POPTASTIC key is used for this. As soon as this key has been exchanged, all e-mails are only sent as encrypted messages. The Spot-On Encryption Suite in which it was developed automatically detects whether the message should be displayed as a chat message or an email message. With this function, Spot-On extended instant messaging to a normal e-mail client and used existing e-mail servers for chat. Other clients have taken over and continued to use this function of using the e-mail infrastructure for encrypted chat and key exchange under the term AutoCrypt. A well-known user of POPTASTIC-Chat (for IMAP) and AutoCrypt is the Delta-Chat-Messenger.

- **Privacy:** In common parlance, private is mostly used as the opposite of »public«. Private stands for the term »personal« or is used in the sense of »in an intimate circle«.

- **Quantum-computer:** Quantum informatics or quantum information processing is the science of information processing that uses quantum mechanical phenomena. With the quantum-computers, some calculations could be carried out much faster than is possible with classic digital or binary computers.

- **Random:** Random is when no causal explanation can be found for a single event or the coincidence of several events.

- **Ransomware:** .. is malware that locks computers and encrypts files.

- **REPLEO:** With a REPLEO, the own public key is encrypted with the other's public key that has already been received, so that the own public key can be safely transmitted to the friend.

- **RSA:** RSA is one of the first practical asymmetric public key cryptosystems. A key for encryption is public and differs from the private key, which is to be kept secret. RSA is based on the difficulty of factoring the product of two large prime numbers. RSA is formed from the first letters of the surnames of Ron Rivest, Adi Shamir and Leonard Adleman, who first publicly described the algorithm in 1977. Since 2016, the NIST authority has called RSA »no longer secure« in view of the development of quantum-computers.

- **Secret Streams:** Secret Streams are a function within the Spot-On application and describe a key pool that is provided by a function that derives short-lived keys that were created by the SMP - Socialist Millionaire Protocol - process for authenticating two people in a chat. With this Zero-Knowledge proof, keys are generated on both sides that do not have to be transmitted over the Internet, similar to the Juggerknaut Keys via the J-Pake protocol.

- **Server:** In computer science, a server (literally servant, in the broader sense also service) is a computer program or a device that provides functionalities, utility programs, data or other resources so that other computers or programs (»clients«) can access them, usually via a Network. This architecture is known as the client-server model.

- **Signatur, digital:** A digital signature, also called digital signature method, is an asymmetric cryptosystem in which a sender uses a secret signature key (the private key) to calculate a value for a digital message (i.e. for any data), which is also called a digital signature. This value allows anyone to use the public key to verify the non-contestable authorship and integrity of the message.

- **Simulacra:** The Simulacra function is a similar function to the Impersonator. While the Impersonator simulates a chat between two people with messages, Simulacra only sends a fake message from time to time. Simulacra messages contain only random characters and are not in the style or aim of mimicking a conversation process.

- **SMP-Calling:** SMP calling is a mode for Cryptographic Calling in which temporary symmetric keys are sent for end-to-end encryption, which are derived from the Socialist Millionaire protocol for authentication. SMP calling is the basis for constantly generated temporary keys, which are also known as Secret Stream Keys.

- **Socialist Millionaire Protocol (SMP):** In Cryptography, the socialist millionaire problem is one where two millionaires want to determine if their wealth is equal without giving each other information about their wealth. It is a variant of the millionaires problem where two millionaires want to compare their wealth to see who has the greatest wealth without giving each other information about their wealth. It is widely used as a cryptographic protocol that allows two parties to verify the identity of the remote party using a shared secret.

- **Symmetric Calling:** Symmetric Calling is a mode for Cryptographic Calling in which temporary, symmetric keys are sent for end-to-end encryption. So it refers to sending a symmetric key over a secured channel.

403

- **Symmetric Encryption:** Symmetric key algorithms are cryptographic algorithms that use the same cryptographic keys for both plain text encryption and cipher text decryption. The keys can be identical or there can be a simple transformation between the two keys. In practice, the keys represent a shared secret between two or more parties with which a private information connection can be maintained. This requirement that both parties have access to the secret key is one of the main disadvantages of symmetric key encryption compared to encryption with public key (asymmetric encryption).

- **TLS:** Transport Layer Security (TLS), also known by its predecessor Secure Sockets Layer (SSL), is an encryption protocol for secure data transmission on the Internet.

- **Token:** A token is a code or physical device that can be used to access an electronically restricted resource. The token is used in addition to or instead of a password. It acts like an electronic key to access something. Examples of this are a wireless key card that opens a locked door or, in the case of customers trying to access the bank account online, the use of a token provided by a bank can prove that the access is authorized. A device can also have a cryptographic token stored and execute commands when this code is addressed.

- **Turtle-Hopping:** Turtle is a free, anonymous peer-to-peer network project that was developed at the Vrije Universiteit in Amsterdam with the participation of Andrew Tanenbaum (initially for the Gnutella network). As with other anonymous P2P programs, users can share files and communicate via third parties without having to fear legal sanctions or censorship. Technically, Turtle is an F2F (friend-to-friend) network. The RetroShare Messenger is based on an F2F and has implemented a »Turtle-Hopping« function inspired by Turtle.

- **Two-Way-Calling:** Two-Way-Calling is a mode for Cryptographic Calling in which temporary, symmetric keys are created for end-to-end encryption, which Alice and Bob each define as 50:50. In the case of a bidirectional Call, Alice sends a password to Bob as a passphrase for future end-to-end encryption, and Bob sends Alice his own password in response. Now the first half of Alice's password and the second half of Bob's password are taken and put together to form a common password.

- **Web-of-Trust:** Network of Trust or Web of Trust (WOT) is the idea of verifying the authenticity of digital keys through a network of mutual confirmations (signatures) by friends, combined with the individually assigned trust in the confirmations of the other (»owner Trust «). It represents a decentralized alternative to the hierarchical PKI system.

- **Zero-Knowledge-proof:** A Zero-Knowledge proof or Zero-Knowledge protocol is based on a protocol in which two parties communicate with one another. One side convinces the other side with a certain probability that a secret is known without disclosing information about the secret itself.

DIDACTIC QUESTIONS •

For each letter in the alphabet: Here are 26 didactic questions.

a. Discuss which **recommendation** to balance the market power of cryptographic messenger services is the most urgent for you. Code: 456D706665686C756E67.
b. Explain the concept of a Trusted Execution Environment (**TEE**). Code: 544545.
c. Does the RetroShare Messenger have more **ephemeral** keys than the GoldBug Messenger? Code: 657068656D6572616C.
d. What **measures** can be used to prevent or reduce crime? Code: 4D61DF6E61686D656E.
e. Check how many characters (**number of entities**) a McEliece key comprises with different moduli. Code: 416E7A61686C.
f. Research whether a one-time pad (**OTP**) is more secure than using GPG and explain why. Code: 4F5450.
g. Look for an alternative program for **steganographic** processes on the Internet. What is the name of this program? Code: 7374656E6F677261706869736368.
h. Select 10 terms from this volume for the game in a Cryptographic **Cafeteria**. Code: 436166657465726961.
i. Select the five most important references from the bibliography and mark them. Explain why it is important to read the original text in **depth**. Code: 76657274696566656E64.
j. Why can a user of RSA keys also read messages from a user of Mc-Eliece keys in a **compatible** manner? Code: 6B6F6D7061746962656C.
k. What did the **Big-Seven** study find out? Code: 42696720536576656E.
l. What is stored with **Juggerknaut** Keys, an SMP or a J-PAKE? Explain this. Code: 4A75676765726E617574.
m. What is meant by **multi-encryption**? Code: 4D756C746965727273636865CFC7373656C756E67.
n. What are the characteristics of the Third Epoch of Cryptography? Code: 45706F636865.
o. **What are Secret Streams?** Code: 53656372657420537472656616D73.
p. What **civil rights** will flourish as encryption expands? Code: 42FC7267657272656368687465.
q. Which three **applications** would you like to test in more detail and why? Code: 4170706C696B6174696F6E656E.

405

r. What features does the **Spot-On** Encryption Suite include?Code: 53706F742D4F6E.

s. What role does **graph theory** play in Exponential Encryption? Code: 4772617068656E7468656F726965.

t. Which encryption is used for **end-to-end** encryption? Asymmetric or symmetric encryption? Code: 456E64652D7A752D456E6465.

u. What is the name of the person with whom you are going to test a new messenger? Code: 4E616D656E

v. How can a friend's key exist without it being **transmitted** over the internet? Code: FC62657274726167656E.

w. What is Cryptography **transformed** into? Code: 7472616E73666F726D69657274.

x. How is the Echo Network different from the Tor Network? What do they have in **common**? Code: 76657262696E646574

y. What is the difference between Smoke-Chat and Delta-Chat **servers**? Code: 536572766572.

z. On which topic would you like to read in more detail and borrow a corresponding **book**? Code: 42756368.

BIBLIOGRAPHIC REFERENCES •

Abdalla, Michel / Lange, Tanja (2012): Pairing-based Cryptography – Pairing 2012, 5th International Conference, Cologne, Germany, May 16-18.

Ackermann, Evelyn & Klein, Michael (2020): Caesura in Cryptography: My first Workshop about Encryption - An Introduction with Teaching and Learning Material for School, University and Leisure, Norderstedt.

Adams, Carlisle / Lloyd, Steve (2003): Understanding PKI: concepts, standards, and deployment considerations, Addison-Wesley Professional, pp. 11–15.

Adams, David / Maier, Ann-Kathrin (2016): BIG SEVEN Study, open source crypto-messengers to be compared – or: Comprehensive Confidentiality Review & Audit of GoldBug, Encrypting E-Mail-Client & Secure Instant Messenger, Descriptions, tests and analysis reviews of 20 functions of the application GoldBug based on the essential fields and methods of evaluation of the 8 major international audit manuals for IT security investigations, English / German Language, ISBN 9783750408975.

AG Kritis (2020): IT-Sicherheitsgesetz 2.0: »Mittelfinger ins Gesicht der Zivilgesellschaft«, 10. Dezember, URL: https://www.heise.de/news/IT-Sicherheitsgesetz-2-0-Mittelfinger-ins-Gesicht-der-Zivilgesellschaft-4986032.html.

AK VDS / Arbeitskreis Vorratsdatenspeicherung: Amnesia CD 1.0 (2007) bis 3.0 (2011), URL: http://www.vorratsdatenspeicherung.de/CD/CD_1.0/akvorrat.html.

Anderson, Ross (2008): Security Engineering - A Guide to Building Dependable Distributed Systems, Wiley.

Arute, Frank / Martinis, John M. & et al. (2019): Quantum supremacy using a programmable superconducting processor, Nature volume 574, pages505–510 (23. October 2019)

Ateniese, G. / Francati, D. / Nuñez, D. et al. (2021): Match Me if You Can: Matchmaking Encryption and Its Applications, J Cryptol 34, 16.

Ayushi (2010): A Symmetric Key Cryptographic Algorithm, International Journal of Computer Applications, s 1(14):1–4, February.

Bacon, Francis (1605): The Proficience and Advancement of Learning Divine and Humane.

Becker, Dirk (2011): OpenVPN – Das Praxisbuch, Bonn.

Becker, Leo (2020): E-Privacy: Apple und sein Software-Chef Craig Federighi pochen auf Ende-zu-Ende-Verschlüsselung, 8. Dezember, URL:

https://www.heise.de/news/E-Privacy-Apple-pocht-auf-Ende-zu-Ende-Verschluesselung-4983045.html.

Bédrune, Jean-Baptiste / Videau, Marion (2016): Security Assessment of VeraCrypt - Fixes and evolutions from TrueCrypt, QuarksLab.

Bellare, M. / Pointcheval, D. / Rogaway, P. (2000): Authenticated Key Exchange Secure against Dictionary Attacks. Advances in Cryptology – Eurocrypt 2000 LNCS. Lecture Notes in Computer Science. 1807. Springer-Verlag. Pp. 139–155. Doi:10.1007/3-540-45539-6_11. ISBN 978-3-540-67517-4.

Bellovin, S. M. / Merritt, M. (May 1992): Encrypted Key Exchange: Password-Based Protocols Secure Against Dictionary Attacks. Proceedings of the I.E.E.E. Symposium on Research in Security and Privacy. Oakland. P. 72. Doi:10.1109/RISP.1992.213269. ISBN 978-0-8186-2825-2.

Ben-Or, Michael / et. al. (1990): Everything provable is provable in zero-knowledge; in: Goldwasser, S. (Ed.): Advances in Cryptology—CRYPTO '88, Lecture Notes in Computer Science, 403, Springer, pp. 37–56.

Bernstein, D. / Chou, T. / Lange, T. / von Maurich, I. / Misoczki, R. / Niederhagen, R. / Persichetti, E. / Peters, C. / Schwabe, P. / Sendrier, N. / Szefer, J. / Wang, W. (2019): »Classic McEliece«, Einreichung zum NIST-Prozess.

Bernstein, Daniel J. (2010): Grover vs. McEliece, URL: http://cr.yp.to/codes/grovercode-20100303.pdf.

Bernstein, Daniel J. / Lange, Tanja / Niederhagen, Ruben (2015): Dual EC - A Standardized Back Door, URL: http://projectbullrun.org/dual-ec/documents/dual-ec-20150731.pdf.

Bertram, Linda A. / van Dooble, Gunther: Transformation of Cryptography, 2019, deutsch: Die Transformation der Kryptographie, ISBN: 978-3749450749.

Beuth, Patrick (2021): Signal-Chef Moxie Marlinspike: »Man kann Kriminellen nicht die Verschlüsselung wegnehmen«, 11. Februar, Spiegel-Online.

BfDi / Der Bundesbeauftragte für den Datenschutz und die Informationsfreiheit (2020): Stellungnahme zur öffentlichen Anhörung des Innenausschusses zum Thema Recht auf Verschlüsselung – Privatsphäre und Sicherheit im digitalen Raum stärken, 27. Januar.

BfJ / Bundesamt für Justiz (2020): Statistiken 2019 über die Telekommunikationsüberwachung und über die Erhebung von Verkehrsdaten, 18. Dezember, URL: https://www.bundesjustizamt.de/DE/Presse/Archiv/2020/20201218.html.

Biermann, Kai (2020): Der Kampf der EU gegen die Verschlüsselung, 26. November 2020, URL: https://www.zeit.de/digital/datenschutz/2020-11/verschluesselung-eu-rat-sichere-kommunikation-messenger.

Biham, Eli / Shamir, Adi (1996): The next Stage of Differential Fault Analysis: How to break completely unknown cryptosystems.

Bitkom (2014): Mehrheit der Lehrer fordert Informatik als Pflichtfach, 24, März, URL: https://www.bitkom.org/Presse/Presseinformation/Mehrheit-der-Lehrer-fordert-Informatik-als-Pflichtfach.html.

Black, Michael (2013): When I first heard of GoldBug – Review of GoldBug Secure Instant Messenger, URL: http://www.lancedoma.ru/, 29 Oct.

Blum, Manuel / Feldman, Paul / Micali, Silvio (1988): Non-Interactive Zero-Knowledge and Its Applications, Proceedings of the Twentieth Annual ACM Symposium on Theory of Computing (STOC 1988), pp. 103–112.

BMI (2014): Wir präsentieren den Entwurf der digitalen Agenda: Wir wollen Verschlüsselungs-Standort Nr. 1 auf der Welt werden. Dazu soll die Verschlüsselung von privater Kommunikation in der Breite zum Standard werden, 22. Juli, URL: https://netzpolitik.org/2014/wir-praesentieren-den-entwurf-der-digitalen-agenda/.

Bolton, Doug (2015): APPLE CEO Tim Cook defends Encryption and Protecting Users from Government Surveillance, December 21, URL: https://www.independent.co.uk/life-style/gadgets-and-tech/news/tim-cook-apple-Privacy-encryption-a6781441.html.

Boskin, Michael (2019): Privacy, power and censorship: how to regulate big tech, April 29, URL: https://www.theguardian.com/business/2019/apr/29/big-tech-regulation-facebook-google-amazon.

Boudot, Fabrice / Schoenmakers, Berry / Traoré, Jacques (2001): A Fair and Efficient Solution to the Socialist Millionaires' Problem, Discrete Applied Mathematics, 111 (1), pp. 23-36.

Boyko, V. / MacKenzie, P. / Patel, S. (2000): Provably Secure Password-Authenticated Key Exchange Using Diffie–Hellman. Advances in Cryptology – Eurocrypt 2000, LNCS. Lecture Notes in Computer Science. 1807. Springer-Verlag. Pp. 156–171. Doi:10.1007/3-540-45539-6_12. ISBN 978-3-540-67517-4.

BRAK / Bundesrechtsanwaltskammer (2020): Stellungnahme Nr. 72/2020 zum Entwurf für einen Beschluss des Rats zur Verschlüsselung – Sicherheit durch Verschlüsselung und Sicherheit trotz Verschlüsselung, November, URL: https://www.brak.de/zur-rechtspolitik/stellungnahmenpdf/stellungnahmen-deutschland/2020/november/stellungnahme-der-brak-2020-72.pdf.

BRAK / Bundesrechtsanwaltskammer / Schöttle, Hendrik / Ludwig, Cédric (2020): Anwaltliche Kommunikation per E-Mail - nur noch mit Ende-zu-Ende-Verschlüsselung?, in: BRAK-Mitteilungen 6/2020, S. 308-315.

Breyer, Patrick (2005): Die systematische Aufzeichnung und Vorhaltung von Telekommunikations-Verkehrsdaten für staatliche Zwecke, Berlin.

Bruchstein, Hubertus (1996): Bittere Bytes - Cyberbürger und Demokratietheorien, in: Deutsche Zeitschrift für Philosophie 4, S. 583-607.

BSI / Bundesamt für Sicherheit in der Informationstechnik (2020): Die Lage der IT-Sicherheit in Deutschland, URL: https://www.bsi.bund.de/DE/Publikationen/Lageberichte/lageberichte_node.html.

BSI / Bundesamt für Sicherheit in der Informationstechnik (2021): Moderne Messenger – heute verschlüsselt, morgen interoperabel?, Bonn.

BSI / Federal Office for Information Security (2020): Security Evaluation of VeraCrypt, November 30, URL: https://www.bsi.bund.de/SharedDocs/Downloads/EN/BSI/Publications/Studies/Veracrypt/Veracrypt.pdf.

Buktu, Tim (2013): NTRU: Quantum-Resistant Cryptography, Independent / not affiliated with NTRU Cryptosystems, Inc.

Bundeskartellamt (2021): Sektoruntersuchung Messenger- und Video-Dienste - Zwischenbericht „Branchenüberblick und Stimmungsbild Interoperabilität", Bonn.

Bünz, Benedikt / Bootle, Jonathan / Boneh, Dan / Poelstra, Andrew / Wuille, Pieter / Maxwell, Greg (2018): Bulletproofs - Short Proofs for Confidential Transactions and More, Stanford University, URL: http://web.stanford.edu/~buenz/pubs/bulletproofs.pdf.

Calderbank, Michael (2007): The RSA Cryptosystem: History, Algorithm, Primes.

Cane (2019): Lasst Jabber/XMPP endlich sterben, URL: https://forum.kuketz-blog.de/viewtopic.php?f=31&t=4839.

Canetti, R. / Dwork, C. / Naor, M. / Ostrovsky, R. (1997): Deniable Encryption; in: Kaliski, B.S. (Ed.): Advances in Cryptology — CRYPTO '97. CRYPTO 1997. Berlin, pp. 90-104.

CEPIS / Council of European Professional Informatics Societies (2020): Right to Encryption instead of a Master Key for Encrypted Communication, Brussels, 1 December, URL: https://cepis.org/app/uploads/2020/11/Right-to-encryption-instead-

of-a-master-key-for-chat-communication-CEPIS-LSI-SIN.pdf &
https://cepis.org/app/uploads/2020/12/Press-Release-CEPIS-
statement-on-the-right-to-encrypt-12.2020.pdf.

Chaos Computer Club (2020): CCC fordert kompromissloses Recht auf Verschlüsselung, 27. Januar, linus, URL: https://www.ccc.de/de/updates/2020/ccc-fordert-kompromissloses-recht-auf-verschlusselung.

Christ, Sebastian (2020): Digitalisierung & KI: Tagesspiegel Background, 17. Dezember, URL: https://background.tagesspiegel.de/digitalisierung.

Christen, Michael (2005): YaCy – Peer-to-Peer Web-Suchmaschine, in: Die Datenschleuder, #86, 54–57.

Cohn-Gordon, Katriel / et al. (2016): A Formal Security Analysis of the Signal Messaging Protocol, Cryptology ePrint Archive, IACR).

Council of the EU (2020): Draft Council Resolution on Encryption-Security through encryption and security despite encryption, Council document 12143/1/20 REV1, November 6, URL: https://www.heise.de/downloads/18/2/9/9/8/5/2/0/783284_fh_st121 43-re01en20_783284.pdf, & earlier version https://www.heise.de/downloads/18/2/9/9/8/5/2/0/eu-council-draft-declaration-against-encryption-12143-20.pdf & public version: https://data.consilium.europa.eu/doc/document/ST-13084-2020-REV-1/en/pdf.

Cremers, Cas / Feltz, Michèle (2015): Beyond eCK: perfect forward secrecy under actor compromise and ephemeral-key reveal, Designs, Codes and Cryptography, 74 (1): 183–218.

Daemen, Joan / Rijmen, Vincent (2011): The design of Rijndael – AES – The Advanced Encryption Standard, Springer, Berlin, London.

Delfs, Hans / Knebl, Helmut (2007): Symmetric-key encryption, Introduction to Cryptography: principles and applications, Springer.

Delgado-Bonal, Alfonso / Martín-Torres, Javier (2016): Human vision is determined based on information theory, Scientific Reports, 6 (1).

Der Spiegel / Bartsch, Matthias et al. (2020): Rechtsextreme bei Polizei und Bundeswehr - Die dunkle Seite der Staatsmacht, 7. August, URL: https://www.spiegel.de/politik/deutschland/rechtsextreme-bei-polizei-und-bundeswehr-die-dunkle-seite-der-staatsmacht-a-00000000-0002-0001-0000-000172378470.

Deutsches Institut für Vertrauen und Sicherheit im Internet (DIVSI) (2014): DIVSI U25-Studie - Kinder, Jugendliche und junge Erwachsene in der digitalen Welt, Hamburg.

Diffie, Whitfield / Hellman, Martin (1976): New directions in Cryptography, 22, IEEE transactions on Information Theory, p. 644-654.

Diffie, Whitfield / van Oorschot, Paul C. / Wiener, Michael J. (1992): Authentication and Authenticated Key Exchanges, Designs, Codes and Cryptography,2(2):107–125.

Dingledine, Roger / et al. (2004): Tor - The Second-Generation Onion Router, in: Proceedings of the 13th USENIX Security Symposium, August 9–13, 303–320.

Dinh, Hang / Moore, Cristopher / Russell, Alexander / Rogaway, Philip (Ed.) (2011): McEliece and Niederreiter cryptosystems that resist quantum Fourier sampling attacks, Advances in cryptology—CRYPTO 2011, Lecture Notes in Computer Science, 6841, Heidelberg, pp. 761–779.

Dobbertin, Hans / Rijmen, Vincent / Sowa, Aleksandra (Eds.) (2005): Advanced Encryption Standard – AES – 4th international conference, AES 2004, Bonn, Germany, May 10-12, 2004: revised selected and invited papers, Springer, Berlin.

Dolev, Danny / Dwork, Cynthia / Naor, Moni (2000): Nonmalleable Cryptography, SIAM Journal on Computing, 30 (2), 391–437, URL: https://dx.doi.org/10.1137%2FS0097539795291562.

Dragomir, Mircea (2016): GoldBug Instant Messenger – Softpedia Review: This is a secure P2P Instant Messenger that ensures private communication based on a multi encryption technology constituted of several security layers, URL: http://www.softpedia.com/get/Internet/Chat/Instant-Messaging/GoldBug-Instant-Messenger.shtml, Softpedia Review, January 31st.

Drehling, Wilhelm (2021): Reingefallen - Asymmetrische Verschlüsselung: Sicher durch Falltürfunktionen, c't 7, S. 60.

Dreyfus, Suelette (2012): The Idiot Savants' Guide to Rubberhose, URL: https://archive.is/20121029045140/http://marutukku.org/current/src/doc/maruguide/t1.html#selection-273.0-282.0.

Edwards, Scott / Spot-On.sf.net Project (Eds.) (2019): Communicating like dolphins with Spot-On Encryption Suite: Democratization of Multiple & Exponential Encryption; Handbook and User Manual as practical software guide with introductions into Cryptography, Cryptographic Calling and Cryptographic Discovery, P2P Networking, Graph-Theory, NTRU, McEliece, the Echo Protocol and the Spot-On Software, ISBN 9783749435067, Norderstedt.

EFF (2016): End-to-End Encryption, EFF Surveillance Self-Defence Guide, Electronic Frontier Foundation.

412

Engelbert, D. / Overbeck, R. / Schmidt, A. (2007): A Summary of McEliece-Type Cryptosystems and their Security, in: J. Math. Crypt. 1 (2007), pp. 151–199.

ENISA / European Union Agency for Cybersecurity (2021): Post-Quantum-Cryptography – Current state and quantum migration, May v02.

ENISA / European Union Agency for Network and Information Security (2015): Privacy and Data Protection by Design, January 12, URL: https://www.enisa.europa.eu/publications/Privacy-and-data-protection-by-design.

Esken, Saskia (2015): Mehr Verschlüsselung wagen, 22. Januar 2015, URL: https://web.archive.org/ web/20150125233354/ http://blogs. spdfraktion.de/netzpolitik/2015/01/22/mehr-verschlusselung-wagen.

Esken, Saskia (2020): Verschlüsselung für jede/n von uns, December 14, URL: https://twitter.com/EskenSaskia/status/1338538749353979911.

Europäisches Parlament (2018): Richtlinie (EU) 2018/1972 des europäischen Parlaments und des Rates über den europäischen Kodex für die elektronische Kommunikation, 18. Dezember, URL: https://eur-lex.europa.eu/legal-content/DE/TXT/HTML/?uri=CELEX:32018L1972#d1e2632-36-1.

EuroPKI (2010): Public key infrastructures, services and applications: 7th European workshop, EuroPKI 2010, Athens, Greece, September 23 – 24.

Europol (2020): Europol and the European Commission inaugurate new decryption platform to tackle the challenge of encrypted material for law enforcement investigations, December 18, URL: https://www.europol.europa.eu/newsroom/news/europol-and-european-commission-inaugurate-new-decryption-platform-to-tackle-challenge-of-encrypted-material-for-law-enforcement.

Even S. / Goldreich, O. (1985): On the power of cascade ciphers, ACM Transactions on Computer Systems, vol. 3, pp. 108–116.

FBI / Federal Bureau of Investigation (2011): Cryptanalysts: Breaking Codes to Stop Crime, Part 1, March 21, URL: https://www.fbi.gov/news/stories/breaking-codes-to-stop-crime-part-1.

Filby, P.W. (1995): Floradora and a Unique Break into One-Time Pad ciphers. Journal of Intelligence and National Security, 10:3, p. 408–422, doi:10.1080/02684529508432310.

Fleißner, Eduard (1881): Neue Patronengeheimschrift - Handbuch der Kryptographie, Wien.

Floyd, S. / Fall, K. (1999): Promoting the Use of End-to-End Congestion Control in the Internet (IEEE/ACM Transactions on Networking, August).

413

Ford, W. / Kaliski, B. (14–16 June 2000): Server-Assisted Generation of a Strong Secret from a Password. Proceedings of the IEEE 9th International Workshops on Enabling Technologies: Infrastructure for Collaborative Enterprises. Gaithersburg MD: NIST. P. 176. CiteSeerX 10.1.1.17.9502. doi:10.1109/ENABL.2000.883724. ISBN 978-0-7695-0798-9.

Fujisaki, E. / Okamoto, T. (1999): Secure Integration of Asymmetric and Symmetric Encryption Schemes. In: Wiener, M. (Ed.) CRYPTO 1999, Heidelberg, LNCS, vol. 1666, pp. 537–554.

Gadimov, Bahtiar (2015): Initial Omemo commit, dev.gajim.org.

Gaines, Helen F. (2014): Cryptanalysis – A Study of Ciphers and Their Solution, Courier Corporation.

Gasakis, Mele / Schmidt, Max (2018): Beyond Cryptographic Routing: The Echo Protocol in the new Era of Exponential Encryption (EEE) – A comprehensive essay about the Sprinkling Effect of Cryptographic Echo Discovery (SECRED) and further innovations in Cryptography, ISBN 978-3-7481-5198-2, Norderstedt.

Gaus, Günter (1983): Nischengesellschaft, in: Ders.: Wo Deutschland liegt - Eine Ortsbestimmung, Hamburg, S. 156–233.

Gematik (2021): Konzeptpapier TI-Messenger, 52. p, 21. Juli.

Gerhards, Julia (2010): (Grund-)Recht auf Verschlüsselung?, Der Elektronische Rechtsverkehr, Band 23, Baden.Baden.

GI / Gesellschaft für Informatik (2029): Stellungnahme der Gesellschaft für Informatik e.V. (GI) zum Recht auf Verschlüsselung, Berlin, 9. Dezember 2020, URL: https://gi.de/fileadmin/GI/Allgemein/PDF/2020-12-09_GI_Recht_auf_Verschlu__sselung.pdf.

GI (2020): Arbeitspapier Schlüsselaspekte Digitaler Souveränität, Berlin.

Goldberg, Ian / Stedman, Ryan / Yoshida. Kayo (2008): A User Study of Off-the-Record Messaging, University of Waterloo, Symposium on Usable Privacy and Security (SOUPS) 2008, July 23–25, Pittsburgh, PA, USA, URL: http://www.cypherpunks.ca/~iang/pubs /otr_userstudy.pdf, & URL: https://otr.cypherpunks.ca/Protocol-v3-4.0.0.html.

Goldreich, O. / Lindell, Y. (2001): Session-Key Generation Using Human Passwords Only. Advances in Cryptology – Crypto 2001 LNCS. Lecture Notes in Computer Science. 2139. Springer-Verlag. Pp. 408–432. Doi:10.1007/3-540-44647-8_24. ISBN 978-3-540-42456-7.

Gultsch, Daniel (2015): OMEMO Encrypted Jingle File Transfer, in: Website der XMPP Standards Foundation, 2. September.

Gultsch, Daniel (2018): Federated Instant Messaging with Jabber/XMPP – FOSSASIA 2018, published 25.03.2018, Min: 8:55, outdated XMPP servers: jabber.systemausfall.org, jabber.hot-chilli.net, elaon.de, jabber.fr, jabber.de, high-way.me, bommboo.de, mail.de; URL: https://www.youtube.com/watch?v=5pJYGQ_oKks.

Hahn, Tobias / Herfert, Michael / Lange, Benjamin (2015): Pro Privacy, URL https://www.sit.fraunhofer.de/fileadmin/dokumente/studien_und_tec hnical_reports/Abschlussbericht-Pro-Privacy.pdf.

Hao, Feng / Ryan, Peter (2019): J-PAKE – Authenticated Key Exchange Without PKI, Springer Transactions on Computational Science XI, Special Issue on Security in Computing, Part II, Vol. 6480, pp. 192-206.

Hao, Feng / Ryan, Peter (2008): Password Authenticated Key Exchange by Juggling, Proceedings of the 16th International Workshop on Security Protocols.

Harvey, Cynthia / Datamation (2015): 50 Noteworthy Open Source Projects – Chapter Secure Communication: GoldBug Messenger ranked on first # 1 position for Secure Communication, URL: http://www.datamation.com/open-source/50-noteworthy-new-open-source-projects-3.html, posted September 19.

Hein, Buster (2016): 11 juicy quotes from Tim Cook's interview on encryption, March 17, URL: https://www.cultofmac.com/418213/tim-Tim-encryption-interview/.

Heuzeroth, Thomas (2020): Messenger weist Forderung nach Zugang zu verschlüsselten Inhalten zurück, 29.11.2020, URL: https://www.welt.de/wirtschaft/webwelt/article221279278/WhatsApp -Rivale-Threema-CEO-weist-Forderung-nach-Zugang-zu-verschluesselten-Inhalten-zurueck.html.

Hildenbrand, Jerry (2016): Everyone is a node: How Wi-Fi Mesh Networking work, URL: https://www.androidcentral.com/how-wifi-mesh-networks-work.

Hoffstein, Jeffrey / Pipher, Jill / Silverman, Joseph H. (1998): NTRU – A ring-based public key cryptosystem, Algorithmic Number Theory, Lecture Notes in Computer Science, 1423, pp. 267–288.

Hohmann, Mirko (2015): D64-Positionspapier - Verschlüsselung als Grundvoraussetzung für unsere Gesellschaft, Berlin.

Honda, Osamu / Ohsaki, Hiroyuki / Imase, Makoto / Ishizuka, Mika / Murayama, Junichi (2005): Understanding TCP over TCP: effects of TCP tunneling on end-to-end throughput and latency.

Hooshmand, Reza / Shooshtari, Masoumeh Koochak / Aref, Mohammad Reza (2014): PKC-PC: A Variant of the McEliece Public Key Cryptosystem based on Polar Codes, URL: https://arxiv.org/ftp/arxiv/papers/1712/1712.07672.pdf

Houmkozlis, Christos N. / Rovithakis, George A. (2012): End-to-end adaptive congestion control in TCP/IP networks; in: Automation and control engineering series, CRC Press, Boca Raton, Fla.

Huang, Yahsin (2019): Decentralized Public Key Infrastructure (DPKI): What is it and why does it matter?, Hacker Noon.

Hudde, Hans Christoph (2013): Development and Evaluation of a Code-based Cryptography Library for Constrained Devices, Master's Thesis, February 7, URL: https://www.emsec.ruhr-uni-bochum.de/media/attachments/files/2013/03/mastersthesis-hudde-code-based-Cryptography-library.pdf.

Hudde, Hans Christoph (2013): Development and Evaluation of a Code-based Cryptography Library for Constrained Devices, Master's Thesis, February 7, Bochum.

Informationweek (2016): Google's Cloud Lets You Bring customer-supplied encryption keys (CSEK), URL: http://www.informationweek.com/cloud/infrastructure-as-a-service/googles-cloud-lets-you-bring-your-own-encryption-keys/d/d-id/1326482.

Joint Committee on Human Rights (2007): Government response to the Committee's fourteenth report of session 2007-08, Data protection and human rights – twenty-second report of session 2007-08, report, together with formal minutes, and an appendix.

Joos, Thomas (2014): Sicheres Messaging im Web, URL: http://www.pcwelt.de/ratgeber/ Tor__I2p__Gnunet__RetroShare__Freenet__GoldBug__Spurlos_im_W eb-Anonymisierungsnetzwerke-8921663.html, PCWelt Magazin, 01. Oktober.

Joux, Antoine (2009): Algorithmic Cryptanalysis, CRC Press.

Kaeser, Eduard (2020): Die verschlüsselte Gesellschaft und ihre Freunde – das Rhizom der Schnüffler breitet sich weltweit aus, 13. Februar, URL: https://www.nzz.ch/meinung/datenklau-die-verschluesselte-gesellschaft-und-ihre-freunde-ld.1540307

Kahle, Christian (2020): GoldBug-Messenger im Interview: Ende-zu-Ende-Krypto unter Beschuss - Verbot ist technisch aber Unsinn, 28.11.2020, URL: https://winfuture.de/news,119739.html.

Karinthy, Frigyes: Láncszemek, 1929.

Katz, J. / Ostrovsky, R. / Yung, M. (2001): «Efficient Password-Authenticated Key Exchange Using Human-Memorable Passwords». 2045. Springer-Vergal.

416

Katz, Jonathan (2015): Public-key Cryptography - PKC 2015: 18th IACR International Conference on Practice and Theory in Public-Key Cryptography, Springer, Gaithersburg, MD, USA, March 30 – April 1.

Kerckhoffs, Auguste (1883): La cryptographie militaire, Journal des sciences militaires, vol. IX, pp. 5–83, January 1883, pp. 161–191.

Koalitionsvertrags der 19. Legislaturperiode des Bundestages (2019): Ende-zu-Ende-Verschlüsselung für jedermann verfügbar machen, Zeilen 1979ff.

Kobara, Kazukuni / Imai, Hideki (2001): Semantically Secure McEliece Public-Key Cryptosystems –Conversions for McEliece PKC, in: Kim, K. (Ed.): PKC 2001, LNCS 1992, pp. 19-35.

Kuder, Matthias (2020): Der Regierende Bürgermeister Berlin - Senatskanzlei Wissenschaft und Forschung: Berlin wird Zentrum für Nationales Hochleistungsrechnen – Zuse-Institut Berlin von GWK in die Förderung aufgenommen, Pressemitteilung vom 13.11.2020.

Lang, Jacqueline (2018): Tim Cook warnt vor Daten als Waffen »mit militärischer Effizienz«, 24. Oktober, URL: https://www.sueddeutsche.de/digital/apple-cook-datenschutz-1.4183262.

Lindner, Mirko (2014): POPTASTIC: Verschlüsselter Chat über POP3 mit dem GoldBug Messenger, Pro-Linux, URL: http://www.pro-linux.de/news/1/21822/poptastic-verschluesselter-chat-ueber-pop3.html, 9. Dezember.

Lobo, Sascha (2015): Geheimdienste lesen nicht mal Zeitung, 25. November, URL: https://www.spiegel.de/netzwelt/web/sascha-lobo-ueber-die-irrationale-ausweitung-der-ueberwachung-a-1064508.html

Lobo, Sascha (2020): Rechte in Polizei und Sicherheitsbehörden - Die dunkle Macht der Chats: Extremisten aller Art lieben Chats – auch bei der Polizei, 2. Dezember, URL: https://www.spiegel.de/netzwelt/web/rechtsextremismus-bei-der-polizei-warum-chats-bei-extremisten-so-beliebt-sind-podcast-a-363826c9-2790-4e1b-ad74-a68dfd962c44.

Locker, Theresa (2015): Die Onionview-Karte zeigt, wo in Deutschland die meisten Tor-Server stehen, 15. September, URL: https://www.vice.com/de/article/gv5743/die-onionview-karte-zeigt-wo-in-deutschland-die-tor-server-stehen-444.

Madore, David (2000): Method of free speech on the Internet: random pads, URL: http://www.eleves.ens.fr:8080/home/madore/misc/freespeech.html.

Marlinspike, Moxie (2013): Advanced cryptographic ratcheting, Signal Blog, November 26.

Marlinspike, Moxie (2016): Reflections: The ecosystem is moving, URL: https://signal.org/blog/the-ecosystem-is-moving/.

Matejka, Petr (2004): Model of Turtle network - Security in Peer-to-Peer Networks, Master Thesis. URL: http://turtle-p2p.sourceforge.net/thesis2.pdf.

Maurer, M. / Massey, J. L. (1993): Cascade ciphers – The importance of being first, Journal of Cryptology, vol. 6, no. 1, pp. 55–61.

McEliece, Robert J. (1978): A Public-Key Cryptosystem Based On Algebraic Coding Theory, DSN Progress Report. 44: 114–116.

McNoodle Library (2016): Implementation of the McEliece Algorithm in C++, Github.

Meinrath, Sascha D./ Vitka, Sean (2014): Crypto War II, Critical Studies in Media Communication, Vol. 31, No. 2, June, pp. 123–128, URL: https://www.tandfonline.com/doi/pdf/10.1080/15295036.2014.921320.

Meister, Andre (2020): BND-Gesetz - Ausspähen unter Freunden wird legalisiert und ausgeweitet, 30. November, URL: https://netzpolitik.org/2020/bnd-gesetz-ausspaehen-unter-freunden-wird-legalisiert-und-ausgeweitet/.

Merkle, Ralph (1978): Secure Communications over Insecure Channels, in: Communications of the ACM, Band 21, Nr. 4, April, S. 294–299.

Mermin, David (2006): Breaking RSA Encryption with a Quantum Computer: Shor's Factoring Algorithm, Cornell University, Physics, 481-681.

Mey, Stefan (2020): 25 Jahre Anonymisierung mit Tor, eine Geschichte mit Widersprüchen, 29. November 2020, URL: https://www.heise.de/hintergrund/ Missing-Link-25-Jahre-Anonymisierung-mit-Tor-eine-Geschichte-mit-Widerspruechen-4972675.html?seite=all.

Meyn, Christian (2013): Verschlüsselung und Innere Sicherheit: Die verfassungsrechtliche Zulässigkeit eines Verschlüsselungsverbots bei elektronischer Datenkommunikation, Berlin

Mezini, Mira et al. (2021): Nationaler Pakt - Gesamtgesellschaftliche Erklärung zur Cybersicherheit, Berlin.

Milgram, Stanley: The Small World Problem. In: Psychology Today, URL: http://measure.igpp.ucla.edu/GK12-SEE-LA/Lesson_Files_09/Tina_Wey/TW_social_networks_Milgram_1967_small_world_problem.pdf, ISSN 0033-3107, pp. 60–67, Mai 1967.

Ministerium Soziales, Integration und Gleichstellung Mecklenburg-Vorpommern (2021): Bildungskonzeption für 0- bis 10-jährige Kinder in Mecklenburg-Vorpommern, Schwerin.

Modadugu, Nagendra / Rescorla, Eric (2003): The Design and Implementation of Datagram TLS, Stanford Crypto Group.

Moechel, Erich (2020): »Five-Eyes« hinter den Entschlüsselungsplänen des EU-Ministerrats, 29. November, URL: https://fm4.orf.at/stories/3009643/.

MOMEDO (2018): Open Source Mobiler Messenger für kommunale und schulische Zwecke mit Verschlüsselung, Internet-Ressource.

Moonlander, Casio (2020): Smoke - An Android Echo Chat Software Application: Personal Chat Messenger / Open Source Technical Website Reference Documentation, Band 1 von 2 in dieser Reihe, ISBN 9783752691993.

Moonlander, Casio (2020): SmokeStack - An Android Echo Chat Server Application: Open Source Technical Website Reference Documentation, Band 2 von 2 in dieser Reihe, ISBN 9783752692006.

Morris, Gemma / Presenter, Swipe (2015): Wiki Boss: Encryption Ban Like Banning Maths, October 8, URL: https://news.sky.com/story/wiki-boss-encryption-ban-like-banning-maths-10343807.

Mundt, Andreas (2020): Bundeskartellamt leitet Sektoruntersuchung zu Messenger-Diensten ein, November 20, URL: https://www.bundeskartellamt.de/SharedDocs/Publikation/DE/Presse mitteilungen/2020/12_11_2020_SU_Messenger_Dienste.html.

Muth, Max (2020): Five-Eyes-Geheimdienste sollen Europa helfen, Verschlüsselung zu umgehen, 29. November 2020, URL: https://www.sueddeutsche.de/digital/geheimdienste-verschluesselung-crypto-wars-messenger-1.5131084.

Narr, Wolf-Dieter (Hg.) (1977): Wir Bürger als Sicherheitsrisiko - Berufsverbot und Lauschangriff, Reinbek.

Needham, Roger M. / Schroeder, Michael D. (1978): Using encryption for authentication in large networks of computers, in: ACM (Hg.): Communications of the ACM. Band 21, Nr. 12, Dezember.

Neue Richtervereinigung (2020): Ende-zu-Ende-Verschlüsselung nicht den Sicherheitsbehörden opfern, 15. Dezember, URL: https://www.neuerichter.de/fileadmin/user_upload/bundesvorstand/2 020_12_NRV_PM_CryptoWars.pdf.

NIST (2001): Announcing the ADVANCED ENCRYPTION STANDARD (AES), Federal Information Processing Standards Publication 197. United States National Institute of Standards and Technology (NIST), URL: http://nvlpubs.nist.gov/nistpubs/FIPS/NIST.FIPS.197.pdf, November 26.

NIST / Chen, Lily / Jordan, Stephen / Liu, Yi-Kai / Moody, Dustin / Peralta, Rene / Perlner, Ray / Smith-Tone, Daniel (2016): NISTIR 8105, DRAFT, Report on Post-Quantum Cryptography, URL:

http://csrc.nist.gov/publications/drafts/nistir-8105/nistir_8105_draft.pdf, National Institute of Standards and Technology. February.

Nomenclatura (2019): Encyclopedia of modern Cryptography and Internet Security: From AutoCrypt and Exponential Encryption to Zero-Knowledge-Proof Keys, ISBN: 978-3748191513 & ISBN: 9783746066684.

Odendaal, Hansie / Sharrock, Cayle / Heerden, SW. (o.J.): Bulletproofs and Mimblewimble, Tari Labs University.

Offsystem: OFF System Introduction about Brightnets, Owner-Less Data and Multi-Use Data, URL: http://offsystem.sourceforge.net/.

Pednault, Edwin / Gunnels, John A. / Nannicini, Giacomo / Horesh, Lior / Wisnieff, Robert: SUMMIT Super-Computer at Oak Ridge National Laboratories - Leveraging Secondary Storage to Simulate Deep 54-qubit SYCAMORE Circuits, IBM T.J. Watson Research Center, NY, URL: https://arxiv.org/pdf/1910.09534.pdf

Perlroth, Nicole / Larson, Jeff / Shane, Scott (2013): N.S.A. Able to Foil Basic Safeguards of Privacy on Web, New York Times, URL: https://www.nytimes.com/2013/09/06/us/nsa-foils-much-internet-encryption.html, September 5.

Piétron, Dominik / Wiggerthale, Marita (2019): Neue Wettbewerbsregeln für die Plattformökonomie, 6. Dezember, URL: https://netzpolitik.org/2019/neue-wettbewerbsregeln-fuer-die-plattformoekonomie/.

Pohl, Michael / Junginger, Bernhard (2020): Gibt es eine rechte Schattenarmee in der Bundeswehr?, 6. Juli, URL: https://www.augsburger-allgemeine.de/politik/Gibt-es-eine-rechte-Schattenarmee-in-der-Bundeswehr-id57678296.html.

Pointcheval, David (2000): Chosen-Cipher-Text security for any one-way cryptosystem, Public Key Cryptography, Springer, pp. 129–146.

Popescu, Bogdan C. / Crispo, Bruno / Tanenbaum, Andrew S. (2004): Safe and Private Data Sharing with Turtle: Friends Team-Up and Beat the System, in: 12th International Workshop on Security Protocols, Cambridge, UK, April.URL: http://turtle-P2P.sourceforge.net/turtleinitial.pdf.

Possony Stefan T. (2013): Zur Bewältigung der Kriegsschuldfrage: Völkerrecht und Strategie bei der Auslösung zweier Weltkriege, Berlin, p. 204.

Preneel, Bart / Bosselaers, Antoon / Govaerts, René / Vandewalle, Joos (1992): A Software Implementation of the McEliece Public-Key Cryptosystem; in: Proceedings of the 13th Symposium on Information Theory in the

420

Benelux, Werkgemeenschap voor Informatie- en Communicatietheorie, pp. 119-126.

Qt Digia (2015): Qt Digia has awarded GoldBug IM as reference project for Qt implementation in the official Qt-Showroom of Digia: https://showroom.qt.io/goldbug/.

Quisquater, Jean-Jacques / Guillou, Louis C. / Berson, Thomas A. (1990): How to Explain Zero-Knowledge Protocols to Your Children, Advances in Cryptology – CRYPTO '89, 435, pp. 628–631.

Referentenentwurf des Bundesministeriums für Wirtschaft und Energie und des Bundesministeriums für Verkehr und digitale Infrastruktur (2020): Entwurf eines Gesetzes zur Umsetzung der Richtlinie (EU) 2018/1972 des Europäischen Parlaments und des Rates vom 11. Dezember 2018 (Telekommunikations-Modernisierungsgesetz), URL: https://intrapol.org/wp-content/uploads/2020/12/201209_BMWi_BMVI_RefE_Telekommunikationsmodernisierungsgesetz.pdf.

Repka, Marek (2014): McELIECE PKC CALCULATOR, Journal of ELECTRICAL ENGINEERING, VOL. 65, NO. 6, pp. 342–348.

Rieffel, Eleanor G. / NASA/TP-2019-220319 (2019): Quantum Supremacy Using a Programmable Superconducting Processor, NASA Ames Research Center, National Aeronautics and Space Administration, Ames Research Center, Moffett Field, URL: https://www.inverse.com/article/59507-full-quantum-supremacy-paper, California, August.

Rihaczek, Karl (1984): Verschlüsselung und Normung, in: Datenverschlüsselung in Kommunikationssystemen. DuD-Fachbeiträge, Wiesbaden.

Ritter, Terry (1995): Ritter's Crypto Glossary and Dictionary of Technical Cryptography, Comments on Multi-Encryption, URL: http://www.ciphersbyritter.com/GLOSSARY.HTM#MultipleEncryption

Rivest, R.L. / Shamir, A. / Adleman, L. (1978): A Method for Obtaining Digital Signatures and Public-Key Cryptosystems, URL: https://people.csail.mit.edu/rivest/Rsapaper.pdf

Roering, Christopher (2013): Coding Theory-Based Cryptopraphy: McEliece Cryptosystems in Sage, Honors Theses. Paper 17, URL: http://digitalcommons.csbsju.edu/honors_theses/17.

Rothblum, Ron D. / Sealfon, Adam / Sotiraki, Katerina (2021): Toward Non-interactive Zero-Knowledge Proofs for NP from LWE. J Cryptol 34, 3.

Rueckert, Phineas / Schilis-Gallego, Cécile (2020): Hacked: The Story behind the Israeli Spyware targetting Moroccan Journalists, June 22, URL: https://forbiddenstories.org/the-story-behind-the-israeli-spyware-targeting-moroccan-journalists/

Saint-Andre, Peter et. al. (2016): Manifesto: A Public Statement Regarding Ubiquitous Encryption on the XMPP Network, URL: https://github.com/stpeter/manifesto/blob/master/manifesto.txt.

Schmeh, Klaus (2017): Versteckte Botschaften – Die faszinierende Geschichte der Steganografie, Hannover.

Schmidt, Jürgen: Lasst PGP sterben, http://www.heise.de/ct/ausgabe/2015-6-Editorial-Lasst-PGP-sterben-2551008.html, Magazin Ct, 20.02.2015.

Schneier, Bruce / Seidel, Kathleen / Vijayakumar, Saranya: A Worldwide Survey of Encryption Products, URL: https://www.schneier.com/academic/paperfiles/worldwide-survey-of-encryption-products.pdf, February 11, 2016 Version 1.0.

Schnorr, Claus Peter (2021): Fast Factoring Integers by SVP Algorithms, received 1 Mar, last revised 3 Mar, Cryptology ePrint Archive: Report 2021/232

Schulz, Jimmy (2016): Ist Verschlüsselung der Schlüssel zur digitalen Souveränität?; in: Friedrichsen, Mike / Bisa, Peter-J. (Hrsg.): Digitale Souveränität - Vertrauen in der Netzwerkgesellschaft, Wiesbaden, S. 161-167.

Schulz, Jimmy (2018): Rede im Bundestag, Privatsphäre und Sicherheit im digitalen Raum, 29.11.2018, URL: https://www.youtube.com/watch?v=es-_7Hsaiaw.

Schulz, Jimmy et al. (2018): Recht auf Verschlüsselung – Privatsphäre und Sicherheit im digitalen Raum stärken, Drucksache 19/5764, URL: https://dip21.bundestag.de/dip21/btd/19/057/1905764.pdf.

Scientists4Crypto / Schiffner, Stefan / Krenn, Stephan et al. (2020): Open letter responding to Council Resolution on Encryption - Security through encryption and security despite encryption, by 373 signatories from 25 countries, December 14, URL: https://sites.google.com/view/scientists4crypto/start.

Sevignani, Sebastian (2016): Krise der Privatheit - Zur Dialektik von Privatheit und Überwachung im informationellen Kapitalismus; in: Hahn, Kornelia / Langenohl, Andreas (Hg.): Kritische Öffentlichkeiten - Öffentlichkeiten in der Kritik, pp 237-254.

Shor, Peter W. (1997): Polynomial-Time Algorithms for Prime Factorization and Discrete Logarithms on a Quantum Computer, in: SIAM Journal on Computing, 26, p. 1484–1509.

Sinkov, Abraham (1966): Elementary Cryptanalysis: A Mathematical Approach, Mathematical Association of America.

Smoke (2017): Documentation of the Android Messenger Application Smoke with Encryption, URL:

https://github.com/textbrowser/smoke/raw/master/Documentation/Smoke.pdf, 2017.

SmokeStack: Server Software for Encrypted Messaging, URL: https://github.com/textbrowser/smokestack.

Snowden, Edward (2019): Permanent Record.

Somavilla, Ilse (2013): Verschlüsselung in Wittgensteins Nachlass, Innsbruck.

Spot-On (2011): Documentation of the Spot-On-Application, URL: https://sourceforge.net/p/spot-on/code/HEAD/tree/, under this URL since 06/2013, Sourceforge, including the Spot-On: Documentation of the project draft paper of the pre-research project since 2010, Project Ne.R.D.D., Registered 2010-06-27, URL: https://sourceforge.net/projects/445nerdd/ has evolved into Spot-On. Please see http://spot-on.sf.net and URL: https://github.com/textbrowser/spot-on/blob/master/branches/Documentation/RELEASE-NOTES.archived, 08.08.2011.

Spot-On (2021): Documentation of the Spot-On-Application, URL: https://github.com/textbrowser/spot-on/tree/master/branches/trunk/Documentation, Github 2021.

Spot-On Encryption Suite (2019): Democratization of Multiple & Exponential Encryption: - Handbook and User Manual as practical software guide, ISBN: 978-3749435067.

Srisakthi, S., Shanthi, A.P. (2020): Towards the Design of a Stronger AES: AES with Key Dependent Shift Rows (KDSR). Wireless Pers Commun 114, 3003–3015 (2020).

Stehlé, Damien / Steinfeld, Ron (2016): Making NTRUEncrypt and NTRUSign as Secure as Standard Worst-Case Problems over Ideal Lattices, Cryptology ePrint Archive.

Stevens, Richard W. (1996): TCP/IP Illustrated, Volume 3: TCP for Transactions, HTTP, NNTP, and the UNIX Domain Protocols.

STOA / Ausschuss Science and Technology Options Assessment des Europäischen Parlaments (2015): Mass Surveillance - Part 2: Technology foresight, options for longer term security and Privacy improvements, January 13, URL: https://www.europarl.europa.eu/stoa/en/document/EPRS_STU(2015)527410.

Straub, Andreas (2016): XEP-0384: Omemo Encryption, XMPP Standards Foundation website.

Stubblefield, Adam / Wallach, Dan S. (2001): Dagster: Censorship-Resistant Publishing Without Replication, URL:

https://www.cs.rice.edu/~dwallach/pub/dagster-tr.pdf &
https://scholarship.rice.edu/handle/1911/96291.

The United Nations / Office of the High Commissioner of Human Rights (2014): What are human rights?

Thomas, Stephen A. (2000): SSL and TLS essentials securing the Web, New York: Wiley.

Thompson, Andi Wilson / Kehl, Danielle / Bankston, Kevin (2015): Doomed to Repeat History? Lessons from the Crypto Wars of the 1990s, June 17, URL: https://www.newamerica.org/cybersecurity-initiative/policy-papers/doomed-to-repeat-history-lessons-from-the-crypto-wars-of-the-1990s/.

Tremmel, Moritz / Grüner, Sebastian (2021): Warum es okay ist, dass Signal Google-Server nutzt, 29. Januar, URL: https://www.golem.de/news/whatsapp-alternative-warum-es-okay-ist-dass-signal-google-server-nutzt-2101-153764.html

Tremmel, Moritz (2021): Onionshare - Einfach anonym Dateien teilen, Golem, 11. Mai.

Tur, Henryk / Computerworld (2018): GoldBug Secure Email Client & Instant Messenger, https://www.computerworld.pl/ftp/goldbug-secure-email-Client-instant-messenger.html, January 11.

Urdaneta, Guido / Pierre, Guillaume / van Steen, Maarten (2011): A Survey of DHT Security Techniques, ACM Computing Surveys 43(2).

USCM / US Conference of Mayors (2019): 87th Annual Meeting Opposing Payment To Ransomware Attack Perpetrators, URL: https://www.usmayors.org/the-conference/resolutions/?category=a0D4N00000FCb3LUAT&meeting=87th%20Annual%20Meeting.

Wake, Mancy A. / Hibernack, Dorothy / Lullaby, Lucas (2020): Echo on a Chip (EoC) – A New Perception for the Next Generation of Micro-Controllers handling Encryption for Mobile Messaging: From Secure Embedded Systems to Separated Secure Embedded Systems (SSES) in Cryptography. Hardware supported Trusted Execution Environments (TEE) for Encryption / Decryption Processes separated from Transport-Processes and Server-Processes respective even other Operational Processes. ISBN 9783751916448.

Waldman, Marc / Mazières, David (2001): Tangler: A Censorship-Resistant Publishing System Based On Document Entanglements, in: Proceedings of the 8th ACM Conference on Computer and Communications Security, p.p. 126-135, URL:

http://www.scs.stanford.edu/~dm/home/papers/waldman:tangler.ps.g
z.

WhatsApp (2020): Encryption Overview - Technical white paper, Version 3 Updated October 22.

Wieduwilt, Hendrik (2021): Mit den Trump-Sperren beginnt ein postmodernes Internet, 02. Februar, URL: https://www.heise.de/news/Mit-den-Trump-Sperren-beginnt-ein-postmodernes-Internet-5034922.html

Wikipedia (2021): Various illustrations and information.

Windelband, Daniela (2018): Welche Messenger dürfen in der katholischen Kirche eingesetzt werden? Bericht zum Beschluss der Konferenz der Diözesandatenschutzbeauftragten der katholischen Kirche Deutschland zu Beurteilung von Messenger-Diensten, 27. September, URL: https://www.datenschutz-notizen.de/welche-messenger-duerfen-in-der-katholischen-kirche-eingesetzt-werden-5621145/ & https://www.kdsa-nord.de/sites/default/files/file/NEU/Beschluesse_DDSB/2018_07_26_B eurteilung_von_Messengern_und_anderen_Social_Media_Diensten.pd f.

Winkel, Olaf (1997): Private Verschlüsselung als öffentliches Problem, Leviathan, Vol. 25, No. 4, pp. 567-586.

Wunderlich-Pfeiffer, Frank (2021): Ein optischer Quantencomputer für eine Million Qubits, Fach-Forum Golem, 7. Mai.

Yao, Andrew (1982): Protocols for secure communications, Proc. 23rd IEEE Symposium on Foundations of Computer Science (FOCS '82), pp. 160–164.

INDEX OF ABBREVIATIONS ●

E2E	End-to-End
EAN	European Article Number
ECO	Verband der Internetwirtschaft
EFF	Electronic Frontier Foundation
ENISA	EU-Agentur für Netzwerksicherheit
EPKS	Echo Public Key Sharing
F2F	Friend-to-Friend
FBI	Federal Bureau of Investigation
FC2C	From Cipher to Conceal
FCZB	Frauen-Computer-Zentrum Berlin
FISA	Foreign Intelligence Surveillance Act
FSF	Free Software Foundation
FVEY	Five-Eyes
FZJ	Forschungszentrum Jülich
GB	GoldBug
GFF	Gesellschaft für Freiheitsrechte e.V.
GI	Gesellschaft für Informatik e.V.
GnuPG	Gnu-Privacy Guard
GPG	Gnu-Privacy-Guard-Verschlüsselung nach PGP
GUI	Graphical User Interface
HRNG	Hardware Random Number Generator
HTTP	Hypertext Transfer Protocol
HTTPS	Hypertext Transfer Protocol Secure
ICC	Interaction-Free Cryptographic Calling
IMAP	Internet Message Access Protocol
loc. cit.	loco citato / ibidem / at the same place
IRC	Internet Relay Chat
ISBN	Internationale Standardbuchnummer
IuK	Information und Kommunikation
JKK	Juggerknaut Keys
J-PAKE	Password Authenticated Key Exchange by Juggling
JPL	Jet Propulsion Laboratory
LGBTQIA	Lesbian, Gay, Bi, Transsexual, Queer, Intersex, Asexual
MAD	Militärischer Abschirmdienst
MELODICA	Multi Encrypted Long Distance Calling
MIC	Machine Identification Code
MIT	Massachusetts Institute of Technology
NIST	National Institute of Standards and Technology
NR	Neue Richtervereinigung e.V.
NSA	National Security Agency

Omemo	Omemo Multi-End Message and Object Encryption
OpenPGP	Open Pretty Good Privacy
OS	Open Source
OTM	One Time Magnet
OTP	One Time Pad
OTR	Off the Record
P2P	Peer to Peer
PAKE	Password Authenticated Key Exchange
PGP	Pretty Good Privacy
PKI	Public Key Infrastructure
POP3	Post Office Protocol, Version 3
POPTASTIC	Chat over Post Office Protocol
PQC	Post-Quantum Kryptographie
QIA	Quantum Internet Alliance
QuBit	Quantenbit
RCP	Rosetta Crypto Pad
RCS	Rich Communication Services
RFC	Request for Comments
R.I.P	Rest in Peace
S/MIME	Secure / Multipurpose Internet Mail Extensions
SAM	Secure Architecture Model
SMP	Socialist Millionaire Protocol
SMS	Short Message Service
SSK	Secret Stream Keys
SSL / TLS	Secure Sockets Layer / Transport Layer Security
STASI	Staatssicherheitsdienst
STOA	Panel for the Future of Science and Technology (STOA)
StPO	Strafprozessordnung
SWOT	Strengths (Stärken), Weaknesses (Schwächen), Opportunities (Chancen), Threads (Risiken)
TCP	Transmission Control Protocol
TCP-E	Transmission Control Protocol over Echo (Protocol)
TEE	Trusted Execution Environment
TH	Turtle Hopping
TKG	Telekommunikationsgesetzes
TKÜ	Telekommunikationsüberwachung
TRNG	True Random Number Generator
TÜV	Technischer Überwachungsverein
UBIT	Fachverband Unternehmensberatung, Buchhaltung, IT
ÜGR	Überwachungsgesamtrechnung

URI	Uniform Resource Identifier
URL	Uniform Resource Locator
USCM	US-Conference of Mayors
VDS	Vorratsdatenspeicherung
VPN	Virtual Private Network
WoT	Web of Trust
XOR	eXclusive OR
ZITIS	Zentrale Stelle für Informationstechnik im Sicherheitsbereich
ZK	Zero-Knowledge

REGISTER •

430

REFERENCES •

1. Comp. a. Thompson (loc. cit.), Gerhards (loc. cit.), Meinrath (loc. cit.), Moechel (loc. cit.).
2. Meyn (loc. cit.).
3. Winkel (loc. cit.).
4. Comp. e.g., NIST (loc. cit.).
5. www.youtube.com/ watch?v=8Jrlqmlzj2U
6. Own illustration.
7. Council (loc. cit.).
8. Moechel (loc. cit.).
9. www.congress.gov/ bill/116th-congress/senate-bill/3398/text
10. Compare for this reasoning the interview with the project GB Messenger, Kahle (loc. cit.).
11. Internet 2020.
12. Boskin (loc. cit.).
13. Becker (loc. cit.).
14. en.wikipedia.org/ wiki/2015_San_Bernardino_attack
15. Snowden (loc. cit.).
16. Esken 2015.
17. Esken (loc. cit.), 1338538749353979911 & 1134540427909091328 & 1402577214768570368.
18. Schulz (loc. cit.), 29.11.2018.
19. Schulz et al. (loc. cit.).
20. Bundesarchiv, Image 183-1990-0116-013 / CC-BY-SA 3.0.
21. BRAK (loc. cit.).
22. BRAK (loc. cit.).
23. BTDS 19/25999.
24. Az. AnwZ (Brfg) 2/20. From a technical point of view, the insecure infrastructure of the lawyer's mailbox could simply be used and an e-mail client with encryption such as Spot-On (exchange of the POPTASTIC key), Spike, GoldBug or Delta simply placed as an overlay over it. After a one-time key exchange, encrypted communication can also take place via the semi-encrypted line of the lawyer's mailbox.
25. NRV (loc. cit.).
26. Statement Nr. 25/2021
27. Comp. Windelband (loc. cit.).
28. kloster-einsiedeln.ch/das-goldene-ohr/
29. Kahle (loc. cit.).
30. Heuzeroth (loc. cit.).
31. Kahle (loc. cit.).
32. Beuth (loc. cit.).
33. tutanota.com/ blog/posts/european-autonomy-in-danger/
34. www.teletrust.de/ uploads/media/210514-Gemeinsamer_Brief_BVerfSchG_-_Artikel_10-G.pdf
35. ripe82.ripe.net/ archives/video/523/
36. www.sz.de/1.5332538
37. Bruchstein (loc. cit.).
38. Narr (loc. cit.).

39 In an Interview with Bolton (loc. cit.).

40 GI (loc. cit.).

41 GI (loc. cit.).

42 Pohl (loc. cit.).

43 mariazweipunktnull.de, compare also interview with Michael Osterheider, in: Nürnberger Nachrichten, April 23rd, 2010.

44 Comp. a. Der Spiegel (loc. cit.), Lobo (loc. cit.).

45 Case C-511/18, dejure.org/dienste/vernetzung /rechtsprechung?Text=C-511/18

46 www.patrick-breyer.de/eu-deal-zur-chatkontrolle-flaechendeckende-und-verdachtslose-durchsuchung-von-privatnachrichten-wird-gesetz/

47 GI (loc. cit.).

48 BfDi (loc. cit.).

49 BfJ (loc. cit.).

50 CEPIS (loc. cit.).

51 ENISA (loc. cit.).

52 www.it-daily.net/it-sicherheit/datenschutz-grc/26734-crypto-backdoors-konterkarieren-ende-zu-ende-verschluesselung?ref=ittagessc hau.de

53 STOA (loc. cit.:1).

54 BMI (loc. cit.).

55 Regierungsvertrag, (loc. cit.):1979ff.

56 IT-Sicherheitsgesetz (loc. cit.).

57 Directive (EU) 2018/1972 of the European Parliament and of the Council, (loc. cit.).

58 Kritis (loc. cit.).

59 www.ccc.de/de/updates /2020/scheinbeteiligung

60 Berliner Anwaltsblatt 05/2021

61 Locker (loc. cit.).

62 OLG Rostock, Decision of March 23rd, 2021, to use a crypto cell phone - 20 Ws 70/21

63 Technische Universität Chemnitz.

64 heise.de/-6026709

65 The e-mail operator POSTEO made this proposed formulation available, which had already been distributed to the operators, compare also the blog of March 2nd, 2021, 5:00 p.m. and posteo.de/FormulierungshilfeB MI.pdf

66 netzpolitik.org/ 2021/tkg-novelle-seehofer-will-personalausweis-pflicht-fuer-e-mail-und-messenger-einfuehren/

67 heise.de/-6022364

68 Council of the European Union, 8519/21 Brüssel, 12 May 2021.

69 Comp. Meister (loc. cit.).

70 Snowden 2013 and (loc. cit.).

71 Comp. BT-DS 19/24785 incl. SÜG.

72 Comp. ASDS 19(4)844D and other in reference to BTDS 19/24785, 19/24900.

73 Constitutional issues regulating the use of source telecommunications surveillance by intelligence services, WD 3 - 3000 - 293/20, February 19, 2021

74 shop.freiheit.org/ download/P2@1025/389073/2 0210316_FNF_Analyse_%C3%9 Cberwachung_final.pdf

75 Sevignani (loc. cit.).

76 Gaus (loc. cit.).

77 Internet.

78 In an interview with Hein, (loc. cit.).

79 Lang (loc. cit.).

80 www.nytimes.com/ 2021/05/17/technology/apple-china-censorship-data.html

81 docs.house.gov/ meetings/JU/JU00/20210630/1 12849/HHRG-117-JU00-Wstate-BurtT-20210630.pdf

82 www.tagesspiegel.de/ themen/reportage/tausende-beamte-in-der-tuerkei-entlassen-erdogan-macht-wieder-jagd-auf-seine-kritiker/19334732.html & www.spiegel.de/politik/auslan d/tuerkei-unter-recep-tayyip-erdogan-entlassen-festnehmen-saeubern-a-1104956.html

83 www.bbc.com/news/ technology-57881364 & www.theguardian.com/news/2 021/jul/19/

84 Rueckert / Schilis-Gallego (loc. cit.).

85 PR 11.11.2020 (loc. cit.).

86 Basic communication rights such as Art. 5, Paragraph 1, Paragraph 3, and Article 10, Paragraph 1 of the Basic Law also bind the legislature through Article 1, Paragraph 3 of the Basic Law. See a. BVerfGE 100, 313 (359); 120, 274 (323). And see Hoffmann-Riem, AöR 134 (2009), 513 ff .; same, AöR 137 (2012), 509 ff.; same, JZ 2014, 53 ff; quoted from Gärditz, Klaus F. (2021): Statement on the draft of a second law to increase the security of information technology systems, February 28.

87 CSW-Nr. 2021-234348-1032.

88 www.eff.org/deeplinks/ 2021/08/apples-plan-think-different-about-encryption-opens-backdoor-your-private-life

89 cdt.org/press/cdt-apples-changes-to-messaging-and-photo-services-threaten-users-security-and-privacy/ & cdt.org/insights/international-coalition-calls-on-apple-to-abandon-plan-to-build-surveillance-capabilities-into-iphones-ipads-and-other-products/

90 GI 09.11.2020, (loc. cit.).

91 Own illustration.

92 Bertram (loc. cit.):182.
93 FBI (loc. cit.).
94 According to Cardan / Fleißner.
95 Xerox Gmbh: Xerox DocuColor® 6060 Digital color printing system. Brochure. Neuss, section »Technical data of the digital color printing system Xerox DocuColor 6060«, S. 8, Col. 2, URL: www.xerox.com/downloads/deu/de/7/708P86985DED.pdf
96 Francis Bacon.
97 github.com/ DavidBuchanan314/tweetable-polyglot-png
98 Dreyfus (loc. cit.). Also: embeddedsw.net/doc/physical_coercion.txt
99 Schmeh (loc. cit.:223).
100 ubit-oesterreich.at/ 2021/04/22/
101 Scientists4Crypto (loc. cit.).
102 Europol (loc. cit.).
103 Europol EncroChat (loc. cit.).
104 Lobo 2015 (loc. cit.).
105 AFuV (loc. cit.).
106 BSI Lagebericht 2020, (loc. cit.).
107 www.funkemedien.de/ de/presse/medienmitteilungen /news/UPDATE-Hackerangriff-auf-die-FUNKE-Mediengruppe-00001/
108 USCM (loc. cit.).
109 zetter.substack.com/ p/biden-declares-state-of-emergency
110 Fact Sheet: President Signs Executive Order Charting New Course to Improve the Nation's Cybersecurity, May 12, 2021.
111 Anderson (loc. cit.), media.ccc.de/v/rc3-11577-what_price_the_upload_filter
112 Hohmann (loc. cit.).
113 WhatsApp (loc. cit.):4.
114 WhatsApp (loc. cit.):13.
115 Thomas Röper under www.anti-spiegel.ru/2021/neue-whatsapp-regeln-zeigen-die-end-to-end-verschluesselung-war-eine-luege/ to Dmitry Belyaev under tass.ru/mezhdunarodnaya-panorama/10439967
116 Government spokesman Steffen Seibert on January 11, 2021, at www.stern.de/politik/deutschland/regierungssprecher-seibert--merkel-haelt-trumps-sperrung-auf-twitter-fuer--problematisch--9561456.html
117 Comp. Moechel (loc. cit.:50).
118 Edwards (loc. cit.).
119 CCC (loc. cit.).
120 Scientists4Crypto (loc. cit.).
121 Kerckhoffs (loc. cit.).
122 In an interview with Morris, (loc. cit.).
123 Cryptography-Workshop.
124 Public Domain Illustration.
125 Public Domain Illustration.
126 Figure Public Domain.
127 Internet.
128 Public Domain Illustration.
129 Public Domain Illustration.

130 Public Domain Illustration.
131 Public Domain Illustration.
132 Internet.
133 Srisakthi / Shanthi (loc. cit.).
134 General Figure of Polychor Schach according to Maack.
135 doi.org/ 10.1080/0161-119291866928
136 Public Domain Illustration.
137 Diffie/Hellmann (loc. cit.).
138 Rivest, Shamir, Adleman (loc. cit.).
139 NIST 2016.
140 McEliece (loc. cit.), NTRU (loc. cit.).
141 General Illustration.
142 Schmidt 2015.
143 Drehling (loc. cit.).
144 lists.gforge.inria.fr/ pipermail/cado-nfs-discuss/2019-December/001139.html
145 mathcenter.ru/en/RSA-232-number-has-been-factored
146 Rivest / Shamir / Adleman, (loc. cit.); Estimates; general and methodologically illustrative compilation.
147 Schnorr (loc. cit.).
148 www.math.uni-frankfurt.de/ ~dmst/teaching/WS2019/SVP9 .pdf
149 heise.de/-5071387
150 NIST 2016, (loc. cit.).
151 www.ecrypt.eu.org/ csa/publications.html und BSI TR-02102-1 »Kryptographische Verfahren: Empfehlungen und Schlüssellängen« Version:

2020-01, 02.04.2020 as well SP 800-133 Rev. 2; Recommendation for Cryptographic Key Generation, June 2020.
152 Migration zu Post-Quanten-Kryptographie, Handlungsempfehlungen des BSI, Stand: August 2020.
153 www.handelsblatt.com/ 26118192.html
154 BSI Richtlinie TR-02102-1 »Kryptographische Verfahren: Empfehlungen und Schlüssellängen« Version: 2020-01, 02.04.2020, Seite 2.
155 www.fz-juelich.de/ SharedDocs/Pressemitteilunge n/UK/DE/2020/2020-11-16-juwels-booster.html
156 Arute / Martinis et al. (loc. cit.), comp. a. Rieffel (loc. cit.).
157 www.techrepublic.com/ article/china-sends-unbreakable-code-from-quantum-satellite-to-earth/
158 www.zdnet.com/ article/quantum-computing-networks-satellites-and-lots-more-qubits-china-reveals-ambitious-goals-in-five-year-plan/
159 news.uchicago.edu/ story/argonne-uchicago-scientists-take-important-step-developing-national-quantum-internet
160 Kuder (loc. cit.).

[161] app.handelsblatt.com/ downloads/26796228/3/road map- quantencomputing.pdf?ticket= ST-12994842- YkQ4VJ7ZdmGerdZZHsTu-ap3

[162] www.ibm.com/ blogs/research/2020/09/ibm- quantum-roadmap/

[163] Comp. aip.scitation.org/ doi/10.1063/1.4962732 & www.globalfoundries.com/pre ss-release, May 5, 2021

[164] Gasakis/Schmidt (loc. cit.). What's under the article "Match me if you can" in 2021 has been described by Giuseppe Ateniese et al. (loc. cit.) for Matchmaking Encryption was previously programmed in the ECHO- Matching and has also been described in the manuals since more than one decade before.

[165] Adams/Maier (loc. cit.).

[166] Comp. Dolev et al. (loc. cit.).

[167] Edwards (loc. cit.).

[168] Further details can be found in the technical manual, comp. Spot-On (loc. cit.).

[169] Gasakis / Schmidt (loc. cit.).

[170] Moonlander (loc. cit.).

[171] Milgram (loc. cit.).

[172] Karinthy (loc. cit.)

[173] Edwards (loc. cit.).

[174] A combination of both paradigms is presented by the Steam protocol for file transfer in Smoke Messenger, which maps the Echo protocol as a TCP variant: TCPe – TCP over Echo.

[175] Buktu (loc. cit.) / Hoffstein et al. (loc. cit.) / Stehlé et al. (loc. cit.).

[176] vgl. die Arbeiten zu diesem Algorithmus von McEliece (loc. cit.), Preneel (loc. cit.), Roering (loc. cit.), Hudde (loc. cit.), Repka (loc. cit.), Kobara et al. (loc. cit.), Engelbert et al. (loc. cit.)

[177] Enisa 2021 (loc. cit.).

[178] Bertam et al (loc. cit.).

[179] Merkle (loc. cit.).

[180] Diffie / Hellman (loc. cit.).

[181] Needham / Schroeder (loc. cit.).

[182] See: Edwards (loc. cit.).

[183] Spot-On (loc. cit.), Ackermann / Klein (loc. cit.).

[184] Comp. Yao (loc. cit.).

[185] Comp. also Bertram et al. (loc. cit.).

[186] Diffie / Hellman (loc. cit.).

[187] Spot-On tech. doc. (loc. cit.).

[188] Hao / Ryan (loc. cit.).

[189] vgl. Bellovin / Merrit (loc. cit.); u.a. Bellare, Pointcheval, Rogaway (loc. cit.) as well Boyko, MacKenzie, Patel (loc. cit.). These protocols proved to be secure in the so-called "random oracle model" (or even stronger variants), and the first real protocols that were proven to be secure under standard assumptions

were those of O. Goldreich and Y. Lindell (Crypto 2001), which, however, serve as a plausibility check and were not efficient, as well as by J. Katz, R. Ostrovsky and M. Yung (Eurocrypt 2001), which were more practicable. The first methods of obtaining keys with password authentication were described by M. Ford and B. Kaliski in 2000. See also IEEE P1363.2.

[190] General Illustration.

[191] General Illustration.

[192] General Illustration.

[193] Ackermann / Klein (loc. cit.).

[194] Blum et al. (loc. cit.).

[195] Bünz et al. (loc. cit.).

[196] Comp a. Mimblewimble: Odendaal et al. (loc. cit.).

[197] Smoke Developer.

[198] Smoke Developer.

[199] GI (loc. cit.), 2020.

[200] N = 254 free & open-source crypto tools of 865 in total, analyzed in 2016 by Schneier et al. (loc. cit.) / own calculations quoted according to Ackermann (loc. cit.).

[201] Wake et al. (loc. cit.).

[202] Own Screenshot.

[203] BSI (loc. cit.).

[204] Fujisaki/Okamoto (loc. cit.).

[205] Pointcheval (loc. cit.).

[206] »Creating a Smart World where technology becomes so pervasive part of society that people are unaware of its presence.«

[207] Moonlander (loc. cit.).

[208] www.weser-kurier.de/deutschland-welt/deutschland-welt-politik_artikel,-merkel-appelliert-in-coronakrise-an-buerger-die-rede-zum-nachlesen-_arid,1903711.html

[209] Comp. Edwards (loc. cit.:210).

[210] Spot-On (loc. cit.).

[211] Edwards (loc. cit.).

[212] Gasakis / Schmidt (loc. cit.).

[213] Spot-On (loc. cit.), Edwards (loc. cit.).

[214] Adams (loc. cit.).

[215] Momedo (loc. cit.)

[216] Comp. a. Gasakis/Schmidt (loc. cit.:67), quoted according to Delta-Chat, in: Nomenclatura 2019:130.

[217] Matejka (loc. cit.), Popescu (loc. cit.), Tanenbaum (loc. cit.), RetroShare (loc. cit.).

[218] Smoke (loc. cit.).

[219] Saint-Andre (loc. cit.).

[220] NIST (loc. cit.).

[221] Gultsch (loc. cit.)

[222] Marlinspike (loc. cit.): Ecosystem is moving.

[223] Cane (loc. cit.).

[224] Tremmel / Grüner (loc. cit.).

[225] See GitHub Issue #11101.

[226] Radio RBB 14. Mai 2021.

[227] element.io/blog/element-on-google-play-store/

[228] Wieduwilt (loc. cit.).

[229] Internet.

[230] Own Screenshot.

[231] Matejka (loc. cit.), Popescu (loc. cit.), Tanenbaum (loc. cit.), RetroShare (loc. cit.).

[232] BTDS 19/26247.

[233] Einführung einer registerübergreifenden einheitlichen Identifikationsnummer, Expert opinion of the Wissenschaftlichen Dienstes des Bundestages, WD 3 - 3000 - 196/20, 2020.

[234] This finding was based on the microcensus ruling of the Federal Constitutional Court of 1969, BVerfGE 27, 1 – Mikrozensus, Juli 16, 1969.

[235] PM of March 2, 2021.

[236] Erich Fromm, 1963d; GA IX, p. 373.

[237] Stadt Pforzheim / Brändle, Gerhard: Menschen statt Namen, 2013.

[238] COM(2021) 281 final 2021/0136 (COD) mit OJ L 257/73 of 28.8.2014

[239] www.spiegel.de/ wissenschaft/entlasst-horst-seehofer-a-a0c5f2c0-496e-47d5-a4a6-4a349bb90407 & www.br.de/nachrichten/deuts chland-welt/linken-politikerin-seehofer-eine-gefahr-fuer-die-demokratie,SR8kmJr

[240] ASDS 19(4)825

[241] BTDS 19/28169

[242] www.fiff.de/presse/ eID_Stellungnahme-ccc-fiff9.

[243] Edwards (loc. cit.:213).

[244] TLP, 5.6, quoted according to Somavilla (loc. cit.).

[245] Offsystem (loc. cit.), Madore (loc. cit.), Waldman (loc. cit.), Stubblefield (loc. cit.).

[246] www.osiris-sps.org/

[247] See above.

[248] Sanatinia / Noubir (loc. cit.), Levine (loc. cit.) quoted according to Gasaski (loc. cit.:167,165).

[249] Levine (loc. cit.)

[250] AK VDS (loc. cit.).

[251] Rihaczek (loc. cit.).

[252] www.statista.com/ statistics/260819/number-of-monthly-active-whatsapp-users/

[253] Internet, own research, 1 = DHT, 2 = pre-compiled Binaries/AWS

[254] Comp. Furthermore e.g. also a VZBZ-Paper of Mai 17, 2021.

[255] Mundt (loc. cit.).

[256] www1.folha.uol.com.br/ internacional/en/world/2013/0 9/1335563-brazil-wants-national-antisnoop-email.shtml

[257] See www.ccc.de/en/updates/2015/ ccc-fordert-ausstieg-aus-unverschlusselter-kommunikation und FN 33 zur Stellungnahme zum Sicherheitsgesetz vom 01. März 2021.

[258] Programm: Nie gab es mehr zu tun, (loc. cit.:37).

441

[259] onlinelibrary.wiley.com/
     doi/10.1002/ijop.12746
[260] Ministerium MV (loc. cit.).
[261] DIVSi (loc. cit.).
[262] Kaeser (loc. cit.).
[263] Mezini (loc. cit.).